Preparing for the Urban Future

Published in cooperation with the United Nations Centre on Human Settlements (Habitat II)

Preparing for the Urban Future

Global Pressures and Local Forces

Edited by

Michael A. Cohen
Blair A. Ruble
Joseph S. Tulchin
Allison M. Garland

WW *Published by The Woodrow Wilson Center Press*
Distributed by The Johns Hopkins University Press

Woodrow Wilson Center Special Studies

The Woodrow Wilson Center Press
Editorial Offices
370 L'Enfant Promenade, S.W.
Suite 704
Washington, D.C. 20024-2518 U.S.A.
telephone 202-287-3000, ext. 218

Distributed by
The Johns Hopkins University Press
Hampden Station
Baltimore, Maryland 21211
order department telephone 1-800-537-5487

9 8 7 6 5 4 3 2 1

Library of Congress Cataloging-in-Publication Data

Preparing for the urban future : global pressures and local forces / edited by
    Michael A. Cohen . . . [et al.].
        p.   cm.—(Woodrow Wilson Center special studies)
    "Published in cooperation with the United Nations Conference on Human
    Settlements (Habitat II)"—Leaf preceding t.p.
    Includes bibliographical references and index.
    ISBN 0-943875-78-1 (alk. paper)—ISBN 0-943875-79-X (pbk.: alk. paper)
        1. Cities and towns—Congresses.   2. Urban economics—Congresses.
3. Urban policy—Congresses.   4. Urban sociology—Congresses. I. Cohen,
Michael A., 1994–.   II. Series.
HT107.U723   1996
307.76—dc20   96-436
                                                               CIP

The Woodrow Wilson International Center for Scholars

The Center is the living memorial of the United States of America to the nation's twenty-eighth president, Woodrow Wilson. Congress established the Woodrow Wilson Center in 1968 as an international institute for advanced study, "symbolizing and strengthening the fruitful relationship between the world of learning and the world of public affairs." The Center opened in 1970 under its own board of trustees.

Woodrow Wilson Center Special Studies

The work of the Center's Fellows, Guest Scholars, and staff—and presentations and discussions at the Center's conferences, seminars, and colloquia—often deserve timely circulation as contributions to public understanding of issues of national and international importance. The Woodrow Wilson Center Special Studies series is intended to make such materials available by the Woodrow Wilson Center Press to interested scholars, practitioners, and other readers. In all its activities, the Woodrow Wilson Center is a nonprofit, nonpartisan organization, supported financially by annual appropriations from the U.S. Congress, and by the contributions of foundations, corporations, and individuals. Conclusions or opinions expressed in Center publications and programs are those of the authors and speakers and do not necessarily reflect the views of the Center staff, Fellows, trustees, advisory groups, or any individuals or organizations that provide financial support to the Center.

Contents

Foreword

The Road to Istanbul and Beyond

Jorge Wilheim

Preparing for the second United Nations Conference on Human Settlements (Habitat II), we have all been struck by the profound changes occurring throughout society as a result of the globalizing economy. These changes are not circumstantial or localized; as the economy is globalized, institutions and individuals network across borders, and effects are found everywhere.

A substantive discussion of the future of cities requires us first to debate the context in which a new paradigm can be developed. This is the intention of the contributors to this volume. Such a debate is certainly timely, as humankind passes through a transition in which a new social contract must be reached and the tasks of development redistributed among all social actors.

The transitional period in which we find ourselves is marked at the individual, institutional, and national levels by uncertainty and nostalgia, which in turn drive intolerance, violence, ethnic hatred, and destruction. Such backward-looking responses to uncertainty often manifest themselves in cities, making us forget that cities are also the core of civilization and of culture—the mirrors of society, reflecting in their social fabric and in their built spaces all the characteristics of their society.

The authors of this volume explore our present urban situation to discover the roots of our future. The important topics they address include the policy implications of the global economy and its effects on cities; new paradigms of an increasingly urbanized world in the

Jorge Wilheim, a Brazilian architect and urbanist, is deputy secretary-general of the United Nations Conference on Human Settlements (Habitat II) to be held in Istanbul in June 1996.

twenty-first century; the role of culture in a globally competitive world; the reshaping of urban life and of ethical values; the new design of democracy; and, finally, the urban landscape as it has changed. The treatment of these issues in this volume contributes to our understanding of cities and to preparations for Habitat II.

Misleading Statements

The current urban discourse has often proceeded from misleading assumptions about our present political situation. Although each of the following statements presents some truth, it would be dangerous to build our plans for the first decades of the next century upon such oversimplifications.

Socialism is dead, capitalism is eternal. The disintegration of the Soviet regime brought an end to undemocratic central planning, discrediting old socialist theories. But there is no reason to think that the ultimate aim of a just society and a more equitable distribution of wealth—the core of socialist theory—has been put aside in some permanent or irrevocable manner.

States are getting weaker, and the market will take over. The weakening of state power is not only a result of discredited central planning but the consequence of a pervasive lack of ethics in society and government, recently brought to light by the spread of democracy and a free press. The weakening of the state is also the consequence of the lack of financial resources at the disposal of the public sector, which is unable to face the increasing challenges of development or the challenges of social welfare aggravated by unemployment and migration. This crisis of the state will have to be resolved through institutional and political change, not by the substitution of the state with private sector market institutions.

The guarantee of development, its sustainability, is forged through ecological balance; or, in other words, "sustainability" is a "green" word. We welcome the growing trend to incorporate in development programs measures that preserve natural resources for future generations. Without attention to human resources, however, truly sustainable development cannot be achieved.

Information technology is the ultimate tool for individual autonomy. Technology has not only brought an incredible acceleration of global linkages and access to information, but a widening gap between the informed and the uninformed in every society.

After global adjustment to a market economy, current social difficulties will be overcome. It would be an error to assume that economic adjustment alone can resolve the issues of unemployment, migration, and inequality.

Aspects of Globalism

New modes of industrial production have had a profound impact on the management of plants, the skills required of labor, the structure of employment, and the size and location of industrial units. Radical advancements in information technology have accelerated all economic and social processes, in turn widening inequalities among and within countries, presenting new forms of social and economic exclusion.

Phenomenally mobile capital is circulating at a rapidly increasing pace through capital markets, funds, and stock exchanges, out of the reach of national governments.

In addition, electronic cash that circulates outside the established channels of private banks and all regulations set by state central banks around the world has weakened governments' ability to monitor and tax capital flows. To this we should add that transnational corporations, which increased from approximately 7,000 in the 1960s to approximately 37,000 by the late 1980s, account for more in sales than all the world's trade exports put together.

Finally, we must address the current crisis of governance. The credibility of states and governments is being undermined not only by a lack of financial resources and by unethical behavior within governments, but by increasing social unrest, tension, and violence. Internal and external migration, giving way to ethnic and cultural intolerance, is yet another consequence of globalism that challenges good governance.

A Proposed Scenario for the Near Future

In preparing background papers for the formulation of the Habitat agenda and its implementation strategy—the Global Plan of Action— we looked beyond this transitional period, speculating on alternatives for the future. It is time to redefine concepts and adopt a new social contract.

To guarantee the future of an enhanced global market, we must narrow gaps and address social exclusion and underdevelopment in poor and wealthy countries alike. By linking the activities of corporations to regional development strategies, both governments and corporations can develop new partnerships with previously excluded social actors to build a new form of governance. The participation of civil society in decision making is a significant aspect of the enabling process that can change values and firmly set human welfare at the center of development objectives.

The Effects of Change in Cities

Structural social changes have had a significant impact on urban life, making cities the main stage during this transitional period. As democracy in the twenty-first century adapts to the changes brought by telecommunications, information technology, urbanization, and a new set of human values, we will see new institutions and different forms of representation. Democracy in the next century will also reflect new institutional arrangements and partnerships. We expect that decentralization in management and decision making will translate to very diversified forms of urban governance and some new kind of public-but-not-state institutions.

The Design of the Road to Istanbul

In conceiving a strategy for Habitat II, we sought to design a road that would lead to a complex and rich conference. The road had to be wide, in order to encompass a variety of interested partners: professionals, researchers, businesses and a range of private-sector entities, nonprofit foundations and NGOs, labor unions, parliamentarians, and local government authorities who deal daily and directly with issues of human settlements. The road had also to incorporate international agencies, including U.N. organizations, because the conference is much more than minor sectoral business.

The strategy was to build a partners' conference at the preparatory stages as well as at the final stage. During 1995, our "learning year," more than fifty international seminars and thematic workshops mobilized all kinds of interested partners. A series of dialogues and round-tables was organized for discussion of the city in the twenty-first century, focusing on critical aspects of urban life such as water, energy, transport, townscape, rural-urban linkages, employment, citizenship and democracy, the information society, and human solidarity. Through their national committees, countries prepared reports, including their crucial five-year commitment for better urban life, and background papers for the international delegates' group appointed to draft the Habitat agenda. Parallel to these activities, this volume was prepared independently to highlight the challenges and opportunities facing the world's cities in relation to globalization.

Outcomes and Beyond

We foresee the following products resulting from the conference: new criteria for financing cities; better legal and functional relationships between central and local authorities; a less sectoral approach to urban policies; the setting up of a permanent electronic catalog of good urban practices as well as a permanent global urban observatory; and agreements to specific declarations and commitments.

Beyond the conference, the international community will probably use its findings to prepare for an urbanized twenty-first century and revise the mandate of its institutions. Istanbul might be, therefore, a turning point. The Istanbul conference will not only be the last and concluding U.N. conference in this century, it might also be the first of its kind, an institutional opening, an illuminating event, to which this volume makes a valuable contribution.

Preface

To complement its longstanding strength in geographic area studies, in 1991 the Woodrow Wilson Center developed three core themes around which research activity would focus. Drawing from the expertise of the Center's Division of Regional and Comparative Studies, which includes the Asia Program, the Kennan Institute for Advanced Russian Studies, the Latin American Program, and the East and West European programs, as well as the Division of United States Studies and the Division of Historical, Cultural, and Literary Studies, scholarly activities at the Center were organized to explore, in a comparative context, issues of fundamental importance to the contemporary world: ethnicity, governance, and urban studies. The Center's urban theme combines a concern for contemporary domestic issues with a broader concern for the evolution of cities throughout the world in the face of technological and economic changes.

The comparative urban program at the Woodrow Wilson Center has organized seminars and colloquia, in which leading urban scholars and practitioners addressed a wide variety of urban topics. In addition, the Center has hosted four sets of Guest Scholars during successive summers working on urban issues. Over the past several years, the Center has published seven major books and over twenty working papers, including its Comparative Urban Studies Occasional Paper Series, about the world's cities.

In June 1994, the Woodrow Wilson Center's comparative urban program, in cooperation with the Urban Development Division of the World Bank, convened academics, practitioners, and officials of national and local governments and international agencies to participate in an unofficial, substantive discussion of the current state and future evolution of the world's cities, parallel to the preparations for the June 1996 United Nations Conference on Human Settlements (Habitat II). Over the course of a year, working group members met to discuss commissioned papers that, after several rounds of circulation, were revised to form the basis of the chapters of this book. The thoughtful participation of each working group member has been key to the success of this project.

The Woodrow Wilson Center is grateful for the intellectual and financial support of the World Bank and its substantial contribution to the design and implementation of this project. We are also deeply indebted to the United Nations Centre for Human Settlements for its support of this project and for its formal endorsement of this volume. In particular, Jorge Wilheim, deputy secretary-general of Habitat II, provided invaluable assistance and encouragement for our working group and its inclusion in the Habitat process.

We want to extend special appreciation to the Latin American Program staff, Ralph Espach and Michelle McCallum, and interns, Meraiah Foley, Aimée Sutton, and Angie Acosta, as well as Monique Principi and Jodi Koehn of the Kennan Institute for Advanced Russian Studies, who provided indispensable help in organizing the workshop series and in preparing the manuscript. Joe Brinley, Robert Poarch, and, in particular, Carolee Walker, of the Woodrow Wilson Center Press must be credited for their extraordinary patience and efficiency in steering the volume through an impossible publication schedule in spite of two government shutdowns and the blizzard of 1996.

Chapter 1

Introduction: Globalism and Local Realities—Five Paths to the Urban Future

Blair A. Ruble, Joseph S. Tulchin, and
Allison M. Garland

Globalization and Local Responses

In her controversial 1984 volume *Cities and the Wealth of Nations,* Jane Jacobs launched a bitter polemical attack on the dogmas of macroeconomics. She concluded her study by explaining precisely why cities— as opposed to nations and empires—are the engines of economic growth:

> In its very nature, successful economic development has to be open-ended rather than goal-oriented, and has to make itself up expediently and empirically as it goes along. For one thing, unforeseeable problems arise. The people who developed agriculture couldn't foresee soil depletion. The people who developed the automobile couldn't foresee acid rain. . . . Economic development [is] a process of continually improvising in a context that makes injecting improvisations into everyday life feasible. . . . Cities are the open-ended types of economies in which our open-ended capacities for economic creation are not only about to establish "new little things" but also to inject them into everyday life.[1]

The decade since the appearance of Jane Jacobs's work has provided a great deal of evidence supporting the importance of open-ended innovation capacities for economic development, and, furthermore, of the role of metropolitan regions and cities in that innovation. Commentators throughout the period have been predicting the end of the urban age due to a seemingly endless stream of somewhat contradictory maladies: new electronic communication technologies will permit everyone to live in splendid isolation, environmental degradation will finally succeed in choking off all urban life-forms, social pathologies will similarly make the city uninhabitable. As Robert Bruegmann notes in this volume, there has hardly been an era of human history in which such predictions have not been made. Yet cities do survive—and will survive—precisely because of their endless capacity to reinvent them-

1

selves. Tudor, Victorian, and Thatcherite London are all extraordinarily different urban forms, and yet London has remained on any list of the world's great cities for half a millenium. Similarly, the classic late–nineteenth century European metropolis may indeed be as extinct as the culture that produced it, but new urban forms are being born before our eyes. The city as a social and economic form is alive and well, even thriving.

Optimism about the urban future must be chastened by concern over the distress that coexists with prosperity in so many cities around the world. One of the most striking aspects of each of the chapters in this volume is that in spite of the diversity of responses, there is unanimous agreement on the need to address the tensions facing cities as a result of globalization, while at the same time emphasizing the local dimension of urban dilemmas and policy choices. Michael Cohen and Hank Savitch draw out the two underlying major themes of this book in their respective chapters, interpreting the impact of globalism on cities and affirming the importance of local realities. Globalism and localism may not be polar opposites at all, but rather two sides of the same coin.

In a global marketplace, as Weiping Wu's contribution confirms, cities have become independent actors that must compete with one another for investment and capital in order to create employment opportunities for their citizens. The success of a city is a function of its ability to integrate itself in the global society, as much as it is a measure of its ability to develop links to the nation or its immediate hinterland or region. As several contributions to this volume demonstrate, cities are hardly dying, nor are they passé. Rather they are changing, creating dynamic and innovative social and spatial configurations by forging direct links to the international system.

These new urban realities challenge traditional notions of the nation-state as an international actor, and pose serious questions about the relevance of national governments to urban problems. Yet, we contend the local is as important as the national and the global. Local responses to new urban dilemmas are often the most effective; answers are rooted in local realities, based on local perceptions, motivations, and culture. Several authors in this volume—María Elena Ducci, Mohamed Halfani, Nezar AlSayyad, and K. C. Sivaramakrishnan among them—emphasize the tension between the local and the global and remind us that not all change is progress. What is significant for all regions of the world is that we all are becoming urbanized. Even most of the Third World is now more than 50 percent urban, and the migration from the country to the city and its surrounding region is most rapid in the most "backward" areas. That means that even if a city wants to remain traditional and has no ambitions to grow or change, it nevertheless almost certainly will receive new population that will force it to renovate its infrastructure and its institutions, and to find jobs for the new residents. It will just as certainly be plugged into a television cable, an electronic web, a telecommunications network, and a financial-markets information service.

Urban Convergence and the New Paradigm

Michael Cohen's convergence theory elaborates a common set of critical economic, social, infrastructural, environmental, and institutional problems that plague urban areas in both the world's North and its South. However, the ability of each city to address these urban dilemmas is determined by national and local culture, affecting its resources, fiscal management capacity, and political organization.

At the same time, a city's historical and cultural roots affect its ability to adapt to the post–cold war globalizing economy. Cities that are prospering in the competitive world system, concludes Savitch, are operating within the context of a new paradigm based on incrementalism, entrepreneurship, and markets. Hank Savitch's "distressed" or "impacted" cities lack the social structures and institutions that provide space for maneuver and facilitate responsiveness and action. Cities must behave as reorganized corporations, Savitch argues, exhibiting flexibility and adaptability in order to insert themselves in the global system.

Richard Stren reviews a vast body of literature developing criteria to measure a city's successful adaptation to the global economy. Most studies emphasize labor force and financial mobility as well as the quality of human capital and infrastructure, particularly communications and transportation networks.[2] It is theoretically possible for a city to direct its efforts to adapt at a surrounding region, rather than at the global economy. Mohamed Halfani points out that some cities may be linked to subordinate hierarchies rather than dominant global hierarchies. Still, the nature of technological change and the driving consumerism of urban elites makes it inevitable that sooner or later at least some portion of every city in every region of the world will want to participate in the global economy. That drive, together with growing population pressures, means that all cities, to some degree or other, will have to confront the dilemmas discussed in this volume.

Successful cities, from Singapore to Charlotte, North Carolina, have transformed investments in natural, human, and man-made capital into job creation and income generation. Furthermore, improvements in education and infrastructure can be converted to build social capital, strengthening social structures that respond to urban dilemmas, expanding a city's capacity to make tough policy choices.[3] We need to better understand success and failure in the new urban world. To do so, Lisa Peattie reminds us, requires that we adopt Aristotelian *phronesis*. We must develop a deeper knowledge of what to do in particular circumstances, through in-depth case studies as well as more generalized observations.

Historical Conditions

History and culture have endowed cities with a diverse set of assets and liabilities that facilitate or hinder their efforts to face the global system and integrate themselves in the world economy. In turn, a city's ability to adapt to the global economy has a direct impact on its capacity to deal with the types of urban dilemmas outlined in this volume— the changing agenda for urban health, the social dimension of technology change, population dynamics, including internal and international migration, issues of governance, and the politics of urban sustainability. Each of the urban dilemmas discussed in this volume presents policymakers with tensions and conflicts that require difficult political and economic choices.

It is clear from the chapters that make up this volume that there is no single set of policy recommendations for cities in a global era. Cities must draw upon their existing reality to confront urban problems. Although a city's historical and cultural roots do not necessarily determine its future, the importance of factors such as political culture, local perceptions, and economic and institutional capacity cannot be underestimated. As Nezar AlSayyad observes in his disagreement with Michael Cohen, similarities in the built environment may be more apparent than real. AlSayyad believes that recent urban developments may be properly interpreted only when grounded in their appropriate cultural and historical contexts.

As we shall detail in our final section, which deals with policy recommendations, the concept of "best practices," which has become popular among urban planners and the development banks, must be understood to encompass issues of governance, infrastructure, quality of life, and equity. Further, it is clear from the studies in this volume that there can be no best practice that will work in all cities. Martha Schteingart observes that the positivist certainty that characterized urban planning in the era of Habitat I (the first United Nations Conference on Human Settlements, Vancouver 1976) no longer holds. We must be eclectic in our search for models and tolerant of difference in our analysis.

Five Paths to the Urban Future

Our thinking about the city in the twenty-first century must begin to become as differentiated as the discrete realities reflected by urban communities and regions. We have organized these distinct realities that cities bring to the emerging era of globalism into five distinct paths based on historical and cultural conditions: the postindustrial city; the New Age boomtown; the postsocialist city; the partially marketized city; and the marginalized city.

This volume seeks to explore the significance of local realities and their implications for a city's ability to adapt to globalism and thus, its capacity to address urban dilemmas. These classifications do not outline five stages in a linear development of world cities, but rather, distinguish five paths to the future city. The complexities of globalization are much more than a hierarchy of cities in the world economic order based on stages of economic development. We suggest this typology as a way of organizing how we believe different cities will deal with the inevitable challenge of globalization.

THE POSTINDUSTRIAL CITY

These cities were among the great industrial centers of the past, located primarily around the North Atlantic Rim. Some major Latin American cities may also come to follow this pattern of postindustrial development. The cities in this category reflect differential rates of adjustment to postindustrial realities. Yet, even in the most successful postindustrial cities, according to various macro-level measures, there is ample evidence of severe social dislocation.

Most growth now takes place in previously underdeveloped areas of the urban region, with abandonment of historic plants and areas under private control leading to the appearance of physical deterioration in a city's most traditional neighborhoods. This pattern of open-field growth has favored previously underdeveloped small and medium-sized cities, simultaneously nurturing the "edge city" phenomenon in North America and more focused urban expansion in Europe.[4] For Robert Bruegmann, one of the more intriguing questions to be answered in the future will be precisely how unique to North America the new decentralized and motorized urban regions of the United

States will prove to be. In crude shorthand, are Los Angeles, Phoenix, and Houston the urban future?

Julie Roqué rightly reminds us in her work that even areas within "successful" urban regions are being left behind in the process of postindustrial development and are increasingly marginalized from the global economy and technological changes that are driving late–twentieth century economic expansion and development. Such neighborhoods frequently become known for social deviance and violence. Jordi Borja suggests that political arrangements remain an important variable in how cities respond to global and internal change. Urbanites are often saddled with obsolete political institutions and arrangements even in the most successful postindustrial cities.[5] Such communities appear at times to be incapable of managing social and economic change even when all looks good according to indicators such as general level of job expansion and gross trade turnover.

The postindustrial city, therefore, is one in which the weight of traditional industrial production in the local economy has fallen whereas the role of the service sector has expanded in both employment and the creation of wealth. It is, in the words of Guy Burgel, a "city of consumption" rather than a "city of production"—or of production of a kind peculiar to the present era.[6] Galia Burgel and Guy Burgel explore these themes further in their discussion of new land-markets trends in Europe and elsewhere.

American urbanologists Paul Kantor and Hank Savitch referred to a postindustrial stage in the history of the city when they wrote in 1993 that

> While the age of global trade is upon us, so too is global diversity. Around-the-clock trading, international stock exchanges, mobile labor pools, and international communications and telecasting generate new roles for cities. Globalism has ushered in an array of functionally diverse cities. New York, London, Paris, and Tokyo have climbed to the financial and managerial command posts of the international economy. Singapore and Rotterdam guard their positions as world port cities. Brussels, Washington, and Moscow are vital for ensuring political agreements. São Paulo, Seoul, and Mexico City challenge the rest with new manufacturing capacity.[7]

Such urban restructuring is often related to the shifting place of the metropolitan economy in the international economic system. Old functions become obsolete, new functions emerge. Hank Savitch, for example, reported in *Post Industrial Cities* that New York City's economy lost almost five hundred thousand manufacturing jobs between 1965 and

1985, whereas it added just over that number of jobs in the service sector during the same period.[8] By the early 1970s, Savitch continues, 53 percent of all jobs in London were outside of manufacturing, a figure that rose to 80 percent a decade later. Meanwhile, the London metropolitan area lost six hundred thousand jobs. Paris also lost jobs during the same period, especially in manufacturing.

Savitch points to the accompanying problems of social adjustment. Even in the best case of macro-level adjustment—that of New York—the five hundred thousand workers who lost their manufacturing jobs did not necessarily fill the jobs that were created in the—primarily financial—service sector. Entirely different skills are required in the postindustrial age, skills frequently outside the experience and training of industrial workers. The postindustrial city thus becomes a tragedy for many individual workers and their families even as advances are being made overall. Edmundo Werna, Ilona Blue, and Trudy Harpham reveal that urban pathologies are not limited to cities in the so-called developing world.

The adaptation of cities to new postindustrial realities has not been uniform, and one may easily identify stark variation in the process of change, institutional response to change, and patterns of inequality.[9] Postindustrial cities include such culturally diverse urban agglomerations as Barcelona, Milan, San Francisco, Singapore, Los Angeles, and the Osaka-Kyoto Kansai region in Japan. Some have remade themselves on the foundation of their earlier success; others have turned largely to service activities; and still others have virtually abandoned their traditional activities to mimic the high-tech, information, and transportation intense successes of the New Age boomtown, discussed below.

There are a handful of truly global cities (e.g., Tokyo, New York, London), which may, in fact, draw more nourishment from one another than from their own national economies. The work of Saskia Sassen has been particularly important in establishing precisely how such cities function.[10]

Sassen argues that the new place of metropolitan urban regions is a direct consequence of the dramatic transformation of the world's economic system since 1970.[11] Adding Paris and Los Angeles to this comparison, urban observer Deyan Sudjic wrote in his 1992 work *The 100 Mile City* that London, Paris, Tokyo, New York, and Los Angeles are the largest, furthest evolved, and most important postindustrial cities.[12] These five metropolitan regions have metamorphosed into an integrated system of interlinked, but also antagonistic, urban communities. Together they dominate the world's economy and cultural life, even while struggling with one another to maintain their position against potential competitors. The postindustrial environment thus becomes a Hobbesean world of unending struggle for survival and dominance.

THE NEW AGE BOOMTOWN

These cities have capitalized on newly developed industries and technologies to emerge as major financial-service production centers, with special reliance on postindustrial technologies. Julie Roqué's discussion of cities and technological change poses a critical perspective on precisely how urban cities are shaped by innovation. These particular cities and regions are driven by global economic forces, are outward looking, and tend to be located around emerging markets—in the Pacific Rim (primarily in Asia, such as Sydney, Singapore, and Hong Kong, but also in North America, around Seattle and Vancouver) and in Latin America (primarily around the Gulf of Mexico).[13] In a few instances, they might focus their energies on information rather than trade, as Borja describes in the cases of Montpellier and Tübingen, both European New Age boomtowns.[14] The New Age boomtown is linked to the global economy with well-developed infrastructure, particularly advanced communications and transportation systems. In addition, these cities draw from a highly skilled and educated labor base. They are consciously and deliberately protagonists in the global economy.

The typical boomtown grew relatively recently, so physical and spatial patterns tend to be more spread out than in earlier industrial cities—although the overall extent of their built-up area may be greater. As strange as it may appear, the 1990 census showed that metropolitan New York and metropolitan Los Angeles have the same overall population density.[15] Cities like Houston and Miami tend to sprawl and have not focused on a traditional center, even where an historical center exists.

Transportation is crucial for any city serving emerging markets and the success of one seems to threaten the well-being of others in the same region. For example, Miami has become a gateway city for Latin America, even taking traffic away from cities such as Caracas, Panama, and Santa Marta that lie on the edge of the Caribbean Basin, and Houston's growth may be undermining economic activity in New Orleans.

Boomtowns in Europe tend to emerge from university centers, which moved early into applied technology. Montpellier became the central European node of the Bitnet and built research parks around the charming historical core. Another form of boomtown is the administrative or bureaucratic city. This is not new—Washington, D.C., and

New Delhi are prime examples—but economic integration is providing the basis for new growth in Brussels as well as giving a tremendous boost to the legal profession in towns along the Texas-Mexico border. Taking into account Halfani's notion of multiple hierarchies of cities, it is possible to add to this list several cities in the developing world, such as Campinas, Brazil, and Nairobi, Kenya, that base their growth either on high-tech universities or international bureaucracies. In each of these cases, the primary driving force has been sufficient to enable the city to diversify its job base and to diversify its function or role.

There is another type of boomtown, most frequently found in the developing world or in the former socialist countries. It is a city that is *becoming* industrial and that is entering the international market immediately and directly, whose entry into the international market is designedly competitive by virtue of inputs of cutting-edge technology, by virtue of explicit policies and actions by the state, or by the international nature of the capital behind its growth. Thus, Seoul, Korea, and São Paulo, Brazil, as a result of deliberate state-sponsored or supported industrial policy and subsidies, produce cars cheaper and faster than Detroit and produce the most sophisticated steel products and push them into the U.S. market in a manner that has both U.S. producers and the U.S. government very concerned. In a similar fashion, Vladivostok and Vostochnyi Port, in Russia; Lodz, Poland; Valparaiso, Chile; and Monterrey, Mexico, have elbowed their way onto the world stage with aggressive competitiveness, but using a different strategy. They have attracted entrepreneurs with a huge appetite for risk, who have placed their investments with an eye on niches in the international market from the very beginning.

THE POSTSOCIALIST CITY

Located throughout the formerly Communist states of East Central Europe and Central Eurasia, these urban communities confront multiple transitions simultaneously. One transformation constitutes a structural reorganization of the economy away from traditional industrial production. Another involves a profound change in the property regime. A third connects with issues of political regime change and nation-building. A fourth is a consequence of the introduction of state-of-the-art technologies into urban environments that had previously lagged behind the technological standards of the West. Cellular telephones and facilities for electronic mail, for example, are being introduced even as more traditional telecommunications services languish in a mire of obsolete equipment. Finally, as the introduction of cellular telephones and electronic mail portends, postsocialist cities are only now becoming subject to the forces of globalization that so dominate the urban scene elsewhere. It is too early to know precisely how global forces will shape urban development in the postsocialist world other than to note the obvious: experience elsewhere indicates that such influence will be momentous.

Old bureaucratic and political methods for negotiating between central authorities and local communities no longer achieve their desired ends in such a quickly changing environment. The logic of city-building decisions becomes quite different. Where personal connections and hidden corruption once enabled city leaders to protect their own interests as well as the interests of their communities, unbridled graft and yet-to-be-mastered financial incentives reign supreme. The conjunction of these profound changes in the organization of economic and urban life forces postsocialist municipal officials and urbanites to overcome a profound sense of disorientation as they seek to chart a new future for their communities.

Facing international competition for the first time in decades, postsocialist societies must reorient their economies toward new niches in the global economy. Managers must upgrade facilities capable of innovation and shut down those that have been rendered obsolete. Urban planning methods are similarly outdated. The preparation of socialist-era general development plans for cities and regions was a mammoth and complex undertaking.[16] Planners were driven to incorporate as much of human existence as possible into their formulas and maps. At the same time, the extensive economic, demographic, and social informational base that existed in every major city of the industrialized world was frequently either nonexistent or sealed from view. The indices and measures used to assess plan-fulfillment conformed to the peculiarities of the centrally planned economy, and are close to worthless when confronting the realities of a market economy. Wholesale revision of city planning is required before municipalities can begin to wrestle with pressing planning issues.

The question of property involves the reintroduction of private ownership of economic and physical capital. Such changes are fostering severe disruptions in the *modus vivendi* of urban communities as well as a dramatic restructuring of urban space as land and buildings are passed from state monopolies to individual and corporate ownership. New cleavages between owners and nonowners, among owners themselves, and between the public and private sectors produce previously unknown—or at least submerged—conflicts and competitions. Institutional structures within and outside the state are insufficiently developed to manage such conflicts. As Galia Burgel and Guy Burgel observe, urban political and economic power are being redistributed together with privatized firms and enterprises.

A number of postsocialist states that did not exist as recently as 1989 now confront the need to construct new states and foster new national identities. Beyond the scope of urban management in the narrow sense, these processes often play themselves out in city streets. City leaders find themselves responsible for controlling behavior and managing conflict resulting from the arrival and departure of large numbers of refugees, demobilized soldiers, and displaced persons. Civic leaders confront social and political groups seeking to confer new identities on their communities. Urban management becomes a task of alleviating tensions resulting from, and fervent searches for, new identity.

The social, economic, and political forces unleashed by the post-socialist transition magnified those problems that existed in the Communist past. Whatever the shortcomings of the prior regimes, informal bureaucratic mechanisms had evolved over the years to keep cities functioning. New coping mechanisms must be developed to insure that urban communities can successfully come to terms with new political, economic, and social realities. The complexity of this process may be seen in the housing sector.

A number of postsocialist regimes have launched ambitious housing privatization programs in an effort to foster new middle classes, alleviate demands on state budgets, and generally improve the housing stock. Yet, few postsocialist cities have been able to mold a comprehensive housing policy around the mantra of privatization. Financial instruments and institutions are nascent at best, construction supplies remain limited in design and availability, whereas quite often the basic legal and administrative supports required of a private housing market have yet to come into place. Basic urban infrastructure—heating, wastewater systems, water supplies, and electricity—once provided on a mass level to gigantic housing estates, cannot service individual apartments and houses without renovation and enormous investment. A robust private construction sector has already emerged throughout the postsocialist world suggesting that, no matter how daunting the impediments, urban communities remain surprisingly vibrant and robust.

THE PARTIALLY MARKETIZED CITY

These are urban communities of the developing world, primarily in Latin America, embedded in statist regimes that have protected private property rights and capital. Like the postindustrial city, with which they share several characteristics, such cities confront a drastic restructuring of their economies. Like the postsocialist city, the partially marketized city has undergone a complete structural reorganization of its economy, moving from a model based on import-substitution industrialization to an opening of the economic system to the competitive world market. The most successful of them, like São Paulo, have many characteristics of the New Age boomtown. Export promotion, trade liberalization, and regional trade agreements mark the significant change that has occurred in Latin America since the mid-1970s. Following the debt crisis of the 1980s, adjustment programs based on fiscal restraint and privatization have dramatically reduced the role of the state in Latin America, with serious implications for the region's urban areas.

Cities have also undergone a political transformation with the consolidation of democracy in Latin America and elsewhere. K. C. Sivaramakrishnan maintains that issues of local governance are even more important in the mid-1990s than they were when Habitat I convened in Vancouver. Decentralization has been a critical aspect of recent efforts to restructure the state and redefine its role. This trend has significant ramifications for the urban populations whose political mobilization and participation demand the attention of local and national government. Political reforms have brought unprecedented numbers of local-level elections, giving rise to a new leadership with strong ties to grassroots community action. As a result of this massive transfer of decision-making and spending power from the central to the local level, Latin American municipal governments are now spending between two and four times as much as they were in 1976.[17]

In spite of these promising developments, "the decline of the state brought on by the debt crisis and restructuring reforms has left cities close to bankruptcy and impotence. No Latin American city has the fiscal and juridical independence to deal with the crisis of education and employment."[18] Municipal governments of partially marketized cities have failed to keep pace with rapid population growth augmented by tremendous rural-urban migration. The poorest citizens are moving further away from the center of employment, living in low-quality housing in illegal settlements in the city's periphery. Municipal governments are incapable of providing adequate public services and infrastructure to these informal or "unintended" cities.

The collapse of the state, combined with harsh structural adjustment programs, has accelerated the process of informality that distinguishes most of the cities of the South from the cities of the North. Social groups are organizing to demand that states, incapable of managing and providing for urban populations, reduce excessive regulation, recognize illegal settlements, and liberate the productive energy of informal entrepreneurs. "In other words, if the city is in fact self-built, it should also be self-governed."[19]

The central issue is not how to reach the entire population with the spectrum of services provided by the institutional city, but how to open the institutional space of the city to create the possibility of improving the urban population's quality of life. The solution turns on improving the cities, creating ties to the global economy, opening them to modern technology, and facilitating innovation and the population's access to education.

However, Latin American cities appear to be falling farther and farther behind on the crucial dimensions of urban adaptability—communications and transportation. Of the large cities in Latin America, only São Paulo has been able to sustain a high correlation between population growth and the creation of jobs in industry. Not coincidentally, São Paulo has the best communications and transportation network in the region. Unless the partially marketized city accepts its linkage to the developed world and increases its ability to adapt to the changes in the global economy, continued deterioration is assured. The future city in Latin America must become more integrated into the rest of the world or risk prolonging the underdevelopment of the entire region.[20]

The Marginalized City

These cities, located primarily in Africa, but found throughout the developing world, have been bypassed to a large degree by technological change and by the emerging global economy. The populations of marginalized cities are increasingly poor and left to survival strategies that draw on local resources. The contemporary African city nonetheless offers the prime example of such communities—there are more telephones in metropolitan Tokyo, for example, than on the entire African continent.

Of course, marginalization is not peculiar to cities in the Third World. There are social groups whose identification is often reinforced by racial or ethnic differences, and geographically definable neighborhoods—ghettos—within cities that are otherwise successfully engaged in the global economy, as well as within the cities of wealthy nations whose residents appear totally marginalized in the process of globalization and who demonstrate levels of social indicators comparable to those of the world's most underdeveloped cities. Rates of infant mortality, literacy, nutrition, and life expectancy might be alarmingly similar between the ghettos of some of the wealthiest cities in the United States and the shantytowns of the poorest cities of Africa. Although these neighborhoods and social groups are the most vulnerable populations of the cities of the developed world, they result from urban phenomena markedly distinct from those that produce marginalized cities. In political terms, the marginalized populations of Savitch's "distressed" cities and of what Manuel Castells called "the dual city"[21]— prosperous cities where there are large social and economic disparities—require a very different approach than that demanded by marginalized cities.

Globalization appears to be exacerbating the gap between the North and the South and, within the North, between prosperous and distressed cities. Hank Savitch broaches the question of increasing inequality among cities in the global system, to which Mohamed Halfani responds from an African perspective. Within the context of a new paradigm, as Halfani and other contributors demonstrate, the world is becoming increasingly divided into cities that are winners and those that are losers. Our task is to examine why some cities are bypassed and others are not.

In his study of African cities in the world economy, David Simon begins with the premise that much of the region's future is rooted in its colonial past. The colonial legacy of sub-Saharan Africa embedded the region's cities "firmly but extremely inequitably within the emerging capitalist world economy."[22] Simon concludes:

> the principal sub-Saharan African cities have experienced far less structural transformation and remain significantly more marginal to international flows and relations than their counterparts in Asia and Latin America, a feature attributable primarily to the continent's continued peripheral global economic position and role.[23]

There is much evidence that marginalized cities are increasingly less engaged in the global system. Foreign direct investment in African cities has steadily dropped and the region's share of world exports has also declined since the mid-1970s. These trends have serious implications for the provision of adequate infrastructure and human capital formation, affecting productivity and ultimately, the city's capacity for the generation of jobs and wealth. Furthermore, as María Elena Ducci and Julie Roqué document, many cities of the South have been forced by a lack of resources to make choices that have resulted in serious environmental degradation. Much of the literature refers to the 1980s and '90s as a period of "urban crisis" throughout Africa, marked by dropping rates of formal employment, deteriorating infrastructure and basic services, and the declining quality of the urban environment, both built and natural.[24] Municipal authorities have demonstrated little capacity for urban management on the scale necessary to confront this crisis.

Yet, marginalization cannot be viewed as a zero-sum game. Indicators such as infrastructure or services, job creation, the environment, and even urban governance fail to capture the element of dynamism in marginalized cities of the South. Mohamed Halfani's chapter in this volume draws attention to the important, yet unmeasured role the informal sector plays in the economy as well as the significance of a vibrant civil society that is key to understanding urban governance and political stability. The rise of the informal sector in marginalized cities is a response to the local government's inability to create sufficient jobs to keep pace with rapid population growth. According to an International Labor Office study, the informal sector employs 60 percent of the urban labor force in the typical African country.[25]

The informal sector has similarly demonstrated resourcefulness and vitality, creatively responding to the absence of adequate public services and infrastructure in the "unintended" city. Like the partially marketized city, the marginalized city's poorest populations are self-building the new city in unserviced, illegal areas located in the outskirts of the city. Halfani estimates that more than 75 percent of the basic needs of the bulk of the population of African cities is provided by the informal sector, including shelter, services such as water, energy, neighborhood security, wastewater removal, and transportation, and in some cases, land. Furthermore, Halfani argues that urban governance has been revitalized by the deployment of social capital embedded in traditional institutions to operate and manage African cities. This process is recognized by and interfaced with the formal system of urban management, indicating the emergence of a new mode of urban governance in Africa.

On a global level, marginalized cities may not be destined to remain on the periphery of an increasingly polarized world. Halfani's chapter details a new international division of labor that has resulted in a system of multiple hierarchies through which the marginalized city is able to insert itself in the global system via nodal linkages to networks, both global and regional. However, it is not clear if this model will prove to be more than a trickle-down approach to distributing benefits in the global system. Marginalized cities, just like partially marketized cities and postsocialist cities, must accommodate the new paradigm outlined by Savitch, placing them under tremendous pressure to compete. We must reconsider the implications of these dominant models and policy prescriptions that offer a market approach and cooperation, at best, as a remedy for human settlements in marginalized cities, particularly for the poorest segments of the population, in the emerging global era.

Governance and Success in the Global System

The lessons of the two-decade period between Habitat I and II have been ambiguous. This has been a period of tremendous change without question. Yet a number of seemingly eternal questions remain, as Martha Schteingart reminds us in her review of what has changed and what has not since Habitat I. Julie Roqué tells us how time has been compressed, whereas Michael White underscores how much more mobile we have all become. Robert Bruegmann cautions us to recall that "individuals in every generation, at least since the birth of the industrial revolution, have thought that they were watching the most rapid changes ever seen in history. They have all been correct."

One of the greatest lessons of the period in question can be drawn from observation of how issues of democracy have affected the ways in which cities make choices. The growth of democratic institutions, particularly at the local level, has eroded the capacity of overall planning. Planners or environmentalists may see zero-sum solutions, but the essence of politics, as K. C. Sivaramakrishnan writes, is the creation of compromise, especially when resources are finite. All of the chapters in this volume emphasize the important role that local institutions must play in urban management.

Jorge Heine, in a study of Benjamin Cole, who served for two dozen years as mayor of the Puerto Rico city of Mayaguez, contended that municipal leaders must learn how to create new resources to overcome small budgets, legislative constraints, and other obstacles. They must become political entrepreneurs who garner resources and allies from the most unlikely places.[26] The contemporary city's stormy diversity and dynamism can thus be converted into a resource. Successful leaders expand their communities' capacities beyond the formal constitutional, legal, financial, environmental, and cultural constraints within which they are forced to function. They convert metropolitan pluralism from a liability into an asset. The increasingly democratic politics of today's city represent just such an accommodation to the social fragmentation created by economic liberalization. But it is frequently a compromise of a peculiarly urban type—with a reliance on local politicians who frequently practice what has become known as "machine" politics.

Politicians of the 1990s throughout the world have been seeking to keep themselves in power by manipulating scarce resources through patronage networks to alleviate some of the local population's worst suffering in a time of economic and social upheaval. Machine politics becomes a means of social compromise by which a political class retains power in exchange for a distribution of resources to favored supporters by nonmarket means. Machine politics and bossism counteract the harshest realities of the unfettered market. "The politics of balance," Edward R. Kantowicz, a Chicago-based historian, wrote, "may sound boring, the stuff of safe-and-sane conservatism; but nothing could be further from the truth. In fact, maintaining a political balance in a rapidly growing, factionalized city is a highly dynamic even daring act." Authority depends on an ability "to accommodate, with amazing dexterity and flexibility, the explosive growth and bewildering diversity"[27] of such volcanic urban centers. Success beyond mere survival in today's global economy rests on the distinctive political resource of balance, of metropolitan pluralism.

Policy Implications

Perhaps most important of all, the sixteen chapters in this volume make arguments with three powerful implications for formulating public policies for cities. First, whether you agree with the convergence hypothesis or not; whether you give special attention to the cultural and historical attributes of cities that emphasize the local and the singular or privilege the global forces impinging on cities, all cities, no matter where they are and no matter what paths they may be following into the future, are faced with the dilemmas outlined in this volume.

Second, these dilemmas, like some mysterious new virus, are not subject to cost-free solutions, no matter what resources are applied to their solution. All solutions to these dilemmas require trade-offs, involve prejudice to groups in the society, and exacerbate other problems. As a consequence, it is our view that there is no single policy prescription for the dilemmas confronting the world's urban communities. The keys to successful urban practice are flexibility and tolerance for a variety of solutions to the same problem together with a willingness to encourage citizen participation in the formulation and execution of public policies. The central issue is no longer the clearest definition of an ideal solution to a precisely circumscribed problem, as it seemed to be during the halcyon days of urban planning. Although it would be an exaggeration to say we have entered a post-planning state, the point is that we approach urban dilemmas with less certitude than we had at the time of Habitat I.

The third suggestion for policymakers is that urban dilemmas almost always are multisectoral. Just as Richard Stren argues that urban problems cannot be understood fully within the constructs or paradigms of a single academic discipline, so, too, in the real world, solving urban problems requires deliberate violation of the traditional bureaucratic categories, such as housing, health, infrastructure, human resources, and employment. Especially among the most vulnerable groups in the urban society, the traditional ministries and the traditional models to alleviate distress do not get at the root of the problem. For the typical shantytown-dweller, it is housing, health, and employment all at the same time. The individual's existential urban dilemma cannot be dealt with effectively within the traditional categories of the ministries or the multilateral agencies charged with solving urban problems.

Today, solutions to problems at the local level, as well as urban success in the global environment, require a nonideological and multisectoral approach that welcomes popular participation in decision-making, that uses existing networks and NGOs (nongovernmental organizations) to define the agenda for action and to help set the priorities for limited resources, that uses those same NGOs or others to carry out decisions and, in appropriate circumstances, to distribute resources to citizen-residents. Rather than think in positivistic terms of solving urban problems, we propose policies that empower citizens to participate in the unending process of resolving urban dilemmas.

But local initiatives and the empowerment of civil society should not for an instant suggest that the state can abrogate its role. However much the national state may shrink or withdraw, the municipal government must be ready to act. In fact, if national governments withdraw from some activities, it may well become necessary for city governments to *increase* their participation. The concept of governance becomes more and more important. "Governance" implies a relationship between the citizen and the state that goes in two directions. Both are responsible and both are accountable. Neither can sit back and expect the other to act on their behalf. Both are engaged in a process, the *same* process. Although it is important for the modern state to provide space for entrepreneurs to invest and create jobs for the city's residents, leadership is more important in the entrepreneurial city of the twenty-first century than at any time in our history. As Borja and Savitch make plain, leadership in the city of the future must combine management skills for dealing with the city's population-citizenry and entrepreneurial skills to make the city competitive in the international economy, with political skills that maximize the accountability of the leader and the emerging civil society.

Even in this framework, certain policy solutions are clearer than others. For example, investment in education and health services are important to any city. They enhance equity, they improve the quality of life of all residents, and they make the city more competitive. No matter how limited the resource base of a city, it should privilege investment in human capital. Other issues are more ambiguous. For example, the consequences of environmental regulation or protection do not appear to fall evenly across the socioeconomic spectrum, so that even with unlimited resources and unfettered will, it may not be possible for a municipal government to satisfy most or all of its citizens. And, in democracies, it will be difficult to construct coalitions of voters to deal with these issues. The best policy prescription we offer in the short run is to distinguish clearly between the green agenda and the brown agenda. As outlined by Ducci, the green agenda centers on global environmental problems such as global warming, ozone-layer depletion, biodiversity, deforestation, and exhaustion of nonrenewable resources, whereas the brown agenda is concerned with the local urban environment, focusing on congestion, problems of water and air pollution, the lack of basic services and green areas, declining infrastructure, and poor housing conditions. Once these agendas are distinguished, the priority given to quality of life and human capital might well call for action on one or both agendas specific to each city.

One of the cruelest lessons to be learned from the experience of the period since Habitat I is that policies and projects that focus resources and political will on a solution to a vital problem and generate employment can, by virtue of their very success, exacerbate problems for that same city, simply by accelerating the rate of migration to the city in which the project is being implemented. Sustainability for cities, especially cities in the developing world, calls for multisectoral policies and projects to prevent asymmetries or disequilibria that might make matters worse in the long run.

Finally, for the sake of argument, we must consider that it is possible that the current bias in favor of markets will change over time and that cities in the former socialist bloc and in the developing world, for different reasons, will rush to return to statism, or, that cities in the more developed countries, disillusioned with open competition, could retreat behind walls of protectionism. Even so, it is our belief that in the short run cities everywhere will have to compete to survive and succeed, whether they compete in a global hierarchy or in regional networks. To compete for resources they will have to offer something—some product or some service—that others want. The basis for success in such a competitive environment will continue to be the human- and natural-resource base and its collective perception of the quality of urban life, the transportation infrastructure, and the ability to deal with information and money. Among the larger and older cities, the human-resource base appears to be linked to high culture and to intellectual activities, such as universities and publishing. These are the traditional attributes of an urban lifestyle. But, it is not enough to offer high culture for a small economic or social elite. Urban success in the future will require better utilization of the entire human-resource base and will require more attention to preserving the quality of life of all citizens and residents. The current trend toward increasing maldistribution of income is morally objectionable, politically unmanageable, socially corrosive, and economically unsustainable. The sustainable and the successful city is not merely a place in which a few get fabulously rich. It is a place in which all groups in the city participate and receive benefit from their participation.

Toward Habitat II

Our purpose in bringing together twenty-two urban specialists from a variety of nationalities and disciplines—academics, practitioners, and officials of national and local governments as well as international agencies—to contribute to this volume is to compile an agenda for cities for the future.

Two years prior to the second United Nations Conference on Human Settlements (Habitat II) in June 1996, the Comparative Urban Studies Program of the Woodrow Wilson International Center for Scholars, in cooperation with the Urban Development Division of the World Bank, assembled a diverse group of over thirty urban experts, to meet parallel to the preparations for the UN conference and define a set of issues critical to an understanding of the current state and future evolution of the world's cities. This working group set out to examine, in a nonofficial forum, how global economic and political changes since the first UN conference on human settlements in Vancouver in 1976 have affected the quantitative and qualitative dimension of cities: their economic prospects, social compacts, demographic composition, political dynamics, and environmental challenges.

The issues that the group found central to the understanding of the urban phenomena serve as the common themes treated by each of the chapters in this book: political change—including the end of the cold war and the shift to democratic forms of government—and its implications, governance, and the role of the state; globalization; contra-global phenomena like xenophobia, cultural specificity, and cultural pride; and the nature of competitiveness and regulation. Most important, our goal was to explore how the very understanding of urban affairs has changed over the past generation, reassessing in a global perspective the intellectual frameworks within which current urbanism discourse occurs.

In some instances, our multidisciplinary, multiregional approach has produced competing ideas, strengthening the argument that there are neither clear definitions nor perfect solutions to urban problems. The key to successful urban practice is flexibility. The chapters of this volume are linked by their exploration of global challenges as they filter through to the local level, and the crucial aspect of dynamic local responses to the urban dilemmas created by globalization. Our collective mission has been to construct a discussion framework for Habitat II based on research and reflections that provides a backdrop against which effective solutions can be found that will be useful to academics and policymakers alike. The ideas presented in this book add up to a powerful agenda, which we hope will move forward in the Habitat process, with positive implications for the future of human settlements.

Notes

[1]Jane Jacobs, *Cities and the Wealth of Nations* (New York: Random House, 1984), 221–25.

[2]See Saskia Sassen, *The Global City: New York, London, Tokyo* (Princeton, N.J.: Princeton University Press, 1991), and Mattei Dogan and John C. Kasarda, eds., *The Metropolis Era* (Beverly Hills, Calif.: Sage, 1988).

[3]Michael Cohen, notes from meeting of Wilson Center Habitat II working group, August 2, 1995.

[4]The term "edge city" was coined in Joel Garreau, *Edge City: Life on the New Frontier* (New York: Doubleday, 1991). On the spatial expansion of European cities, see Michael Parkinson, Alan Harding, and Jon Dawson, "The Changing Face of Urban Europe," in *European Cities Towards 2000: Profiles, Policies, and Prospects*, ed. Alan Harding, Jon Dawson, Richard Evans, and Michael Parkinson (Manchester, UK: Manchester University Press, 1994), 1–16; and Paul Cheshire, Dennis Hay, Gianni Carbonaro, and Nick Bevan, *Urban Problems and Regional Policy in the European Community* (Brussels: ECSC-EEC-EAEC, 1988).

[5]A point developed further in reference to the United States in David Rusk, *Cities Without Suburbs* (Washington, D.C.: Woodrow Wilson Center Press, 1993).

[6]Guy Burgel, *La ville aujourd'hui* (Paris, France: Hachette, 1993), 119–23.

[7]Hank V. Savitch and Paul Kantor, *Urban Mobilization of Private Capital: A Cross-National Comparison*, Woodrow Wilson Center Comparative Urban Studies Occasional Paper no. 3 (Washington, D.C.: Woodrow Wilson International Center for Scholars, 1993), 1–2. São Paulo and Seoul actually display characteristics of the New Age boomtown as well. Although these categories should not be considered mutually exclusive, we tend to see these cities primarily as boomtowns rather than postindustrial cities.

[8]H. V. Savitch, *Post-Industrial Cities: Politics and Planning in New York, Paris, and London* (Princeton, N.J.: Princeton University Press, 1988), 290–94.

[9]For such a comparison of U.S. cities, see Neal R. Peirce, *Citistates: How Urban America Can Prosper in a Competitive World* (Washington, D.C.: Seven Locks Press, 1993).

[10]Saskia Sassen, *The Global City,* and *Cities in a World Economy* (Thousand Oaks, Calif.: Pine Forge Press, 1994).

[11]Sassen, *The Global City,* 337.

[12]Deyan Sudjic, *The 100 Mile City* (San Diego, Calif.: Harcourt Brace, 1992).

[13]Derek Davies, "Traveller's Tales," *Far Eastern Economic Review* 151, no. 18 (May 2, 1991): 22; and Lily Kong and Brenda S. A. Yeoh, "Urban Conservation in Singapore: A Survey of State Policies and Popular Attitudes," *Urban Studies* 31, no. 2 (March 1994): 247–65.

[14]Michael Parkinson, "The Rise of the Entrepreneurial European City: Strategic Responses to Economic Changes in the 1980s," *Ekistics* 58, nos. 350–51 (Sept.–Dec., 1993): 280–99.

[15]As Judith A. Martin and Sam Bass Warner point out in an unpublished paper, the Census Bureau has, over the decades, enlarged its metropolitan boundaries: "New York from 4,000 square miles in 1950 to 7,600 square miles in 1990, Los Angeles from 4,900 to more than 6,700. . . . The 1990 density of Los Angeles was about 2,170 persons per square mile, New York 2,371. The addition of the Riverside–San Bernardino PMSA in 1990 obscures the density estimates for Los Angeles because this PMSA covers 27,270 square miles and was inhabited by only 34,000 persons. The density estimate given is without Riverside–San Bernardino." Judith A. Martin and Sam Bass Warner, "New Planning Goals and the Experience of Chicago's West Suburbs" (paper presented at the Woodrow Wilson International Center for Scholars, September 23, 1994), 5.

[16]For further discussion of this point, see R. A. French and F. E. Ian Hamilton, *The Socialist City: Spatial Structure and Urban Policy* (New York: Wiley, 1979), James H. Bater, *The Soviet City* (London, U.K.: Edward Arnold, 1980), and Judith Pallot and Denis J. B. Shaw, *Planning in the Soviet Union* (Athens: University of Georgia Press, 1981).

[17]"A Survey of Cities," *The Economist* (July 29–August 4, 1995): 17.

[18]Joseph S. Tulchin, *Global Forces and the Future City,* Woodrow Wilson Center Comparative Urban Studies Occasional Paper no. 4 (Washington, D.C.: Woodrow Wilson International Center for Scholars, 1994), 11.

[19]Ibid., 13.

[20]Ibid., 15.

[21]Manuel Castells, "The Rise of the Dual City: Social Theory and Social Trends," *Documento de Trabajo No. 9,* (Madrid, Spain: Instituto Universitario de Sociologia de Nuevas Tecnologias, Universidad Autonoma de Madrid, February 1990).

[22]David Simon, *Cities, Capital, and Development* (London, U.K.: Belhaven Press, 1992), 3.

[23]Ibid., 16.

[24]Richard Stren, "Urban Changes in Africa, 1960–1995," (paper prepared for IIED, London and Global Report on Human Settlements, Toronto, March 1995), 17. See also Richard Stren, *African Cities in Crisis: Managing Rapid Urban Growth* (Boulder, Colo.: Westview, 1989).

[25]International Labour Organisation, *The Informal Sector in Africa* (Addis Ababa, Ethiopia: Jobs and Skills Programme for Africa, 1985), 13–15.

[26]Jorge Heine, *The Last Cacique: Leadership and Politics in a Puerto Rican City* (Pittsburgh: University of Pittsburgh Press, 1993), 12–15.

[27]Edward R. Kantowicz, "Carter H. Harrison II: The Politics of Balance," in *The Mayors: The Chicago Political Tradition,* ed. Paul M. Green and Lelvin G. Holli (Carbondale and Edwardsville: Southern Illinois University Press, 1987), 16.

PART I

Urban Convergence and a New Paradigm

WITH A FOCUS ON improving living conditions of the world's poor and achieving more equitable access to resources, the recommendations emanating from the 1976 United Nations Conference on Human Settlements (Habitat I) in Vancouver centered on comprehensive settlement planning, with great faith in the government as an instrument of reform. Twenty years later, strategies for intervention are being formulated in a changing climate that embraces neoliberalism with the conviction that markets are the best way to promote social progress. In addition, the two-decade period between Habitat I and Habitat II has been marked by the process of globalization. Boundaries have been obscured by growing cultural and political linkages, economic integration, and increasing interdependence among nations. These global processes highlight the need for a broad, comparative analysis of cities that examines not only common dilemmas, but more importantly, the local dimension of shared urban problems. The first part of this book outlines how our understanding of the world's cities has changed since the Vancouver conference, and as a result, how new policy objectives and prescriptions have evolved.

Cities of the North and South are becoming increasingly similar in their most important characteristics, argues Michael Cohen, citing areas of convergence such as growing unemployment, declining infrastructure, deteriorating environment, and institutional weakness. This common set of critical problems facing urban areas translates in political terms to a collapsing social compact, reflected in crime, violence, racism, and xenophobia. While these problems are shared by the North and the South, regardless of level of national development, Cohen writes, "it is precisely the variations in economic, financial, and institutional capacity that account for the differential prospects for improvement over time." In drawing conclusions about urban convergence and commonalities of urban phenomena at the global level, it is essential to recognize the importance of "local perceptions, motivations, and culture" as well as "the specificity of place and landscape" as a basis for policy and action, concludes Cohen.

The very way in which these urban dilemmas are perceived has changed since 1976, with important implications for urban policy and practice. Hank Savitch outlines a new social paradigm centered on "incrementalism, entrepreneurship, and markets" that replaced the "rational, comprehensive, government centered" approach that dominated Habitat I. Cities by nature, argues Savitch, are capable of flourishing in this new environment, particularly in the context of increasing globalization. Savitch details the rise of "delocalized" cities that have assumed new roles as autonomous entrepreneurs, seeking their own businesses, joining together to form consortia, and even adopting their own foreign policies. On the flip side, however, disparities are bound to ensue from the process of globalism and its relentless pace of competition, creating winners and losers. Following investment patterns and financial flows, Savitch concludes that the gap between richest, rising, and poorest economies appears to be increasing. By calling on government to undertake only what it can do well, by building social capital, and by forming cooperative and collaborative relationships, cities can improve their prospects for adapting to delocalized and global status and "take up a place at the leading edge of the new social paradigm."

The socioeconomic mechanisms behind access to land, social division, segregation, and housing problems have fundamentally remained the same during the twenty-year period between Habitat I and II. However, there has been a dramatic change in urban discourse, argues Martha Schteingart, noting the absence of discussion of these issues—the structural problems of underdeveloped cities—in preparation for the 1996 UN Conference on Human Settlements. This change has profoundly affected the goals, implementation, and administration of urban policy. Urban policy is now centered on new formulas for community organization with an emphasis on nongovernmental organizations and on the relationship between the state and civil society, writes Schteingart. While the most important instrument for social change embraced in 1976 was state-centered planning on all levels, the Istanbul conference focuses on enabling strategies that emphasize neoliberal reforms such as decentralization and privatization and the principles of empowerment and equity. Schteingart argues that such policies imply the acceptance of poverty, leaving the solutions to serious social problems in the hands of the poor themselves. The importance of enabling strategies and the notions of governance and leadership cannot be ignored, Schteingart concludes, however, they are not sufficient in a world where access to basic resources is increasingly inequitable and where international relations are more and more asymmetrical.

Chapter 2

The Hypothesis of Urban Convergence: Are Cities in the North and South Becoming More Alike in an Age of Globalization?

Michael A. Cohen

A first-time visitor from São Paulo to Los Angeles remarked: "It's all very familiar. I've been here before."

A taxi driver in Bangkok proudly commented to a client: "With all of our traffic, we have become modern. We are just like New York!"

"A recent survey of 150 mayors from around the world revealed that all of them listed the most serious problem affecting their city was unemployment." (*New York Times*, August 19, 1994).

This chapter examines the hypothesis that cities in the North and South are becoming more alike in their most important characteristics: growing unemployment, declining infrastructure, deteriorating environment, collapsing social compact, and institutional weakness. Although the degrees of similarity and the meanings of these shared features differ between any two cities and between northern and southern cities, the chapter argues that a common set of critical economic, social, infrastructural, environmental, and institutional problems beset urban areas regardless of level of national development. The assertion that these problems are shared does not imply that urban areas in the North and South also share equal capacities to address and to resolve them. In fact, it is precisely the variations in economic, financial, and institutional capacity that account for the differential prospects for improvement over time. Moreover, important differences in national and local cultures result in popular assignment of dissimilar meanings to apparently similar characteristics.

Understanding of local conditions and the process of convergence has been complicated by the globalization of the world economy. Growing linkages, interdependence, and diffusion of cultural patterns through mass media have led to a widespread perception of growing homogeneity of economic and social phenomena. Local responses to local problems and processes, when they appear similar across cities, are frequently ascribed to the forces of globalization. However, these responses may in fact be rooted in local realities, for example, local labor or environmental conditions, and may have nothing to do with global processes. Similarly, the impact of global processes on individual cities does not necessarily imply a resulting similarity in urban conditions. Assessing the significance of convergence, therefore, requires an appreciation of causality and of factors contributing to patterns of change, including local responses to external and/or global pressures.

Paradoxically, the chapter also shows that convergence may be affected by processes of marginalization whereby specific localities, such as East African cities, may not be included in global patterns of exchange and communications. Declining infrastructure or reduced private investment in an African city, for example, may be both a cause and an effect of geographical or economic exclusion; that is, cumulative disadvantages may exacerbate existing conditions.

In addition, the appearance of converging phenomena may be a result of unintended consequences. For example, governments have frequently ignored the need of the poor to be located near income-generating opportunities, and they are surprised by ubiquitous street vendors and the informal sector. Governments bulldoze slums in Nairobi or Jakarta, destroying the assets of the poor, and then are taken aback when new slums appear.

Finally, the use of the terms "North" and "South" is admittedly problematic. As Pasqual Maragall, the mayor of Barcelona, says frequently, "I come from a city which is on the North of the South and the South of the North. And in every northern city, there is a southern city, and the opposite is also true."[1] This reality suggests that using such a dualism as North and South may distract the reader from the main line of the argument presented here. Nevertheless, this oversimplification can also help to strengthen this argument and provoke the needed discussion about those cases that do not confirm the original hypothesis.

Unemployment and the Absorption of Labor

Significant unemployment is a problem shared by most cities of both North and South. Despite a range of measurement problems in determining labor force participation rates, it is a common perception that large numbers of the labor force in most cities are unemployed.

Although the origins of this phenomenon vary from industrialized to developing countries, it nevertheless exists.[2]

In the North, slow economic growth in many cities has reduced the rate of new job formation. This overall reduction in labor absorption has been accompanied by increased labor productivity in some sectors as a result of technological change. The demand for labor in manufacturing jobs has decreased significantly in most industrialized countries, most visibly in sectors that have experienced major technological revolutions in production processes, such as the automotive industry in Detroit or steel in Pittsburgh. Reduced demand in the North, however, has also occurred in industries in which labor is still needed but can be found more cheaply in developing countries. The export of manufacturing jobs, whether from the United States to Mexico, or Sweden to Thailand, has contributed to a reduced demand for labor at a time when there have also been large increases in the female potential labor force. Changed lifestyles, the need for second incomes, and expectations of women raised through a generation of post–World War II education have all resulted in a changed composition of the demand for jobs. While some of this growing labor force is absorbed through an expanded tertiary sector, including service industries, many of these jobs are also low-paying and therefore do not satisfy the need for income.

The net economic effects of high levels of urban unemployment, reaching 15 percent in France, 22 to 24 percent in Spain, and almost 50 percent of African-American males in some U.S. cities, are reduced incomes and levels of well-being frequently below the level of the previous generation. This has become a first-order political priority. In sharp contrast to a generation ago, in the 1990s mayors are leading trade missions that seek direct foreign investment and are actively competing for new economic opportunities for their populations. Mayor Richard J. Daley could keep the Chicago economy strong through federal investment in infrastructure in the 1960s. But his namesake son, as mayor, must now go to Japan to compete for investment with other North American and European mayors.

In contrast to the situation in the North, demographic pressures, low levels of productivity of capital and labor, and macroeconomic contraction fuel the unemployment crisis in cities in the South. Continuing high birthrates and the relative youth of most urban populations assure a steady flow of potential entrants into the labor market in developing countries. The urban population increase projected for developing countries from 1990 to 2020 is 2.4 billion people, from 1.5 to 3.9 billion, or one million per week for thirty years. This is equivalent to one

Goma, Zaire (the town that received the flow of Rwandan refugees in the summer of 1994), a week, which would also be without water supply and sanitation, but obviously not all in one place. Nevertheless, the "invisible" one million begin to show up on the urban landscape at some point. One such entry point is the labor market.

Being available for entry into the labor market, however, is very different from securing employment. A job search is normally a long and very frustrating experience. In many cases these new entrants lack training and skills required for formal sector employment. Indeed, formal sector jobs themselves are frequently rationed through complex labor regulations and informal practices. Increasing proportions of this potential labor force, therefore, turn to the informal sector and often lower levels of productivity and income.

Whether jobs are found in the formal or the informal sector, workers encounter serious constraints on their productivity resulting from infrastructure deficiencies, such as a lack of public provision of water supply, electricity, garbage collection, and transport.[3] Substantial levels of private capital investment by entrepreneurs are required to provide needed inputs for production. A survey of small and medium-sized firms in Lagos, Nigeria, showed that employers were spending an average of 20 percent of fixed capital investment on infrastructure, thereby reducing profits and the possibility to generate more jobs.[4] Not surprisingly, smaller firms feel the impact of public sector deficiencies more acutely than larger firms because the investment in infrastructure represented a greater share of their total investment. Therefore, this situation has serious distributional impacts in addition to limiting the growth of firms.

Other constraints on productivity include excessive regulation, as documented by Hernando de Soto in Lima, Peru,[5] and by many studies of the process of obtaining official permits for various types of economic activity. In 1990, it took fifty-five steps and up to five years to obtain a construction permit in Kuala Lumpur.[6] These constraints operate at the city level and reduce the overall level of productivity of urban-based economic activities in many developing countries. As one observer has noted, "an inefficient Cairo means an inefficient Egypt." Bangkok loses a large share of its product in traffic delays. The average car in Bangkok spends forty-four days a year stalled in traffic. São Paulo has twice as many cars as telephones, resulting in traffic congestion and environmental costs that increase the cost of doing business in the metropolitan area. These examples are not caricatures, but represent actual outcomes of prevalent tendencies in many, if not most, urban areas in the South.[7]

Demographic pressures (fueling a high demand for jobs) and severe constraints on productivity both contribute to an urban employment crisis in the South. This process is much worsened in economies that themselves may be contracting as a result of global recession, debt crises, macroeconomic adjustment, and shifting global patterns of demand for items produced in Southern cities. Continued recession in the North, exacerbated in Germany and central Europe by the political and economic collapse of the Eastern bloc, has sharply reduced the demand for products from the South. This drop has fostered frequent waves of protectionism in northern countries. At the same time, Latin America and Africa have experienced macroeconomic crises of accelerating debt service, runaway inflation, fiscal deficits, and growing trade deficits. All of these have contributed to plummeting levels of public and private investment in cities and a sharp contraction in new job creation. Lower subsidies to urban populations for energy, water supply, transport, and social services have further reduced urban real incomes, even while producer prices for food have increased in rural areas, thereby correcting earlier urban biases in income and levels of well-being.[8] Dropping urban real incomes further reduce economic multipliers, the demand for goods and services in urban areas, and hence the demand for labor.

These patterns at the national and urban levels are exacerbated by the globalization of production in many industries. Footloose investors move industries away from middle-income developing countries when wage levels increase too much. They trade off lower labor costs against better infrastructure in the belief that infrastructure will improve over time. This has certainly been true in the cases of Indonesia and Thailand, while it is less apparent in sub-Saharan Africa. Free-trade agreements such as NAFTA; the Asian-Pacific Accord reached at Bogor, Indonesia, in November 1994; and the MERCOSUR framework in the southern cone of Latin America also speed up patterns of employment dislocation.

In summary, while the causes of urban unemployment in the North and South are certainly different, their manifestations and consequences are similar, if not identical. Increasing numbers of low-income earners, working in the service sector, face rising prices for many needed urban services and the satisfaction of basic needs. Homelessness, youth unemployment, and growing social problems of the poor, including crime and drugs, are evident in both northern and southern cities. In economic terms, the unemployed continue to consume various public services in the cities, but they do not contribute tax revenue for the operation and maintenance of those services.

The Decline of Urban Infrastructure

The slow growth of the economic base of cities in both the North and South is also immediately reflected in the slow growth of public investment in infrastructure such as roads, water supply, sanitation, liquid waste treatment, solid waste collection and disposal, electricity, and telecommunications. In the North, certainly in North America and to a lesser extent in Europe, there has been a decade of debate about whether there is an *infrastructure crisis*.[9] This debate has reflected the common experience of the public with collapsing bridges in Connecticut, failed water and sewer systems in Chicago and Washington, electricity blackouts on the eastern seaboard, and the increasing number and size of potholes due to ineffective road maintenance throughout urban areas. Although many of these physical indicators of the decline of infrastructure are certainly discernible and accurate, they do not capture the more important point that infrastructure in many cities in the North does not serve the new economic needs and community preferences of the urban population.[10] Moreover, many infrastructure investments seem to come at very high financial and environmental costs, which are increasingly apparent to and hardly appreciated by urban residents. The range of common negative reactions to infrastructure, from shoot-from-the-hip NIMBY (Not in My Back Yard!) reactions and BANANA (Build Absolutely Nothing Anywhere Near Anybody!) responses to more sophisticated assessments, and fear of environmental damage from electromagnetic waves, are all based on a growing mistrust of state and bureaucratic motivations and behavior at the local level.[11] As one Hispanic, middle-aged, female resident of the South Bronx appealed at a 1993 community meeting with local officials, "Please, please, at least don't hurt us. We're so tired of getting hurt."

While this description is certainly too summary and there are many important works which pose a finer-grained analysis of the situation, the consequences of infrastructure decline in cities reinforce constraints on the productivity of labor and capital and add to negative externalities through insensitivity to environmental and social consequences.

Similarities of this situation to circumstances in the South lie primarily in three areas: (1) the poor performance of infrastructure in meeting local needs without causing environmental damage, (2) the apparent limited financial resources for investment, and (3) the surprisingly weak institutional capacity for management.[12] As noted previously, there is almost global dissatisfaction with the performance of urban infrastructure. For example, despite substantial capacity to pay for urban water supply, water utilities and other public institutions seem unable to put together reasonably efficient service for which urban residents are willing to pay. More than 170 million urban residents in the South now lack clean water supply, even though they frequently pay between fifteen and twenty times more per liter of water than do those households served by water connections in their homes.[13] People obviously must and do consume water to survive, yet public institutions are unable to meet increasing demand. Curiously, experts complain that half of the water produced for urban consumption in the South is lost between the production source and the intended consumer, yet roughly the same amount is unaccounted for in Montgomery County, Maryland, raising the question asked by one Nigerian water engineer, "Is 50 percent of water lost a high or low number?" Clearly this is a high number in economic, financial, environmental, and engineering terms.

Another indicator of poor infrastructural performance in the South is urban sanitation. While millions of urban households receive piped water supply or use communal water-supply sources such as standpipes, many of those millions lack effective on-site sanitation facilities.[14] This applies not only to human waste, but also to other forms of solid and liquid waste. A 1994 survey of infrastructure in Latin America noted that only 2 percent of all urban waste was treated before disposal.[15] This imbalance between the provision of water supply to communities and the lack of facilities to move waste water out is fundamental in terms of its consequences for environmental sanitation, pollution of natural resources, and human health.

The cost of urban transport is yet another important indicator of insufficient urban infrastructure in the South. In many large cities, households spend close to 25 percent of their income on transport. As one observer noted, "With 35 percent of income devoted to housing, people spend 60 percent of their income before they even put a meal on the table and a shirt on their backs." The physical sprawl of cities and long commuting distances, often more than an hour of travel each way, have made urban transport a major constraint on income generation and social mobility. The demand for mobility is reflected in an accelerating rate of motorization in southern cities, which in turn exacerbates traffic congestion and increases the pressure on infrastructure performance. In the mid–1970s, Robert Hackenberg suggested that the spatial growth of cities in the Philippines had created a concentric distribution of income, with poorer households living in the peripheral rings, unable to afford the transport costs needed for more than one family member to earn income.[16] In Bangkok in 1994, the poor could not afford to live outside the central city so they further densified crowded slums.

The second broad similarity between North and South is *the apparent lack of financial resources for investment in infrastructure.*[17] As suggested earlier in the distinction between capacity and willingness to pay, urban residents have income that can be devoted to financing infrastructure. Yet somehow, even in cities within countries with sharply contrasting levels of development and disposable income, there is the common claim that there are no resources for road repair, sewage treatment, or infrastructure extension. Although the public treasuries of developing countries are certainly less endowed than their counterparts in the North, the same language is inaccurately used to argue that there are no public revenues for these purposes. In both cases, however, funds are devoted to expensive prestige projects such as airports, bridges, and tunnels, which may be useful for some portion of the population but frequently will not serve the needs of the most needy.

All of these points lead to the third similarity, which is the surprisingly weak capacity for infrastructure management in both North and South. There are certainly fewer trained personnel working in the public institutions responsible for urban infrastructure in the South, and coupled with the lack of spare parts and operating budgets, this is reflected in poor management. Yet the biases of infrastructure managers in both North and South, regardless of national wealth, are shared: They prefer large capital-intensive projects that emphasize investment and construction rather than efforts to improve operations and maintenance. This is particularly striking when one considers that the stock of urban infrastructure investments is about US$3 trillion in developing countries with annual investment at about US$150 billion. (External contributions to new investments are about US$5 billion.) There are, therefore, enormous benefits to be obtained from better operations and maintenance. The shared common indicator of these biases is the low level and quality of service to consumers, despite often enormous sunk investments.

The Deteriorating Environment

A third broad area of convergence between the North and the South is the deteriorating urban environment.[18] In the North, the "discovery" of the urban environment over the past twenty years has led to many efforts to reduce industrial and automotive emissions into the air, curtail pollution of waterways and lands, and preserve the fragile ecosystem. Many of these initiatives have been successful, such as controlling transport-related air pollution in Amsterdam, and limiting industrial emissions in Pittsburgh and Tokyo and Kitakyushu in Japan.[19] Increasingly stringent regulations governing the disposal of toxic and medical wastes and new levels of sensitivity to other environmental risks are all evidence of growing public sophistication concerning, and accountability for, the urban environment. The rapid spread of recycling in the Organization for Economic Cooperation and Development (OECD) countries in the early 1990s is a remarkable behavioral change. Yet, with only a few exceptions, the absolute quality of the urban environment continues to deteriorate in terms of depletion of natural resources, pollution of neighboring areas through disposal of urban waste, and weakness of environmental governance.

This last point is crucial. In political terms, there is no effective political consensus that could establish a set of rules concerning sustainable levels of consumption of natural resources in the North. Almost all cities consume inordinately high levels of energy and water that are not sustainable over time.[20] Yet efforts to significantly restrain private car use through gasoline taxes, and to favor mass transit alternatives, are not under serious consideration. Similarly, many cities face rising marginal costs for water that has to be harvested at greater distances from final consumption. Los Angeles consumes water from sources some five hundred miles away. However, few communities have modified the practice of watering lawns or begun conserving water for other priority uses. Environmental fundamentalists can wage *jihads* over the spotted owl, yet few are prepared to fight the political battles over increasing salinity in the Central Valley of California or air pollution in Los Angeles. It is simply incomprehensible that, as a 1994 White House paper reported, one in four American families lives within four miles of a toxic waste site.[21] And yet, relatively few communities mobilize against this threat.

On one issue, however, there does seem to be an implicit political consensus among the majority, that it is *acceptable* for the poor to bear a disproportionate share of the impact of urban environmental deterioration. This implicit agreement is manifest in the siting of infrastructure and other environmentally unfriendly facilities such as waste dumps and sewage treatment plants. The tardy call for environmental justice, although growing, is hardly a murmur against the roar of bulldozers and construction machinery working on such facilities.[22]

There is an important gap, therefore, between the rhetoric of environmental protection in the cities of the North and the gradual spread of negative impacts, initially felt by the poor and eventually by the population as a whole. This growing gap is reflected in public awareness of the fact that the arrangements for urban governance, whether municipalities or metropolitan frameworks, do not meet the needs of protecting the natural resource bases of cities. Questioning by city authorities of the efficacy of the Metropolitan Toronto government at managing the environmental resources of the Toronto region suggests that even where metropolitan government is seen to be effective in providing infrastructure and social services, it may not be able to effectively control natural resource flows that go beyond metropolitan jurisdictions.

This debate in the North has only recently begun in the South. Nevertheless, rapid demographic and spatial growth of cities and towns in the South has placed great pressures on the environmental resources in these urban regions.[23] As suggested earlier, the relatively widespread absence of environmental infrastructure, such as water and waste treatment facilities, has created serious pollution and environmental sanitation problems. The absence of data about air and water quality, moreover, adds to these problems by making it impossible to establish meaningful and attainable standards for environmental protection. And indeed, even if meaningful standards could be formulated and adopted by local authorities, there are no personnel or instruments to enforce these standards in most communities in the developing world. In this respect, continuing urban environmental decline is very much related to the absence of urban environmental governance.[24] The prospects for improvements on a wide scale in the urban South are therefore very limited.

A Collapsing Social Compact

It is not surprising that the concurrence of declining prospects for employment, infrastructure services, and the environment should lead to accentuated social conflict in both North and South.[25] In the first instance, there is simply more competition for fewer jobs and income-earning opportunities. In European or North American cities there are increasing pressures from new entrants into the labor force, whether women from the North, or male and female migrants, often from the South. Differences among African-Americans and Hispanic-Americans now go beyond racial competition for jobs and housing, to extend to new definitions of "affirmative action" or "fair share," in which social differences have become wrapped up in efforts to compensate for past and present disadvantages. Similarly, new social or environmental costs become further reified by public policy. Another category under attack is welfare mothers, whose reproductive behavior, literacy, job searches, and food consumption are all considered eligible arenas for social policy and social engineering.

The emergence of the Contract With (or on) America and its effort to institutionalize such moves under the rubric of "reform," policy to avoid pressing unfunded mandates onto the states, and Proposition 187 in California, are all likely to accelerate the collapse of a broad-based social compact that includes the poor. The administration's "Middle Class Bill of Rights" may have some electoral justification from a political perspective, but it encourages neither cooperation among traditional Democratic constituencies nor social cohesion. Blaming the victim occurs on many levels, including dressed-up academic treatises such as *The Bell Curve.*

These same political and social forces are manifested in Europe, where debate has reemerged in Sweden, Italy, Spain, France, and even in the Netherlands about how great an effort can be made to retain social cohesion through public policies and programs. Waves of immigrants from Turkey, North Africa, and the former Yugoslavia have been a key stimulus for this debate. Xenophobic behavior in most countries is a good barometer of perceived social mobility among urban residents.

Similar, if not identical pressures are being experienced in southern cities. Ethnic and class violence are more prevalent, even expected in many cities, as so-called criminality among the poor is understood as rational behavior in a time of economic crisis. As one Malian official explained to me in Bamako in 1995, when the government is perceived to have fewer means to provide for the people, the people express their disappointment and need for assistance by fighting each other. African cities have long traditions of expelling migrants from neighboring countries when their own economies contract. Similarly, the militancy of demands by Latin American social groups for their "rights" to occupy the city or specific urban spaces has also increased. Caste differences have emerged even more sharply in Indian cities as the structure of economic opportunity narrows. Ethnic conflict flourishes across the border in Karachi where the city seems to be lurching toward a Beirut-like situation. A variant on this process is growing Islamic fundamentalism in urban Algeria, where religious zealots are able to enlist broad-based support from a disaffected urban citizenry. All of these examples lead to the conclusion that it is only a matter of time before authoritarian forces will have well-justified excuses to intervene and topple fragile democracies.

Institutional Weaknesses in Both North and South

The set of problems outlined in this chapter result, to a significant degree in many countries, from the perceived, and hence actual weakness of urban (and national) institutions. The impact of a cumulative decline of economic opportunity, public infrastructure, environmental conditions, and social cohesion on the capacity of local institutions to initiate remedial actions is profound. Declining economic fortunes reduce revenue bases at times when new steps are required to rehabilitate infrastructure and protect environmental resources. At the same time, the political consensus required to mobilize new financial resources to solve these problems is absent. Italian-like stalemates develop and are reflected in many cities by a perceived status quo, masking a gradual decline at best.

These trends raise the question of whether national governments continue to be relevant to urban problems. In general, many national governments seem to deny the importance of the local as a decision variable in the management of many national policies and programs.

The Urban Paradox

The observation that cities in the North and South are converging in some of their most significant objective characteristics is important in the broad comparative understanding of cities. It is also a radical departure from the common-sense perception of great differences that existed in the 1960s or 1970s when urban analysis became a priority issue in public policy, at least in the northern countries. It is important to underline the shared problems of policy and institutional performance to demonstrate to officials and observers of urban life that they face common dilemmas and that there may be surprising sources of experience and learning in far away cities.

In presenting these shared phenomena, I have sought to distinguish between objective conditions and the perceived meanings of those conditions. This juxtaposition poses what might be called "the urban paradox": Even as objective conditions are becoming more similar and shared at a global level, their meanings are becoming more local and subjective. This paradox is reflected in the observation of Charles Correa, the Indian architect, that even as Bombay's environment and physical conditions are deteriorating, it is becoming an increasingly interesting and vibrant place in which to live.[26] This statement is reminiscent of that of the New Yorker who refers to "the city" as if there were only one urban area deserving this honored appellation. The local is sacred.

Over the past twenty years, this local dimension—the specificity of place, landscape, and culture of urban places—has increasingly been acknowledged as the most critical feature that makes urban life worthwhile, despite the hassle. Alice Coleman writes of local public housing in Britain as "utopia on trial," showing how poorly designed physical environments destroy social prospects.[27] Richard Sennett movingly reminds us of "the conscience of the eye," which is profoundly local and immediate, as the basis of social and personal judgment about whether cities are morally and esthetically acceptable.[28] More recently, Witold Rybczynski elegantly explains in his book, *City Life: Urban Expectations in a New World*, how our expectations of urban life are very great even when the historical and physical conditions for success may not be present.[29]

All of these perspectives emphasize the importance of the "subjective" in understanding the significance of convergence. Above all, they suggest that even when there appear to be clear conclusions about the causes and manifestations of urban processes, and their commonality across a global range of cities is appreciated, the basis for policy and action itself must be rooted in local perceptions, motivations, and culture. Indeed, the very assertion of convergence at the global level should provoke an affirmation of the local, wherever it occurs. The widespread character of this reaction, interestingly enough, is another example of the similarity of processes—objective and subjective—which are becoming the most important recognized features of urban life.

Notes

[1]Pasqual Maragall, mayor of Barcelona, speech to Association of Ibero-American Mayors, Barcelona, December 1993.

[2]World Bank, *Workers in an Integrating World*, World Development Report, 1995 (Washington, D.C.: Oxford University Press for the World Bank, 1995).

[3]Kyu Sik Lee and Alex Anas, "Manufacturers' Responses to Infrastructure Deficiencies in Nigeria: Private Alternatives and Policy Options," discussion paper no. 50 (Washington, D.C.: World Bank, 1989).

[4]Ibid.

[5]Hernando de Soto, *The Other Path* (New York: Harper and Row, 1989).

[6]World Bank, *Malaysia: The Housing Sector: Getting the Incentives Right*, report no. 7292-MA, World Bank, 1989.

[7]Michael A. Cohen, *Urban Policy and Economic Development: An Agenda for the 1990s*, World Bank policy paper (Washington, D.C.: World Bank, 1991).

[8]Michael A. Cohen, "Macro Economic Adjustment and the City," *Cities* (February 1990): 49–59.

[9]National Academy of Sciences, *In Our Own Backyard: Principles for Effective Improvement of the Nation's Infrastructure* (Washington, D.C.: National Academy Press, 1993).

[10]See community case studies by William Morrish and Catherine Brown, publications of the Design Center for the American Urban Landscape, University of Minnesota, 1994–95.

[11]National Academy of Sciences, *In Our Own Backyard*.

[12]World Bank, *Infrastructure for Development*, World Development Report, 1994 (Washington, D.C.: Oxford University Press for the World Bank, 1994).

[13]Ismail Serageldin, *Toward Sustainable Management of Water Resources* (Washington, D.C.: World Bank, 1995).

[14]Letitia Obeng and Alain Locussol, "Sanitation Planning: A Challenge for the 1990s," paper presented at the Union of African Water Suppliers Congress, Cotonou, Benin, 1992.

[15]See World Bank, *Infrastructure for Development*.

[16]Robert Hackenberg, *The Poverty Explosion: Population Increase and Income Decline in Davao City, 1972* (Davao City, Philippines: Davao Action Information Center, 1974).

[17]See World Bank, *Infrastructure for Development*.

[18]See Ismail Serageldin and Michael A. Cohen, *The Human Face of the Urban Environment: A Report to the Development Community* (Washington, D.C.: World Bank, 1995).

[19]Carl Bartone, Janis Bernstein, and Josef Leitmann, *Towards Environmental Strategies for Cities* (Washington, D.C.: World Bank and the Urban Management Program, 1994).

[20]Lester R. Brown, Nicholas Lenssen, and Hal Kane, *Vital Signs 1995* (Washington, D.C.: Worldwatch Institute, 1995).

[21]Robert Watson and Julie A. Roqué, "The Superfund Experience: Hazardous Wastes Cleanup in the United States," in *The Human Face of the Urban Environment: Proceedings of the Second Annual Conference on Environmentally Sustainable Development*, ed. Ismail Serageldin, Michael A. Cohen, and K. C. Sivaramakrishnan (Washington, D.C.: World Bank, 1995).

[22]Philip Shabecoff, *A Fierce Green Fire: The American Environmental Movement* (New York: Hill and Wang, 1993).

[23]Serageldin and Cohen, *Human Face: A Report*.

[24]K. C. Sivaramakrishnan, "Urban Environmental Governance: An Overview," in *Human Face: Proceedings*, ed. Serageldin et al.

[25]*The Urban Age* 4 (Summer 1993).

[26]Charles Correa, "Great City, Terrible Place," in *Human Face: Proceedings*, ed. Serageldin et al.

[27]Alice Coleman, *Utopia on Trial: Vision and Reality in Planned Housing* (London: Hillary Shipman, 1985).

[28]Richard Sennett, *The Conscience of the Eye: The Design and Social Life of Cities* (New York: Knopf, 1990).

[29]Witold Rybczynski, *City Life: Urban Expectations in a New World* (New York: Scribner, 1995).

Chapter 3

Cities in a Global Era: A New Paradigm for the Next Millennium

H. V. Savitch

It is the responsibility of Governments to prepare spatial strategy plans and adopt human settlement policies to guide socioeconomic development efforts.

Report of Habitat: United Nations Conference on Human Settlements, Vancouver (1976)

People have become informed and clever as a real consequence of living in a truly global information era. And now governments have become the major obstacle for people to have the best and the cheapest [goods] from anywhere in the world.

Kenichi Ohmae, *The Borderless World* **(1990)**

Old and Emerging Social Paradigms

It is not always easy to separate the rise and fall of ideas. The paradigms of one period may be left over from another time. They may have barely perceptible beginnings and accelerate over time.[1] Even the issue of how we separate periods is up for debate. Is it by decade? by portions of a century? by "defining moments"? by catastrophic events? or by gradual shifts in culture and social mores?

Such are the dilemmas of trying to pinpoint the intellectual genesis of the Vancouver Habitat I conference, held in 1976. Whatever can be said of that era, its perspective reached back into the 1950s and 60s, and it dealt with the world as it existed in those years. Its modus operandi was to identify the most pressing urban problems (squalid living conditions, intolerable disparities of wealth, and cities clogged with an exodus of peasants) and pronounce policy objectives (subsidize housing, redistribute resources, and plan new settlements). The prescriptions were ambitious, couched in the language of social equity, the responsibilities of government, and the value of an overarching international organization to guide rehabilitation.[2]

Given the colossal scope and magnitude of the problems, how might we make sense of the Vancouver deliberations? The suggested approach is to turn to the idea of a social paradigm. A social paradigm refers to the identification of means-ends relationships, core values, and composite perceptions that are used to organize people for action. In another sense, a paradigm illustrates a path toward problem solving. It is a way of identifying and reconstituting elements of a problem with an eye toward creating solutions.[3]

Habitat's social paradigm can be described as one that placed faith in a rational, comprehensive, government-centered strategy. Government and centralized planning were to be used as major instruments for bringing about social and economic opportunity. The *process* of problem solving was placed on government agencies, specifically on their ability to plan, cajole, and command. The *substance* of problem solving centered on the redistribution of wealth and resources. If people were poor, the solution lay in transferring assets from one group to another. If environmental degradation threatened the planet, the idea was to arrest the threat by government regulation.

Much has changed since 1976. The belief that futures could be predicted through techniques such as trend analysis and *delphi* methods gave way to a notion that events were the result of random and chaotic admixtures of circumstance.[4] The idea that society and its organizations could be managed in some comprehensive form collapsed in favor of isolating pieces of a larger problem and managing them individually.[5] Faith in government as an instrument of social reform seemed to vanish as the Thatcher and Reagan revolutions dismantled the welfare state.

The shedding of a rational, comprehensive, government-centered paradigm has not been without pain, but neither has there been a void of ideas. Foremost among the replacements is a paradigm that is centered on incrementalism, entrepreneurship, and markets as the best way to promote social progress. The approach is inductive and views problems piece by piece. Prosperity is to be propelled by the actions of discreet participants. Solutions cannot be commanded, but should be produced by voluntarism and free trade. While governments can be enlisted in this venture, they best function when put at the service of privately owned enterprise—building roads, training workforces, and supplying funds for research and development. Solutions can best be discovered through individual or group initiative, flourishing within an environment of deregulation and privatization and a liberal economy.

As we approach the millennium, the incremental, entrepreneurial, market-centered paradigm is gathering momentum, partially due to its seeming democratic and antiauthoritarian virtues, although East Asian nations have given it a different flavor. Another element of its appeal can be traced to a Western-oriented desire to limit the powers of government and increase private autonomy. The recent popularity of free capital, privatization, nongovernmental organizations, and individual mobility illustrate the attractions of the new paradigm. Much of the new paradigm's steam can also be attributed to a phenomenon that accelerated shortly after the 1970s and has now come to be known as "globalism."

Globalism and Cities

Globalism consists of a bundle of interrelated ideas. First, it refers to the integration of national economies, and the notion that capital, products, and services transcend national boundaries. This universality is manifested in the increasing reliance upon common global standards, whether for electronic components or patent regulations. Trade, currency exchange, and financial transactions undergird the global patterning, and have been used to demonstrate the changing nature of economic relationships.[6]

Second, globalism is political, and connotes an intensification of interaction and interconnection between states, localities, and societies across the world.[7] Its residue can be seen in the rise of multilateral organizations, regional pacts, and talk of a borderless world. States, localities, nongovernmental organizations, and labor have obliterated old boundaries and are driven by the seemingly contradictory stimuli of cooperation and competition.

Third, globalism is sociocultural and conveys the idea of an open, multipolar, and multicultural society.[8] Immigrant and ethnic cultures are now said to thrive in "transnational space" in which language, habit, and tradition continue regardless of geography. Transnational space has also been made possible by the communications revolution. Electronic communication has penetrated entertainment and information monopolies with everything from Sony Walkmans to CNN newscasts and Internet services.

A general idea unifying all aspects of globalism is the mutual vulnerability it fosters between nations, localities, and organizations. These entities now depend upon one another in ways thought inconceivable a century ago. In a matter of minutes, a crisis in a single great bank can upset finance at the other end of the world. Disease travels as swiftly as airline flights and has acquired an international character. Vulnerability also has an opposite side which can be found in cross-national synergy. This kind of complementary interdependence has brought about joint ventures in space exploration, multinational research collaboration, and the rise of multinational corporations.

Table 3.1 provides an indication of the economic side of globalism. The table shows the movement of goods and currency throughout the world and begins with an already substantial base in 1972. The world has changed a good deal since the conference in Vancouver and the numbers are revealing.

TABLE 3.1
EXPORTS FROM TWENTY-FIVE NATIONS, 1972–1992
(in millions of U.S. dollars, adjusted for inflation)

	1972	1992	% Increase	Avg. Annual % Increase
OECD Member Countries				
Australia	6,461	42,824	565	28
Austria	3,803	47,270	1,115	56
Canada	21,185	134,435	535	27
France	26,467	235,871	790	40
Germany	46,736	422,271	805	40
Ireland	1,607	28,331	1,665	83
Italy	18,609	178,550	860	43
Japan	28,591	339,492	1,085	54
Netherlands	19,163	139,945	630	32
Norway	3,203	35,178	970	49
Portugal	1,298	18,350	1,315	66
Spain	3,817	63,334	1,585	79
Sweden	8,769	49,857	470	24
Switzerland	6,867	58,687	755	38
United Kingdom	23,987	180,180	650	33
United States	48,979	420,812	760	38
Non-OECD Member Countries				
East Asia/Pacific:				
China	3,693	84,940	2,200	110
Hong Kong	3,436	119,516	3,380	169
Indonesia	1,778	33,816	1,800	90
Korea	1,616	76,394	4,625	230
Malaysia	1,722	40,705	2,265	113
Singapore	2,181	63,386	2,805	140
Taiwan	2,914	81,395	2,695	135
Thailand	1,039	32,473	3,025	150
Latin America:				
Mexico	1,845	27,166	1,370	69

SOURCES: *World Tables 1994*, World Bank, table 7, 26–29; table 19, 74–77; *International Financial Statistics Year Book*, 110–13.

We can appreciate the magnitude of change by considering the nations involved. Twenty-five nations either exceeded $40 billion in exports or experienced a tenfold increase in their exports over the last two decades. The average industrial nation increased its exports more than ninefold in just twenty years. Among OECD members, Germany and France increased exports eight times, while Spain's exports exploded more than fifteenfold. The United States and Japan rose equally as much, to surpass $300 billion in trade. Pastoral nations such as Ireland and Portugal joined the ranks of exporters with twentyfold rises. The gains were even more dramatic in East Asia, particularly China, Korea, Singapore, Taiwan, and Hong Kong.

How do cities fit into this picture? As markets become larger and more open, so do opportunities. The agglomerative features of cities make them natural centers for coordination and direction. In effect, cities have become the strategic nodes through which the new economy can be planned and facilitated.[9] They provide the critical spaces needed to organize a dizzying array of functions; they hold the infrastructure needed to support millions of white-collar workers; and they furnish the conduits for rapid transfer of goods, money, and information.

Currency has always played an important role in urban life, but it is now the fuel that drives all else. The ability to process capital through "trade centers" and "smart buildings," the availability of financial and business services, access to capital markets, and proximity to sources of information and investment are the stuff of today's world cities. Whether a city can make use of and exploit these assets has a great deal to do with how it will fare in the decades ahead.

We can get a glimpse of how cities sort themselves out on at least one financial dimension—banking. Table 3.2 lists cities around the globe according to major banks and their holdings.

The leading cities are hardly surprising. Tokyo, Paris, Frankfurt, London, New York, Brussels, Amsterdam, Zurich, and Milan have traditionally been at the forefront of the banking industry. Many of the newcomers, however, are lodging themselves in East Asia (Osaka, Beijing, Hong Kong) or the South Pacific (Sydney, Melbourne). Judging from the list, the axis of financial power appears to stretch from northwestern Europe across to North America, veering sharply into the South Pacific and up into East Asia. Indeed, this matches global exports shown in table 3.1, where much of the existing and growing trade encompasses northwestern Europe, North America, the South Pacific, and the eastern corners of Asia.

Several points then guide our understanding of what has changed since the 1970s. First, the coupling of the incremental, entrepreneurial,

TABLE 3.2
RANKING CITIES BY MAJOR BANKS AND BANK HOLDINGS, 1994
(Headquarters locations of the top 100 banks)

Rank	City	Country	# Banks (top 100)	Assets	Deposits
				(billions of U.S. $)	
1	Tokyo	Japan	17	4,686.8	3,846.2
2	Paris	France	8	1,520.9	988.8
3	Osaka	Japan	4	1,383.8	1,102.1
4	Frankfurt	Germany	6	892.5	774.2
5	London	United Kingdom	5	723.0	615.3
6	New York	United States	4	419.1	282.1
7	Munich	Germany	3	412.8	385.5
8	Brussels	Belgium	5	364.5	297.0
9	Amsterdam	Netherlands	2	361.9	224.2
10	Zurich	Switzerland	2	299.9	253.4
11	Nagoya	Japan	1	272.9	204.1
12	Milan	Italy	3	262.0	210.4
13	Beijing	China	1	247.9	106.7
14	Toronto	Canada	3	238.7	195.6
15	Rome	Italy	2	217.6	168.4
16	Montreal	Canada	2	192.3	163.5
17	Düsseldorf	Germany	1	165.3	134.9
18	Turin	Italy	1	161.0	122.5
19	Stockholm	Sweden	2	137.8	76.2
20	Basel	Switzerland	1	137.0	114.6
21	Madrid	Spain	2	133.9	103.0
22	San Francisco	United States	1	132.2	106.9
23	Sydney	Australia	2	128.3	96.4
24	Utrecht	Netherlands	1	127.7	83.6
25	Melbourne	Australia	2	126.3	96.1
26	Hong Kong	Hong Kong	1	125.5	108.7
27	Yokohama	Japan	1	105.2	78.7
28	Siena	Italy	1	97.2	77.1
29	Hannover	Germany	1	92.7	86.5
30	Sapporo	Japan	1	90.5	75.1
31	Bilbao	Spain	1	87.8	77.9
32	Naples	Italy	1	75.4	61.8
33	Chiba	Japan	1	73.8	61.6
34	Stuttgart	Germany	1	69.3	37.9
35	Brasilia	Brazil	1	69.1	15.2
36	Shitzouka	Japan	1	65.8	58.1
37	Toyama	Japan	1	63.8	54.1
38	Mito	Japan	1	62.7	56.0
39	Santander	Spain	1	61.4	51.5
40	Edinburg	United Kingdom	1	61.3	52.3
41	Utsunomia	Japan	1	57.9	50.2
42	Fukuoka	Japan	1	57.3	51.7
43	Wiesbaden	Germany	1	56.6	53.3
44	Barcelona	Spain	1	56.2	43.6

SOURCE: "The Top 500 Banks in the World," *American Banker*, July 29, 1993.

market-centered paradigm to globalism fits the character and basis of cities. After all, cities are corporations. From the time of the ancient marketplace, to the Italian and Hanseatic trading ports, up through modern office complexes, cities have specialized in promoting enterprise. By nature, cities are small, flexible collections of economic activity and quite capable of flourishing in this new environment.

Second, give or take modifications in national habits, localities have lined up behind the new paradigm. They have striven to supply entrepreneurs with staffing, infrastructure, and strategic space. When cities have been unable to incubate their own industries, they have welcomed new ones from abroad. National and local policies are now based on private enterprise, the barometer of the marketplace, and sheer growth.

Third, globalism produces differential impacts between cities. The global economy is increasingly competitive, and not all cities share the same fate. The new era has sharpened urban differences and produced multiple networks that carry out certain divisions of labor. Networks of cities span the globe and underscore the relationship between national economic power and urban preeminence. The most powerful cities are to be found in the developed economies of North America, western Europe and Japan; rising cities also exist in the transitional economies of East Asia and Latin America; whereas the least powerful cities are located in the less-developed economies of Africa and parts of Latin America.

Fourth, globalism produces different impacts within cities. Even the most powerful cities have their underside and are blighted by unemployment, substandard housing, and an underclass. By the same token, rising and less-powerful cities have propagated industry, affluence, and a growing middle class. The sketch is not so much one of contrasts falling on one or another side of a border, but of multiple subcomponents whose components vary.

The following sections trace patterns between and within different urban networks. I examine cities in developed economies (prosperous and distressed), turning next to cities in rising economies (transitional), and finally to cities in less-developed economies (impacted).

Developed Economies, Growth Machines, and the Seamy Side of Globalism

Since the 1960s, scholars have talked about the demise of central cities, and the predictions continue.[10] Central cities are seen as vestiges of an era when proximity was crucial and when limitations of transportation and communication placed a premium on highly concentrated space. Why maintain congested cities, when business transactions can be consummated within the time span of an electronic message and executives can move across continents on Concorde jets? Indeed, some might argue that cities impede economic progress and clog development.[11]

The truth is, cities are extraordinarily efficient. They optimize the use of human and mechanical energy; they allow for fast, cheap transportation; and they provide flexible, highly productive labor markets.[12] In addition, cities facilitate a diffusion of products, ideas, and human resources between urban, suburban, exurban, and rural spaces. We can appreciate how cities optimize their work by examining their economic performance over a period of time.[13]

Urban centers have always led in the creation of national wealth, and many now occupy a special place in the global era. Cities are the international growth machines of the new economy and their pace has accelerated. In 1990, Barcelona held 7 percent of its nation's GDP, Frankfurt held 4 percent, Seoul held 23 percent, Sydney held 19 percent, and New York contained 2.5 percent. As the last column in table 3.3 shows, all of these were explosively up from the previous two decades. The increases are impressive and in most cases exceed 1000 percent.

Moreover, international growth machines are efficient and getting better at what they do. Cities are the workhorses of the world. In 1970, 44.5 percent of the population within the above-listed cities were part of the labor force. By 1990 that figure had climbed to 59.7 percent. Imagine an advanced, high-tech, high-density society in which nearly 60 percent of a well-educated population is gainfully employed.

Much of this productivity has poured back into the city. The most prosperous cities now profit from new skylines, converted waterfronts, and rejuvenated neighborhoods. A new urban middle class, trained in high technology, blankets great cities and earns a livelihood that would be the envy of their medieval trading forbears.

Central cities have not only grown outward from their old cores, but they nurture people who have moved into surrounding suburbs and exurbs. Cities and their surrounding regions are connected by transportation, business, and fiscal networks. Over two million commuters pour into Manhattan each day and acquire more than half the income earned in the city. Washington, D.C.'s commuter population exceeds its inhabitants, and they too collect more than half the earnings made in that city.[14] Much the same story can be told of Paris, Frankfurt, and Tokyo. Even medium-sized cities such as Pittsburgh, Strasbourg, and Cologne are closely linked with and sustain outlying areas.

TABLE 3.3
GROSS DOMESTIC PRODUCT FOR EIGHTEEN CITIES,
1970–1990

City	City GDP* 1970 (billions of U.S. $)	City GDP* 1990 (billions of U.S. $)	% Increase 1970–1990
Barcelona	.74	36.65	4,952
Chicago	19.13	181.12	947
Cleveland	3.98	46.59	1,171
Detroit	7.97	92.34	1,159
Frankfurt	9.67	60.85	629
Hamburg	20.42	38.57	189
Hong Kong	31.78	119.00	374
London	10.75	112.39	1,045
Los Angeles	16.46	184.59	1,121
Louisville	1.95	24.50	1,256
Montreal	6.02	69.64	1,157
New York	9.82	159.49	1,624
San Francisco	4.47	44.76	1,001
Seoul	4.67	99.32	2,127
Singapore	19.06	42.40	222
St. Louis	3.26	56.74	1,741
Sydney	12.07	65.97	547
Tokyo	22.23	643.27	2,894

*City GDP is calculated as $\dfrac{\text{Labor Force (city)}}{\text{Labor Force (national)} \times \text{GDP (national)}}$ = City GDP

Special Note: Labor force data for Hamburg and Sydney were not available. Mean fraction of labor force (out of total population) in each year was applied.

SOURCES: (1970 data): Labor force for each city: U.S. Cities — *County and City Data Book: A Statistical Abstract Supplement, 1972;* Hong Kong and Singapore — *The Statesman's Year-Book: Statistical and Historical Annual of the States of the World, 1971;* others — *Cities of the World,* Vols. I–V, 1988. U.N. Exchange Rate: Hong Kong and Singapore — *Wall Street Journal,* January 1970; others — *Statistical Abstract of the U.S., 1972.* Labor force and GDP for each country: Hong Kong and Singapore — *The Statesman's Year-Book: Statistical and Historical Annual of the States of the World, 1971;* others — *Statistical Yearbook Annual Statistique,* 1981. (1991 data): Labor force for each city: U.S. Cities — *County and City Data Book: A Statistical Abstract Supplement, 1994;* Hong Kong and Singapore — *The Statesman's Year-Book: Statistical and Historical Annual of the States of the World, 1992;* others — *The World Fact Book,* 1994. Labor force and GDP for each country: Canada and United States — *The Europa World Yearbook,* 1994; Hong Kong and Singapore — *The Statesman's Year-Book: World,* 1992; others — *The World Fact Book,* 1994.

For prosperous cities in developed economies, the key to survival is to manage a conversion from an earlier industrial base (manufacturing, processing, shipping, or warehousing) to what has been termed "postindustrial employment" (finance, services, and information processing). Successful cities find ways to pick up the slack in their economic base, nurture mixed land use, and promote synergies between traditional manufacture, high technology, and research and information. The conversion to postindustrialism need not be total. Economic diversity is a sure asset, and it is important to modernize and retain traditional industry.

While experiences with economic conversion may differ, the most successful cities follow a pattern of diversity and incorporate features of the new social paradigm. In North America, Pittsburgh is an example of a single industry (steel) town that managed a successful conversion to postindustrial activity. The city enlisted business (the Allegheny Conference), diversified its economic base, and coupled high technology and information services to an export strategy. In western Europe, Hamburg stands out as a port city that managed a successful conversion. A combination of moderate politics and the city's merchant tradition helped to bridge class differences. This allowed business and labor to rationalize port facilities, diversify the economy, and take the lead in robotics and media services. Today, Hamburg is one of Europe's most aggressively competitive cities.[15]

There is, too, another side to urban productivity, and that is the relentless pace of competition, its acceleration during the last five years, and the disparities that ensue. As in most races there are winners and losers; developed economies have no lack of losers. Many of these are former sites of heavy manufacture, or have ports that are no longer in use. Often characterized as "rust belts," they appear to have been left in a time warp. Their signals are obvious—underutilized or closed factories, dilapidated docks, scarce capital, and long lines of people seeking work. Some distressed cities tried to recuperate by appealing to tourist trade. After the automobile factories closed, Flint, Michigan, converted its historic remains into an automobile museum, and heralded a first-class hotel. Both establishments are now closed.

Distressed cities in the developed world include Detroit, Liverpool, Belfast, Naples, and Valenciennes.[16] These cities are characterized by shrinking private resources and lack the political capacity to mobilize investment. This puts them at odds with powerful paradigmatic and international currents. Detroit and Liverpool are two abject examples of how cities in developed economies can get swept aside by this tide.

Once the leading automotive production center of world, Detroit's share of the international market fell from 76 percent in 1950 to just 19 percent three decades later.[17] During those same years, real wages tumbled, jobs evaporated, and Detroit fell apart. These losses affected every part of the city, as it lost 45 percent of its population and more than one-fifth of its people fell below the poverty line.[18] Through the 1990s median household income and retail sales have been stagnant.[19] For the most part, the city has been unable to recruit private capital or win its confidence. Mostly white suburbs have rejected collaboration with Detroit, and the city's mayors have been forced to grant business corporations huge concessions in order to slow their exodus.[20]

Shipping is to Liverpool what autos are to Detroit. After the United Kingdom turned eastward and emigration from Ireland slowed, Liverpool lost its appeal as the westward gateway. Automation and containerization did the rest, and the city gradually became an early casualty of global expansion. By the 1980s the city had shrunk to nearly half its earlier size. More than one-third of the population fell below the poverty line and unemployment hit 27 percent. Liverpool's condition became a cause célèbre when radical Labour (Militant Tendency) won control of city hall and tried to reverse disinvestment. With few sources of private capital, Militant Tendency turned to public coffers and tried to spend the city into bankruptcy. Although these efforts failed, government still bears a heavy responsibility and accounts for 15 percent of the city's job base.[21]

Observing cities in the context of global change, the disparities are quite substantial. Indeed, it may be useful to think of world cities as located at different points within a regional network. Some cities (New York, London, Paris, Tokyo, and Frankfurt) may be at the hub; they operate as global cities with dense national and regional linkages, complemented by a much larger net of global relationships. Other cities (Pittsburgh, Hamburg, Osaka, Brussels, and Lyon) occupy lesser stations; they rely mostly on regional relationships but are able to take advantage of a thinner economic mesh. Still other cities (Detroit, Liverpool, Belfast, Marseilles, and Naples) are on their way to marginalization; caught in a steady attrition of industry, they can no longer generate an economic surplus and must rely on external sources of support.

Rising Economies and Transitional Cities

Transitional cities in rising economies are in the process of adapting economic activities and land uses to globalism and the new social paradigm. Again, the key factors are the ability of cities to modernize and retain a traditional industrial base; to generate additional activities in tertiary sectors; and to promote synergies with high technology, research, and information.

The most dramatic examples of transitional cities are in East Asia. Hong Kong, Singapore, and Seoul represent a few of Asia's growth machines. Hong Kong has been able to capitalize on the region's prosperity and serve as its trade nexus. During the last two decades Hong Kong's gross domestic product rose fifteenfold, and exports rocketed twenty-sevenfold, placing it among the top ten exporters in the world. It has retained 57 percent of its (mostly light industry) manufacture and growth of 5.5 percent annually. Hong Kong is one of the few cities in the world that has a negative rate of unemployment and actually imports workers.

All this was accomplished by emphasizing a strong entrepreneurial spirit (*Fortune* magazine rated Hong Kong one of the "World's Best Cities for Business") and by embracing an independent role as a free-trade city. Hong Kong has also built on its existing locational advantage through massive investments in airport facilities and cultivation of a strong tertiary sector (Asia's largest stock exchange).

Seoul is another example of a city working in a global environment that has begun to transform itself. It holds 23 percent of Korea's gross domestic product, and through the early 1990s its nonagricultural employment grew by more than 8 percent annually. Seoul's median household income shot up by 17 percent each year and retail sales climbed 16 percent annually.[22] These figures are impressive, despite a national inflation rate that peaked at 10 percent.

Seoul has the added advantage of being South Korea's capital city, and its service sector has grown on the crest of politics and business. It also retained its role in manufacture, holds one-third of the country's industrial plants and has a vigorous television and electronics export industry. The city also receives a heavy dose of infrastructure investment (extensive subway lines, office towers, and sewage facilities). All this is coupled with indigenous entrepreneurs and a powerful economic elite, known as the *chaebol*.

Less-Developed Economies and Impacted Cities

Located in less-developed economies, impacted cities are unable to produce diversified industry or mix different land uses or generate a substantial tertiary sector out of their economic base. As a result, their capacity for converting local resources into an export sector is diminished and, therefore, interaction with the global economy is limited. Many of these cities are located in sub-Saharan Africa; some are in North Africa and Latin America.

Typically, these cities are the outgrowths of agricultural economies, built out of single crops or a scant number of products. Government is the surest type of employment—and, for high-level officials, a source of great privilege. A substantial part of the economy is taken up by the informal sector: small scale, unlicensed businesses that neither pay taxes nor have specifically established locations.

It is not uncommon for people to shift between regular and informal work. Aside from crop exports, few goods or services are converted into externally generated income. Yet despite the hardships, migration continues from the countryside and swells the city with squatter settlements. Nairobi and Dar es Salaam exemplify this pattern.

Nairobi should be the "jewel" of African cities. It was chosen by the British as the national capital because of its cool temperature and natural attractions. In times gone by, the Nairobi river was a resting place for Masaii herders, and its name means "cool waters." Today, the river has turned into an eyesore and an environmental hazard. The city has spread from its plush green origin into the Eastland, which is flat, deforested, and known as the "grey" area because of its desolation and poverty.[23]

Nairobi has become the seat of several international organizations and companies wishing to do business in Africa. Its population soared from just 500,000 in the 1960s to 2.5 million people in the 1990s. Despite the seeming opportunities, 40 percent of residents live in shanties as squatters. Many settlements are composed of makeshift cardboard houses or shelters built of mud, grass, and sheets of tin.

A substantial portion of the economy is driven by the informal sector. This includes vending, street hawking, carpentry, tailoring, welding, and tinsmithing. The meager earnings of these workers (approximately $12 per month) hardly sustain a family. More often than not, those who work at informal jobs also live as squatters. Government campaigns to clear the street of illegal vendors or eliminate squatter settlements invariably target the same unfortunate people.[24]

This picture can be contrasted against a fragment of great wealth. The rich live in guarded compounds, surrounded by high fences. Two years ago, the fear of carjacking and pilferage were enough for the United Nations to downgrade Nairobi from a "Category A" city to "Category B" (less safe, less secure, and occasioned by violence).[25]

Tanzania's leading city, Dar es Salaam, shares many features with its East African sister, but is nonetheless grimmer. Over the last three decades Tanzania's population soared from 128,000 to over 2 million. The influx continues amid deteriorating conditions. Roads are in disrepair, telephones do not always function, the supply of electricity is sporadic, and consumer and pharmaceutical goods are scarce. According to one estimate, Dar es Salaam remains one of the poorest places on earth.[26]

The economy chugs along through a combination of formal and informal work. Vendors and street hawkers dot the city, and according to one report eke out the barest living ($8 to $12 per month).[27] Informal work is not just the domain of marginal people; it is also conducted by those who receive wages at regular jobs. Per capita GDP is reported as $110 annually.[28]

Living conditions are difficult. Most of the population consists of tenants who occupy squatter settlements. One survey revealed that only one-third of the homes in these settlements were built as permanent dwellings. Floors are typically made from tamped earth; walls from mud and poles; and roofs from grass or leaves. Most dwellings lack both electricity and piped water.[29]

As in Nairobi, the elites of Dar es Salaam live well—in luxurious beach houses surrounded by guards, with access to expensive automobiles and consumer goods. They frequently gain their livelihoods and privileges from positions as ministers, party officials, senior civil servants, or military officers.

Global Conditions, Paradigm Shifts, and Urban Responses

One way or another, all major cities are affected by globalism and its paradigmatic motif. Some cities have profited by the change, others have persisted, and a number have suffered damage. Whereas the stimulus of change has been constant, the responses vary. Not all cities are alike, and it is reasonable to expect that results will differ; however, variation is also contained by distinct patterns and we can discern global effects.

Prosperous cities generally experience rising employment and income, escalating land values, and affluence amid social polarization. The inner cores of prosperous cities de-densify. Distressed cities lose in all categories. Their economies plummet, social conditions worsen, and the populace flees. Transitional cities have an altogether different experience. High demand forces almost everything up—income, jobs, social conditions, and population. By contrast, an absence of demand within impacted cities leads to stagnation, uncertainty, or long-term depression. Jobs remain scarce, income is marginal, and land value is unsure. Only the number of inhabitants increases, and impacted cities continue to grow from the outside.[30]

Table 3.4 summarizes these responses as nominal categories (for data on specific indicators see table 3.5 and figures 3.2–3.8 in the appendix). Economic responses, shown by plus or minus signs, mean higher or lower income and employment. Differing social responses, shown in the same manner, signify higher rates of poverty and a rising number of homeless. Demographic responses are shown as rising or falling populations within urban cores.

TABLE 3.4
URBAN RESPONSES: DEVELOPED, RISING, AND LESS-DEVELOPED ECONOMIES

	Economic (Employment, Income)	Social Distress (Poverty, Housing)	Demographic (Growth, Densification)
Developed Economies Prosperous	+	+− (bipolar)	−
Distressed	−	−	−
Rising Economies Transitional	+	+	+
Less-Developed Economies Impacted	−	−	+

There is, then, no necessary relationship between urban development and population growth or densification. Cities can enhance their development and lose population, much as they can stagnate and absorb huge populations. By the same token, cities can follow a classic pattern of development coupled with population increase. How a city responds depends on its level and phase of maturation.

Evidently, cities do not have a free hand in choosing a response. Historical circumstance, location, resources, and sheer luck account for a good deal of a city's fate. New York and London have long histories as banking centers and are likely to profit from agglomerative tendencies in the current era of international finance. Hong Kong and Singapore have the good fortune to be port cities located in a high-growth region during an era of international trade. Paris and Tokyo enjoy the blessing of being capital cities in regions where politics and commerce mix well.

Investors seek profit and it is natural that money would flow into the most promising locations. Figure 3.1 bears out this proposition, showing foreign direct investment between 1970 and 1993. Investment is measured on a national basis for cities in developed, rising, and less-developed economies.

The lion's share of investment is still made in developed economies. While proportions slid a bit in developed economies, the absolute amount of foreign direct investment rose substantially in each type of economy. Although we have no systematic way of knowing where these funds actually flow, available banking data skew toward the most prosperous cities. Distressed cities appear to be subject to continued disinvestment.[31] The rising economies show a gain over the last twenty-five years, moving from 9 percent to 16 percent of the total. The most

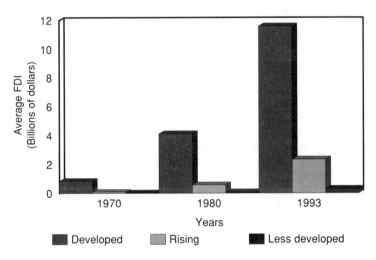

Figure 3.1. Foreign direct investment by type of economy (*Balance of Payments Statistics Yearbook*, Part 2, vol. 28, Washington, D.C.: International Monetary Fund, 1994: 41–43, 45)

surprising finding is that less-developed economies incurred a proportionate loss, falling from 4 percent to just 2 percent of total foreign direct investment.

At least in relative terms, the gaps between richest, rising, and poorest economies appear to be widening. Writers have noted that Asia progressively accounts for an increasing, if not majority, share of foreign dollars.[32] Although this is true, the real distinction may revolve around level of development rather than geography.[33] Some Asian cities may be on the verge of joining the most prosperous ones and at least one (Tokyo) is already there.

As a rule, developed areas fare even better than transitional ones and less-developed areas shrink in the relative attention given to them. At best, less-developed cities are at the rim of powerful networks—well behind most transitional cities. At worst, they are often excluded and occasionally tied to the rest of the world by the good graces of government-sponsored organizations.

Finally, although investment patterns follow the natural advantages of location and resources, we should recognize that cities do have latitude. They can establish priorities and put together development strategies. After World War II, Singapore was down on its heels with a paucity of capital and little foreign aid. Seoul was the national seat of a poor country with few resources, high illiteracy, and a ravaged economy. Cities are resilient, capable of exploiting their natural advantages, combining assets, and coordinating activities. Globalism accentuates this potential, enabling cities to penetrate markets that were once unavailable to them.

Delocalization and Policy Strategies

As globalization melts national borders and intensifies competition, cities assume new roles. They become progressively delocalized, and take up a place at the leading edge of the new social paradigm that preaches global action, market awareness, and entrepreneurship.

We can think of delocalization as a process that continues with globalization. Cities may be delocalized in varying degrees. The most delocalized are prosperous cities of the developed economies. Next, transitional cities are becoming more delocalized. Finally, the least delocalized are impacted cities of the less-developed world.

Delocalized cities are profoundly affected by global changes in economics, technology, and culture. Their central business districts are tied together by a net of multinational corporations and financial and brokerage houses. Their waterfronts receive tourists, and their neighborhoods house foreign executives, guest workers, migrants, and transients. Although delocalized cities refract national habits and mores, their reference points are international and compete for capital and prestige.

Delocalized cities seek their own business, and in doing so are apt to recruit internationally and carry a broad portfolio of activities. Since the 1970s cities have adopted their own foreign policies, establishing representation across the world. In the 1990s over 1,000 American localities participate in some kind of microdiplomacy, by establishing trade representation in foreign countries, creating "sister city" exchanges (of students, business delegations, conventions, and fairs), or adopting resolutions on issues (such as nuclear-free zones or sanctuary for refugees).[34]

The challenge for major cities is to adapt to delocalized and global status. This will not be easy, especially for impacted and distressed cities. The new social paradigm conveys a message of self-help through private capital. Given investment patterns, private finance will likely flow to cities that are least in need. Unless impacted and distressed cities can radically shift by themselves, the gaps will continue to widen. Also, in order to function globally cities will have to balance the imperatives of competition against the need for cooperation. This requires that cities increase local productivity, while collaborating with their counterparts to avoid destructive practices. Cities must be careful to avoid raiding one another for capital, bargaining away assets to potential investors, and falling into a pattern of "place wars." Last, the rules of international intercourse are changing. Old bonds are breaking apart, and new ones will have to be forged. New relationships will have to be built while cities are in the process of birth, adaptation, and maturation. Although these conditions pose difficulties, they also present opportunities.

Impacted and distressed cities may be constrained by the new paradigm, but they need not be thwarted by it. In some instances they will do best by playing by the rules and adopting conforming strategies. In other instances cities may be able to maneuver around the existing paradigm by using regional urban networks for economic, social, and political cooperation.

The objective is to optimize opportunities and convert them into relationships in which cities view the prosperity of others as good for themselves. To reach this end, cities should employ strategies that are flexible enough to accommodate individual as well as collective objectives. The following urban strategies are designed to realize that potential:

- Cities must recognize that government-induced development has substantial limits. Although government cannot efficiently create development, it can foster conditions for its success. Government can steer better than it can row, and it should undertake only what it can do well.

  —Government can build or rebuild local infrastructure, particularly mass transit facilities, highways, streets, utilities, and general modes of access.

  —Government can promote "supply-side" incentives, designed to lure capital from abroad.[35] This can be done by lowering the cost of private investment through tax abatements, training workers, or contracting with potential employers to train workers.

  —Government can promote "demand-side" incentives by identifying foreign markets and alerting private enterprise to customers and business opportunities.[36] Still another way to pursue demand-side techniques is for delocalized states to become equity investors—risk takers willing to lend or invest public money in new ventures such as port facilities or housing.[37]

- Cities should play to their natural advantages. These include strategic location (near ports, highway junctures, and strategic passages), access to local markets, economies of agglomeration, and opportunities for commercial or technical interaction.

—Government can couple locational advantages with potential development. Businesses, universities, and research centers can be clustered within specific areas. This can be facilitated through zoning, establishing special districts and transportation linkages, and targeting public investment.

—Government can assist business in paying attention to local markets. Most business develops by producing for and selling to home markets, allowing exports to grow afterward.[38]

—Government can stimulate competition between local businesses. Internal competition is healthy and leads to stronger, more resilient enterprise. Competition can be fostered by creating opportunities for related enterprise (such as low-rent areas), or providing special amenities (better transportation, higher security, or more frequent sanitation services).

—Government can recognize the value of the informal sector. This sector often incubates businesses and serves as a valuable source of innovation. Impacted and distressed cities should encourage informal work by relaxing licensure requirements and providing sliding scales for business taxes. In less-developed economies, conditions within squatter settlements should be improved so that informal job holders can strengthen ties between living space and workplace.

- Government should support and enhance social capital. The most important component of city-building is its stock of human relationships. A city's future is determined by the skill, training, and capacity for mutual assistance lodged within its people. Government must approach this task gingerly, taking care not to substitute itself for individual and private initiative. Localities can work to facilitate these forces of pluralism.

    —Government can work in tandem with private enterprise to train workers. Schools can be linked to private enterprise and education carried out in conjunction with performance of a job.

    —Vocational and technical education should be valued, and apprenticeships carried out in conjunction with labor unions, not-for-profit organizations, and private enterprise.

    —Private enterprise and voluntary organizations can be enlisted in determining certification and graduation. This can be carried out on a contractual basis among public, nonprofit, and private sectors.

- Cities should re-create relationships with each other. They should use regional networks to form consortia and exploit common opportunities. In most cases this can best be done by encouraging dissimilar types of cities to collaborate, and complementing their resources. Impacted cities can work with prosperous and transitional cities; distressed cities can and should collaborate with prosperous and transitional counterparts.

—Cities can use cooperative relationships to further common investment and training. They can establish regional development banks, agree to avoid destructive competition, and ease the plight of migrant labor.

—Cities can coordinate their work with, and support nongovernmental organizations. These organizations can work with migrants to train workers, establish social networks, and create entrepreneurial and labor pools for economic development.

—Cities can conduct research and share information on policy development and evaluation. At present there is neither the information nor the institutional capacity to determine whether adopted public policies are effective. Most cities do not know whether tax abatements and supply-side measures accomplish their objectives. Cities often spend billions of dollars pursuing uninformed hunches. This should be changed so that hunches are converted into informed choices.

The world is changing—perhaps faster than in any previous era. We do know something about the operation of globalism, and new paradigms grow out of experience. The irony is that in some ways these conditions are reminiscent of the fifteenth, sixteenth, and seventeenth centuries. City-states in those periods found they could keep the narrowest autonomy and also prosper in a wider world. We should expect no less of ourselves.

Appendix

Table 3.5 and figures 3.2 to 3.8 were derived from a variety of standard sources. As with all cross-national data collection, categories change meaning depending on context and culture. Thus, conceptions of owner-occupied housing may differ in North America, Europe, Latin America, Asia, and Africa. Also, definitions of what constitutes a city may differ as well as how city boundaries are drawn. Given these limitations, the data need to be read in the context of the case and category. In all instances data were collected with an eye toward consistency. Distinctions were made between the municipal boundaries of a city and the functional boundaries of an economy (or an agglomeration), and the figures designated accordingly.

TABLE 3.5

GLOBAL CITIES IN DEVELOPED, RISING, AND LESS-DEVELOPED ECONOMIES

Developed Economies *Prosperous and Distressed Cities*	*Rising Economies* *Transitional Cities*	*Less-Developed Economies* *Impacted Cities*
Amsterdam	Bangkok	Abidjan
Chicago	Beijing	Accra
Detroit	Bombay	Algiers
Frankfurt	Buenos Aires	Baghdad
Glasgow	Guangzhou	Bangalore
Hamburg	Hong Kong	Bogota
Houston	Istanbul	Cairo
Liverpool	Jakarta	Calcutta
London	Johannesburg	Casablanca
Los Angeles	Kuala Lumpur	Dakar
Madrid	Leningrad	Dar es Salaam
Marseilles	Manila	Dhaka
Milan	Mexico City	Kinshasa
Naples	Moscow	Lagos
New York	Nanjing	Lima
Paris	New Delhi	Nairobi
Philadelphia	Rio de Janeiro	
Rome	São Paulo	
San Francisco	Seoul	
Stockholm	Shanghai	
Sydney	Singapore	
Tel Aviv	Taipei	
Tokyo		
Toronto		
Washington		
Zurich		

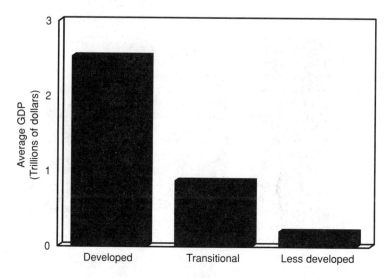

FIGURE 3.2. Average GDP by type of economy, ca. 1993 (*World Almanac and Book of Facts: 1995*, Mahwah, N.J.: Funk and Wagnalls, 1995)

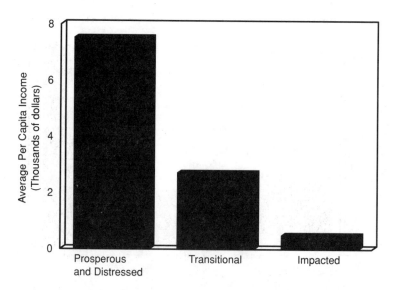

FIGURE 3.3. Average per capita income, by type of city, 1980 (*Book of World City Rankings*, New York: Free Press, 1986)

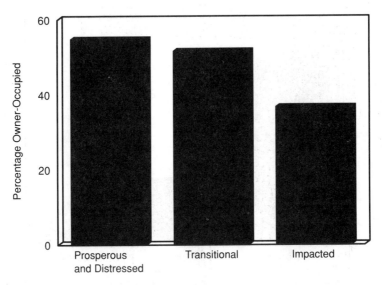

FIGURE 3.4. Percentage owner-occupied housing, by type of city, 1995 (*The Housing Indicators Program*, vol. 2, indicator tables, Washington, D.C: World Bank, 1995)

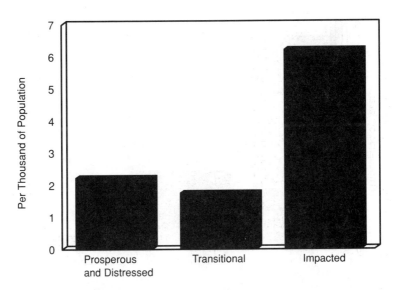

FIGURE 3.5. Homelessness by type of city, 1995 (*The Housing Indicators Program*, vol. 2, indicator tables, Washington, D.C: World Bank, 1995)

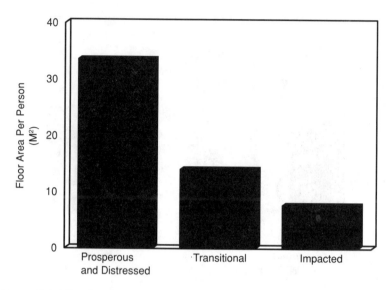

FIGURE 3.6. Housing space per person by type of city, 1995 (*The Housing Indicators Program*, vol. 2, indicator tables, Washington, D.C: World Bank, 1995)

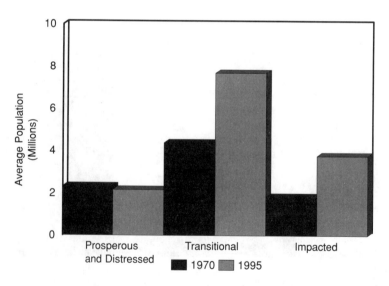

FIGURE 3.7. City population by type of city, 1970 and 1995 (U.N. Population Fund, Institut d'estudis Metropolitana de Barcelona, Barcelona, 1988; *World Almanac and Book of Facts: 1995*, Mahwah, N.J.: Funk and Wagnalls, 1995)

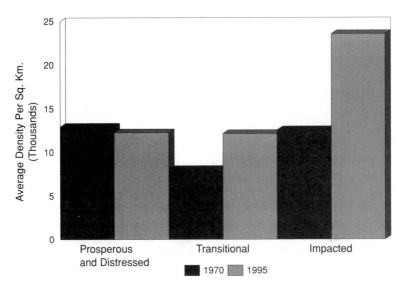

FIGURE 3.8. Population density by type of city, 1970 and 1995 (U.N. Population Fund, Institut d'estudis Metropolitana de Barcelona, Barcelona, 1988; *World Almanac and Book of Facts: 1995*, Mahwah, N.J.: Funk and Wagnalls, 1995)

Notes

[1]Thomas Kuhn, *The Structure of Scientific Revolutions*, 2d ed. (Chicago: University of Chicago Press, 1970).

[2]United Nations, *Report of Habitat: United Nations Conference on Human Settlements*, (United Nations policy paper presented at conference, Vancouver, British Columbia, Canada, 1976).

[3]Kuhn, *Structure of Scientific Revolutions*.

[4]See L. Douglas Kiel, "Nonlinear Dynamical Analysis: Assessing Systems Concepts in a Governmental Agency," *Public Administration Review* (1993): 143–53; H. R. Priesmeyer, *Organizations and Chaos: Defining the Methods of Nonlinear Management* (New York: Quorum Books, 1992); James Gleick, *Chaos: Making a New Science* (New York: Viking, 1987).

[5]See Tom Peters, *Thriving on Chaos: Handbook for a Management Revolution* (New York: Knopf, 1988); Charles Lindbloom, "Still Muddling, Not Yet Through," *Public Administration Review* 39 (November/December 1979): 517–26.

[6]See Saskia Sassen, *Cities in a World Economy* (Thousand Oaks, Calif.: Pine Forge Press, 1994); Sassen, *The Global City: New York, London, Tokyo* (Princeton, N.J.: Princeton University Press, 1991).

[7]D. Held, "Democracy, the Nation-state and the Global System," *Economy and Society* 20 (Winter 1991): 138–72.

[8]Richard Knight and Gary Gappert, eds., *Cities in a Global Society* (Newbury Park, Calif.: Sage, 1993).

[9]Sassen, *Global City* (1991); H. V. Savitch, *Post-industrial Cities: Politics and Planning in New York, Paris, and London* (Princeton, N.J.: Princeton University Press, 1988); Daniel Bell, *The Coming of Post-industrial Society: A Venture in Social Forecasting* (New York: Basic Books, 1976).

[10]Joel Garreau, *Edge City: Life on the New Frontier* (New York: Doubleday, 1991).

[11]Robert Bruegmann, *Urban Aberration or Glimpse of the Future* (unpublished manuscript, 1995); Melvin Webber, "Order in Diversity: Community without Propinquity," in *Cities and Space: The Future Use of Urban Land,* ed. Lowden Wingo (Baltimore, Md.: Johns Hopkins University Press, 1963).

[12]Peter Newman, *Urban Environmental Quality and Economic Competitiveness: An Australian Perspective* (paper prepared for the OECD conference "The Economy of Cities," Melbourne, Australia, 1994; Remy Prud'homme, *On the Economic Role of Cities* (paper prepared for the conference "Cities and the New Global Economy" organized by the Government of Australia and the OECD, Melbourne, November 20–23, 1994).

[13]I am grateful to Remy Prud'homme for bringing this to my attention. Professor Prud'homme calculated city GDP somewhat differently and used larger urban agglomerations to show urban productivity. See Prud'homme, *On the Economic Role of Cities.* I use a more narrowly based definition of the city to gather this data, relying instead on municipal boundaries.

[14]H. V. Savitch and Ronald Vogel, *Regional Politics: America in a Post City Age* (Newbury Park, Calif.: Sage, 1996); Bureau of Economic Analysis, *U.S. Department of Commerce Survey of Current Business* (September 1992): Table 3.

[15]Jens Dangschat, "Case Study: Hamburg" (unpublished paper for the University of Hamburg Center for Comparative Urban Research, 1990).

[16]Franco Bianchini, *Urbanization and the Functions of Cities in the European Community-City Case Study: Naples* (unpublished research report, 1991); Paul Cheshire, Gianni Carbonaro, and Dennis Hay, "Problems of Urban Decline and Growth in EEC Countries: Or Measure of Degrees of Elephantness," *Urban Studies* 2 (1986): 131–49; Joe Darden, Richard Child Hill, June Thomas, and Richard Thomas, *Detroit: Race and Uneven Development* (Philadelphia: Temple University Press, 1987).

[17]Kent Trachte and Robert Ross, "The Crisis of Detroit and the Emergence of Global Capitalism," *International Journal of Urban and Regional Research* 9 (1985):186–217.

[18]Mark Nethercut, *Detroit Twenty Years After: A Statistical Profile of the Detroit Area since 1967* (unpublished research report submitted to Center for Urban Studies, Wayne State University, Detroit, 1987); Darden et al., *Detroit.*

[19]Urban Land Institute, *ULI Market Profiles* (Washington, D.C., 1994).

[20]Darden et al., *Detroit;* Brian Jones and Lynn Bachelor, *The Sustaining Hand* (Lawrence: University of Kansas Press, 1986).

[21]Michael Parkinson and Hillary Russel, *Economic Attractiveness and Social Exclusion: The Case of Liverpool* (paper prepared for the report "Europe 2000+" for the European Commission, 1994); Richard Meegan, *Liverpool—Sliding Down the Urban Hierarchy: From Imperial Pre-eminence to Global and National Peripherality* (paper presented at the conference "A New Urban and Regional Hierarchy?" sponsored by the International Sociological Association Research Committee #21 and the Lewis Center for Regional Studies, University of California at Los Angeles, April 23–25, 1992).

[22]*ULI Market Profiles.*

[23]Kinuthia Macharia, "Meeting the Challenge in an African City: Nairobi's Informal Economy," *In the New Urban Challenge and the Black Diaspora*, ed. Charles Green (Albany: State University of New York Press, 1995).

[24]Ibid.

[25]Joe L. P. Lugalla, "Where the Majority Live in Tanzania: Why and How?" in *In the New Urban Challenge*.

[26]"Asia and Africa: The Root of Success and Despair," *In the Washington Post*, July 12, 1992, p. 1.

[27]Lugalla, "Where the Majority Live in Tanzania."

[28]*Dar Es Salaam* (United Nations Centre for Human Settlements and the World Bank, 1993).

[29]Lugalla, "Where the Majority Live in Tanzania."

[30]Richard Stren, *The Study of Cities: Popular Perceptions, Academic Disciplines, and Emerging Ideas* (unpublished manuscript, 1995).

[31]John Marlin, Emanual Ness, and Stephen Collins, *Book of World City Rankings* (New York: Free Press, 1986), and *ULI Market Profiles*.

[32]Hooshang Amirahmadi and Wu Weiping, "Foreign Direct Investment in Developing Countries," *The Journal of Developing Areas* 28 (1994): 167–90; Yue-Man Yeung, "Globalization and the World Cities in Developing Countries," in *Urban Research in the Developing World*, ed. Richard Stren (Toronto, Canada: Centre for Urban and Community Studies, University of Toronto, forthcoming).

[33]Some studies use geographic areas rather than level of development to categorize foreign direct investment. Thus, Tokyo is counted along with Guangzhou and Kuala Lumpur as part of Asia, and not part of the most developed economies. Once places are categorized according to their developmental level, proportions change and the gap is larger.

[34]John D. Stempel, "The Decentralization of American Foreign Policy," *Journal of State Government* 54 (1991): 122–24; Michael H. Shuman, "Dateline Main Street: Local Foreign Policies," *Foreign Policy* 10 (winter 1986/1987): 10; Ivo D. Duchacek, "The International Dimension of Subnational Self-Government," *Publius: The Journal of Federalism* (fall 1984): 5–31.

[35]Peter K. Eisinger, *The Rise of the Entrepreneurial State: State and Local Economic Development Policy in the United States* (Madison: The University of Wisconsin Press, 1981).

[36]Ibid.

[37]John Rose, "Foreign Relations at the State Level," *Journal of State Government* 64 (1991): 110–17.

[38]Michael Porter, "The Competitive Advantage of the Inner City," *Harvard Business Review* (May–June 1995): 55–71.

Chapter 4

What Has and Has Not Changed since Habitat I: A View from the South

Martha Schteingart

Habitat II provides an opportunity to reflect both individually and jointly on the situations, phenomena, and processes in cities that have remained the same or have been altered since Habitat I; on differences in the way urban problems are viewed and interpreted over time; and on the proposals introduced to address these problems.

Such an endeavor could prove to be a tremendous, or impossible, task, unless it is limited geographically or by subject, since the way change is viewed and the very nature of change undeniably varies between the countries of the North and the different regions of the South. There is also great variation in the perception of change depending on what aspect of urban problems is observed. For the purpose of this chapter, I shall focus on analysis of what has occurred in Latin America regarding some aspects of urban problems: (1) how the internal organization of cities has evolved, with particular emphasis on the most notable contradictions and conflicts, and on the segregation of different social groups in the urban setting; (2) what has become of poverty and the settlements where the vast majority of the urban poor live; and (3) what has or has not changed as a result of proposals or strategies for intervention applied by governments of the region.

In my view, the subjects selected touch upon key aspects of urban problems in the countries of the region, given that different studies have pointed to greater inequality and a rise in poverty as manifestations of the harsh social reality Latin America has been experiencing. Accordingly, there have been changes in the proposals to address the problems, and these in turn should be seen in the context of the sweeping economic and political transformations since Habitat I.

This chapter is based mainly on review and analysis of documents produced by international agencies, because of the comprehensive data they deal with on a regional basis and for groups of countries and, more importantly, because through these agencies we have been able to follow up on the views, analysis, positions, and proposals put forth regarding the problem at hand. This output is interpreted and, in some instances, compared or argued, taking into account the conclusions of scholarly research and my own experience, research, and practice in the field of urban studies.

Contradictions, Social Differences, and Conflicts in Latin American Cities

In 1950, 30 percent of the world's population was living in cities; by 1995 this percentage had risen to 45 percent of the total world population; and it is estimated that by the year 2005, the figure will reach 50 percent. This overall situation, however, varies greatly from region to region. Three-quarters of the population of developed countries and Latin America live in urban areas, whereas in Asia and Africa the urban population does not even represent one-third of the total number of inhabitants, although the rate of urbanization in these regions is increasing. In developing countries, generally speaking, the urban population grows at an annual rate of at least 3.6 percent. In other words, it increases by 170,000 people a day; whereas in rural areas the increase is around 60,000 inhabitants per day; and by the year 2030, the urban population in developing countries will reach two-thirds of the total population. Although Latin America as a whole is a region with a highly urban population, it also contains areas that deviate significantly from this generalization. By 1985 three groups of countries had been identified according to population concentration in urban areas. The first group is made up of the countries with the highest concentration of urban population: Argentina, Chile, Uruguay, and Venezuela, with an average urban population of 82 percent. The second group includes six nations: Brazil, Mexico, Colombia, Peru, Cuba, and Nicaragua, with 69 percent of the population in urban areas. Last we find Ecuador, Bolivia, Paraguay, and the rest of Central America with a significantly lower percentage, an average urban population of 42 percent.[1] I must note that in the 1980s there has been a sharp decline in the pace of urban influx in the countries of the second group (which includes almost all of the most populous nations of the region) and also in the pace of growth of the largest metropolises in Latin America. In previous decades these larger cities had been characterized by intense population growth.

Although the more serious urban problems in these countries worsened partly due to the high concentration of people in urban areas and the vertiginous growth of large cities, those problems mainly result from economic situations of a structural nature that are tied to urban income distribution and prevailing development styles. Accordingly, analyses of changes in income distribution in some Latin American countries show that since the beginning of the 1980s quite a lot of ground has been lost and that the gain in the early 1990s in countries such as Argentina, Brazil, Costa Rica, Mexico, Panama, and Venezuela was not enough to overcome the heightened social inequality of the previous decade.[2] Furthermore, wasteful spending, air pollution, transportation problems, and poverty in cities have more to do with the contradiction between the privatization of benefits and the socialization of urbanization costs than with the demographic size of metropolises.[3]

Wasteful economic, social, and environmental spending is rampant. We see it, for example, in the way highways are planned, and it is apparent when buildings in good shape are prematurely dubbed obsolete and demolished only to be replaced by buildings that allow for higher-density occupation yielding higher rents. Wasteful spending can also be seen in the abuse or inefficient use of energy resources and materials from by-products, generally associated with consumption by the wealthier classes. Last, we see our collective labor potential go to waste. At the same time, it is extremely difficult for the low-income population to gain access to land for housing, due to the get-rich-quick mentality so prevalent in real estate management today. This way of thinking is imposed on the market by the owners of vacant lots who keep their properties off the market awaiting better prices, and by real estate developers who base their profits on land-use changes they promote through their own projects. In so doing, developers perpetuate and intensify the social division of space and the segregation of the poorest groups. In other words, if profiting from changes in land use is what determines the price of urban property, then speculation by developers only serves to raise land prices in anticipation of future land use. This pattern tends to eliminate any possible land use that does not command the profits required to pay such high prices.[4]

In this economic context, investments tend to be concentrated in some social groups as economic policies encourage increases in utility rates and restrictions on social spending. This will only lead to greater inequality. While poor and even middle-class families have a difficult time coping with higher prices for basic urban services, the wasteful lifestyles of the upper class will remain unchanged. Furthermore, this pattern perpetuates and intensifies spatial segregation of the most impoverished segments of society due to rate increases for public transportation and fuel, and the small pool of investment resources, which are concentrated in the "formal" city, particularly in areas where the wealthier classes live.[5] These facts and tendencies have given rise to social unrest and protest movements in Latin American countries, including Venezuela, Colombia, Brazil, Argentina, and Mexico.

Although the growing differences between social groups in southern cities appear to be a universal phenomenon also found in cities of northern countries, what stands out about the differences in Latin America is that a poor majority has not managed to substantially improve its living conditions (at times they have even become worse) and in many instances new waves of poor people have been added to this majority as a result of spatial and social readjustments. The living conditions of these people stand in stark contrast to spaces occupied by the more affluent segments of society, whose consumption sometimes surpasses the level and sophistication of the most privileged segments of society in developed countries.

Employment, Poverty, and Irregular Settlements

In Latin America during the 1970s there was a perception that blue-collar workers' income would increase in the short term in tandem with the fast pace of urbanization. A varied occupational structure was found in cities, and at the same time the prospect of on-the-job training could help a poor family leave a life of abject poverty behind.[6] Nevertheless, during the crisis of the 1980s, employment and salaries dropped sharply in the countries of the region; unemployment shot up considerably in cities, reaching 11 percent in 1985. There was also an increase in the number of people working in the informal sector due to diminished supply of quality jobs on the market, and for this reason informal, urban employment expanded to such an extent that it canceled out the advances achieved in the past three decades.[7]

Although in some countries the 1990s saw the economy pick up again as unemployment dropped, in others unemployment figures continued to soar or dipped only to rise again (as in the cases of Mexico and Argentina).[8] Also, according to the Economic Commission for Latin America (ECLA) statistics on the evolution of poverty, particularly in urban areas, the overwhelming majority of countries in the region had a higher percentage of households below the threshold of poverty in 1994 than at the end of the 1970s.[9]

Turning to housing, we find that between 30 and 50 percent of the urban population in Latin American countries live in illegal settlements or in crowded slums. The housing needs of the low-income population in cities have been met neither through the formal real estate market nor through public housing programs. This population has managed to gain access to plots of land, set up homes, and minimally satisfy its housing needs on the periphery of cities by means of de facto occupation (squatting) or through extralegal land transactions, as well as by self-built housing. The sheer breadth and recurrence of this irregular and informal modality of land appropriation and development—dubbed "popular urbanization"—together with the fact that it is executed in a standardized fashion has caused it to be recognized as a primary type of production in cities.

Studies show that a very high percentage of the houses in these settlements are partially or totally built by the occupant family. Unlike studies in the 1960s that tended to idealize houses built by the dwellers themselves, more recent analyses have stressed the relatively high cost of this type of housing. Old-fashioned production methods, low productivity, and the do-it-yourself builders' lack of experience lead to slow-moving production and home-improvement processes, and this entails great sacrifice for the families involved.[10] Finally, residents of these settlements must wait an inordinately long period of time before urban infrastructure is installed and basic services are provided and both are usually received only after a lengthy struggle to gain government support and require dwellers' contribution of labor. To live in these urban settings for many years without services exacts a high social toll on the families involved, particularly on women and children, who are the group most sensitive to the problems of popular settlements.[11]

This type of development started in the 1950s or 1960s in most Latin American countries and was considered at first to be an urban cancer; so the residents were the object of repeated attempts at eviction. It then came to be accepted and tolerated, and only lately did it become the model for solving the housing problems of the poor in the Third World.

One positive note that emerged from this type of settlement for the poor deserves attention. As a result of this phenomenon several movements and social organizations have come to life, and through their struggles, community activism, and experience at self-management have in some way contributed to strengthening civil society and furthering local democracy; in some cases they have formed the basis for alternative models of city management.[12]

Responses to Urban Regional Development: Settlement Planning and Management

Human settlement planning includes measures that affect, modify, or adapt the "socio-spatial process of territorial occupation, use, and organization, to improve the quality of life of the population." Planning is also viewed as a process for streamlining a national development project implemented on the local and regional levels, since it is on these levels that the specific mechanisms that bring about social inequality are located, and where social participation can be developed.[13]

The history of planning in Latin American countries includes different institutional modalities. There have been national and regional, urban and/or metropolitan planning efforts; proposals for comprehensive rural development; economic infrastructure plans and programs; and social plans to address the problem of poverty. Planning on a national level began as a tool for centrally determined resource distribution under the banner of "the first decade of development" launched by the United Nations in 1955. However, we acknowledge that this over-centralization created apoplexy at the center and anemia on the periphery of cities, and that perhaps the best way to proceed must include a combination of innovative measures on the local level hand in hand with central strategic guidance, aimed at efficient and equitable use of scarce resources. It is agreed, however, that it is not a good idea for solutions to come from the center of power, through a pyramid-shaped organizational structure, nor should they come solely from local planning, which often reflects preferences of local interest groups in power and thus does not ensure efficient and equitable use of limited resources. Central authorities can make settlements better by introducing structural changes and redistribution policies, but they should also stimulate or encourage autonomy and local initiative or it is unlikely that many problems in cities will find sound solutions.[14] The most frequent goals of regional planning are directed toward territorial integration, correction of the imbalance in housing production for certain population groups, control of metropolitan growth, and development of specific territories, although these goals tend to be more an ideological discourse than proposals for viable action. Regional planning has rarely been tied to other development efforts such as change in land ownership, industrial development, natural resource policies involving the environment and ecosystems, transportation and communications, or policies for improving living conditions of extremely poor groups in society. Furthermore, planning has not been efficient enough to make social participation possible.[15]

Following in the footsteps of First World nations to a certain extent, there was an attempt to achieve greater balance in urban land development, through macrospatial plans, such as core regions, satellite cities, new population centers, and development corridors. All these alternatives were predicated on the same assumption: since socioeconomic forces, generally speaking, have an effect on spatial forms, government could also reform socioeconomic forces through spatial strategies. Such strategies were difficult to implement, and in only a very few instances was there any hope of success for them. Experts say that if rural and urban strategies are well thought out, they do not preclude one another from working, but rather complement each other and both contribute to the productive base of rural and urban areas.[16]

Urban and/or metropolitan area planning has been developed with an emphasis on mechanisms like zoning, densification, and urban expansion control, especially through master plans. These were introduced in many Third World countries during the 1950s and 1960s, and were an attempt to coordinate urban development through long-term spatial proposals with superficial treatment of economic, demographic, and social issues. For this reason they proved to be quite inappropriate for these countries, where many settlements experienced explosive growth. Starting in the 1970s, static master plans geared more toward land use were gradually replaced by the action-plan approach. More dynamic, short-term government action became customary, and projects were selected on the basis of socioeconomic cost benefit analyses. Action plans paid greater attention to public financing, overcoming delay in providing basic services and proper sanitary and environmental conditions to the urban poor. More recently there has been growing interest in strategic management in an effort to strike a balance between dynamic, intersectorial, spatial strategies in the long term and development programs and action plans in the short term. This type of planning is based on recognition that decisions made by one agency can have an effect on matters under another agency's purview, and costs and benefits related strictly to one sector can differ considerably from those relating to society as a whole.[17] Nevertheless, there have been times when short-term projects have ignored the balance with broader strategies.

Although Latin American countries favored centrally planned government action until the beginning of the 1980s, subsequently, strategies involving some type of decentralization appeared. These include electing local authorities and strengthening municipalities by expanding those authorities' duties and functions and increasing financial resources. Such strategies have been particularly important to medium-sized cities despite certain problems and limitations that have emerged in managing these urban centers, including lack of financing to promote economic activity, poor quality of local technical personnel, weakness of decision-making bodies, political cronyism, and a lack of real popular participation.[18]

Different approaches to social-program planning have emerged and they encompass both sectorial views (with heavy emphasis on health, education, and housing) and address extreme poverty through compensatory programs such as social investment funds and PRONASOL, the Solidarity Program implemented in Mexico. This type of target-based program is designed to make the beneficiaries themselves take part in the organization of the program. These beneficiaries are defined by territory and community and there is emphasis on transparency in the management process. Nevertheless, there have been numerous evaluations of this program in Mexico, and they have underscored how very difficult it is to apply many of the principles articulated by PRONASOL, especially in the context of an authoritarian political system with a high degree of corruption.[19] Social investment funds have been replicated throughout the region in accordance with World Bank guidelines to ameliorate the intensification of poverty resulting from structural adjustment programs.

On the subject of solving housing problems of the poor, the United Nations acknowledges in its 1986 "World Report on Human Settlements" what has been asserted in this chapter: Since the end of the 1970s the prevailing view on urban development, migration, and poverty is much more positive than it was in the 1950s and at the beginning of the 1960s. Due to studies conducted on these phenomena, irregular settlements have ceased to be considered the greatest problem of cities and are viewed instead as an answer to unsatisfied housing needs. The main objective of "Global Housing Strategy for the Year 2000," adopted by the General Assembly of the United Nations in December 1988, is to make adequate housing available for everyone. The strategy acknowledges that the housing situation in developing countries has not improved despite decades of direct government intervention; it therefore calls on governments to leave housing production to the private sector and community efforts, and to provide legal, financial, and institutional support to this process. Although this strategy is in place in many countries, it is widely acknowledged that the needs of the poorest groups have not been adequately fulfilled. The instances in which the poorest groups have benefited from housing policies have all involved deliberate government action such as direct subsidies or special assistance. Therefore the proposal is for enabling strategies to be directed toward the less-impoverished population, which would free up resources for the most needy groups. These strategies strive to reduce the role of government and public authorities to facilitating housing production by establishing more appropriate rules and suitable financing mechanisms, a role that would enable the private sector, nongovernmental organizations, and grassroots and community-based organizations to contribute effectively to the solution of the problems.[20]

Urban Problems and Their Solutions:
The Views from Habitat I and Habitat II

Habitat I was part of the International Development Strategy for the United Nations' Second Decade with the objective "to exchange experiences, stimulate innovation, and ensure the broadest collaboration and dissemination of new ideas and technologies related to the setting of man's coexistence: his habitat."[21]

During the general debates a wide variety of countries discussed the challenges of development and the need to improve quality of life, to achieve more equitable and fair access to resources, and to create better living conditions for the most disadvantaged groups. Emphasis was placed on the poverty and human degradation suffered by the majority of the population in a world of sharp disparities in economic and social opportunities. The problem with human settlements is only part of a much broader and deeper problem: the poor living conditions of more than three-quarters of the world's population (which faces serious problems of nutrition, water, employment, health care, and education). During the conference focus was given to the need to improve the quality of life for all mankind in the context of the New International Economic Order. Concern was also clearly expressed over the demographic explosion of the past three decades, massive migration into cities, and the sharp increase in the number of people living in cities. It was mentioned that since 1950 almost 300 million people have moved into urban areas in underdeveloped countries.

The main recommendations for settlement planning made at the conference were the following: (1) economic and social development planning should provide a framework for comprehensive settlement planning on the national, regional, and local levels; (2) rural area planning should be directed toward revitalization and overcoming disadvantages of dispersed populations; (3) urban renewal and rehabilitation should respect the rights and pursuits of new beneficiaries and preserve their cultural values; (4) special attention should be paid to providing essential services on the neighborhood level; and (5) planning on all levels should be redefined as an ongoing process that requires observation, evaluation, and research.

Diverse studies and opinions are pessimistic, however, about whether the Vancouver recommendations had a direct impact. In Latin American countries, for example, the right socioeconomic conditions have not come about for the adaptation of a reform-minded approach and concrete steps toward the improvement of human settlements.[22] Furthermore, the economic crisis of the 1980s has caused an increase in poverty and worsened socio-urban contradictions and conflicts, making it more difficult to achieve the proposed objectives.

Habitat I took place during a period marked by the struggle of Third World countries to achieve a more just position in the world order. The meeting took place at the same time as the "Charter of Rights and Duties of the Nations" was proposed to the United Nations. Habitat II, on the other hand, will be held during much tougher times. National economies are more interdependent, but their ability to adopt policy decisions and regulate their own economies independently has also been weakened. This is particularly true in the case of the countries of the South. The costs of structural adjustment have proven that economic growth is indispensable but is not enough to ensure social development. Strategies should take society into account and not just the economy. In other words, it is not possible to achieve macroeconomic stability at the cost of the needs and interests of the poorer and more vulnerable sectors of the population.[23] On the other hand, the foreign debt service burden is rapidly becoming more onerous, and in many countries requires economic resources that could be used to fund social programs. Moreover, most capital for future investments will come from private sources, and these sources mainly do business in the very few countries where average incomes run mostly in the middle range.[24]

In light of this bleak outlook for Third World countries, the content of the Global Plan for Action (GPA) for Habitat II focuses on people and their settlements, and on the commitment of government leaders and nongovernmental organizations to develop enabling strategies in different countries to give their residents a chance to exercise their rights and fulfill their responsibilities by working to improve their own environment. This includes the notions of "governance" and "leadership" as basic tools to achieve these goals. To define urban problems the GPA mainly addresses the antisocial behavior of individuals (e.g., crime and corruption) that provides the backdrop to our cities, instead of shedding light on the relationship between the socioeconomic framework of the cities and their cultural, political, and psychosocial aspects. Therefore a new ethic is needed, perhaps emerging from enabling strategies, whereby political leaders and community representatives engage representatives from the poorest segment of society to work with governments, the private sector, and nongovernmental organizations in order to determine together the future they desire, by deciding on their own what measures to take, and in what order of priority.

At Habitat I the most important tool used to address the pressing problems of human settlements in the 1970s seemed to be state intervention and planning on all its levels. At Habitat II, at a time when the neoliberal mentality is flourishing, the prevailing philosophy pins its greatest hopes on enabling strategies, the new magic tool of the nineties, where government plays less and less of a role, poverty is accepted, and there is an attempt to create new forms of community organization and a new relationship between state and society.

Assessment of What Has and Has Not Changed between Habitat I and Habitat II

In Latin American cities, contrasts and differences between rich and poor have become even sharper and social conflicts have intensified. While some live in luxury, others lack even the most basic necessities. Although poverty has always been present in Latin American cities and irregular settlements date back in time, they cannot be described as passing phenomena, but rather as part of a permanent structural problem of underdeveloped cities, a problem that has intensified with an increase in unemployment and informal employment, and a drop in the real value of salaries. What has not changed, however, are the processes that cause different people to have such varied degrees of access to urban services, and the shortages and hardship that afflict the neediest classes. Although there is less and less discussion about socioeconomic mechanisms for gaining access to land, social division of space, sociospatial segregation, the housing problem of the poor, and so on, these problems have not changed fundamentally and continue to pervade our cities. Comparing texts produced at Habitats I and II makes the lack of discussion on these issues apparent. These problems are noticeably absent from discussions of pressing topics in the field of urban research.

What has or has not changed regarding housing, for example, since 1976? Among the things that have *not* changed are the rationale behind the need for a housing policy, the justification of government involvement in this sector, and the role of housing in the economy. Providing housing to the poorest people requires a government strategy specifically designed for these people. Housing is part of the productive sector of the economy and therefore should be seen as a key component in any transitional phase, to be used as a tool to drive economic growth. What *has* changed, on the other hand, is that now international agencies and governments fashion strategies targeted toward different population groups. This has lead to a significant change in direction that has a profound effect on policy goals, on the means chosen to implement that policy, and on the organization of government housing administrations.[25]

Planning, on its diverse levels, has been criticized either because it has not been implemented or because it has brought about few positive results for the population. The process of decentralization and the drive to empower municipal governments have been significant trends but are still very limited in practice. This should not be taken to mean that planning should necessarily be dropped as a practice, rather that it should be more flexible and realistic.

On this score there still is no valid reason why government intervention in territorial organization to support poor groups should be dropped. Neoliberal rhetoric in official speeches and a change in the attitude of both international agencies and governments of the region regarding the proper function of government is behind many of the negative comments on planning and government intervention. According to that rhetoric, this function should be limited in order to allow private groups, nongovernmental organizations, and the population itself to take care of social problems. This change of attitude is quite evident when we compare the principles and statements approved or proposed in 1976 with those put forth in the 1990s. At Habitat I there was ongoing discussion of government intervention and planning, whereas more recently the battle cry is "enabling strategies" and the application of a set of principles such as empowerment, equity, etc. The importance of these principles cannot be denied, but by themselves they do not appear to be enough in a world where access to basic resources is more and more inequitable and international relations are more and more asymmetrical (if not almost a nontopic). Habitat I was held under the banner of the "Charter of Rights and Duties of the Nations," whereby more fair treatment for countries of the Third World was demanded. Habitat II, on the other hand, is being held at a time when this broader issue seems to be ignored in favor of individual, local, and private initiatives and so-called new ethics.

These proposed principles and plans are consistent with the neoliberal rhetoric that calls for redefining the roles and responsibilities of families, grassroots organizations, businesses, and so on, in order to attain smaller, more efficient, and less meddlesome government. Evidently, the influence of neoliberalism in social policies is the product of a complex combination of factors. Both the fall of real socialism as well as the crisis of the welfare state, especially in more developed countries, have helped to bring about a change in the course of events and this has manifested itself through measures that reflect a tradition of privatization. This tradition has always existed in our societies and its adoption is not only a consequence of economic necessity but also echoes the age-old idea that private is better than public, despite careful study and experience that often prove the contrary.[26]

We can identify two different directions in which these so-called enabling policies are heading from their position at the center of the proposals for habitat. One direction emphasizes the freeing up of markets, deregulation, and privatization, which is at the core of neoliberal reforms. The other direction, by contrast, proposes addressing housing problems of the most impoverished groups, taking into account community-organization development and the democratization of citizen life. Naturally, these two directions can involve different degrees of government intervention and different points of view concerning what course this intervention ought to take.

Nevertheless, I would like to draw attention to the unoriginal nature of these proposals. Many of the principles involved were put to the test more than a decade ago and the results were not always positive, particularly for the most disadvantaged segments of urban society. Moreover, in some cases enabling policies imply a lapse into acceptance of poverty, which leaves the solutions to the serious social problems of poor people in the hands of the poor people themselves.

In light of what was learned from many experiences that followed the same course as some proposals for Habitat II, I believe it is essential to issue a warning about the danger of falling for trickery and creating great expectations for "new" strategies whose content is still not very clear.

Notes

[1] Alejandro Rofman and Nora Marqués, "Tendencias en el proceso de Urbanización," in *Construcción y Administración de la Ciudad Latinoamericana* (Buenos Aires, Argentina: IIED-AL, Grupo Editor Latinoamericano, 1990), 21–78.

[2] Economic Commission for Latin America (ECLA), *Panorama Social de América Latina* (Santiago, Chile: United Nations, 1994).

[3] ECLA, *La Crisis Urbana en América Latina y en el Caribe: Reflexiones Sobre Alternativas de Solución* (Santiago, Chile: United Nations, 1989).

[4] Ibid. See also Martha Schteingart and Antonio Azuela, "Habitat Popular," in *Construcción y Administración*, 351–90.

[5] ECLA, *La Crisis Urbana*.

[6] Bertrand Renaud, *The Task Ahead for the Cities of the Developing Countries*, World Bank staff working paper no. 209 (July 1975).

[7] Hector Szretter, "Empleo e Ingresos Urbanos en América Latina," in *Construcción y Administración*, 117–74.

[8] ECLA, *Panorama Social*.

[9] Ibid.

[10]Jorge Legorreta, *La Autoconstrucción de Vivienda en México: El Caso de las Ciudades Petroleras* (Mexico City: Centro de Ecodesarrollo, 1984). See also Alberto Lovera, "Indagaciones Sobre la Construcción de la Vivienda en los Barrios de Ranchos: el Caso de Caracas," in *Revista Interamericana de Planificación*, SIAP 12, no. 65 (Mexico, 1983): 9–29; Mario Zolezzi and Julio Calderón, *Vivienda Popular, Autoconstrucción y Lucha por el Agua*, DESCO (Lima, Peru: Centro de Estudios y Promoción del Desarrollo); and Schteingart and Azuela, "Habitat Popular."

[11]Martha Schteingart, ed., *Pobreza, Condiciones de Vida y Salud en la Ciudad de México* (Mexico City: El Colegio de México, forthcoming).

[12]Willem Assies, Gerrit Burgal, and Ton Salman, *Structures of Power, Movements of Resistance: An Introduction to the Theories of Urban Movements in Latin America*, CEDLA, Latin American Studies, no. 55 (Amsterdam, 1990).

[13]United Nations Center for Human Settlements (UNCHS), Habitat, *Planificación de los Asentamientos Humanos en América Latina y el Caribe: Teorías y Metodologías* (Nairobi, Kenya: United Nations/ECLA, 1984).

[14]Lloyd Rodwin and Bishwapriya Sanyal, eds., *Shelter, Settlement, and Development* (Boston: Department of Urban Studies and Planning, Massachusetts Institute of Technology, 1987).

[15]UNCHS, Habitat, *Planificación de los Asentamientos*.

[16]Lloyd Rodwin and B. Sanyal, "Shelter, Settlement, and Development: An Overview," in *Shelter, Settlement, and Development*, ed. Lloyd Rodwin (United Nations, 1987), 3–31.

[17]Programa de las Naciones para el Medio Ambiente (PNUMA) and UNCHS, *Directrices Ambientales para la Planificación y Gestión de Asentamientos* (Madrid, Spain: Ministerio de Obras Públicas y Transporte, 1987).

[18]UNCHS, Habitat, *Gastión Urbana en Ciudades Intermedias de América Latina* (Nairobi, Kenya: United Nations/ECLA, 1993).

[19]Emilio Duhau and Martha Schteingart, "Governance and Poverty at the Local Level: Mexico, Colombia, and Central America" (document prepared for the GURI Project, University of Toronto/Ford Foundation, Toronto, Canada, 1995).

[20]UNCHS, Habitat, *National Experiences with Shelter Delivery for the Poorest Groups* (Nairobi, Kenya: UNCHS, 1994).

[21]United Nations, *Declaración de Vancouver sobre Asentamientos Humanos y Plan de Acción de Vancouver* (United Nations, 1976).

[22]UNCHS, Habitat, *Planificación de los Asentamientos*.

[23]United Nations, *World Summit on Social Development* (declaration of project, Preparatory Committee for the World Summit on Social Development, United Nations, New York, 1994).

[24]United Nations, *World Summit*.

[25]Economic Commission for Europe, *Housing Policy Guidelines: The Experience of ECE with Special Reference to Countries in Transition* (New York: United Nations, 1993).

[26]Timothy Barnekov, Robin Boyle, and Daniel Rich, *Privatism and Urban Policy in Britain and the United States* (London, England: Oxford University Press, 1989).

PART II

From Local to Global

ALL CITIES ARE UNDER tremendous pressure from forces that are global in scope. The information revolution, the growing mobility of capital and people, and an emerging video culture all undermine the long-standing importance of place—as well as those social and cultural characteristics tied to a specific community in a particular setting. Social arrangements predicated on place, such as the city, appear to be endangered.

The most powerful and effective responses to the dislocations generated by contemporary global transformations often are rooted in local realities, based on local perceptions, motivations, and culture. "Global" and "local" may not be contradictory phenomena but, rather, linked responses to identical processes. The globalization of the late twentieth century may well prove to present a fatal challenge to the nation-state. The local community, especially at the level of the metropolitan region, may prove to be a beneficiary of that contest.

The contributions of Mohamed Halfani, Nezar AlSayyad, and Wei-ping Wu explore such dynamic relationships between the global and the local. Halfani explores those cities that have been "dislocated from the global system." Examining his native Africa, Halfani argues that some cities are not effectively participating in the "new mode of global accumulation" because of the absence of an adequate infrastructure. The result is that "the overall morphology and the functioning of urban centers have been distorted." Yet, even as African cities appear to be left behind the global production of wealth, caught in a "vicious circle of crisis and marginality," a number of urban communities on the continent are demonstrating remarkable resilience and sustainability. This vitality is based not in the global, but in the resurgent power of local customs, traditions, and practices that dominate so-called informal economies. It is, he concludes, "at the lower level of the neighborhood and primordial community where there is a discernible increase of civic engagement."

Nezar AlSayyad grapples with the limits of global perspectives from a different direction, the cultural. AlSayyad argues that despite superficial similarities in the physical environments of cities, underlying historical relationships and cultural patterns ensure that cities around the world are not just becoming alike. Colonial legacies, conflicts between the traditional and the modern, and issues of ethnic identity, for example, all mediate the meaning of an increasingly "place-less" physical environment. Urbanism, AlSayyad continues, "will continue to be a vibrant arena where it will be possible to observe how the forms of global domination are mediated by local struggles." While not denying the emergence of a "globally compressed world," AlSayyad points to the "distinctive cultural and unequal conditions under which the notion of the 'global' was constructed." In this manner he urges all who think about cities to appreciate the centrality of questions of identity. Precisely because culture is becoming increasingly placeless, "urbanism will become an arena where one can observe the specificity of local cultures and their attempts to mediate global domination."

Weiping Wu approaches issues of globalism and localism through the window of economic competition. Wu notes that cities around the world are increasingly connected with one another through global financial and production networks. A number of strategic functions in the international market have been recentralized in a small number of cities at the top of a new urban hierarchy. New York, Tokyo, London, Paris, Los Angeles, and Hong Kong "now function as focal points of the global economy." Competition for eminence within this system is intense. Meanwhile, many cities are struggling to replace their old manufacturing base by service industries. Although such trends may be global, the manner in which cities and regions secure their niche in this new hierarchy are local. "Each city," Wu reports, "often has its own unique production functions as a result of its history, location, and factor endowment." How coalitions in cities mobilize resources around their strengths is often an issue of local leadership. Hence, the success of cities in a new global economy is based on intensely local factors. "To compete effectively," she counsels, "a city's governing coalition needs to crystallize and endorse a vision of the future that is acceptable to both business and citizens. Public and private sectors must collaborate so as to share the burden of risks."

Urban realities thus challenge the increasingly widespread belief that all change is from the global "down" to the local. Rather, how local communities and institutions are organized may influence the precise manner in which people thousands of miles away live out their lives. The customs of Tokyo's Tskiji Fishmarket determine how fishermen in Surabaya and on Long Island live out their lives. The precise configuration of London financial markets as determined by national law and local regulation influences how neighborhood banks can operate on distant continents. By focusing on these concerns, the chapters of this section elucidate the complex relationship between the global and the local.

Chapter 5

Marginality and Dynamism: Prospects for the Sub-Saharan African City

Mohamed Halfani

In the second half of the last decade of the twentieth century, Africa finds itself at the confluence of two major trends that exert tremendous pressure on the development of its urban centers. The first trend is associated with shortcomings of past development strategies. The failure to rectify sectoral and regional imbalances inherited at independence created a negative impetus that continues to accelerate the rate of urban growth. Not only have urban systems in the various countries been rendered incapable of accommodating the rapidly increasing population, but their own ecological sustainability is also in jeopardy.

Persistence of the agrarian crisis in the region, characterized by low productivity, low incomes, negative terms of trade, and absence of services, precipitated a massive influx of the rural population into the urban centers, which are perceived (especially since the 1980s) to have retained a space for human survival. The consequence of such rapid growth is an acute crisis of urbanization indicated by housing shortages, environmental degradation, severe unemployment, extreme poverty, and critical infrastructural deficiencies.

As the population shifts from one dominant form of habitat to another, the combination of rapid demographic change with the weak economic and ecological base of the receiving habitat creates a crisis of unprecedented magnitude. It alters spatial structures, dislocates markets and internal economies, transforms social and political relations, and impinges on welfare.

The second trend exerting pressure on urban development relates to changes in the global system of industrial production that drastically altered the international division of labor and dislocated Africa's competitive advantages. The traditional function of supplying industrial raw materials and cheap labor to global industrial establishments has been overtaken by rapid advances in technology and communication systems. Agricultural primary inputs lost their significance in industrial processing and distance ceased to be an impediment for industrial location. Africa's cheap labor, agricultural raw materials, and large market are no longer sufficient factors to maintain its incorporation into a new global system of accumulation.

The new level of industrial sophistication favors highly skilled labor and high-income markets. It valorizes and gives prominence to the corporate service component of industrial accumulation—the "symbol economy" as compared to the "real economy." Within such a context of realignment, the African urban centers that used to serve as the main conduits for the export-import economy are the major losers.

Although cities and transnational corporations are acknowledged to be the main driving forces behind the new mode of global accumulation, African urban centers do not share this qualification because they lack the infrastructural base to effectively participate in the new engagement. Thus, since the early 1980s most African cities have been dislocated from the global system.

The impact of these two forces has virtually crippled the formal economic and managerial structures. Both the overall morphology and the functioning of urban centers have been distorted. In the 1990s, whether in scholarly discourse or in policy circles, African urban systems are mostly addressed in terms of their crisis features and through the attributes of external marginalization. Their overall resilience and even their sheer capacity to grow in the midst of marginality and degeneration are feats that have been obscured.

Urban centers in Africa are perceived as dreaded nightmares of the future—sources of illegal immigrants to the West, potential incubators of disease, potential sites of instabilities in an otherwise converging world, even as habitats that perpetuate environmental destruction. The viable mode of intervention prescribed in some quarters is for the affluent nations to provide more charity and philanthropy.

This chapter attempts to shift away from this perspective, which overemphasizes the vicious circle of crisis and marginality in explaining the predicament of the African city. The chapter focuses on factors and processes that account for the resilience and sustainability of political and socioeconomic life in urban centers at this conjuncture when the formal structures are seemingly stressed, degenerated, and globally marginalized. The main objective is to identify the forces whose reconfiguration provides an opportunity for African cities to reconstitute their global linkages and, more importantly, to deploy their constricted dynamism so as to initiate sustainable growth and development.

An Urban Crisis

Although it is the region of the world with the highest concentration of its population still living in rural settlements, since the early 1970s sub-

Saharan Africa (SSA) has also exhibited the highest urban growth rate; by 1990 close to two-thirds of the population was still living in rural settlements, but the annual rate of urban growth was 5 percent (the highest regional average in the world). In fact, one subregion (East Africa) had an annual rate of urban growth (6.8 percent) that was more than twice the world average.[1]

In terms of absolute numbers, there has been a six- to tenfold increase of the urban population in the twenty years since the first Habitat conference. And it is estimated that the urban population will increase from 240 million people in 1994 to 804 million people by 2025. With such a rapid rate of growth, urban centers have been unable to prepare appropriate land-use systems, to provide basic social and economic services, to deploy the rapidly growing labor force in an organized way, and to become competitive in a rapidly globalizing world.[2]

Urban centers of almost all sizes in SSA manifest an acute failure to cope with the stress of rapid growth. In a majority of urban centers the rate of population increase far exceeds the rate of formal sector investment growth. In fact, while population has been increasing at an exponential rate, investments in the most critical areas of human habitat— land servicing, social and economic infrastructural development, as well as jobs creation—have been declining significantly. For example,

> In Dar es Salaam, there was a decline in expenditure on services and infrastructure of 11 percent a year from 1978–79 through 1986–87, measured in constant currency units. . . . While the Tanzanian economy as a whole was stagnating during much of this period, the decline of the urban infrastructral fabric was occurring at a much more rapid rate. To the north, Nairobi's services have also been deteriorating along with its revenue base. The capital expenditures of the Nairobi City Commission (in real US dollars per capita) for water and sewerage fell from US$7.29 to $2.30 over the same period when calculated in a similar manner. Over a six year period, this represents an average annual decrease of approximately 28 percent, compounded, when both capital and maintenance expenditures are added together. Similar calculations for expenditures on public works over the same period show an annual decrease of 19.5 percent, compounded; and for social services an annual decrease of 20 percent, compounded.[3]

The process of land development for housing construction also reflects the impact of demographic pressure. Again in Dar es Salaam, where the state (and not the market) is the overall custodian of urban land, between FY 1978–79 and FY 1991–92, the city council received

261,668 applications for plots but was able to produce (survey and register) only 17,751 plots![4] Only 6.8 percent of the official demand for land was met. More than 90 percent of those who wanted to build houses were forced to obtain land from other "nonofficial" sources, which obviously meant building in unsurveyed and unregulated areas.

By the late 1980s the formal structures of the SSA cities were described to be in a crisis of sustainability; they could not support the social and economic reproduction of the people and their habitat. The *Global Report on Human Settlements* captures four dimensions of this crisis: a severe shortage of decent housing; a decline in levels of formal employment, and a corresponding rapid increase in informal sector activities in many key areas of the urban economy; a deterioration in both the quality and distribution of basic services; and a decline in the quality of the urban environment, both built and natural.

Housing is a critical requirement for a major shift of population from one habitat to another, such as is taking place in Africa. But as Richard Stren computes,

> In a city such as Abidjan which was growing at the rate of approximately 10 percent per annum during the 1960s and 1970s, some 818,000 people were added to the city's population over the seven year period from 1973–80. This averages out to 116,871 persons per year, or—at the rate of five persons per household—23,374 households. Most of these households were in the low-income groups; and approximately 40 percent were from other countries. But the public supply of housing averaged only 4,000 units per year during this period; none of the public housing was available to non-Ivoirians. The modern private sector produced only 900 units per year over the same decade.[5]

A survey carried out by the World Bank and the United Nations Center for Human Settlements (UNCHS) confirms that the situation in Abidjan is not atypical. For example, in 1990 the percentages of unauthorized and squatter housing in Dar es Salaam were 64 and 51 respectively; in Lilongwe, 71 percent and 71 percent; in Nairobi, 75 percent and 37 percent; in Dakar, 67 percent and 30 percent; Ibadan had 75 percent unauthorized housing, and Accra had 40 percent of the same.[6] The housing deficiency is aggravated by the poor condition of both the authorized and the unauthorized houses. They lack basic facilities such as toilets, water, electricity, and basic infrastructure, and most of the unauthorized houses are built of impermanent material. Without question, the high densities of accommodation and the poor housing conditions promote health hazards and social maladies.[7]

The urban crisis also manifests itself in the employment situation. A survey carried by the International Labor Organization (ILO) shows that as of the mid-1970s, when African economies attained their highest level of performance for the period 1960–90, only 40 percent of the urban labor force was engaged in the formal wage sector.[8] With the overall economic downturn of the 1980s and the accompanying retrenchment of public services that followed, it is unlikely that the situation has improved by the mid-1990s. Survey results from selected countries and urban centers seem to point out that the majority of the urban labor force earn their living outside the formal sector.[9]

One symptom of an intensification of the labor crisis in the formal sector of African urban centers is the increasing informalization of the socioeconomic activities in the centers. In a majority of African cities today, more than 75 percent of the basic needs of the bulk of the population are provided by the informal sector. These include shelter; subsistence incomes; services such as water, energy, neighborhood security, wastewater removal, and transportation; and, in some cases, land. This implies that most urban residents are accommodated in squatter housing, derive their incomes in petty commodity production activities, and do not have direct access to basic services. Indeed, the pervasiveness of informalism has reduced the scope of formal management to a very small sphere of urban life.

The inability of urban management authorities to cope with the rapid growth rate and to establish and regulate an effective system of service provision has forced urban communities to devise alternative modes of survival in a context of acute service deprivation. Unfortunately, these alternatives have been damaging to the urban environment.[10] For example, the high concentration of population in poorly regulated settlements has increased the incidence of communicable diseases such as tuberculosis, malaria, cholera, and sexually transmitted diseases. At the same time, poor wastewater and sanitation facilities add to surface- and groundwater pollution, leading to frequent, serious intestinal maladies.

Similarly, the high demand for firewood, charcoal, and building materials in the urban centers has intensified the rate of deforestation. While it is true that the energy consumption per capita may be the same whether the consumer is in the rural settlement or has migrated to an urban center, the areal intensity of deforestation is much higher near urban centers. The rural population is more widely dispersed and thus can be less damaging to the ecology. In addition, the close connection between rural production culture and nature has helped to maintain a certain degree of conservation awareness. In rural cultures there are a number of taboos and rituals associated with maintaining the harmony between human beings and nature.

Other urban environmental damages include widespread soil excavations for gravel and sand, destruction of coral reefs for building-stones, and more seriously, pollution due to a lack of appropriate and adequate household and industrial waste disposal systems. Furthermore, the advent of urban agriculture, bringing with it pesticide use, animal husbandry, and cultivation near already-contaminated waterways, poses serious health hazards such as tetanus, malaria, and poisoning; it also exacerbates soil erosion.

In the 1990s, some urban centers are beginning to suffer the consequences of environmental destruction. Cultivation around water sources and the destruction of vegetative cover around these areas has gradually dried out the rivers and streams that feed urban centers. Many Tanzanian urban centers have experienced extended power cuts and severe water shortages as a result of damage to the water sources.

It is not only rapid growth that fosters the crisis in urbanization. The skewed nature of population distribution also compounds the situation. In almost every African country, the urban system is characterized by a dominance of a large primate city that has 30 to 40 percent of the urban population, flanked by numerous towns of fewer than 200,000 people whose main function is to service and administer a large rural hinterland. In a study of African cities in the world economy, David Simon made the following observation:

> Apart from the only two major metropolitan cities—Lagos and Kinshasa—which have estimated populations of 6 and 5 million people respectively, there are only 10 other capital cities with populations of 1–2 million each. The majority of the people who live in urban centers are found in settlements which are small in size (ranging from 0.5 million to 10,000 people).[11]

On the basis of the latest UN population statistics, 59 million of the 154 million people in sub–Saharan Africa (38 percent) are concentrated in forty-two urban centers of more than a million people. The remaining urban population—95 million—are dispersed in more than two thousand (our estimates) small and medium-sized towns.[12] Such a distribution pattern has serious economic as well as political implications for urban governance.

The coexistence of primacy and dispersion in the same system complicates the management of urban development. While the primary cities suffer from the stressful effects of overpopulation, the small towns are handicapped by the constraints of underpopulation. The concentration of investments in the large urban center provides a resource base that can be harnessed for service provision and infrastructural improvements. At the same time, the low population base in the small centers, which is additionally handicapped by very low incomes, limits the ability of such centers to provide even the basic level of services and infrastructure. In the words of one Tanzanian town director,

> Even if I collect all the fees, rates, and levies in my district for two years, and suspend all other expenditures, I will not be able to buy one septic tank.[13]

No wonder most of the urban centers, which have not devised alternative modes of service provision, have almost abdicated from providing facilities such as wastewater removal, garbage collection, fire control, and ambulance services. There are a number of urban centers whose municipal authorities cannot even afford to name their streets, or to conduct a cadastral survey and maintain a housing registry.

An additional complication arising from the pattern of population distribution relates to the political marginalization of urban social issues. Throughout the postindependence period the rural population has been the main political base of the reigning state power. Despite the apparent concentration of capital investments in urban spaces, improvement of urban welfare has not been favorably considered in policy circles and it has been given only symbolic attention. In most cases, privileges associated with "urban bias" benefited the few elites. Interests of the nonelitist sphere of the city (which constituted the main part of the city) were neglected, or even criminalized.

Even as we enter the twenty-first century, the situation has not changed significantly. The bulk of human settlements on the African continent still remains in the rural areas. By 1990, it was estimated that out of a total population of 633 million people, only 203 million (i.e., close to one-third) live in some form of urban settlement. Slightly more than two-thirds of the population—430 million people—are still in rural settlements.[14] Demographic projections indicate that the dominance of rural population will persist throughout the first quarter of the twenty-first century, and that is where the political power base will remain.

In fact, in the few pluralistic elections that have been conducted thus far, results have confirmed the traditional political allegiance of the rural population. For example, in both Kenya and Senegal, the urban population voted overwhelmingly in support of the opposition, and their counterparts in rural areas were the main supporters of the incumbent parties. It is very likely that the success of the former opposition in Zambia—the Movement for Multiparty Democracy—in defeating the ruling party was largely due to the high level of urbanization in that country.

The advent of political pluralism has also generated hostilities between municipal authorities and central governments. In the case of Kenya, for example, the opposition's success in winning a majority of seats in municipal elections, which led to gaining the mayorship in many towns, has fueled incessant conflicts between urban councils and central government ministries to the point of almost jeopardizing favorable policy considerations for urban development. Municipal authorities are increasingly deprived of power and resources for urban management. In some urban centers there is open hostility between mayors and central government ministers responsible for local government and urban development.

The political situation in African urban centers is also complicated by the sociopolitical fragmentation of the towns. Since the 1960s, urban centers have been spreading outward, forming a multi-nuclear pattern of (mostly squatter) settlements that are not fully integrated into municipal authority domain. Over the years, each of these diverse communities has developed a local leadership and an authority system that is not necessarily part of the formal municipal structures. Aside from the promotion of local development activities and the protection of community interests (largely against the central and local government), one leadership function is to lobby for resources to provide basic infrastructure and services in these areas. Many such demands from diverse communities complicate the process of urban planning and management.

The centrifugal tension embedded in some of these local communities is so powerful that it creates an impression that the community is not part of the larger city. Abdou Simone, a social anthropologist, describes the neighborhood of Medina, which is the largest in Dakar, Senegal:

> Medina is a hodgepodge of small-scale housing developments (working man's mansions) interspersed with cardboard shacks, chickens and goats, young preteens fighting police in [M]adonna outfits before changing clothes to attend obligatory religious instructions. Religious fundamentalists coincide with communists coincide with fashion models and gangsters—all share the conviction that the integrity of the community is maintained only because everyone is coming and going to and from somewhere else. . . . A neighborhood such as Medina [may appear] ungovern-

able from the point of view of rational urban planning. Walking through Medina, it is easy to conclude that the whole place will explode at any moment—yet it is an explosiveness on which everyone seems to thrive. As one teacher eagerly points out, "there is no place in the world where you can be lost and found so many times in 24 hours."[15]

Based on the above socioeconomic and environmental profile, it seems that African urban centers have been poor human habitats in the last twenty years. However, to what extent are they "engines of growth" in relation to their national and regional economies? In other words, do cities add value to agricultural products, stimulate production, and increase productivity through the diffusion of technology and skills? Have urban centers in Africa in the last two decades been able to mobilize capital for outward investment and provide employment for surplus population? To what extent have they been able to offer higher-order welfare services to the population? I shall explore only some of these elements.

The available statistical evidence is sketchy but the heavy reliance on primary commodities in merchandise exports suggests that urban centers continue to play the traditional role of facilitating exports. In 1970 primary commodities accounted for 93 percent of all exports; by 1991 the level was still at a high of 89 percent. This means that the economic base of the region remained essentially rural throughout those twenty years. In fact, a close look at table 5.1 shows that the value added by urban-based sectors (industry and services) declined throughout the 1970s and 1980s.

The process of urban growth was not accompanied by increased technological development. Urban centers went through a process of de-industrialization in the 1980s.

Almost the same pattern was exhibited in the sphere of labor productivity. Figure 5.1 shows that whereas productivity per worker

TABLE 5.1
SECTORAL GROWTH RATES, 1965–89
(Average Annual Percentage Change of Value Added)

	1965–73	1973–80	1980–89
Agriculture	2.2	−0.3	1.8
Industry	13.9	4.2	−0.2
Services	4.1	3.1	1.5

SOURCE: *World Development Report 1990* (Washington, D.C.: World Bank, 1990), 162.

Percent per year

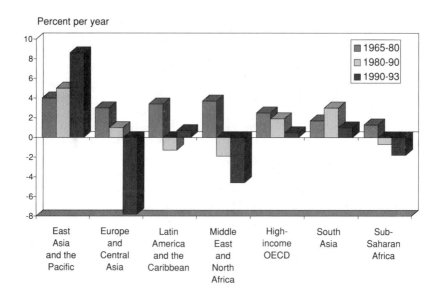

FIGURE 5.1. Growth of GDP per worker by region, 1965–1993. (World Bank, *World Development Report 1995*, Washington, D.C.: World Bank, 1995, 13).

between 1965 and 1993 trebled in East Asia, there was a consistent decline in Africa and the Middle East beginning in 1980. Such evidence demonstrates the failure of urban systems in the region to stimulate labor productivity.

Of course, one of the underlying causes of low productivity is the low level of urban infrastructure. And the developmental implication of this condition is captured in a conclusion of a World Bank research report:

> Unreliable infrastructure services impose heavy costs on manufacturing enterprises. Virtually every manufacturing firm in Lagos has its own electric power generator to cope with the unreliable public power supply. These firms invest 10 to 35 percent of their capital in power generation alone and incur additional capital and operating expenses to substitute for other unreliable public services. The burden of investment in power generation, boreholes, vehicles, and radio equipment in lieu of working telephones is disproportionately higher for small firms. In Nigeria and many other low-income countries, manufacturers' high costs of operation prevent innovation and adoption of new technology and make it difficult for them to compete in international markets.[16]

Marginality

Whereas the failure of domestic policy played a part in generating the crisis of urbanization in Africa, the macroeconomic situation at the global level seriously inhibited the region's capacity to overcome the crisis. Negative terms of trade, rising interest rates, and massive disinvestment all colluded to forestall internal accumulation, contributed to deindustrialization, and undermined revenue mobilization for investments.

By the end of the 1980s Africa's marginal position in the international economic system was more entrenched. Its share of direct foreign investments and total international trade remained negligible throughout the 1980s. The region seem to be increasingly marginalized in an increasingly globalized world.

As table 5.2 shows, the volume of investment in Africa in 1983 was almost the same as it was in 1990. During the same period, East Asia trebled its volume, Latin America's had doubled, and only the Middle East—which had a stronger domestic resource base, with a high share in international trade—showed a similar lack of growth.

Africa's trading position also worsened. In 1992, more than 50 percent of SSA exports went to industrialized Western countries, which supplied in turn 80 percent of its imports. However, protectionism and restrictive agricultural practices on the part of the European Community and the United States have created an oversupply of some agricultural commodities, dampened worldwide demand, and weakened world prices. At the same time, imports from African countries have been restricted by tariff and nontariff barriers. Table 5.3 shows the sharp decline in Africa's share of total world exports.

In 1995, the subregion's share of total world exports was a third of what it had been in the 1950s. Its share of total world imports showed the same trend. Imports fell from a high of 3.1 percent in 1955 to a low of 1 percent in 1992. According to the trade figures, developed market economies—the United States, Europe, and Japan—essentially traded among themselves in the 1990s, and South and Southeast Asia joined that league. The other region of the Third World—Latin America—performed slightly better than SSA, with a share of 3.6 percent in 1992. This showed SSA to be the subregion that traded the least with the rest of the world.[17]

The implications of such a situation for urban growth and competitiveness are serious. The lack of foreign investments, a negligible involvement in international trade, and a steep decline in export revenue, coupled with limited domestic savings and investments, imply that the region cannot share in the mostly urban-based technological

TABLE 5.2
DEVELOPING COUNTRIES: FOREIGN DIRECT INVESTMENT INFLOWS BY REGION, 1983–91
(Billions of U.S. Dollars)

Region	1983	1984	1985	1986	1987	1988	1989	1990	1991	Total	% of Developing Countries' Total 1983–91
Developing Countries	16.13	15.91	12.06	13.02	18.19	24.86	30.08	27.46	61.14	218.85	100.0
Africa	1.19	1.11	0.75	0.55	1.39	1.20	2.68	1.20	2.54	12.61	5.8
Asia	5.84	5.47	5.06	7.06	12.67	16.15	18.80	18.55	19.45	109.05	49.8
Middle East	5.59	6.10	2.23	2.29	-0.14	1.45	1.87	0.39	27.15	46.93	21.4
Western Hemisphere	3.51	3.23	4.02	3.12	4.22	6.06	6.73	7.32	12.0	50.21	22.9

SOURCE: *Balance of Payment Statistics Yearbook* (Washington, D.C.: International Monetary Fund, 1992), 68–69.

TABLE 5.3
SSA PERCENTAGE OF WORLD EXPORTS, 1950–92

1950	1955	1960	1965	1970	1975	1980	1985	1988	1989	1990	1991	1992
3.1	3.1	2.8	2.7	2.4	2.3	2.4	1.7	1.0	1.1	1.2	1.1	1.0

SOURCE: United Nations Conference on Trade and Development (UNCTAD), *Handbook of International Trade Development Statistics* (New York: UNCTAD, 1993), 29.

advances attained in the modern era. The subregion is virtually cut off from the cluster of innovations associated with the microelectronic-chip technology. The basic structure of the African city, with its reliance on import substitution industries, resource processing, and primary exports, is obsolete within a global economy entering its "fifth kon-dratieff cycle" in technological development.[18]

A Synergetic Potential for Change

In the 1990s, a synergetic potential exists that could stimulate positive change and reverse the developmental setbacks of cities in SSA. The new international division of labor and the resulting realignment of the global accumulation system have reached an advanced stage of development. At the same time, responses of the urban population in SSA to the crisis situation and to the process of marginalization have crystallized into dynamic organizational systems. These developments expose new opportunities that might contribute to the revitalization of crisis-ridden and marginalized African urban systems.

One of the opportunities arising from globalization at its advanced stage is the consolidation of a multiple hierarchy of cities that are the nodal linkages of the accumulation process. The reconstituted system creates new opportunities for SSA cities to participate in and gain from the globalizing system.

Although hierarchical profiles are not unique to this epoch of global capitalism, the reconstitution of functions and the prominence of city linkages make this hierarchical system distinct. In the words of R. B. Cohen, "the old order was characterized primarily by the production of manufactured goods in Western Europe, the United States, and Japan, and the production of raw materials by Asia, Africa, and Latin America. The attributes of the new international division of labor include: the international spread of manufacturing and corporate related services such as multinational banks, law firms, accounting firms, advertising firms, and contracting firms; the development of a system of international financial markets less subject to regulation by nationally based banks but tied to the needs of major international firms and large multinational banks."[19] Cities have become important components of the new system because

since World War II there has been a great acceleration in the processes by which capitalist institutions have freed themselves from national constraints and have proceeded to organize global production and markets for their own intrinsic purposes. . . . The activities of transnational corporations and the fact that capital has become almost instantaneously mobile over the entire globe contributed to the spatial articulation of the emerging world system of production and markets through a global network of cities.[20]

Within the new international division of labor, the "real economy" of production, manufacturing, and trade continues, but the "symbol economy" is highly valorized. Production of primary commodities, Africa's main preoccupation, is given a low value because of the declining share of material inputs in the production of high-value manufacturing products such as automobiles, machinery, and electronic goods. The fast growth and dominating sectors in the industrialized countries (microelectronics and communication, robotics technology, biotechnology) are resource-saving in nature and therefore consume minimum resources. Fu-Chen Lo cites the case of Japan, where it was estimated that in the early 1990s only 50 to 60 percent of resource inputs were required to produce the same level of GNP as in 1980.[21]

Taking into account the functional and locational diversifications as well as the uneven development of the new global system, John Friedman suggests the mapping of the hierarchy of world cities in figure 5.2, which identifies at least one nodal linkage for Africa.

This hierarchy also recognizes the regional subgroups—European Union, North American Free Trade Agreement (NAFTA), Association

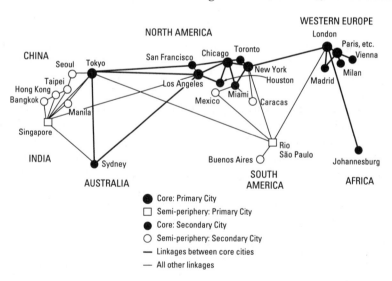

FIGURE 5.2. The world relations of cities (John Friedmann, "The World City Hypothesis (Editor's Introduction)," *Development and Change* 17, No. 1, (1986), 74

of Southeast Asian Nations (ASEAN), and Asian Newly Industrialized Countries (NICs)—and the urban linkages that they develop. However, in the case of Africa, alongside the erratic connections from the core (which is part of the 5 percent direct investments), Johannesburg seems to be the potential linkage. In fact, as figure 5.3 illustrates, the prospects of that connection are gradually being realized in the 1990s.

Less than five years after South Africa joined the community of nations, it began to jump-start the regional economy. In 1995 Howard French of the *New York Times* reported that

> South Africa's pent-up enterpreneurial energy is exploding all over Africa. South African industry is rushing in to build railroads in Zaire, sink mines in Ghana, put up hotels in Kenya, and provide the entire continent with enough jets and telephone lines to help revitalize its sagging economy. South African trade with the rest of Africa is booming, with exports up 50 percent in two years to nearly $2.5 billion in 1994 and imports tripling to $664 million from $220 million.[22]

The urban investments from South Africa associated with the "symbol economy" are in banking, fiber-optic lines and satellite television, hotels and tourism, airline services, ports and railway lines, and processing industries such as breweries.

Prospects for more pivotal links look even brighter when the rapidly growing connection with the Gulf States and the Asian-African diaspora are also taken into account. There has been a growing tide of capital flow from the Gulf States that is fostered by cultural affinities between a sizable African population of Arab ancestry and the Gulf Arabs. This is especially notable in the coastal cities of East Africa, where a lot of real estate development is financed from Gulf remittances and investments. The same applies to investments coming from the Asian-African diaspora; relatives based in Canada and Europe are reconnecting, through business ventures, with relatives who remained in the subregion. The tightening competition in the West is also forcing weak capital of this type to seek easier markets in Africa.

The number of nodal links proliferates when activities of multilateral agencies are taken into account. David Simon, for example, compiles data on location of international organization secretariats and the volume of civil aviation, which reflects business travel and international tourism. He shows that in cities such as Nairobi, Dakar, Addis Ababa, Abidjan, Lagos, and Accra there are more than a dozen global

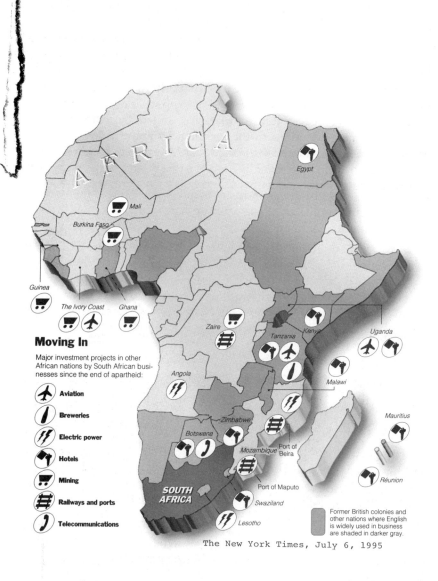

Moving In

Major investment projects in other African nations by South African businesses since the end of apartheid:

Aviation

Breweries

Electric power

Hotels

Mining

Railways and ports

Telecommunications

Former British colonies and other nations where English is widely used in business are shaded in darker gray.

The New York Times, July 6, 1995

FIGURE 5.3. Apartheid's end is helping revitalize a continent.

and regional organizations. In fact, Nairobi has more such institutions than Bangkok, Manila, or even New Delhi.[23]

The importance of the location of international organizations in a given city is illustrated in Nairobi, site of half of the United Nations Environment Programme (UNEP), whose annual budget of $40 to $50 million is injected directly into the city economy in the form of wages, purchases of goods and services, and support for local projects.[24] UNEP's presence also generates multiplier effects in retail business, real estate, and services. Furthermore, the presence of a large number of international organizations has attracted smaller, nondiplomatic institutions to Nairobi to benefit from proximity and networking. All these accrue at different scales to other cities that are homes to the activities of international agencies.

The volume of air traffic in African cities is only a tiny fraction of that handled by major cities in other regions. However, the fact that cities such as Abidjan, Accra, Addis Ababa, Dakar, Lagos, and Nairobi received more than forty-seven thousand international flights in 1988, carrying more than three million passengers and more than eighty-seven thousand tons of freight and mail is a demonstration of a lively global linkage. In fact, the prominence of a city such as Nairobi, which has become a central location for international organizations and a major hub for international air traffic, points to the prospects of this city in assuming a global transactional status. Nairobi is rapidly growing into a negotiation and command center for the international public-sector operations in the African region.

The dynamic spread-effects of all these nodes and subnodes in the global hierarchy are promoted by the growth of subregional organizations such as the Southern African Development Community (SADC), the Preferential Trade Agreement, Economic Community of West African States (ECOWAS), and a few others that allocate coordinating functions to various city capitals. Activities of these organizations also promote closer interaction between places and facilitate the redistribution of resources.

Toward Revitalized Governance

The second synergetic potential for change in SSA cities is revealed in the revitalization of modes of urban governance that nurture and harness the exuberant and yet untapped local energy and use it to create socioeconomically robust and sustainable urban systems.

Since the 1980s, important insights have been brought to bear on the demonstrated effectiveness of traditionally based institutions in ameliorating the impact of the urban crisis.[25] While traditional institutions and organizational arrangements have always been part of the social existence of urban communities, they have only been treated as elements of a fringe culture deployed mainly to ensure survival. It was mostly the marginal social groups in an urban context who needed to invoke traditional structures to facilitate their settlement and advancement in the hostile urban setting.

The marginalism associated with traditional institutions also applied to the informal sector. In the few instances when this sector was accorded positive recognition, as was the case in the various programs of the 1970s, it was treated as an accommodative measure to absorb a surplus labor force or to provide shelter to the urban poor. Essentially, traditional institutions and the informal sector were both considered recalcitrant appendages of the formal system. The latter used traditional institutions simply as a way of buying time while it strengthened its capacity for a more effective legal-rational approach to managing the city.

At the height of the crisis period in the 1980s, the failure of the formal sector to continue with its exclusionary approach to urban governance became more evident. Neither central government ministries responsible for urban development nor municipal authorities were able to effectively maintain law and order, provide services, and regulate socioeconomic activities. It was at this point that urban communities extensively deployed the "social capital" embedded in traditional institutions and informal transactions.

By the early 1990s, traditional institutions as well as informalism were not only survivalist institutions; they were gradually taking over some of the responsibilities of the formal sector. In fact, in some countries, senior functionaries of the state and municipal authorities relied on these nonformal institutions for their own developments.

In various African cities principles that derive from traditional institutions of kinship have been adapted to operate effectively in the heterogenous setting of the modern city. Organized systems of land management, capital mobilization, maintenance of law and order, infrastructural investment, stocking and disposal of merchandise, and even welfare services are provided with relative effectiveness along the principles of trust and generalized reciprocity within a market context.

Accounts of land acquisition in squatter settlements abound.[26] In all those cases transfer of land takes place without using the bureaucratic and legal instruments of the modern state. The unregistered piece of land is passed over to the new owner simply on the strength of local witnesses who vouch for the authenticity of ownership, delineation of boundaries, and terms of payment, and who act on behalf of the community to recognize the new resident. In a place like Tanzania, such deals have been more reliable than the heavily sealed documents provided by the formal system.

The traditional virtues of trust and mutual confidence are also invoked in the system of rotating credit—which seems to be prevalent throughout the Third World.[27] The rotational sharing of a collective fund among urban residents on the basis of trust and associations establishes both a banking and an insurance system. In addition to lending money, the group becomes an insurance organ that can rescue its members in case of a calamity.

On the whole, there is a marked increase in associational life in the urban centers. The bases of such associations range from primordial identities such as ethnicity and hometown origins, religion, trades and occupations, neighborhoods, arts and sports, and gender, to philanthropy. Ethnic and religious institutions have assumed a more functional role in the wider society in terms of providing education, health care, and even mediation assistance with the state.

The authority commanded by some of these associations surpasses that of the local state; in some cases the associations are able to develop wider institutions, or even global networks. Abdou Simone describes the power and organizational scale of the Mouriddiyah, an Islamic spiritual fraternal organization, in the following words:

> Its center, the city of Touba, is a sovereign state unto itself. No Senegalese state authorities are allowed access without permission. . . . The Mouriddiyah has parleyed its traditional organization of groundnut production into a world-wide network of traders who sell watches, Gucci bags, and brass ornaments in every large city of the world. Income derived from these activities has been invested in large real estate acquisitions in New York, Paris, Dakar, and more recently, Tokyo and Hong Kong.[28]

I agree with Professor Akin Mabogunje that the main problem with the prevailing systems of urban management is in the disjuncture between the rules, enforcement mechanisms, and norms of behavior underpinning the mode of living of the majority of urban residents in Africa, and those that are embedded in the formal institutions of urban management. According to Mabogunje, the former are based on remnants of traditional kinship relations, whereas the state and municipal institutions operate on the basis of property rights and contractual relations. The tragedy of postindependence institutional history has been in the failure to effect the necessary "institutional radicalization" of the traditional systems to make them adaptable to the challenges of modern urban development.[29]

The fact that the formal system of urban management is beginning to recognize and interface with some of these civil institutions is an indication that a new mode of urban governance is emerging. The incorporation of a traditional security system (*sungusungu*) in the form of community policing in Tanzania, or the incorporation of the traditional concept of a nonlinear street (which actually refers to a sociological neighborhood) into the municipal administrative structure in the same country are both evidence of the new approach to urban governance. Such initiatives have been taken in Uganda, where nonpartisan culture-sensitive "Resistance Councils" established at various levels constitute the new framework of local governance.[30]

In Nigeria, the principles embedded in the rotating credit system have been successfully deployed in the establishment of modern community banks. The "first one was opened on December 31, 1990, and by December 1992 there were 401 banks opened, out of which 304 had between them built up assets of Nigerian Nairas 981 million, mobilized over N640 million in savings and deposits, and disbursed some N150 million as loans and advances to small-scale informal sector producers."[31] Other examples include integrated systems of managing land in secondary towns where traditional structures are also deployed.[32]

In the city of Nairobi, most of the major hospitals are run by nongovernmental organizations (NGOs), which also provide 9 percent of all primary education and 27 percent of all secondary education.[33] A high point of civil action in Kenya took place early in 1994, when the First Nairobi Convention brought together people from the private sector, voluntary organizations, community groups, academic institutions, civil servants, council officers, elected representatives, and concerned individuals. The goal of this convention, under the rallying cry "The Nairobi We Want," was to develop a vision and a strategy for the development of a city that its people can relate with.[34]

Another prominent interface has been in the provision of commuter transportation. The system that used to serve in the informal sector (and which was therefore illegal) has now formally assumed the function of providing cheap and efficient transport services. Results of a ten-city survey of urban passenger transportation show that on average the informal sector has taken over almost 75 percent of mass transit service in these cities. In cities such as Dar es Salaam, Bamako, Lagos, and Brazzaville, the *dala-dalas, durunis, molue,* and *fula fulas,* as the informal systems are respectively known, provide more than 90 percent of the services.[35]

The vitality of the informal sector has been demonstrated in a long-term-perspective study of West Africa jointly coordinated by the Organization for Economic Cooperation and Development (OECD) and the African Development Bank (ADB). It was convincingly argued that with a sixfold increase of urban population from 13 to 78 million from 1960 to 1990, public and private investment to house the growing population, or population-related investment, had to be the foremost type of capital accumulation (especially due to the absence of urban real estate investment in the colonial past).

Using a Social Accounting Matrix (SAM), which uses expenditure values to compute formal and informal sector incomes and investments, the OECD/ABD study showed that the gross regional product in the subregion has tripled during the postindependence period to a sum of $3 trillion and the total population-related investment of around $500-600 billion, "with a net value (even deducting 'white elephants') somewhere around $400 billion. . . . This capital accumulation amounts to several times the total cumulated net transfers of resources to the region over the last thirty years."[36]

The study argued that Africa is not abnormal in prioritizing population-related investment:

> [T]he region has proceeded in much the same way as today's developed countries did at a comparable stage in their history. In the USA for example, at least half of total investment was financed from outside resources until 1860–70, and more than a third of that total investment went to settling the population. On the eve of World War II, infrastructure and housing still accounted, respectively, for 40 and 34 percent of total investment.[37]

Has this all led to an increased level of civic engagement? Unfortunately, the available evidence is not strong enough to make any definitive postulations. As a tentative postulation, however, it is possible to distinguish two levels of civic engagements: the broader city level, and the community level.

At the city level a growth of civic engagement could be demonstrated by such developments as increased participation in municipal affairs; stronger associations and identification with city-level institutions such as soccer clubs, jazz and traditional music bands, and social clubs; and a rise in the sense of duty, obligations, and rights of the population as citizens of the wider city community. Yet in all these spheres, there is no evidence of increased engagement. The turnout in municipal elections has remained low; interest in municipal decision-making remains marginal unless a local issue is involved; and in some cases even awareness about municipal leadership and structures is seriously lacking. Even the "Nairobi We Want" movement was short-lived. The dynamic mayor who initiated it resigned less than six months after the convention.

The close affinity of city-based cultural and social institutions has waned. Sports clubs and other cultural groups have lost their city identity and the traditional competitions between city-based institutions are no more. The sense of ownership of the city does not exist. And even more seriously, the demise of civics as a subject in schools (and its replacement with political and ideological education) has completely undermined the sense of urban citizenship. Urban residents are not aware of their rights and duties at the national and at the city level.

At the lower level of the neighborhood and primordial community there *is* a discernible increase of civic engagement. Most of the notable developments surface at this lower level where the sense of belonging still thrives and where association, trust, reciprocity, and networks of social exchange are still operational. Of course, the problem of increased engagement at this level is that it fosters localism, especially when the higher levels are weak. Perhaps the galvanized engagement created by multipartisanism will ultimately channel this pent-up energy toward an integrative engagement at the city level.

Conclusion

Confronted with a simultaneous occurrence of a crisis and marginalization, African urban systems must grapple with two daunting tasks. The first is to strengthen internal economies by enhancing productive linkages with the rural hinterland as well as by building new competitive advantages that will attract domestic and foreign investments.

The treatment of urban centers as important economic units has not been given its due attention. The predominance of a sectoral and project approach to urban development has perpetuated the structural disarticulation of the city to having increased investment without raising productivity. Increasing urban productivity involves systematic investment in improved infrastructure, development of high-level skills and industrial discipline, as well as promotion of good governance at the city level.

The enhancement of productive linkages between urban and rural areas involves investing in industrial technology that will boost both agricultural productivity and the competitiveness of rural commodities in global markets. The experience of some Latin American countries in modernizing agricultural production in conjunction with urban-based industries is instructive in this regard.

The second task is to streamline the system of urban management, reconciling and developing proper interfaces among the multiple regimes of governance. The incongruous juxtaposition of trust-based traditional systems, reciprocative and modified market-based informal systems, property and contract-based municipal structures and private sector, and the other outright criminal activities that conform to none of these logics, undermines the very effectiveness of urban management.

The success of the few initiatives aimed at streamlining the operations of governance regimes proves that the task is viable. However, underlying a long-lasting integration of regimes of governance is the need to treat the city as a policy object and, more importantly, to develop a partnership approach in a governance system that is grounded on the decentralization of power, authority, and resources. Although in the specific context of Africa it would not be prudent to adopt Jane Jacob's extreme position of suggesting that "cities be freed from the constraints that states place on their economic activity, enabling them to be more autonomous units in the worldwide economy," the devolution of power is still an important prerequisite for effective urban governance, even in Africa.

Notes

[1] United Nations, *World Urbanization Prospects* (New York: United Nations, 1994), 154.

[2] Ibid., 118–19.

[3] Richard Stren, "Urban Changes in Africa, 1960–1995," (Toronto, Canada: Center for Urban and Community Studies, University of Toronto, 1995), 12.

[4] J. M. Lusugga Kironde, "The Governance of Urban Development in Tanzania" (paper presented at the workshop "Governance of Urban Development in East Africa: A Research Perspective," Institute of Development Studies, University of Dar es Salaam, Tanzania, 1–2 August 1994), 12.

[5] Stren, "Urban Changes in Africa," 13.

[6] World Bank, *World Development Report* (Washington, D.C.: World Bank, 1994), table 4.

[7] A. G. Onibokum, *Governance and Urban Poverty in Anglophone West Africa* (Ibadan, Nigeria: Center for African Settlement Studies and Development, 1995), 2–19; Kironde, "The Governance of Urban Development," 17–23.

[8] Stren, "Urban Changes in Africa."

[9] United Republic of Tanzania, *The Informal Sector Survey* (Dar es Salaam, Tanzania: Planning Commission and Ministry of Labor and Youth Development, 1991); Kinuthia Macharia, "Meeting the Challenge in an African City: Nairobi's Informal Economy in the

1980s and 1990s," (1995), 12; Abdou Toure, *Les petits métiers à Abidjan. L'imagination au secours de la (conjuncture)* (Paris, France: Karthala, 1985), 18.

[10]United Nations Center for Human Settlements (UNCHS), *Managing the Sustainable Growth and Development of Dar es Salaam: Environmental Profile of the Metropolitan Area* (Dar es Salaam, Tanzania: UNDP, 1992); and A. Nuwagaba, "Urbanization and Environmental Crisis in Uganda: Implications for Environment Management and Sustainable Development" (working paper prepared for the African Research Network for Urban Management, Nairobi, Kenya, 1994).

[11]David Simon, *Cities, Capital, and Development: African Cities in the World Economy* (London, England: Belhaven Press, 1992), 75.

[12]United Nations, *World Urbanization Prospects*, 96–97.

[13]Town director of Songea Town Council, communication with the author, May 1991.

[14]Ibid., and a forthcoming document by the UNCHS (1995).

[15]Abdou M. Simone, *Civil Societies in an Internationalized Africa*, (Cape Town, South Africa: Foundation for Contemporary Research, 1993), 6.

[16]World Bank, *Urban Policy and Economic Development: An Agenda for the 1990s* (Washington, D.C.: World Bank, 1991), 38.

[17]United Nations Conference on Trade and Development (UNCTAD), *Handbook of International Trade Development Statistics* (New York, UNCTAD, 1993), 29.

[18]These are 40- to 60-year cycles of long waves of technoeconomic changes associated with clusters of innovations that pervade the entire economy and provide the scope for productivity increase. See Fu-Chen Lo, "The Impacts of Current Global Adjustment and Shifting Techno-economic Paradigm on the World City System," in *Mega-City Growth and the Future*, ed. Roland J. Fuchs, Ellen Brennan, Joseph Chamie, Fu-Chen Lo, and Juha I. Uitto (Tokyo, Japan: United Nations University Press, 1994), 119–29.

[19]Chadwick F. Alger, "The World Relations of Cities: Closing the Gap between Social Science Paradigms and Everyday Human Experience," *International Studies Quarterly* 34 (1990): 498–99.

[20]Ibid., 496.

[21]Fu-Chen Lo, "Impacts of Current Global Adjustment," 109.

[22]Howard French, "Out of South Africa, Progress," *New York Times*, 7 July 1995, p. D1.

[23]David Simon, *Cities, Capital, and Development: African Cities in the World Economy*, 84.

[24]Ibid., 90.

[25]Akin L. Mabogunje, *Perspectives on Urban Land and Urban Management Policies in Sub-Saharan Africa*, World Bank technical paper no. 196 (Washington, D.C.: World Bank, 1992); Akin L. Mabogunje, (paper presented at the final meeting of the "Local Institutions and an Urban Agenda for the 1990s" Urban Research in the Developing World project, held at the Social Science Research Center, American University in Cairo, Egypt, 14 February 1993); UNCHS, *Managing the Sustainable Growth and Development of Dar es Salaam*; Larissa A. Lomnitz, *Networks and Marginality: Life in a Mexican Shantytown* (New York: Academic Press, 1977); Hernando de Soto, *The Other Path: The Invisible Revolution in the Third World* (New York: Harper & Row, 1989); E. A. Pierterse and A. M. Simone, *Governance and Development* (Cape Town, South Africa: Foundation for Contemporary Research, 1994); and John W. Haberson, Donald Rothchild, and Naomi Chazan, eds., *Civil Society and the State in Africa* (Boulder, Colo.: Lynne Rienner, 1994).

[26]J. M. Lusugga Kironde, "The Access of Land by the Urban Poor in Tanzania: Findings from Dar es Salaam" (paper presented at the workshop "Urban Poverty Alleviation and Governance in Tanzania," Ardhi Institute, Dar es Salaam, Tanzania, 14 April 1994); UNCHS, *The Management of Secondary Cities in Sub-Saharan Africa: Traditional and Modern Institutional Arrangements* (Nairobi, Kenya: UNCHS, 1991), 38–74; Mabogunje, *Perspectives on Urban Land;* and Stephen Kituuka, *Urban Land Management in Uganda: The Issues* (Kampala, Uganda: Ministry of Land, Housing, and Urban Development, Government of Uganda, 1992).

[27]Lomnitz, *Networks and Marginality.*

[28]Simone, *Civil Societies in an Internationalized Africa,* 5.

[29]Mabogunje, "Local Institutions and an Urban Agenda."

[30]Expedit Ddungu, *Popular Forms and the Question of Democracy: The Case of Resistance Councils in Uganda,* publication no. 4, (Kampala, Uganda: Center for Basic Research 1989).

[31]Mabogunje, *Perspectives on Urban Land,* 12.

[32]UNCHS, *The Management of Secondary Cities,* 38–74.

[33]N. Bubba and D. Lamba, "Urban Management in Kenya," *Environment and Urbanization* 3 (1) (1991): 37–59.

[34]Davinder Lamba, *Nairobi Action Plan: City Environment and Sustainable Development* (Nairobi, Kenya: Mazingira Institute, 1994).

[35]Xavier Godard and Pierre Teurnier, *Les transports urbains en Afrique a l'heure de l'ajustement* (Paris, France: Karthala, 1992), 51.

[36]Ibid., 34–35.

[37]CINERGIE, *The Real Economy of the West Africa Region: Retrospective Analysis 1960–1990 and Alternative Visions for 2020,* working paper no. 2 (Bamako, Mali: RESADOC, Institut du Sahel, 1994), 35.

Chapter 6

Culture, Identity, and Urbanism in a Changing World: A Historical Perspective on Colonialism, Nationalism, and Globalization

Nezar AlSayyad

One of the principal objectives of Habitat II, the United Nations Conference on Human Settlements, will be to review current global trends in economic and social development as they affect the planning and management of cities and to make recommendations for future national and global action.[1] The purpose of this chapter is to bring the issues of history, culture, and identity to the discourse on urbanism and housing in the era of globalization.

In chapter 2 of this volume Michael Cohen cites several socioeconomic convergence areas to argue that "cities in the North and the South are becoming more alike in their most important characteristics." Although this may indeed be the case, I suggest that in terms of urbanism, the similarities in the built environments of those cities are only apparent, and not real. By tracing the historical relationship between cities of the North and the South, I identify three distinct phases: colonization, independence/nationalism, and globalization. Much of the physical development of cities in the most recent phases may be properly interpreted only when grounded in their appropriate cultural and historical contexts. From this perspective, I suggest that urbanism, defined as the form and culture of cities, may encounter little change under the New World Order. In the era of globalization, when culture is becoming increasingly placeless, urbanism will maintain some relevance because of its ability to explain the specificity of local cultures. Urbanism will continue to be a vibrant arena where it will be possible to observe how the forms of global domination are mediated by local struggles.

As the twenty-first century approaches, looking at the problems of cities today, one must not ignore the revolutionary developments that have occurred in the world since the 1960s. Trends like the transnationalization of capital, the internationalization of labor, the steady increase in global trading and communication, and the ensuing competition between cities have led individuals, businesses, industries, and governments to attempt to position themselves globally.[2] It follows that in a globally compressed world, constituted of national societies that are becoming increasingly aware of their ethnic and racial roots, the conditions for the identification of individual and collective selves become very complex.[3] It is important to take into account that any theory of globalization[4] must recognize the distinctive cultural and unequal conditions under which the notion of the "global" was constructed. It also becomes difficult to comprehend globalization without recognizing the historical specificity of traditional cultures, their colonization, and their later emergence as nation-states.

At the heart of all of these issues is the question of identity. Of course, the connection between the identity of a people and the form and culture of the cities they produce has been the subject of much research. Family, ethnicity, religion, language, and history have all been identified as identity-constituting elements that are handed down in a process normally referred to as "tradition."[5] Tradition is based on valuing constraint, and in a technological world of limitless choices the conflicts between the traditional and the modern in the urbanism of cities becomes unavoidable. To cast the traditional as good and the modern as bad, or vice versa, would be naive. As much research has demonstrated, the traditional/modern dialectic is very problematic. Dichotomies such as East vs. West, North vs. South, First World vs. Third World, core vs. periphery, and developed vs. underdeveloped nations may be considered artificial categories. An approach that takes into account the discursive constitution of cultures would recognize that societies are constructed in relation to one another, and that they are produced, represented, and perceived through the ideologies and narratives of situated discourse.[6] For example, Stuart Hall has observed that the dominant term in each of the above dualities (West, North, core, etc.) is mainly defined in difference, constructed in opposition to the other; none constitutes a monolithic, preexisting real subject itself.[7] The subordinate term (East, South, periphery, etc.) is equally an invention, produced in a variety of postcolonial and anticolonial discourses. The only purpose of these dualities for scholars is to force an articulation of theoretical positions beyond the realm of binary opposition, in the process opening for discussion the complex dimensions of what is being categorized—in this case the underlying political bases of urbanism.

In studying the relationship between these two realms and its effect on the identity of people and their cities, I discern three historic phases:

the colonial period, the era of independence and nation-state building, and the most recent phase of globalization. These phases have been accompanied by three respective urban forms: the hybrid, the modern and pseudomodern, and the postmodern.

Before the era of colonialism in most of the developing world, settlement largely took the form of traditional communities in preindustrial and often insular conditions. Although some form of economic exchange occurred between this world and that of the developed world, curiosity about the "other" was limited. Vernacular forms of settlement were shaped more by sociocultural concerns and the surrounding natural environment. They also reflected, possibly at a subconscious level, the identity of their inhabitants.

Colonialism and the Hybridization of Settlements

Around the middle of the nineteenth century the world witnessed the rise of modern industrial capitalism and the emergence of organized political dominance represented by colonialism. Under this colonial paradigm, the world became divided into two kinds of people and two types of societies: powerful, administratively advanced, racially Caucasoid, nominally Christian, and principally European *dominant nations;* and powerless, organizationally backward, traditionally rooted, and mainly nonwhite *dominated societies.*[8]

The paradigm shift from the traditional to the colonial created a relationship of unequal cultural and socioeconomic exchange. And if one analyzes the issues of identity in the cities of the developing world, one must take this fact into account and understand the processes by which identity was violated, ignored, distorted, or stereotyped throughout history. Jean-Léon Gérôme's painting "Reception of the Siamese Ambassador at Fontainbleau" (figure 6.1) is one of the clearest expressions of the unequal relationship between the newly dominant and the newly dominated. In 1850 the Siamese were forced to open their ports to European trade and to exchange ambassadors with France. When Gerome was commissioned to document the ceremony, he chose to depict the moment when the Siamese envoys kneeled down to the representatives of Western imperial might.

Here the problem of representation becomes central, because such artistic creations contributed to the creation of the "other" and enlarged the gulf between the dominant and the dominated. Once the "backwardness" of the traditional population was established (at least in the minds of the great mass of citizens in the colonial motherland), reform was legitimized. Colonial regimes proceeded to eradicate the ethnicity

FIGURE 6.1. Jean-Léon Gérôme (French, 1824–1904), *Reception of the Siamese Ambassador in Fontainbleau*, 1888, oil on canvas, 33 in. × 48 in. (Musée Nationale de Versailles)

of the colonized cultures. When they failed to do so by force, they resorted to the psychological technique of hypnotizing the middle class, as demonstrated by the Goa House sculpture in New Delhi, which shows a white settler subjugating the Buddha. This series of events necessarily had an effect on the physical fabric of cities; everywhere they went colonists introduced their own brand of settlement.

The colonization process affected the overall planning model that determined the pattern of urban developments in both the core and the peripheries. This was the era when modernist ideas flowed from the countries of the North to the South. Ironically, in the 1950s and 1960s when the countries of the South launched their wars of liberation and independence, the North resorted to an age-old urban strategy. Thousands of traditional villages were destroyed in order to regroup the population in checkerboard resettlement towns under the banner of modernization. This uprooting operation was meant to break the subversive influence of the rebels. There was little desire to improve conditions for the local population.

The colonial era thus resulted in a hybrid urban condition. A certain architecture and urban language began to emerge that, at least at a visual level, unified the lands of colonial empires. For example, variations of the bungalow, a hybrid type of dwelling introduced by the British in India, began to appear all over the British Empire, making it difficult to identify its origins.

Independence, Nationalism, and Modernity

When the people of the dominated societies started to rebel against this colonial world order, they had little conceptual language to employ in their drive to establish sovereignty. Usually they were forced to use the terms of the existing order, with all its baggage of physical realities and ideological constructs like the nation-state. Groups of people living in one region under a colonial power (but of different religions, languages, ethnicities, and traditions), sharing little more than a colonial history, had to band together to achieve this new, "more advanced" stage of independence. The new political bodies highlighted what few commonalities existed, whereas they suppressed differences in pursuit of the noble goal of freedom. A national identity based on short-term political interest and the ideology of struggle emerged as the driving force behind most nationalistic movements. Once independence was achieved, the glue that bound together the various groups no longer held. Indeed, the events of the late 1980s and early 1990s in places such as the former Soviet Union and Yugoslavia are a testament to the true associations of these people, as ethnic origin, race, and religion are reemerging as the prime definers of collective identity.[9]

This second phase of independence and nationalism did not necessarily improve the quality of cities in the developing world, nor did it resolve the conflicts that plagued the traditional settlements of those societies. During the era of colonialism, important and irreversible decisions were made that affected the production of the built environment. In the Arab Middle East, for example, new building codes requiring setbacks (based on Western norms) forced the traditional courtyard house out of existence. New construction often took the form of banal single-family dwellings that were unsuited to the climate. Because of a host of cultural complexities, however, traditional people often preferred the modern units, despite the need for bizarre adaptations (such as building into the street to protect possessions). In a society that cherishes privacy, some people had to build freestanding walls as high as forty feet to shield themselves from their neighbors. In some countries entire efficient systems of construction were abandoned because they did not suit the modern era. The urban system fell grossly out of balance, and the urban environment of many developing societies became pseudomodernized.

Figure 6.2 shows the puzzling image of a lamppost popping out of an apartment building in Al-Khobar, Saudi Arabia. At first glance one might wonder if this is not some new type of postmodern architecture. In reality, as architect Jamil Akbar explains in *Crisis of the Built Environment*, such infringements on public property are common, because in traditional cultures people often are used to a more fluid relationship with the public realm, taking over parts of it without necessarily violating it.[10] Modern codes and the presence of utility lines deny this traditional freedom. But in the case pictured (perhaps due to both disrespect for the law and fear of the authorities), a building owner has resolved the conflict by incorporating the utility pole into his private space without interfering with its public function. There are many other examples of similar arrangements that have emerged from either ignorance of the regulations or a failure of coordination among regulatory bodies.

The obsession with modernity that accompanied the early years of nationalism and independence has preoccupied most governments in the developing world. As a result, the Western pattern of urban development has continued to serve as the reference model for indigenous populations, particularly the urban middle classes who stepped in after independence to run the bureaucracies of developing countries.

FIGURE 6.2. Integration of a public utility light pole in formal residential construction, Saudi Arabia (*Courtesy Jamel Akbar*)

During this time the construction of public housing was seen in many parts of the Western world as an approach to achieve social justice. Among these efforts was the now infamous Pruitt-Igoe housing project in St. Louis, Missouri. Built as part of the urban renewal movement in the 1950s, the project was meant to house low-income residents of the downtown area. Yet after a few years the project deteriorated dramatically, and attempts to improve living conditions and lower the crime rate in its residential towers failed despite the allocation of millions of dollars in rehabilitation funds. By the early 1970s the effort was written off as hopeless, and the project was demolished by the government in an attempt to eliminate the social problems it represented. The demise of Pruitt-Igoe was considered by some to signal the end of the Modern movement in architecture.[11]

Despite such public failures, the international influence of modernism was strong, and Western public housing models were often copied in the developing world without question. Developing world governments, however, used public housing projects as an instrument of nation-building in an attempt to buy the allegiances of their citizenry. Thus, at the same time as Pruitt-Igoe was being torn down, projects were being completed on the outskirts of several cities of the developing world with mixed results. In some places this public housing was reappropriated by the people. Egypt serves as a good example; under the socialist and nationalist regime of Gamal Abdel Nasser thousands of public housing blocks were built across the country. Suffering under the usual problems of such development—lack of maintenance, empty and unused spaces, the need to accommodate expanding families— many residents took matters into their own hands. Thus, one resident would decide to add a room to an apartment on the ground floor. Once built, this would provide the person above with an excellent balcony. What then would prevent the upstairs resident from making it into a room as well? Figure 6.3 shows the result of such a series of events.

Of course, the usual response on the part of the government would be to send a bulldozer to remove such infringements on public property. But residents could also remain one step ahead. They might erect a mosque in the path that a bulldozer would travel, knowing the government would not hesitate to demolish residential infringements, but

FIGURE 6.3. Informal appropriations of public space by residents of public housing, Egypt (*Courtesy Basil Kamel*)

would never dare demolish a mosque. Thus, as informal additions continued, the original blocks would be totally absorbed. This example further shows the tendency of citizens of developing countries to resort to the power of religion to achieve their goals. Together with ethnicity and race, religion is becoming one of the preeminent forms of community identification in both the developed and developing worlds.

Globalization and the Postmodern Urban Form

Globalization is the third phase in the relationship between the dominant and the dominated. Life in formerly colonized societies has arrived at an era in which the search for and the reconstruction of identity has become paramount. Now that independence has been achieved and the dust from the struggle has settled, problems of national and community harmony have begun to surface. Where these issues have not been resolved, religious and political fundamentalisms have begun to flourish. To understand the impact of these forces on urbanism, closer attention must be paid to the difficulties associated with defining national identity. The primary elements of national identity—race, language, religion, history, territory, and tradition—have always been essential but unequal components in its formation. The political units formed as nations after World War II were expected to be homogeneous entities with common cultures. But the reality was otherwise, because these nation-states were mainly put together by international deals that displayed little interest in the will of the people who inhabited these lands.

Of course, national identity as perceived by a government is inherently tied to the image a government wishes to project in the international arena. In sociologist Immanuel Wallerstein's view, the state, through its monopoly of policies and resources, can create a national culture over time, even when it lacks one to begin with.[12] But can one design national identity? And can this national identity be designed by a foreign power? These are questions that were often faced by the politicians who governed the newly independent states. Architecturally speaking, they were also faced by the architects and planners who worked for those politicians. Since cities are composed of forms that convey specific meaning, it is important to examine this physical dimension.

The relation between architectural form and national identity becomes especially important in terms of new "monumental" architecture. For example, Danish architect Jorn Utzon states that the roof of the national assembly building he designed for Kuwait specifically evokes the traditional Bedouin tent and contains a plan based on the Islamic bazaar. Meanwhile, some have argued that the form of Louis Khan's dramatic assembly building in Dacca, Bangladesh, may have been more appropriate for a country with closer links to Western classicist architecture. Nevertheless, Khan's building has also become a national symbol. About this ambiguity Lawrence Vale, a historian of nationalism and the built environment, has written: "At what point, one may ask, did the pyramid become an Egyptian form? Like the pyramids of Giza or the Eiffel Tower, the Citadel of Assembly may someday be seen as being quintessentially of its country as well."[13]

Of course, identity cannot be based on some myth from precolonial times. Many nations and their planners have resorted to a past around which identity may coalesce as a solace against the perceived dominator. Architectural historian Gwendolyn Wright rightfully warns that "the past cannot simply mean a retreat to a golden age before the Europeans, before modern industrialization, for these factors have changed us irrevocably."[14] Respect for the past in the developing world must include accepting and coming to terms with the colonial urban legacy.

If one accepts that national identity is a social construct tied to temporal events, as Louis Snyder[15] the theorist of nationalism has repeatedly argued, then it follows that the urbanism that accompanies it can only symbolize national identity as observed by a single individual or groups of individuals at a specific point in time. One must also recognize that there comes a point in the life of all formally colonized peoples when they must cease to perceive their history as colonial and start absorbing this heritage as their own. When is this point reached? When did the forms of the British colonizers become the vernacular heritage of the eastern United States? When did the Spanish colonial settlement forms in many parts of Latin America emerge as the traditional architecture heralded to tourists by these societies today?

The problem of national identity is further complicated by extensive global economic exchange. Not only do nations have to mediate between precolonial and colonial legacies, between the traditional and the modern, but they must also deal with the effects of globalization and the New World Order. "Globalization" here refers to the process by which the world is becoming a single economic entity, characterized by information exchange, interconnected modes of production and exchange, and transnational flows of labor and capital within a predominantly capitalist world system. It would be convenient to adopt modernist Anthony Giddens' view that globalization has introduced new forms of world interdependence, "in which once again there were no 'others.' "[16] However, since capitalism thrives on the construction of difference, such an economic universalism, under the confines of a world constituted of national units, can only lead to further cultural division. Culture, then, becomes the globally authoritative paradigm for explaining difference as a means of locating "the other."[17]

Indeed, the considerable migration from the former colonies to the lands of the former colonizers and the infiltration of ethnic subcultures into mainstream First World Western societies cannot be dismissed. In fact, this phenomenon has often been the cause of social conflict, as these local subcultures have often resorted to ethnic, racial, or religious allegiances to keep from being swallowed up by the majority culture. The current struggles of multiculturalism and gender politics in the United States may be a good example of an attempt to embrace differ-ence as a fundamental constituent of national identity. It is ironic that the national identity of the former colonizers is undergoing major change, often becoming more inclusive, whereas the national identity of the formerly colonized nations is moving in the opposite direction, often becoming more exclusive and more directly linked to national ori-gin or religious association. Indeed, the twentieth century has wit-nessed the return of states where belonging to a particular religion or ethnic identity is a prerequisite for nationality.[18]

National identity is always engaged in a process of transformation and flux. While the often contradictory forces of globalization are play-ing havoc with traditional loyalties and values, and challenging the older ideologies and practices, a single "world culture" remains a dis-tant prospect. Two controversial works of art that illustrate this posi-tion and demonstrate the complexity of the postmodern era are Salman Rushdie's novel *Satanic Verses* and Saddam Hussein's Victory Arch.

Rushdie, a naturalized British citizen of Muslim-Indian origin, wrote his novel in 1988 employing analogies and using names drawn from the development of Islam. Although hailed in the West for artistic merit, the novel offended many Muslims in India, Pakistan, and Iran, resulting in the infamous Iranian death sentence against Rushdie. As historian Janet Abu-Lughod points out, events such as the Rushdie affair bring home "how globalized and yet unglobalized culture has become."[19] Had Rushdie written *Satanic Verses* before the compression of time and space that now characterize global cultural exchange, it might have caused few ripples.

In similar fashion, symbols that new states inherit from history are often trapped in their old garb whereas their new ones are decontextu-alized. In this light, Saddam Hussein's Victory Arch, shown many times on television during the Gulf War, acquired many negative con-notations in the West. Ironically, these connotations were derived

FIGURE 6.4. Saddam Hussein's Victory Arch (television image)

totally out of context. The arch (see figure 6.4) was built in 1989 to com-
memorate Iraqi victories in the Iran-Iraq war. It consists of two fore-
arms and fists representing the arms of Saddam, the leader.

Samir al-Khalil, the Iraqi dissident and author of *The Monument*, has
compared these enlarged arms to gigantic "bronze tree trunks . . . [that]
rise with their firmly grasped swords to an apex forty meters above
ground. War debris in the shape of five thousand Iranian helmets taken
fresh from the battlefield are gathered up in two nets," and are embedded in the concrete base which supports the arms.[20] Al-Khalil considers
this monument a reflection of a bloody dictatorial regime. In truth, it is
difficult to defend such an abominable piece of art or architecture, but,
understood in its proper context, the arch is at best a product of popular culture, and at worst a monumental piece of design kitsch. As the
gate for a military parade ground, might the arch not have seemed
almost appropriate? And in terms of design, the arch builds on the role
of the sword as a symbol for honor, valor, and pride in Arab culture. A
similar form of two interlocking swords is, in fact, the official seal of
Saudi Arabia, a country that participated in the alliance *against* Hussein
in the Gulf War. The fact is that Western judgments, though justifiable
in political terms, have been uninformed on the basis of content.

Such cultural conflicts show that meanings can be easily lost in
cyberspace and that careful dissection is necessary in order to understand the effects of a single-world system on cities. Furthermore, in
every person it is likely that two conflicting sentiments exist toward

culture. The first is to resort to culture and tradition out of fear of change—change that in and of itself may be inevitable. Protectionism against the unknown does, however, turn into fundamentalism. The second sentiment, characterized by interest in the culture of the mysterious "other," emerges from a totally different feeling: the desire to have the choice to merge with the "other" and share in a wider or a different collective consciousness. The tremendous movement of citizens across borders and the rise of protected ethnic minorities demonstrate that the two sentiments, both legitimate, are not necessarily contradictory. In fact, they may indeed happen simultaneously or, alternatively, based on time and place.

Culture and Urbanism in a Global Era

For those interested in the study of culture and urbanism in a global era, there are some lessons to be learned.[21] First, one may argue that even if there is a world culture, it is a culture marked by the management of diversity rather than the replication of uniformity. A world culture is also essentially a culture of dominant groups, in which the persistent diversity of the constituent local cultures is often a product of globalization itself. This may imply that any convergence indicators only reflect the self-representation of the dominant particular and not a true integration of the cities of the South into a world system.

The second lesson involves the connection between world culture and space, for the latter is a placeless culture created through the increasing interconnectedness of local and national communities. Social theorist Manuel Castells was indeed on target when he pointed to the rise of the "space of flows in opposition to the space of places," in which organizations are connected by flows of information whose logic is largely uncontrolled by any specific local society, but whose impact is likely to shape the lives of all these local societies.[22] The impact on urbanism is that cultural experience will likely become less place-rooted and more information-based. Some will argue that identity cannot be placeless and that culture cannot be swallowed up by informational flows. Indeed, some identities will remain place-based. However, in the present technology-crazed communication era, experience is increasingly shaped by "virtual reality" environments rather than actual places.[23] It is important to come to terms with the effect of this change on the form of cities in the twenty-first century.

Finally, and despite academic preoccupation with globalization, the history of the world demonstrates a movement toward cultural differentiation and not homogenization, in which each individual belongs to many cultures and people have multiple cultural identities. In this sense, identity is always under construction and in constant evolution. For if hybridity is accepted as an inherent constituent of national identity, then the ensuing urbanism must be accepted as only a reflection of a specific transitional stage in the life of any society. Indeed, globalization has made the issues of identity and representation in urbanism very cumbersome and has cast doubt on urbanism's ability to fully represent the peoples, nations, and cultures within which it exists. But since culture has become increasingly placeless, urbanism will become an arena where one can observe the specificity of local cultures and their attempts to mediate global domination.

As the nations of the globalized world order become more conscious of their religious, ethnic, and racial roots, they are likely to seek forms and norms that represent these subidentities, even if these send confused messages to a global audience that will ultimately experience it through the space of flows. The challenge for urban policymakers in the twenty-first century is in confronting these realities.

Notes

[1]United Nations General Assembly resolution 47/180 calls for holding the United Nations Conference on Human Settlements (Habitat II) in Istanbul, Turkey, June 3–14, 1996.

[2]Anthony King, ed., *Culture, Globalization, and the World-System* (London, UK: Macmillan, 1991).

[3]Roland Robertson, "Social Theory, Cultural Relativity, and the Problem of Globality," in *Culture, Globalization, and the World-System*, 69–90.

[4]Many conceptions of globalization have been developed in the social sciences or are rooted in economic theories. This chapter mainly builds on the discourse in the field of cultural studies.

[5]Nezar AlSayyad and Jean Paul Bourdier, *Dwellings, Settlements, and Tradition* (New York: University Press of America, 1989).

[6]Janet Wolff, "The Global and the Specific: Reconsidering Conflicting Theories of Culture," in *Culture, Globalization, and the World-System*, 161–74.

[7]Stuart Hall, "Old and New Identities, Old and New Ethnicities," in *Culture, Globalization, and the World-System*, 41–68.

[8]King, ed., *Culture, Globalization, and the World-System*.

[9]Nezar AlSayyad, "Urbanism and the Dominance Equation," in *Forms of Dominance: On the Architecture and Urbanism of the Colonial Enterprise*, ed. Nezar AlSayyad (London, UK: Avebury, 1992), 1–26.

[10]Jamel Akbar, *Crisis in the Built Environment* (Singapore: Concept Media, 1988).

[11]For more details on this subject, see Kate Bristol, "Pruitt-Igoe Myth," *Journal of Architectural Education* (May 1991): 163–71.

[12]Immanuel Wallerstein, "The National and the Universal: Can There Be Such a Thing as a World Culture?" in *Culture, Globalization, and the World-System*, 91–106.

[13]Lawrence Vale, *Architecture Power and National Identity* (New Haven, Conn.: Yale University Press, 1992).

[14]Gwendolyn Wright, *The Politics of Design in French Colonial Urbanism* (Chicago: University of Chicago Press, 1991).

[15]Louis Snyder, *The Meaning of Nationalism* (Westport, Conn.: Greenwood Press, 1954).

[16]Anthony Giddens, *The Consequences of Modernity* (Stanford, Calif.: Stanford University Press, 1990).

[17]Robertson, "The Problem of Globality," 69–90.

[18]AlSayyad, "Urbanism and the Dominance Equation."

[19]Janet Abu-Lughod, "Going Beyond Global Babble," in *Culture, Globalization, and the World-System*, 131–38.

[20]Samir al-Khalil, *The Monument: Art, Vulgarity and Responsibility in Iraq* (Berkeley: University of California Press, 1991).

[21]Many of these are based on the work of Anthony King, Stuart Hall, Roland Robertson, Immanuel Wallerstein, Ulf Hannerz, and Janet Wolff, presented at a symposium held at the State University of New York, Binghamton, in 1989, and appearing in the edited volume *Culture, Globalization and the World-System*.

[22]Manuel Castells, "The World Has Changed: Can Planning Change?" in *Landscape and Urban Planning* (Amsterdam, Netherlands: Elsevier, 1992), 29–40.

[23]The term "virtual reality" was introduced in computer science in the 1980s to designate nearly exact simulations of audiovisual experience. The field is now growing to include simulations of holistic environments.

Chapter 7

Economic Competition and Resource Mobilization

Weiping Wu

The period since Habitat I has brought significant changes in both the context and the strategies of urban competitive development. Foremost among these is the emergence of a global production and financial network that transcends national boundaries. Cities around the globe are connected with each other more than ever through various economic linkages. These linkages include transnational networks of affiliates and subsidiaries of multinational corporations in manufacturing and specialized services, and the rapidly expanding international financial markets and transactions.[1] With the intensified globalization and recentralization of some strategic functions in major cities, a new global urban hierarchy is forming, on top of which are such contemporary world cities as New York, Tokyo, London, Paris, Los Angeles, and Hong Kong. These cities now function as focal points of the global economy.[2] Alongside this hierarchy, an increasing number of cities in both industrialized and developing countries, many of which used to be centers of manufacturing, are becoming the new periphery. Competition among these cities to regain their eminence in the global system by promoting foreign investment, multinational corporations, and international market functions is becoming explicit. Many of them, as well as a host of other cities, have gone through a similar structural change—replacement of manufacturing with service industries.

To be competitive in the new global economy, a city needs to be able "to produce goods and services that meet the test of international markets while simultaneously maintaining and expanding the real incomes of citizens."[3] However, definitions of competitiveness may vary by the unit of analysis. For a firm or industry, competitiveness may mean high productivity and profits. For a city, I agree with the Center for Economic Competitiveness's definition—competitiveness comprises three goals: prosperous industries, rising real incomes, and improved quality of life.[4] But these three goals are often at odds with one another, and some cities that are widely considered competitive may in fact see deteriorating quality of life. New York serves as a good example in this respect. Prosperous industries, however, are a necessary condition for the achievement of the other two goals and overall competitiveness.

Growth of an urban economy is ultimately reducible to flows of capital and labor, their allocative efficiency, and technological change. As it is in the context of a national economy, growth accounting can be a useful framework for urban analysis. Each city has unique production functions as a result of its history, location, and factor endowment. Although it has been shown that physical capital accounts for one-third to one-half of aggregate growth, recent literature suggests an important role of human capital and technological innovations.[5] Like nations, most cities go through a factor-driven stage of development. Those few that reach an innovation-driven development compete more on the ground of productivity, often derived from high skill levels and advanced technology, than on factor costs.[6] In the 1990s world economy, there will be a decline in competitive advantages based on natural resources and low-wage labor, and such advantages will be transferred to new manufactures and services in which quality, design, and capacity for incorporation of advanced technology are of increasing importance. The rise of information technologies since the 1980s has fundamentally altered patterns of work, productivity, and economic competitiveness.[7]

Factors of production can be made to work for a city by means of policy. Except for geography, none of a city's factor endowment is immutable; all can be modified by policy actions.[8] For instance, cities that have tried to create an environment of training and research are attractive to technology- and knowledge-intensive industries. Here, the role of infrastructure needs to be brought out. It is generally accepted that infrastructure contributes to economic growth and rising quality of life; in particular strong infrastructure is essential to create the productivity gains from urbanization and raise the economic returns of labor.[9] In addition to physical infrastructure, growing attention is paid to the so-called economic infrastructure,[10] which embraces a complex array of factors including diffusion of technology and ideas, industrial organization, regulatory environment, and institutions that affect the efficiency of markets. The essential function of such economic infrastructure is to increase the productivity of factor combinations.

Policy-making that affects economic competition often remains in the public domain, but effective urban governance does not always lay in the hands of elected government. What often exists is a governing coalition or urban regime whereby public and private agents come together to make and carry out governing decisions. Private agents include not only business interests, but also labor unions, nongovernmental organizations, community groups, and religious leaders. The exercise of a power or capability by collective agents or coalitions such as municipal governments, business elites, or civic groups depends on a coordination of actions to accomplish concrete goals.[11] The balance of power among members of the coalition varies by place and over time, making urban governance a complex and often uncertain endeavor. Whoever best solves the problem of collective action will be likely to enjoy a substantial power advantage. As shown in the case of Atlanta and a host of other U.S. cities (including Dallas and to some extent Pittsburgh), what makes governance effective is not the formal machinery of government but the business elite that encourages various groups to act together. On the other hand, Chicago, Boston, and Barcelona are well-documented cases of the effectiveness of entrepreneurial mayors. Urban leadership (in this chapter) refers to a city's governance coalition, which may be dominated by any member of the coalition.

The approach used in this chapter is both historical and comparative. I will first look at the new global context for urban competitive development: transnational flows of capital, the global labor market and immigration, and new information and communications technology; and then at ways that the urban landscape is affected by globalization: a new geography of centralization and decentralization, a new global urban hierarchy, and structural convergence among cities. Alternative strategies of economic competition used by different cities from different regions will be presented, focusing on New York, Barcelona, Santiago (Chile), and Shanghai. Finally, the driving forces of urban economy—capital, labor, and infrastructure, common threads underlying all cities—will be discussed. The chapter concludes with a discussion of two alternative routes to regaining urban economic competitiveness and of the role of urban leadership.

A New Context of Economic Competition

It was not until the 1960s and 1970s, that a "global economy" seemed to emerge, despite a long history of international flows of capital, labor, goods, and services. What marked the difference was the intensity of such flows. For instance, the trade component of national outputs on average rose from about 8 percent in 1950 to 15 percent in 1980, with the most pronounced growth occurring during the 1970s. Since then, the growth of foreign direct investment (FDI) surpassed that of international trade and national outputs.[12] As a worldwide phenomenon, FDI began in the late nineteenth century and early twentieth century. But for decades it made up only a small portion of the total stock of global capital investment, and only started growing rapidly after World

War II, particularly after FY 1973/74. Between 1975 and 1985, worldwide FDI inflows more than doubled in nominal terms, reaching a peak in 1981 and rising thereafter at an annual average rate of 41 percent.[13] In addition to the increasing flows of FDI, key features of the new global economy include the emergence of a global labor market, growth of international financial markets, and expansion of international trade in services as against in goods.

Cities have since been prime locations of transnational capital flows and the sites of production for many international industries. The kind of industries attracted to them depends on their level of development. Postindustrial cities such as New York, London, and Tokyo are centers of producer services, financial and information services, and other specialized services. Research shows that business services, particularly those with a great deal of innovative and strategic content, tend to have a high-order urban concentration. This is mainly the working of agglomeration effects, as scale economies ensure high information densities and rapid circulation of knowledge. Proximity to other specialized services is also important, as business services make intensive use of external economies. Newly industrializing cities, including Hong Kong, Singapore, and Seoul, are actively promoting high-end and knowledge-intensive manufacturing industrial investment, and moving in a more service-oriented direction. A vast number of cities in developing countries, however, are still competing for labor-intensive, standardized industrial investment, which in many cases involves only simple assembly and processing operations. A new category of cities that are exclusively engaged in export processing and manufacturing has grown up; increasingly these cities have the effect of reducing the central role of primary cities in developing countries and becoming new growth poles.[14]

Compared to capital, labor is still much less mobile; in fact, there is a growing disparity between capital and labor mobility in the globalization process. But a global labor market is emerging, with both micro and macro dimensions.[15] For instance, transnational corporations frame their human resource development policies from a viewpoint of a global internal labor market in their worldwide operations. On the macro level is the concern about the delocalization of jobs; high-cost labor is at risk when jobs are redistributed to low-cost locations. In part the internationalization of the labor market overcomes the relative labor immobility that is often caused by political and government barriers. A somewhat positive impact of the new global economy is that countries and cities no longer need to have the full range of locational assets to participate in international production. Labor market specialization, one of the two imperatives of a so-called new paradigm of competitive development,[16] is aided by the possibility of breaking down the production process into clearly separated stages and engaging foreign subsidiaries in only some activities of a firm's global value chain.

However, the mobility of one segment of the global labor market is increasing—that of high-skilled workers and professionals. A study by the Pacific Economic Cooperation Council (PECC) showed that almost all of its twenty-one participating economies have an evident shortage of high-skilled workers in professional and technical occupations.[17] Countries with the lowest immigration barriers have been the main receivers of labor migration: By 1994 the United States reported the largest expatriate population at around 1.1 million, followed by Australia at 1 million. Such flows of professionals are facilitated by two new, important trends: the internationalization of major cities, which become centers for coordination and management of a global economic system; and increasing levels of FDI in the migration-receiving countries. But Tokyo, a major city in the former sense, has claimed a very small number of expatriates since Japan has traditionally kept its doors closed to immigration and discouraged inflows of FDI.[18] Government immigration policies have played a critical role; a number of countries, such as the United States and Singapore, have laws that actively encourage migration of professionals. These countries benefit from the employment of foreign, skilled, experienced workers without having to bear the human capital investment costs. In a tight labor-market situation, foreign labor can also help reduce wage pressure and increase productivity.[19]

Technology has helped produce two parallel processes: reinforced centralization in major cities on a global scale of a few strategic functions that depend on propinquity, and simultaneous decentralization of other functions at more local levels. The advanced development in information, transportation, and communications technology has created the possibility of complete or partial production of goods at any site. As a result, one sees a tendency toward the decentralization or spatial dispersal of some economic activities, particularly those production processes and operations with large amounts of labor inputs. Old industrial cities with narrow ranges of specialization have suffered continuing losses of employment and income from their declining traditional sectors. There are many examples of this decline in Western Europe and North America, particularly in cities dependent on the production of basic metals, transport equipment, and textiles. On the other hand, agglomeration of certain centralizing activities has increased. The development of transnational corporations and their massive par-

ticipation in the world market have made planning, internal administration, product development, and research increasingly important and
complex.[20] So top-level management and control operations, financial
and producer services, publishing, media conglomerates, advertising,
and high fashion are finding homes in major cities where they can take
advantage of well-endowed skills and cultural institutions. Technological innovation again assisted this process; high-quality telecommunications networks allow these centers to interface instantly with other
localities and high-speed transport networks bring them into even
closer contact with each other.[21]

A new global urban hierarchy has emerged as the result of these parallel processes of centralization and decentralization, a hierarchy that
transcends national urban systems. A city's role in this hierarchy is
likely to profoundly influence its character. Topping the hierarchy are
the multinational cities and their metropolitan regions, a contemporary
version of world cities; they act as transnational locations for investment, corporations, services, financial activities, and various international markets. Meanwhile, a large number of other major cities that
used to occupy important positions in national urban systems are losing their role as centers for manufacturing due to decentralization of
production. Cities such as Chicago, Detroit, Manchester, Dortmund
(Germany), and Osaka are all struggling to fit into the new global urban
hierarchy. At the bottom of the hierarchy is a growing number of
peripheral cities, which in aggregate are receiving fewer resources and
less investment world- wide and/or in their respective countries. It is
evident that sheer size is not sufficient to account for a city's level of
economic power in the global hierarchy, which explains why such
megacities as Mexico City, Calcutta, and Bombay are not world cities.
As Hank V. Savitch points out in chapter 3, one result of this global
urban hierarchy is an elevated competition, in which the largest cities
will compete directly with each other to attract high-level functions and
other cities will fall along different points of a steep hierarchy.

However, the fate of peripheral cities is not necessarily so bleak, as
the global hierarchy is not all-encompassing: subcontinental or regional
centers are still important pivots. Trends similar to those evident in
global cities are also emerging in other major cities, though at a smaller
geographical scale and lower levels of complexity, and based on
regional rather than global processes. For instance, Singapore now
serves as the financial and business center of the East Asian region as
does São Paulo for Latin America. Shanghai's aggressive competition
for the mantle of China's and the East Asian region's premier metropolis is an admirable example. Santiago's experience in economic recov-

ery is also encouraging for cities in developing countries often plagued by poverty, mismanagement, and deteriorating quality of life. Furthermore, if Barcelona can pull out of the downward spiral of industrial restructuring and regain prosperity, other old industrial cities may also be able to follow suit; in fact, some have already shown signs of vitality: Pittsburgh, Rochester, and Dortmund, for example. But on the whole, globalization has relatively greater impacts on cities in industrialized countries than on those in developing countries.

There is also a structural convergence among major global and regional cities; services have become initiators of urban growth, particularly producer services.[22] These cities have always been centers of commerce, finance, and business, but the magnitude and importance of services have only grown rapidly during the past few decades. For instance, in Hong Kong, the share of the industrial sector (including manufacturing and construction) in total employment fell from 50 percent in 1980 to a mere 36 percent in 1991, whereas employment in the service sector increased from 48 to 63 percent. Every branch of the service sector has experienced steady growth in employment, and real-wage growth is also much higher than in the manufacturing sector.[23] Within the service sector, producer services have probably contributed the most to urban growth, in part because of their strong tendency to seek agglomeration economies. Moreover, as a result of the possibility of producer services being less dependent upon proximity to their consumers, their concentration in major cities is often export-driven, which can have large multiplier effects.[24]

Alternative Strategies and Practices

NEW YORK

In the early twentieth century, New York's economy was based on the manufacture of clothing, food processing, printing, and its role as a transport hub. These industries financed the development of an efficient infrastructure, growth of urban services, and a good university system. However, many of the industries that once buttressed New York's prosperity, such as textiles and meat packing, have long since deserted the city. It has also ceased to be a regional transportation hub. But all those activities that depend on propinquity, including finance, publishing, and the manufacture of fashion garments, have remained because New York is the ideal urban arena in spite of the many drawbacks posed there by congestion, crime, and deteriorating quality of services.

The expansion and reorganization of the international financial industry contributed directly to the economic restructuring of New York City. Several changes are significant: the 1982 debt crisis, increasing importance of nonbank financial institutions, and massive expansion of the volume of financial transactions. Another trend in the early 1980s was the shift from the tendency toward the development of regional centers and offshore locations to the reconcentration of the management of the financial industry in a limited number of major locations. Inevitably, cities that occupied strategic positions in the international financial industry benefited from this shift. The United States has become a leading recipient of foreign capital since the early 1980s and New York houses the largest number of financial institutions. Over 40 percent of the worldwide capitalization was concentrated in New York.[25] The volume of transactions, a specialized infrastructure (the New York Stock Exchange and a high concentration of corporate headquarters), and the availability of a skilled financial service workforce all help offset other high locational costs.

New York has always been a center of business and finance; what has changed is the magnitude and weight of the service sector in the urban economy. In 1960, manufacturing accounted for close to one-third of total employment, a figure that rapidly fell to 12 percent by the early 1990s.[26] By 1987, the service sector was providing over 60 percent of the city's employment (see table 7.1). Now a large number of highly specialized service firms and nonbank financial institutions are the core of this sector, within which a concentration of foreign firms grows rapidly. New York's role as a leading import-export center further stimulated trade-related service activities, such as warehousing, wholesaling, and distribution. The majority of service establishments are housed in a rather small section of Manhattan, from 60th Street to the southern tip of the island. This pattern reflects the trend toward high physical concentration of finance and certain producer and business services in the downtown areas of major international financial centers around the world. There are at least three factors that contribute to the high concentration of financial activities: access to professionals, access to support services, and personal contacts.

New York has been able to live off services for several reasons: (1) It stands at the apex of the world of finance; (2) It is well endowed with skills; and (3) The city's cultural resources remain exceedingly rich.[27] Nevertheless, the virtual disappearance of manufacturing industries and the concentration of services have led to a dichotomized economy and labor force, with highly rewarded professionals at one end and service workers from the lowest reaches of the income scale at the other.

TABLE 7.1
MACRO INDICATORS OF NEW YORK CITY

| | Employment Structure (% of annual total) | | | |
	Manufacturing	Services*	Government	Others
1970	20.5	52.9	15.0	11.6
1980	15.1	59.2	15.6	10.9
1987	10.8	63.5	16.5	9.2

| | Occupation of Resident Population (% of annual total) | | |
	Professional & Technical	Clerical & Sales	Blue-Collar & Service
1960	21.0	28.0	50.0
1970	24.0	34.0	43.0
1980	28.0	34.0	38.0

Fastest-Growing Sectors, 1977–1984 (% change in employment)	
Securities	71.5
Legal services	50.3
Business services	36.9
Credit agencies	36.6

SOURCES: Susan S. Fainstein and Norman Fainstein, "New York City: The Manhattan Business District, 1945–1988," in *Unequal Partnership*, ed. Gregory D. Squires (New Brunswick, N.J.: Rutgers University Press, 1989); and Saskia Sassen, "Finance and Business Services in New York City: International Linkages and Domestic Effects," *International Social Science Journal* 42, no. 3 (August 1990): 287–306.
*Services include wholesale and retail trade, finance, insurance, real estate, and other services.

The city's growing service sector increasingly relies on a group of new elite professionals as well as a vast reserve of low-skilled, often foreign, office workers (see Table 7.1). The former group, whose members include lawyers, managers, brokers, accountants, and others, is a new class of hardworking, high-income workers and, unlike the wealthy top-level executives, has relatively little corporate control power. On the other hand, immigrant workers have filled most low-wage jobs in services, as almost half of jobs in financial services are low-paying, from cleaner to stock clerk.[28] Corporations in the city are taking advantage of this low-cost labor force to offset other high business costs without having to relocate.

A related problem of increasing magnitude in New York is the gap between the demands of the workplace and the skills of the workforce.[29] Many of the city's new jobs require a college degree, yet a great number of young people never finish high school; employers are los-

ing confidence in the ability of schools to produce work-ready gradu-
ates; and firms have little incentive to retrain the workforce. If these
problems remain untackled, they will not only threaten the city's economy, but will also deepen the income gap and social inequality that are
already evident.

Ever-increasing public expenditure by the municipal government
also seems to play against the city's revival. The city's transformation
to a service base was accompanied during the mid-1970s by fiscal problems so severe that they brought New York to the edge of bankruptcy
in 1976. As Harvard professor of education Nathan Glazer asserted, the
things a city government can do best include keeping its streets and
bridges in repair, building new facilities to accommodate new needs,
picking up the garbage, and policing the public environment. But looking at the spending pattern of New York since the 1960s, one sees that
the city's spending rose from about 10 percent of local value-added to
19 percent by 1989; during the same period the urban infrastructure
steadily deteriorated.[30] In other words, the city has become much less
efficient at what it does the best. Part of the rising expenditure was
based on some good intentions, such as public assistance, health and
social services, and housing. But the costs have been so high, through
seemingly endless additions of personal income tax, commercial rent
tax, business income tax, and sales tax, that businesses were inevitably
driven out of the city.

The city's economy may also have been too reliant on the financial-
services sector, which has historically experienced volatile growth. The
uncertainty of New York's economic sustainability is reflected in the
1995 change in the city's bond rating by Standard & Poor's. Citing both
the sluggish economy and the fiscal gimmicks employed by Republican Mayor Rudolph W. Giuliani, the agency lowered the city's rating
from A− to BBB+ (among the lowest ratings of any major U.S. city).[31]
The feeble local economy has shown some signs of slowing down and
of distress, including a loss of nine thousand jobs in the first quarter of
1995, and projects a weak prospect for continued job growth.

BARCELONA

Far more than just the second largest city in Spain, Barcelona has been
a great international trading city and a regional center, and is the capital of the fiercely independent Catalonia. It has long sought to emphasize its international status and its detachment from the rest of Spain.[32]
If Barcelona cannot escape Spain, it may transcend it. The city has
thrived on its industrial, commercial, and cultural traditions. Another

great asset of Barcelona is its port, which received autonomous status in 1978. Mainly because of management efficiency, which encouraged diversification of traffic, commodities, and geographic areas served, Barcelona has remained highly competitive with other French and Italian ports in the Mediterranean. It is already the Mediterranean's largest container port and a serious rival to Rotterdam, which dominates European port trade.

Barcelona went through the same economic ups and downs as other traditional industrial cities. The 1973 international economic crisis brought severe difficulties for the city and revealed the structural limitations of the industrial expansions of previous decades. In particular, the wave of unemployment proved challenging for the city due to the lack of welfare and social services.[33] Between 1970 and 1985, Barcelona lost 42 percent of its industrial jobs and 69 percent of construction jobs, although the service sector grew by 12 percent. In 1980, the Catalan regional government launched a program of "Economic Action" aimed at combating unemployment, improving the city's major infrastructure, and encouraging the restructuring of some industrial enterprises. But the results proved disappointing. The turning points in Barcelona's recent economic history are the takeover of the socialist administration and creation of a long-term development plan in the mid-1980s, and the Olympic Games (and related events) hosted in 1992.

Metropolitan Barcelona has a long tradition of manufacturing industrial activities, but services are becoming more and more important (see table 7.2). Early this century Barcelona's economy was based on textiles, which remained the leading industry until more foreign investment helped further develop the chemical, metallurgy, and food industries. But during the mid-1970s, the structure of capital investment started to shift away from sectors with more domestic capital, such as textiles, food, and construction.[34] By 1986 the city of Barcelona, as against the metropolitan region and Catalonia, had a much higher concentration of services where 63.4 percent of all employment was in tertiary sectors. The city is especially attractive to business services requiring high levels of skill since over one-third of the workforce has higher education qualifications. As a result, over 80 percent of all such services in the metropolitan region are now housed in the central city. Their concentration has also stimulated the development of suppliers of these services because proximity to supporting services is a great advantage.

Small and medium-sized enterprises have always been an important force in the urban economy. There are some twenty thousand such enterprises in and around Barcelona, making up over three-quarters of all service establishments. These enterprises are thriving now that pro-

TABLE 7.2
MACRO INDICATORS OF METROPOLITAN BARCELONA

Indicator	
Land area (square kilometers)	3,245
Population (millions), 1986	4.23
City of Barcelona	1.70
Metropolitan employment structure (%), 1986	
Industry and Construction	41.2
Services	46.8
City of Barcelona employment structure (%)	
1986 Industry and Construction	27.0
Services	53.5
1990 Industry and Construction	32.2
Services	61.5
Share of employment in tertiary activities (%), 1986	
Metropolitan	52.4
City of Barcelona	63.4
Catalonia	49.0

SOURCE: T. C. Marshall, "Environmental Planning for the Barcelona Region," *Land Use Policy* 10, no. 3 (July 1993): 227–40.

duction and services are demanding higher levels of specialization and flexibility. The location of these firms is an interesting combination of "metropolitanization" and more localized segmentation particularly in some freestanding towns.[35] Barcelona has long been the favored site for foreign investment, with more than two hundred American firms dotting the region including Warner Lambert, Pepsico, United Technologies, Black and Decker, and Bristol Myers Squibb. Japanese firms, such as Sony and Nissan, have followed. Almost half the ownership of large enterprises, and consequently half the output, is in foreign hands. The central government decided to grant a subsidy to Volkswagen to help it maintain the factories of its Spanish subsidiary, which is the main employer in the area.

Barcelona's political leaders in the post-Franco period have been instrumental in promoting competitive development by establishing visions for the city, building public consensus, and encouraging public-private cooperation.[36] The public sector is dominant as its actions motivate other agents, whereas the private sector appears to be dragged along. The first democratically elected administration showed great courage, launching an important fifty-point plan that combined public and private initiatives for the city's development in the mid-1980s.[37]

The four most significant development actions took place in the post-1985 period: (1) Actions performed to promote economic development focused on creating economic and social development systems through occupational training, community cooperation, capital-labor accord, and cooperative societies; (2) Municipal funds were used to generate companies that would produce investments needed by the city. Forty-two such companies have been created (each with private participation) in such areas as infrastructure, telecommunication, information, and research that otherwise would not have been developed; (3) Great effort has been put into the development of external accessibility systems including large transport networks, the European-gauge railway, high-speed trains, and port expansion; and (4) Special attention has been paid to the development and management of support infrastructure for economic, commercial, and distributional activities, such as distribution centers, free-trade zones, and industrial estates.[38] The "Barcelona 2000 Economic and Social Strategic Plan" has also been conceived since 1988; it is strongly based on societal consensus. A major goal of the new plan is to make Barcelona the gateway to southern Europe and a European cultural center.

External factors have contributed significantly to the recent phase of economic expansion in Barcelona, particularly those related to the 1992 Olympic Games. The political leaders of the city were determined that the Olympic Games would pay off over the next several decades. They used this occasion for a major publicity-building program (or city marketing policy) to provide the city with resources it lacked during the Franco regime when the entire Catalonian region was repressed. Two chief goals, which have practically been achieved, were to improve Barcelona's infrastructure and to establish bases for the development of advanced, high-value-added services through upgrading communications systems and telecommunications. To prepare for the Olympics, the city spent approximately £1.2 billion on basic infrastructure alone, paid for by government ministries and a public holding company formed especially for the Olympics. A rebuilt airport, new roads, vastly improved telecommunications, and new hotels all gave the city a real boost. In addition, a substantial amount was spent on public open space, making the city clean and green.[39] Such substantial investment in infrastructure greatly alleviated the problem of serious shortfalls in social capital created during Spain's rapid growth era prior to the 1970s. At that time, the emphasis was on the rapid expansion of production, with a minimum of investment in nonproductive infrastructure. Sometimes even basic services such as electricity, water, wastewater systems, and flood control had to be laid and paid for by residents. Barcelona has been experiencing the alarming emigration of members of all social groups from the center city to peripheral towns in the metropolitan region as finding housing has become increasingly difficult for most people in the city proper.

Barcelona is now taking advantage of the new global system and changes in the European Union (EU). The city council has been actively collaborating in the creation of transborder regions. Domestically, Barcelona has created the C-6 network, including Valencia, Zaragoza, Palma de Mallorca, Montpellier, and Toulouse as capital cities of the group of regions sharing borders. The aim is to establish a cooperative process among productive systems that can contribute to a balanced territory. Internationally, Barcelona is a leader of the Eurocities Movement, an effort to establish urban group networks, which is facilitated by changes in EU policies concerning the role of cities that allow cities to reach independent international agreements.[40] The integration of Spain into the EU also has a significant effect on Barcelona, which occupies an advantageous position between the Iberian peninsula and the rest of Europe.

SANTIAGO

The growth and development of metropolitan Santiago has been closely related to the national economy of Chile and has been affected particularly by the series of reform measures introduced since 1982. As the capital city, it houses nearly 40 percent of the country's population of 13.6 million. In 1983, to rescue the manufacturing sector from a crisis that was due to the collapse of some major conglomerates, restructuring policies were implemented at the national level.[41] Since 1985, annual GDP growth has averaged 6.1 percent, the highest in the Latin American region, and reached a record high of 9.2 percent in 1992. Actual foreign investment in the country is also growing rapidly, averaging more than $1 billion a year since 1989. The government's commitment to reform, its good accountability, and its firm control of the economy were all important factors for the economic recovery. The shift from an import-substitution regime to an export-oriented strategy was particularly instrumental since the country has plentiful natural resources such as timber, and mineral deposits such as copper, for export.[42] In fact, mining has been not only the country's most important hard-currency generator, with copper alone contributing close to half of Chile's exports, but also its biggest draw for FDI. Furthermore, the Chilean government's efforts to put financial matters in order also helped increase public-sector saving and in turn a recovery of investment, with the help of declines in domestic interest rates, during the mid-1980s. The rise in savings was achieved through both increases in revenue, largely due to improvements in the administration of tax collection and reductions in expenditure. Gross fixed investment increased at a double-digit rate. The government also restricted investment to the most profitable projects and scaled down some nonessential investment projects.[43]

Municipal reform has brought much greater latitude and flexibility to Santiago in municipal revenue collection and investment expenditure. Before 1974, municipalities had only limited responsibilities and incomes due to the central government's monopoly. As a result, municipal financial resources were scarce and the provision of urban services was limited. The reform introduced changes in the legal framework, beginning in 1975, that gave municipalities new responsibilities, particularly regarding social services, and granted them increased sources of funds.[44] One of the important features of the new legal framework was the progressive flexibility given to cities over their budgets, whereby they can raise revenues through a much wider range of sources. Between 1976 and 1988, the overall revenues of all municipalities multiplied over six times. Municipal investment expenditures also increased substantially after 1979, and they represented over 40 percent of municipal expenditures by 1988. More autonomy in spending practice and fund-raising has allowed cities to finance some large infrastructure projects.

Riding this wave, Santiago commenced a tremendous effort in the mid-1980s to revive the city's economic viability.[45] The city has seen the highest concentration of commercial, financial, cultural, and administrative activities in the country, with most of these dynamic activities clustering in the small downtown area proper. The most specialized sectors include insurance, retail commerce, transportation services, real estate and professional services, and public administration. The image of economic prosperity, however, was in sharp contrast to physical decay, poor environmental quality, insecurity, traffic congestion, and residential emigration. In effect, the location of activities in central Santiago was already changing because of steady outflows of firms as well as residents. To combat these ills, the city devised a strategic plan, which was adopted in 1991. Two of the principal instruments of the plan to achieve both the functional and environmental goals were the improvement of the transportation infrastructure and the organization of public-private development corporations at the neighborhood level. The goal of the plan was to strengthen and expand the existing activities through improvement of the location advantages of the center city.

Eleven major projects in the transportation system and infrastructure were identified as necessary to achieve this goal.

Between 1985 and 1991, metropolitan Santiago recovered its economic edge over the rest of Chile in terms of the number of industrial establishments (both small and large firms), average employment, and value added. Its shares in the country in all three measures witnessed significant increases (see table 7.3). It seems that agglomeration economies have regained their importance in the location decisions of many firms, creating a trend toward concentration of capital and production especially in manufacturing and service sectors—metropolitan Santiago is the preferred location of the most dynamic industries and their headquarters. The city also saw the proliferation of nonbanking, advanced financial services, and gradually became a financial center for the Latin American region. This resembles the course of events in many industrialized countries as well as a host of developing countries: all the regions of Chile are being incorporated into the global economy through Santiago, although some localities have been marginalized.

TABLE 7.3
MACRO INDICATORS OF METROPOLITAN SANTIAGO

| | Metro Santiago (as % of national total) | |
	Industrial Value Added	Employment
1985	37.2	55.0
1988	38.6	
1991	43.8	58.0

| | Metro Santiago (as % of national total) | |
	GNP	Exports
1990	40.0	11.2

| | Population Classified as Poor (%) | |
	Metro Santiago	Chile
1987	38.7	44.6
1992	25.5	32.7

| | Growth of Industrial Establishment (%) | |
	Metro Santiago	Chile
1991	12.2	9.9

SOURCES: Carlos A. de Mattos, Fernando Soler R., and Francisco Sabatini D., "Globalización, Territorio y Ciudad: El Caso de Chile," *Serie Azul* 7 (Instituto de Estudios Urbanos, Pontificia Universidad Católica de Chile, 1995); and Antonio Daher, "Santiago, Segunda Inflexión," (Instituto de Estudios Urbanos, Pontificia Universidad Católica de Chile, June 1994).

Santiago has benefited greatly from the adequate social, legal, and physical infrastructure built by the military regime. Faced with restricted budgets, the government decided to build some basic infrastructure such as water supply and sewerage systems for the city, sometimes at the expense of housing programs. Despite funding difficulties, many housing programs as well as other social programs yielded admirable results. Spared from the social crisis common in Latin American cities, Santiago is gradually gaining momentum to become a center of multinational production and services for the region. The most urgent task is the elimination of extreme poverty; nearly all Chileans see poverty as the country's greatest ill. For Santiago, an additional concern is the increasing degradation of the urban environment. Its air quality ranks among the world's worst, along with that in Mexico City and São Paulo.[46] To combat the dangerous, rising level of air pollution in Santiago, Chile has imposed a city driving ban on 20 percent of all vehicles, based on rotating license plates.

Santiago's steady growth has also generated rising levels of employment and improved standards of living. In metropolitan Santiago between 1969 and 1985, job creation was insufficient in relation to the growth of the available labor force, and this was the major cause of the rise in unemployment.[47] But the level of unemployment declined substantially by the early 1990s, to about 5 percent in 1993, followed by upward pressure on salaries. As the result of the severe measures dictated by the authoritarian regime since 1973 and particularly after Augusto Pinochet's labor reform of 1979, the labor force is quite disciplined and nonconflictive. The informal sector is no longer important as unemployment is virtually nonexistent and people desire formal jobs to obtain fringe benefits. Although per capita income may seem lower than in some other Latin American countries such as Mexico and Argentina, living conditions in Santiago are much better as most residents enjoy decent housing (which is often provided through housing programs), urban utilities, and healthcare provisions.[48]

SHANGHAI[49]

Modern industrial development, as well as trade, modern banking, and other services, commenced in Shanghai in the late nineteenth century and the city remains China's foremost industrial center. The city is strategically situated at the mouth of the Yangtze River and on the east coast; its hinterland is one of the most densely populated regions of the country and among the richest in natural resources. The city impresses with its size and by the sheer density of its population. The city core

TABLE 7.4
MACRO INDICATORS OF METROPOLITAN SHANGHAI

Indicator	
Land area (square kilometers)	6,341
Population (million), 1993	12.95
Per capita housing (sq. meters), 1993	7.3
GDP annual growth rate (%), 1979–93	7.9
Industrial annual growth rate (%), 1979–93	9.1
Utilized foreign investment (billion $), 1979–93	10.75
Foreign loans	5.10
Foreign direct investment (FDI)	5.13
Other foreign investment	0.52
Gross value of industrial output (billion yuan), 1993	298.98
1993 top five industrial subsectors (share, %)	60.36
Metallurgy	20.52
Machine building	16.24
Transport equipment	9.39
Textiles	8.46
Chemicals	5.75

SOURCE: Shanghai Statistical Bureau, *Shanghai Statistical Yearbook 1994.*

covers just 300 square kilometers out of a municipal total of 6,341 (see table 7.4). In 1980 it had a population of 11.5 million, rising to 13 million in 1993, 8.9 million of whom reside in the city proper. The density is in excess of 43,000 people per square kilometer in parts of the center city. Manufacturing has been and remains the lifeblood of the municipality. The city accounted for 10 percent of the national industrial output in 1980, which had declined to a still impressive 7 percent in 1991, with the bulk of the manufacturing facilities crowded into roughly a quarter of the city's built-up area. The city was also where institutions of higher learning were first established. By all accounts, it was the cultural capital of China before 1949. Its lead over other cities, however, was somewhat reduced because of the urban policy introduced in China after 1949. Now, with the permission of the central government, Shanghai has finally tapped into a full range of reform possibilities and is competing aggressively to retain its premier status.[50]

Shanghai's industrial reach is quite extraordinary and extends into virtually all subsectors. This was the inevitable result of China's development policy, which emphasized industrial independence prior to the reform. An enormous range of industries spanning 140 of the 146 listed subsectors was established in Shanghai. By Chinese standards, Shanghai's state enterprises were also among the best equipped and most efficient producers in the country. As reform proceeded, they strived to introduce new product lines, upgrade their output, and restructure production. The wealth of skills was just one factor. Equally important, especially for the production of such items as automobiles and computers, is the fact that with some effort it is possible to source an extremely wide range of components from within the municipality. Industrial depth has been a huge asset for the city, attracting foreign investment in electronics, chemicals, and transport equipment industries, which in turn have sent externalities through the entire urban economy. The sheer richness of skills and industrial tradition is also the basis for the spread of producer services, banking, finance, consulting, and information, which further contribute to industrial efficiency and provide an additional impetus to the growth of the urban economy.[51] Aside from the producer services that are closely associated with industry, Shanghai's agglomeration economies are a stepping-stone into other services, including advertising, book publishing, fashion design, and media conglomerates.

Industrial specialization is a major pursuit of the city in the reform period, with high priorities assigned to several key industries such as automotive and other transport equipment, precision machinery, chemicals, shipbuilding, and electronics (see table 7.4). In the case of the auto industry, a joint venture was formed between the China Auto Industry Group and Volkswagen of Germany in 1984. Volkswagen brought its Brazilian-designed Santana—a mature model that had been customized for developing-country markets. The city provided tariff protection and guaranteed market for vehicles produced in the initial years. The combination of bureaucratic support, investment funds, and foreign technology made the venture the most productive and profitable automaker in the country.

The city is also set to utilize its vast reserve of human capital, including its pool of skilled workers, technicians, and research facilities, undoubtedly the largest in the country. There are at least 266 independent research institutes, of which 173 specialize in applied research and development (R&D). In addition, there are over fifty universities and colleges located in the city, which have become the cradle for technological innovations.[52] But a shortage of funds prevented the commercial development of many promising ideas. To correct this, Shanghai's leaders have now set up a small fund to be used by local scientists to attract larger sums from outside sources. The municipal Science and Technology Commission also administers a series of grant programs, helping Shanghai scientists compete at the national level. Shanghai's research institutes, particularly those specializing in applied R&D, are beginning to develop some commercial linkages. For example, earnings from technical transfers, engineering services, and business operations amounted to 2.1 billion yuan in 1992, almost three times the government's funding. An even more encouraging phenomenon is the emergence of nonstate-owned technological enterprises, which were estimated to number over five thousand by mid-1994.[53]

The state of urban infrastructure, which was starved of capital throughout the Maoist era, however, makes it harder for Shanghai to realize the full extent of its competitive advantage. Urban services, such as water, heat, sewerage, schools, and hospitals, also lag far behind need or demand, although Shanghai may be better provided for than the rest of the country. Living conditions are inadequate, and transport as well as communications facilities fall far short of standards reached by other East Asian countries. The housing shortage reflects steady population growth that has outpaced the expansion of the urban area. Shanghai's population density, mixed pattern of land use, and its relative prosperity have also led to an increasingly tight supply of land. In fact, in 1992 Shanghai ranked third, after Hong Kong and Tokyo, in net office rents.[54] The first priority in improving the urban infrastructure system must be to use the existing infrastructure more efficiently. To relieve spatial pressure on old Shanghai, a new development zone of 522 square kilometers—Pudong—was also constructed east of the center city. It is designed to become the new center of Shanghai's industry and commerce, particularly for high-tech industrial and trading activities, and to draw foreign investment by offering concessionary policies. Urban land reform also provides the city the opportunity to raise funds by leasing land and to use those funds to finance new construction and upgrade urban infrastructure.[55] Whereas land sale revenues are one-time phenomena, rents and property taxes will yield continuous income.

Shanghai has managed to negotiate a favorable fiscal arrangement with the central government that gives the city more autonomy in revenue collection and municipal expenditure. Between 1949 and 1980, roughly 86 percent of Shanghai's revenue was submitted to the central government, making it the country's largest revenue base. What was left for the city were limited user fees on public services and some surcharges. After several rounds of hard-pressed negotiation, Shanghai was awarded a higher retention ratio (about 25 percent) in 1983, which permitted the city to take the first few steps toward improving urban infrastructure and housing.[56] The city used its political ties to push for an even better agreement and, finally, in 1988 it was able to get a lump-sum term for the next three years. This proved to be a good start and it has been buttressed by subsequent actions to mobilize funds through such measures as increasing user charges, levying land-lease fees, and enhancing local property values. Shanghai's story demonstrates that there is even hope for an old city. But the city has not been successful in cutting down expenditure—the other half of the fiscal equation—because of its unwillingness to push for widespread closures of money-losing state enterprises.

Driving Forces of Urban Competitive Development

The experience of cities from different regions in competitive development is multidimensional. Some have relied more on a long history of industrial and commercial development, a rich culture of business and entrepreneurship, and agglomeration effects resulting from industrial networks. Others have benefited from a conducive national environment, economic reforms, and changes in development policies. Still others are sustained with the help of international capital flows, availability of low-cost labor, support of vast and resourceful hinterlands, and efficient transport systems. For a few cities, such as Barcelona and Osaka, external context and international events are strong stimuli for development. Looking through the lens of growth accounting, one will find some common threads underlying all cases. The driving forces of urban growth inevitably hinge upon finances, human capital, and infrastructure.

URBAN FINANCES

To sustain long-term economic competitiveness, a city needs to draw financial resources through four different channels: municipal tax bases, central or regional governments, financial markets, and capital sources outside of the city. Cities are more frequently looking for new ways to finance businesses and development. One option may lie in the use of venture capital. It is a different form of capital in that institutionalized venture capitalists provide equity rather than debt financing, and frequently they also take an active role in management.[57] Many new companies and technologies in the United States, such as Fairchild, Intel, and Apple Computer, would neither have been launched nor have achieved success without such capital.

Venture capital can be conducive to development because venture capitalists often bring technical skills, operation experience, and a network of contacts, along with their equity investment. Geographical proximity and the existence of a mass of researchers and universities can be significant locational advantages. A network of special suppliers and service providers also facilitates the start-up process. Cities that possess some or all of these elements could resort to venture capital to finance technological innovations and competitive enterprises. But venture capital is just one of many factors contributing to technology-intensive economic growth. For instance, a large amount of venture capital originates from New York and Chicago but ends up in other areas; the presence of abundant venture capital does not always lead to high-tech development.

On the other hand, a successful model for inner-city investing will probably not look like the type of venture capital that caters primarily to technology enterprises.[58] It may instead resemble the equity funds operating in some former socialist countries like Russia and Hungary—investing in such ordinary but potentially profitable businesses as supermarkets and small neighborhood services. In addition, philanthropic efforts targeted at inner cities may be more effective if they also focus on building businesses that, in the long run, will reduce the need for social services.

Foreign investment can also have some substantial, positive impact on the development of cities.[59] It presents an opportunity for cities to finance their economic growth. Cities in developing countries may also access the technological and managerial assets of foreign investors through foreign investment, the diffusion of which can have a substantial impact on productivity growth. In particular, direct investment tends to bind foreign investors to the operation of the investment projects and should enhance their willingness for technology transfer and job training. Moreover, the introduction of efficient and internationally competitive foreign enterprises into an economy can stimulate local entrepreneurship by providing increased competition, a demonstration effect, and opportunities for subcontracting. The more dynamic gains from the industrial development induced by foreign investment include more employment, a better-trained labor force, a higher level of income, more innovations, and access to foreign markets.

Resource mobility can be stimulated with measures that eliminate entry and exit barriers for firms, make markets more flexible, reduce transaction costs, improve access to information, and eliminate regulations that impede transfers of assets. In the case of labor markets, such mobility can be facilitated by improving information dissemination and encouraging flexibility through such means as profit-sharing and flexible working hours. Successful cities have also achieved balanced trade-offs between public finances and regulations. For instance, regulations to preserve high environmental standards can ensure a city's livability, but they can also saddle firms with high costs. Cities that offer the winning combination are usually efficient with their expenditures and ingenious in getting the private sector to fund a variety of capital projects. Guangzhou's move to sell off some stock rights of bridges, tunnels, and waterworks to private enterprises may be a workable alternative to maintain the aging urban infrastructure under tight budget constraints.

HUMAN CAPITAL AND SKILL FORMATION

The changes in urban economic structure in many cities, such as the shift from manufacturing to services and the rise of specialized service functions, will require an adaptable labor force. In an economy with accelerating technological innovations, the ability to learn may be more important than any job-specific skills. Human capital accumulation can be thought of as an improvement in technology because it can raise productivity. A human capital strategy should (at least) build a system of lifelong learning, reconnect work to education, and accommodate the new workforce, such as migrant workers. It is not necessarily the public sector's obligation to provide actual training. However, the public sector does have an important role to play in stimulating and aiding the formation of training firms and organizations.

Events in Rochester, New York, show that educational reform is critical for regaining urban competence, and that a city can achieve a high degree of success within a less-than-conducive context. The root of Rochester's reform was a report released in the early 1980s that painted a very negative picture of the school system and led warring factions in the community to unify.[60] They believed that real progress in restructuring education would come only from shifting decision-making responsibility from the school system's central bureaucracy to individual schools. To accomplish this shift, the new system established a career ladder and new responsibilities for educators. Since then, some substantial progress has been made. For instance, the number of students who passed state competency tests rose steadily, and high school dropout rates declined for the first time in nearly a decade. The improvement of the education system has become a building block in the city's set of core competencies and provided a more work-ready labor force. Rochester's experience also indicates that education must become much more responsive to local needs.

It is becoming increasingly evident that universities with extensive science and engineering programs are indispensable assets for urban industrial health, as technological innovation is one of the most important factors, along with capital, labor, and land, that contribute to the growth of production. Universities and research institutions have often served as seedbeds of technological innovation due to substantial concentrations of talent and facilities. This is evident in the creation of new industrial districts or science parks, often close to major universities, as a means of drawing new industries. The subsequent development of the given locality tends to be very rapid, facilitated by the spillovers from universities or government incentives. Silicon Valley in California, the Research Triangle in North Carolina, and the Route 1 cluster in New Jersey are such cases. On the other hand, large cities are often the places where agglomeration forces are strong and pools of specialized resources are concentrated, such as corporate labor, R&D capabilities, universities, a skilled labor force, and well-developed financial institutions. Large urban centers are able to spawn and nurture new industries, to renew and regenerate old ones to ensure their sustained growth, and to lead the surrounding regions, as seen in the cases of Boston and Washington, D.C.

Nevertheless, the usefulness of technology does not stop at innovation, and a variety of institutions are involved in the management and diffusion of technology. Most notable are those related to technology infrastructure and local support systems, such as financing mechanisms, banks, producer services, and technical consulting services. It is generally accepted that a low level of cooperation among individuals and organizations is an obstacle to technological innovation and improved industrial performance.[61] Technological innovation is a process that can be stimulated by strengthening links and feedback mechanisms within firms, among them, and among research centers and universities. A merit embedded in industrial networking is its capacity to provide such stimulus. A municipal government can adopt a technological development policy that incorporates an element designed to improve the linkages between technology supply and demand. This can be achieved through wide dissemination of technological information and formation of local markets for technology and skilled labor. Policies for attracting and motivating talent are also important, including mobilization of knowledge resources already in the city, encouragement of individual and organizational commitments, investment in support facilities, and development of exchange relations with other centers of knowledge resources.

INFRASTRUCTURE BUILDING

One of the most important functions performed by the public sector is the provision of efficient infrastructure, both physical and economic. Why is efficient urban infrastructure important? By permitting smooth flows of goods and services, it enables modern, competitive industries to develop. It can reduce the cost of and time necessary for the transport of goods and services, and in turn raise overall productivity. By relieving the private sector of the need to develop infrastructure in-house, it saves resources for more productive investments. Cities with aging infrastructure may bear a substantial amount of risk as the deterioration of roads, bridges, sewerage systems, waste treatment facilities, and telephone systems will diminish their attractiveness for economic expansion. Because infrastructure investment tends to be long term, continuous improvements and adaptation are particularly important in order to avoid an accumulation of problems in the future. The new technological paradigm also calls for other infrastructure provisions, such as cable networks for advanced telecommunications, highway access, energy-saving structures, and high-speed trains.[62]

Research indicates that infrastructure is likely to be more cost-effective and have favorable impacts on urban environment when it is subject to user charges based on marginal costs of supply and willingness to pay.[63] In order to achieve the greatest benefits from its ability to raise the returns of other factors of production, infrastructure provision should be priced to reflect resource scarcity and investment costs. User charges are necessary to ensure efficient use of infrastructure and discourage wasteful consumption. The absence of such charges often tends to reduce both quality and availability of infrastructure facilities. Furthermore, in some cities where financial constraints are tight, user charges can be a substantial source of funding for new public utilities.

Regarding economic infrastructure, industrial networking is becoming an essential condition for successful industrial development.[64] Networking is a means of pooling information, capital, expertise, and infrastructure, and it has many layers. On the surface, there is "social organization" based on social or kinship relations, which operates on the ground of trust. Local banks, credit unions, venture capitalists, and informal financial groups form the next layer. At another level of the network are circuits and mechanisms that transmit R&D, and services that generate technical and market information; the latter is often organized on a community base as in the Third Italy. Such networking arrangements are particularly useful for industries in which production is small-scale or specialized and where interfirm collaboration and clustering are efficient and imperative.

Conclusion

For mature industrial cities in need of restructuring, such as New York, Barcelona, and Shanghai, there may be two distinctly different approaches to meeting the challenges of international competition. The first may be called the "low road" to restructuring, defined as seeking competitiveness through low labor costs and a deregulated labor-market environment. The rationale is that cost-cutting will raise productivity and profits. The "high road" to restructuring is a kind of constructive competition strategy, based on efficiency enhancement and innovation. The keys to this approach are better organization and a better mobilization as well as utilization of labor to increase productivity.[65] An acute problem with the low road approach is that it is often short-lived, as lower-cost locations will always emerge. These two alternatives in many ways resemble what Michael Porter, a Harvard University professor of business, prescribes as factor-driven and innovation-driven competitive development. The consensus now is that the high road or innovation-driven approach is far more economically viable.

Cities need to identify their industrial strength or clusters and seek market niches, as there are still tendencies toward specialization among different cities within a country as well as within the global system. The experience of reviving cities in developed countries shows that there is no industrial sector that is intrinsically obsolete or inherently bad, even at high wage levels. Some textile and garment manufacturers are still flourishing in the United States, Italy, Germany, and Japan. The ability to adapt to changing conditions is key to sustained urban growth. Cities with a more diversified industrial structure tend to fare better than those relying on a narrow range of specialization. This is because, in conjunction with scale, diversification is a built-in stabilizer.[66] Here the role of services, particularly producer services, is worth some emphasis, as they often contribute to industrial efficiency and provide an additional impetus to the growth of urban economies. Over the last decade, producer services have become the most dynamic, fastest-expanding sector in many cities around the world, and have sustained or revived the growth of many traditional industrial cities.

Civic vision and political will can be enabling forces for cities in competitive development, as shown in Barcelona, Shanghai, Pittsburgh, and Rochester. These cities have actively pursued and achieved the rejuvenation of their economies. Urban problems are tackled and perceptions altered for the better through real institutional change, such as fiscal practice encouraging commercial development. Led by a popular mayor and a progressive elite, Pittsburgh forged an alliance between business and labor to diversify its economic base and embarked on the road to successful restructuring. Pittsburgh's recovery was also facilitated by the city's wider industrial reach beyond steelmaking, which had already become peripheral to the urban economy by the late 1980s. Several leading universities, including Carnegie

Mellon University and the University of Pittsburgh, and knowledge-intensive industries were seen as the new engines of growth. A similar story unfolded in Rochester, N.Y., where companies and individuals with deep community ties came together to build a common future based on technological and managerial cooperation, using quality as a core competence. On the other hand, the history of New York City urban leadership is more fragmented and sometimes conflicting. Some major development projects have proved successful, including Battery Park City and the Stock Exchange. But other measures, such as the tax system, are strongly biased against commercial use. The city as a whole has been short on vision.

To compete effectively, a city's governing coalition needs to crystallize and endorse a vision of the future that is acceptable to both businesses and citizens. Public and private sectors must collaborate so as to share the burden of risk. The public sector should return to what it does best: keeping urban infrastructure in good maintenance and repair, building new facilities to accommodate new needs, and policing the public environment. It should also encourage the establishment of training facilities, facilitate access to university research institutions, and ensure that public money is spent on the right projects. By the same token, the private sector will be most effective if it also focuses on what it does the best: creating and supporting economically viable businesses and generating a high level of employment.

Notes

[1] Saskia Sassen, *Cities in a World Economy* (Thousand Oaks, Calif.: Pine Forge Press, 1994).

[2] Research using network analysis, based on volume of airline passengers, shows that London, New York, and Tokyo, in descending order, are the most central global cities. On the other hand, John Friedmann ("The World City Hypothesis," *Development and Change* 4, (1986): 12–50; and "Where We Stand: A Decade of World City Research," paper presented at the Conference of World Cities in a World-System, Center for Innovative Technology, Sterling, Va., April 1993) identifies a more extensive list of world cities, which are grouped into four categories. London, New York, and Tokyo are "global financial articulations"; Miami, Los Angeles, Frankfurt, Amsterdam, and Singapore are "multinational articulations"; Paris, Zurich, Madrid, Mexico City, São Paulo, Seoul, and Sydney are "important national articulations"; and a host of cities including Osaka, Chicago, Boston, Hong Kong, Barcelona, and Munich are "subnational, regional articulations." See David A. Smith and Michael Timberlake, "Conceptualizing and Mapping the Structure of the World System's City System," *Urban Studies* 32, no. 2 (1995): 287–302.

[3] Council on Competitiveness cited in DRI/McGraw-Hill, *Competing to Win: DRI/McGraw-Hill's Approach to Competitiveness* (Chicago: Economic Competitiveness Group, 1994), 2.

⁴SRI International and DRI/McGraw-Hill, *Economic Leadership in Illinois: New Approaches for the 1990s* (prepared for Illinois Department of Commerce and Community Affairs, 1993).

⁵On the contribution of capital, see Edward F. Denison, *Why Growth Rates Differ: Postwar Experience in Nine Western Countries* (Washington, D.C.: Brookings Institution, 1967); on the role of human capital, see Paul M. Romer, *What Determines the Rate of Growth and Technological Change?*, World Bank policy, planning, and research working paper no. 279 (Washington, D.C.: World Bank, 1989); and "Two Strategies for Economic Development: Using Ideas vs. Producing Ideas" (paper presented at the World Bank Annual Conference on Development Economics, Washington, D.C., 1992).

⁶In Michael E. Porter's widely acclaimed book *The Competitive Advantage of Nations* (New York: The Free Press, 1990), he identifies four stages of national competitive development: factor-driven, investment-driven, innovation-driven, and wealth-driven. Because of differences in scale, I argue that not all stages apply to urban economies.

⁷Kasarda argues that the speed of production and distribution will become critical competitive factors; in particular competitive success will require vision regarding the role of aviation, and job creation will depend on cities' ability to move people, information, and capital. See John D. Kasarda, "Global Air Cargo–Industrial Complexes as Development Tools," *Economic Development Quarterly* 5, no. 3 (August 1991): 187–96; and Joseph S. Tulchin, *Global Forces and the Future of the Latin American City*, Comparative Urban Studies Occasional Paper Series no. 4 (Washington, D.C.: Woodrow Wilson International Center for Scholars, 1994).

⁸Shahid Yusuf and Weiping Wu, "Prospering Coastal Cities: Shanghai, Tianjian, and Guangzhou" (unpublished manuscript).

⁹Infrastructure is often defined to include the sectors of transport, water and sanitation, utilities, power, telecommunications, and irrigation. For a full discussion of the contributions of infrastructure to economic development, see Christine Kessides, *The Contributions of Infrastructure to Economic Development: A Review of Experience and Policy Implications*, World Bank discussion paper (Washington, D.C.: World Bank, 1993).

¹⁰DRI/McGraw-Hill, *Competing to Win*, 10. This economic infrastructure (sometimes called "social organization") embraces similar factors including local and regional networks, competitive entrepreneurship, and differentiated industrial structure. See Werner Sengenberger and Frank Pyke, "Industrial Districts and Local Economic Regeneration: Research and Policy Issues," in *Industrial Districts and Local Economic Regeneration*, ed. Frank Pyke and Werner Sengenberger (Geneva, Switzerland: International Institute for Labor Studies, 1992).

¹¹On the role of governance and urban regime politics, see Clarence N. Stone, *Regime Politics: Governing Atlanta, 1946–1988* (Kansas City: University of Kansas Press, 1989); and Kevin R. Cox, "Globalization, Competition and the Politics of Local Economic Development," *Urban Studies* 32, no. 2 (1995): 213–24.

¹²Duncan Campbell, "Foreign Investment, Labor Immobility and the Quality of Employment," *International Labor Review* 133, no. 2 (1994): 185–204.

¹³See United Nations Center on Transnational Corporations (UNCTC), *World Investment Directory 1992: Foreign Direct Investment, Legal Framework, and Corporate Data* (New York: United Nations, 1992). The stock of FDI, a measure of the productive capacity of transnational corporations in foreign countries, was some $2 trillion in 1992. See UNCTC, *World Investment Report 1993: Transnational Corporations and Integrated International Production* (New York: United Nations, 1993).

[14]See Saskia Sassen, "The Urban Complex in a World Economy," *International Social Science Journal* 46, no. 1 (February 1994): 43–62; and Hooshang Amirahmadi and Weiping Wu, "Export Processing Zones in Asia," *Asian Survey* 35, no. 9 (September 1995): 828–49.

[15]See Campbell, "Foreign Investment."

[16]This new paradigm is distilled in Michael E. Porter, *The Competitive Advantage of Nations*, which argues that the new competitive development is based on productivity and specialization, instead of factor endowment.

[17]The twenty-one members of the PECC, founded in 1980, include Australia, Brunei, Canada, Chile, China, Colombia, Hong Kong, Indonesia, Japan, South Korea, Malaysia, Mexico, New Zealand, Peru, the Philippines, Russia, Singapore, Taiwan, Thailand, the United States, and the Pacific Island nations. See Pacific Economic Cooperation Council, *Human Resource Development Outlook 1994–1995: Investment and Labor Flows in Selected Pacific Economies* (Singapore: Time Academic Press, 1994).

[18]For a full discussion of migration in Japan and the United States, see Saskia Sassen, "Economic Internationalization: The New Migration in Japan and the United States," *Social Justice* 21, no. 2 (summer 1994): 62–82.

[19]See Pang Eng Fong and Linda Lim, "Foreign Labor and Economic Development in Singapore," *International Migration Review* 16, no. 3 (1982): 548–76.

[20]See Saskia Sassen, "Finance and Business Services in New York City: International Linkages and Domestic Effects," *International Social Science Journal* 42, no. 3 (August 1990): 287–306; and *Cities in a World Economy.*

[21]Roberto Camagni et al., "Europe's Regional-Urban Features: Conclusions, Inferences, and Surmises," in *Industrial Change and Regional Economic Transformation: The Experience of Western Europe*, ed. Lloyd Rodwin and Hidehiko Sazanami (London, UK: HarperCollins Academic, for the United Nations, 1991).

[22]A full definition of producer services should include financial, legal, and general management matters; innovation, design, and development; administration and personnel; production technology; maintenance; transport and communication; wholesale distribution; advertising; cleaning services; security; and storage. See Sassen, *Cities in a World Economy.*

[23]See Yin-Ping Ho and Y. Y. Kueh, "Whither Hong Kong in an Open-Door, Reforming Chinese Economy?" *Pacific Review* 6, no. 4 (1993): 333–51; and Yin-Ping Ho, *Trade, Industrial Restructuring, and Development in Hong Kong* (Honolulu: University of Hawaii Press, 1992).

[24]P. W. Daniels, "Services and Urban Economic Development," in *Urban Regeneration in a Changing Economy: An International Perspective*, ed. Joanne Fox-Przeworski, John Goddard, and Mark de Jong (Oxford, UK: Clarendon Press, 1991).

[25]Sassen, "Finance and Business Services in New York City."

[26]DRI/McGraw-Hill, *The Tri-State Competitive Region Initiative: Diagnostic Assessment* (prepared for the Regional Plan Association, New York, 1994).

[27]World Bank, *China Industrial Restructuring: A Tale of Three Cities*, report no. 10479-CHA (Washington, D.C.: World Bank, 1992).

[28]More than a quarter of the city's population in 1995 is foreign-born and they, as well as minority groups like African-Americans and Latinos, are holding a disproportionally large number of low-paying jobs. See Saskia Sassen, *The Global City: New York, London, Tokyo* (Princeton, N.J.: Princeton University Press, 1991).

[29]Regional Plan Association, *The Third Regional Plan: An Overview* (New York: Regional Plan Association, May 1995).

[30]In fact, the spending reached a peak of 22 percent of local value-added in 1975, but the following fiscal crisis forced it down to around 17 percent in 1983. See Nathan Glazer, "Fate of a World City," *City Journal* (autumn 1993): 18–26.

[31]"In Blow to Mayor, Credit Agency Lowers New York's Bond Rating," *New York Times*, 11 July 1995, sec. A, p.1.

[32]Kenneth Powell, "Barcelona: Arena of Vision," *The World & I* 6, no. 12 (December 1991): 214–19. Such detachment was largely rebuffed during the Franco regime given the hostile attitude of the government toward the potentially autonomist regions of Spain. At that time, planning for the growth of Barcelona was always subordinated to the interests of the central government. See John Naylon, "Anteroom to a Madhouse: Economic Growth and Urban Development in Barcelona in the Franco Era," in *Economic Growth and Urbanization in Developing Areas*, ed. David Drakakis-Smith (London, UK: Routledge, for the IGU Commission on Third World Development, 1990).

[33]Armando Montanari, "Barcelona and Glasgow: The Similarities and Differences in the History of Two Port Cities," *Journal of European Economic History* 18, no. 1 (spring 1989): 171–89.

[34]Soledad Garcia, "Big Events and Urban Politics: Barcelona and the Olympic Games" (paper presented at the XIII World Congress of Sociology, Bielefeld, Germany, 1994).

[35]T. C. Marshall, "Environmental Planning for the Barcelona Region," *Land Use Policy* 10, no. 3 (July 1993): 238; and Alan Tillier, "An Elegant, Hardworking Euro-City," *Europe* (November 1994): 32–34.

[36]It is even argued that a salient feature of Barcelona's economic success in recent years has been the determined pursuit of a political consensus among all social and economic forces involved. See Garcia, "Big Events."

[37]For details of the plan, see Gary McDonogh, "Discourses of the City: Policy and Response in Post-Transitional Barcelona," *City & Society: Journal of the Society for Urban Anthropology* 5, no. 1 (June 1991): 40–63.

[38]See Manuel De Forn, "Barcelona: Development and Internationalization Strategies," *Ekistics* 59, nos. 352–53 (1992): 65–71.

[39]Gregory Wilson, "Regenerating Barcelona," *The Planner* 79, no. 7 (July 1993): 24.

[40]De Forn, "Barcelona: Development."

[41]Alejandra Cox Edwards and Sebastian Edwards, "Markets and Democracy: Lessons from Chile," *World Economy* 15, no. 2 (March 1992): 203–19. The most striking economic changes associated with the reform were in the areas of fiscal matters, finance, labor, and state ownership; among these fiscal decentralization has affected municipalities significantly. See United Nations Conference on Trade and Development (UNCTAD), *Trade Liberalization in Chile: Experiences and Prospects*, Trade Policy Series no. 1 (New York: United Nations, 1992).

[42]A somewhat negative impact of this shift on Santiago was that the "substituting" industries were located mainly in Santiago and their stagnation and disappearance affected metropolitan Santiago more than other parts of the country. See Carlos A. de Mattos, Fernando Soler R., and Francisco Sabatini D., "Globalización, Territorio y Ciudad: El Caso de Chile," *Serie Azul* 7 (Instituto de Estudios Urbanos, Pontificia Universidad Católica de Chile, 1995).

[43]See Cristian Moran, "Chile: Economic Crisis and Recovery," in *Restructuring Economies in Distress: Policy Reform and the World Bank*, ed. Vínod Thomas et al. (Oxford, UK: Oxford University Press, for the World Bank, 1991).

[44]Tarsicio Castaneda, *Combating Poverty: Innovative Social Reforms in Chile during the 1980s* (San Francisco: International Center for Economic Growth, 1992).

[45]See Jaime Valenzuela G., "Urban Decay and Local Management Strategies for the Metropolitan Center: The Experience of the Municipality of Santiago, Chile," in *Latin American Regional Development in an Era of Transition: The Challenges of Decentralization, Privatization, and Globalization*, United Nations Center for Regional Development (Nagoya, Japan: United Nations, 1994).

[46]See *The Economist*, 27 November 1993; and Lauren Bradbury, "Environmental Reform is Under Way in Chile," *Business America* (23 August 1993): 6.

[47]Molly Pollack and Andras Uthoff, "Poverty and the Labor Market: Greater Santiago, 1969–95," in *Urban Poverty and the Labor Market: Access to Jobs and Incomes in Asian and Latin American Cities*, ed. Gerry Rodgers (Geneva, Switzerland: International Labor Office, 1989).

[48]Interview with Maria Elena Ducci, Profesora Investigadora, Instituto de Estudios Urbanos, Pontificia Universidad Catolica de Chile, 7 July 1995.

[49]This section draws from "Shanghai: Renaissance City," in *Prospering Coastal Cities: Shanghai, Tianjian, and Guangzhou in the Era of Reform*, ed. by Shahid Yusuf and Weiping Wu (forthcoming).

[50]Because of Shanghai's importance as the country's largest revenue base, the central government did not permit the city to carry out until the end of the decade the kind of sweeping reforms undertaken in South China throughout the 1980s.

[51]The city has designated six service industries as top priorities of development, including finance and insurance, commerce and trade, telecommunications and transportation, real estate, tourism, and information. The first three subsectors have already become driving forces behind the city's service industry, accounting for 73 percent of the sector's value-added in 1993. See Foreign Broadcast Information Service—China (hereafter FBIS-CHI) 94167, 29 August 1994: 69.

[52]FBIS-CHI-93117, 21 June 1993: 60; and FBIS-CHI-94096, 18 May 1994: 78.

[53]See FBIS-CHI-93117, 21 June 1993: 60; FBIS-CHI-93079, 27 April 1993: 52; and FBIS-CHI-94096, 18 May 1994: 78.

[54]See "Economic Focus in Shanghai: Catching Up," *New York Times*, 22 December 1993, p. A1.

[55]China has chosen to preserve public ownership of urban land while permitting user rights to be leased out and giving leaseholders most of the significant rights of freehold ownership. This is similar to the systems prevailing in Hong Kong, Singapore, Amsterdam, Stockholm, the inner city of London, and Honolulu.

[56]See Zhimin Lin, "Reform and Shanghai: Changing Central-Local Fiscal Relations," in *Changing Central-Local Relations in China: Reform and State Capacity*, ed. Jia Hao and Lin Zhimin (Boulder, Colo.: Westview, 1994).

[57]Venture capital is often defined as capital that is provided by institutional venture funds, including private venture capital, limited partnership, and venture funds affiliated with banks, financial institutions, and large industrial corporations. See Richard

Florida and Donald F. Smith, Jr., "Venture Capital's Role in Economic Development: An Empirical Analysis," in *Sources of Metropolitan Growth*, ed. Edwin S. Mills and John F. McDonald (New Brunswick, N.J.: Center for Urban Policy Research, 1992).

[58]Michael E. Porter, "The Competitive Advantage of the Inner City," *Harvard Business Review* (May–June 1995): 55–71.

[59]See Hooshang Amirahmadi and Weiping Wu, "Foreign Direct Investment in Developing Countries," *Journal of Developing Areas* 28, no. 2 (January 1994): 167–90.

[60]For a detailed portrait of Rochester's story, see Andrea Gabor, "Rochester Focuses: A Community's Core Competence," *Harvard Business Review* (July–August 1991): 116–26.

[61]Michael L. Dertouzos, Richard K. Lester, and Robert M. Solow, *Made in America: Regaining the Productive Edge* (Cambridge, Mass.: MIT Press, 1990).

[62]See Joanne Fox-Przeworski, John Goddard, and Mark de Jong, "Key Factors for Success in Urban Regeneration," in *Urban Regeneration in a Changing Economy*.

[63]Kessides, *The Contributions of Infrastructure*.

[64]The concept of industrial networking has its intellectual antecedents in Alfred Marshal's view that the matrix of production was a region or industrial district and not a firm, and external economies should be obtained through the concentration of a large number of small firms in a single sector. This is echoed in the experience of new industrial districts, represented most appropriately by the Northern Italy region of Emilia Romagna (Third Italy). See Jonathan Zeitlin, "Industrial Districts and Local Economic Regeneration: Overview and Comments," in *Industrial Districts and Local Economic Regeneration*.

[65]See Sengenberger and Pyke, eds., *Industrial Districts and Local Economic Regeneration*.

[66]Harold M. Hochman, "New York and Pittsburgh: Contrasts in Community," *Urban Studies* 29, no. 2 (April 1992): 237–50.

Economic and Social Dilemmas

PART III BRINGS ATTENTION to economic and social dilemmas facing the world's cities and the tough choices that must be made to resolve them. These "problems without policies" are simultaneously exacerbated by globalization and by adverse conditions at the local level. The most successful and sustainable urban policies must strike a difficult balance between what is local and what is global with attention to issues of equity and the most vulnerable groups of society. Edmundo Werna, Ilona Blue, and Trudy Harpham argue that as national and regional actors become less important in an era of globalization, local actors assume pivotal importance in responding to the specific needs of each locality.

Although urbanization implies many negative consequences, cities play an important role in economic development, environmental conditions, and social life, offering overall beneficial effects, argues Michael White. Urbanization speeds the demographic transition, contributing to a shift from a regime of high fertility and high mortality to one of low fertility and low mortality. White also considers the relationship of urban poverty to population growth, tracing a shift in distribution of income resulting from the economic development and industrialization that accompany the demographic transition. In the long run, argues White, the demographic transition may produce improvement in the standard of living; however, the transition may see a period of widening disparities due to a lag in the convergence of fertility to lower mortality. Research indicates that in addition to factors such as education, family planning programs, and nonagricultural occupational opportunity, urbanization reduces fertility rates, contributing to lower urban growth rates. Finally, White suggests that the tensions surrounding the immigration debate reflect a misunderstanding of international and domestic migration. With increasing globalization, "highly advanced nations may have a more limited choice between importing labor or exporting capital."

While technological advances have indisputably improved the quality of urban life, we must closely weigh adverse, secondary consequences of new technologies with the benefits they bring. Furthermore, technological development can exacerbate disparities, argues Julie

Roqué, outlining the negative and often unanticipated impact of new technology on economic development, social and cultural patterns, and on the quality of health and the environment. Roqué cautions against continuing a trend of uneven technological development that has created "growing disparities between those who benefit from new technologies and those who do not—those, who, in fact, may disproportionately bear the burdens of technological development as well." Roqué concludes with a call for the establishment of social and political institutions to manage technology safely and equitably, within a framework of strong national policies that "promote research, development, and the deployment of technologies that will improve urban life."

Edmundo Werna, Ilona Blue, and Trudy Harpham similarly disaggregate statistics to reveal the inextricable links between inequalities in wealth and inequalities in health. Intraurban differentials illustrate how the urban poor suffer disproportionately from infectious diseases and malnutrition characteristic of the underdeveloped world as well as from chronic and social diseases associated with the industrialized world. Werna, Blue, and Harpham establish the relationship between socioeconomic and environmental conditions associated with rapid urbanization and "new" public health problems such as mental disorders and violence that plague vulnerable urban populations. "Due to the close connection between the overall process of development of a city or town and the health status of its population," they argue, "an integrated approach to urban health should be, in fact, an integrated approach to urban development." A holistic, flexible, and multisectoral approach to urban management that is based on strong local actors and institutions, conclude Werna, Blue, and Harpham, is the best way to address the social factors affecting urban public health.

Chapter 8

Urbanization and Population Dynamics: City as Villain, Savior, or Bystander?

Michael J. White

In discussions of the world's problems, cities are often cast as the villains. This is especially true when the problem or crisis under review has an environmental twist. Is this portrayal justified? Cities are sites of crime, pollution, and the erosion of traditional values. Even when urbanization is seen more positively, there is often concern about the rate of urban growth or the balance in growth across different levels of geography.

Cities rarely get the best reviews. American cities, especially large ones, tend to produce lower levels of satisfaction among their residents than suburbs or small towns.[1] Although I am unaware of opinion polls for cities in less-developed settings I suspect they recapitulate some of the negative, even Dickensian, portrayals of cities in highly industrialized societies. In chapter 2 of this volume Michael Cohen suggests that cities are becoming more alike (or at least beset by very similar problems) in both the more- and the less-developed regions. Still, urban areas are often seen as the places to get jobs and where the levels of amenities and services are high.

In this chapter I assess the relationship between urbanization and overall population change. I examine the implications of this dynamic interplay between urbanization and demography for patterns of settlement, land use, and issues of economic development and socioeconomic well-being.

Malthusian and Revisionist Models

The conventional, or Malthusian, view sees population growth as negative for the well-being of humankind and the natural environment. Often this is expressed in terms of the PAT (Population Affluence Technology) paradigm advanced by biologist Paul Ehrlich and others,[2] although work has moved well beyond that simple view.[3] In the PAT model, population, affluence, and technological development interact to bring adverse outcomes for the environment. Another part of the conventional view, although less generally subscribed, is that rapid population growth (due to high fertility) engenders poverty. Indeed, concern that rapid population growth might induce environmental degradation, decelerate economic development, and exacerbate social inequality undergirds many of the antinatalist policies of population and development aid. Indeed the notion of the "population bomb" and the effort to defuse it speak to the orientation of the conventional view.

Urbanization is, perhaps, the bombardier in this scenario. Cities are seen as ravenous consumers of land, polluters of air and water, and unhealthy stewpots of social conflict and disease. Less often is urban growth—sometimes of stunning proportions in developing countries— seen in a beneficial light.

Another viewpoint, the "revisionist model," has developed in recent years. Population growth is seen as benign, indifferent, or beneficial to the social well-being of the populace. This view, mainly articulated by a group of economists, argues (to oversimplify) that market forces, if allowed to act, can serve to allocate resources efficiently. Proper pricing through the market can result in incentives to conserve resources. Meanwhile technology can be developed to help use existing resources more successfully.

Consider the writings of a select panel of experts for the U.S. National Academy of Sciences (NAS) in their slim volume *Population Growth and Economic Development: Policy Questions*.[4] The NAS panel poses for itself this question: Will slower population growth facilitate the absorption of workers into the modern sector and alleviate problems of urban growth? The NAS argues for the overall beneficial effects of urbanization in the process of development but notes that rapid urbanization does impose "externalities," social adjustment and congestion costs not paid by the migrant. The NAS argues further, in a manner consistent with a substantial pool of writing in the field, that the *public* sector has exacerbated urban problems through various kinds of taxes, subsidies, trade restrictions, and other vehicles that hamper the efficient functioning of the market.

In sum, the stage is set. The seemingly inexorable growth of cities and the spread of those cities over a wider territory raises concern— even alarm—in many quarters. Population dynamics are implicated in such concerns both broadly (considering societal resources) and narrowly (taking into account urban sprawl). It would seem prudent to try to examine directly the relationship between population growth and urbanization. I now turn to this task.

Urbanization and the Demographic Transition

The demographic transition offers a key descriptive paradigm for the evolution of populations through time. Simply stated, the demographic transition describes the shift from a regime of high fertility and high mortality to one of low fertility and low mortality. Regimes of high fertility and high mortality, "pre-transition," usually describe populations at lower levels of socioeconomic development. Regimes of low fertility and low mortality, "post-transition," are usually found in highly industrialized populations. Birth and death rates are quite close in pre- and post-transition societies, producing little or no overall population growth.

It is the passage through the transition that attracts interest and concern. The transition itself, in most historical populations, has proceeded with fertility reduction *following* mortality reduction. The gap between birth and death rates drives population growth. In contemporary developing societies at the onset of the transition, annual growth rates can reach about 3 percent, enough to double the population in less than twenty-five years.

As conventionally interpreted, the demographic transition is usually accompanied by economic development, industrialization, and urbanization. Although few quarrel with the paradigm of the transition, the exact route fertility and mortality rates trace through time; the degree to which those vital rates can be maneuvered by public policy; and the roles of urbanization, economic development, and public sector interventions (such as family planning and maternal and child health programs) have been subject to debate.

What interests us here is the role that urbanization and urbanity play in that monumental population transformation. Cities could be just the site of population accumulation, and all the action (and policy intervention) may be directed elsewhere, or cities may play a more integral role in population change.

Urban Development and Demographic Change

In contemporary developing countries the pace of urban growth astonishes many observers. Every day, thousands of migrants arrive in the world's urban centers—Mexico City, São Paulo, Shanghai, Bangkok. Figure 8.1 shows that growth is so manifest in urban areas of less-developed countries (LDCs) that by 1990 eight of the thirteen largest urban agglomerations in the world were located in developing countries.[5] Moreover, cities in these industrializing nations will absorb a disproportionate share of urban growth in the decades to come.

Although cities in many developing countries are growing rapidly, we should not confuse overall urban growth with the pace of urbanization. Urban growth is the rate of change in the urban population; the

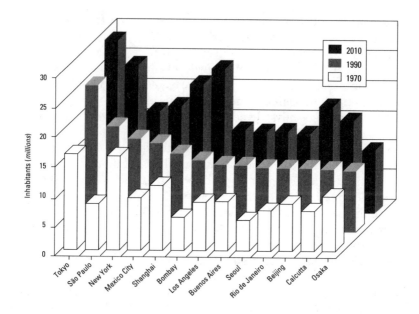

FIGURE 8.1. The largest urban agglomerations in the world. (United Nations, *World Urbanization Prospects* [New York: United Nations, 1993])

pace of urbanization is best measured by the rate of change in the proportion of the population that is urban. This distinction is important for an understanding of the relationship between demographic and urban dynamics.

Consider the observation of demographer Samuel Preston regarding the historical and contemporary pace of urbanization: Countries now classified as more developed underwent rapid urbanization in the late nineteenth century and in a span of twenty-five years increased by about 10 percent in urban concentration. From 1950 to 1970 contemporary developing nations experienced a parallel shift in the *percentage* urban.[6]

About 40 percent of urban growth is attributable to net rural–urban migration and reclassification of rural locations into urban sites. Still, a closer look reveals that national urban growth rates are very highly correlated with overall population growth rates.[7] High rates of natural increase in *both* urban and rural areas help fuel urban growth. The phase of the demographic transition (the excess of fertility over mortality) will have much to say about the process of urban growth in a nation. To the extent that societal intervention with medicine, public health measures, and improved nutrition to bring mortality down is *not* accompanied by reduction of the fertility rate, the population will balloon as the two curves tracing the demographic transition diverge.

In developing regions there is often the desire to curb the growth of urban areas. This is extremely difficult to do. China has succeeded in directing the settlement patterns of its population more than most countries. Under the movement to a more market-oriented economy, efforts to slow urban growth while encouraging town and village enterprises have had only partial success. Temporary migrants continue to flood China's largest cities and find economic niches.[8] Provinces with more rural enterprise activity have actually experienced more outmigration.[9]

Urbanity and Fertility

Once the demographic transition is underway, fertility change becomes the engine of overall population change. It is useful to examine the relationship between urbanity and fertility. By "urbanity" I mean the level of urban agglomeration at which a person lives or that is exhibited by society. By "fertility" I mean the rate of childbearing. Despite the negative interpretation of urbanization (increasing urbanity) found in many quarters, urban settlement may have some ameliorative effects on the overall rate of population growth.

Consider figure 8.2, which describes the relationship between proportional urban and fertility rates around 1990 for nineteen populous nations representing all major world regions.[10] It is evident from the

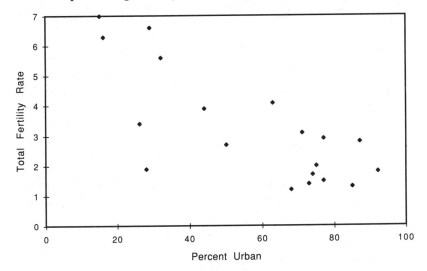

FIGURE 8.2. Fertility versus urbanization

graph that the higher the level of urbanization in a population the lower the total fertility rate (TFR). Nations of sub-Saharan Africa and South Asia have low levels of urbanization and high fertility. Highly urbanized, high-income nations (the United States, the United Kingdom, Germany, and Japan) have fertility rates below the replacement level. It is worth noting that countries once associated with high fertility and population problems (Colombia, Mexico, and Brazil) now exhibit moderate levels of both urbanization and fertility.

Of course this relationship is not due solely and simply to urbanization. Rather urbanization itself accompanies other forms of economic and social change, most notably economic development and industrialization. To be sure, one pole of the great debate in population policy is that fertility decline cannot be achieved without attendant socioeconomic development. (The other pole argues that family-planning programs can lower fertility substantially even in the face of low levels of development.) The decline in the TFR in many settings has been matched by a corresponding decline in the movement of workers out of agriculture, but the pace of the transformation in LDCs is not matching that of the more-developed nations.[11] It is this very industrialization that generates companion concerns about environmental quality, occupational health and safety, provision of public services, and the like.

When we look more directly at the relationship between urbanity and fertility, what do we find? My research with two colleagues can help answer that question. We were able to look at the fertility of women in Peru,[12] a low-income country that exhibits conventional urban-rural fertility differentials (rural TFR=6.3; urban TFR=3.1). We matched each woman's childbearing history to her locality (rural, town, or city) and controlled for other traits, such as education and age, known to influence childbearing and confound aggregate statistics. We found that (otherwise equivalent) women living in towns bore children at a rate 14 percent below the rate of rural women. Women living in cities bore children at a rate 33 percent lower than that of rural women.

These findings are important. When the statistical refinements are peeled away, these results indicate that urbanity does reduce fertility. Other changes such as education, the advent of family-planning programs, and nonagricultural occupational opportunity are also known to reduce fertility rates. Thus urbanization—along with these other changes—can help reduce the overall population growth rate and hence the rate of growth of urban areas themselves. It remains to be seen what the relative strength of each of the contributors is.

This brings us back to fertility and the debate about the "best" way for developing regions to reduce their fertility. This review suggests that urbanization can help speed the demographic transition.

Population Growth, Urbanization, and Poverty

A quick visit to many developing nations with high growth rates would impress the visitor with the coincidence of poverty and rapid population growth. Moreover, such urban environments often provide clear windows on social disadvantage. Hence, the visitor might be led to conclude that high rates of population growth, urban growth, and an increasing incidence of poverty (as an outcome of the former) are closely linked. A contrarian might point to the persistence of rural poverty and particularly emphasize the subsistence conditions that existed before the onset of the demographic transition. So, does the demographic transition and associated urbanization generate urban poverty, or does it merely make a transitional phenomenon more visible?

This question returns to the very origins of Malthusianism and Malthus' own *Essay on the Principle of Population.* A central tenet of the original Malthusian perspective is to view population growth as closely intertwined with poverty. Indeed, one version of Malthusianism holds that regardless of gains made in agricultural productivity, population growth always condemns a society to operate at a subsistence level.

Rigid Malthusian prophecy did not hold. Demographer Massimo Livi-Bacci offers the more contemporary and alternative interpretation of the relationship between population growth and poverty in his *Population and Poverty:* "In the long run—and at the aggregate level—the acceleration of growth does coincide with transformations that change favorably the patterns of life, and improve living conditions.[13]

Livi-Bacci and other demographic observers acknowledge that rapid population growth (often spurred by a welcome decline in mortality at the onset of the transition) produces various sorts of stress. A flood of migrants to urban areas during this transition can lead to urban unemployment or underemployment, and increasing density of low-income individuals (creating *favelas* and shantytowns).

Several considerations bear on any evaluation of the relationship of urban poverty to population growth. First, it is important to note the stage at which we observe a society. Usually, the transition is accompanied by economic growth and fairly rapid population growth, until fertility declines. During this time there is likely to be a shift in the distribution of income—witness contemporary China, Malaysia, and Brazil. It is important, therefore, not to confuse increasing disparities in income (of concern in themselves) with increasing poverty by some absolute standard. In any case, the demographic transition and accompanying industrial changes can be expected to shift the distribution of income.

A second consideration is the implication of individual incentive structures. The conventional view is that in agrarian societies the incentives for high fertility are great, both to offset expected infant mortality and to invite labor and secure old-age support. The exact magnitude of these effects and their precise manifestations may differ substantially in accordance with the economic and cultural setting.[14] For instance, economist Mead Cain argues that access to land generates demand for more labor (and higher fertility), whereas landownership offers old-age security and decreases pressures on fertility.[15] Thus tenure and social security systems may have an influence on fertility. The combination of direct and indirect effects can be quite complicated. One recent study of an agricultural development project in the Sudan found that program participation increased marital fertility and reduced infant mortality. By themselves these events would increase local growth rates, but indirect effects (child survival, female employment, and family income) partially offset the pro-growth effect of the project.[16]

The general result that the more educated, the urbane (not just the urban), and those employed in the modern sector all reduce their fertility more quickly and to lower ultimate levels suggests that high fertility may be associated with negative well-being. Thus, although in the long run the demographic transition may produce improvement in the standard of living for many or all, the transition phase itself may see a period of widening disparities, and one in which those who bear the most children (and no longer reap agricultural rewards for having large families) fare the worst.

Immigration and the Urban Labor Force

International migration has come to prominence as a major demographic phenomenon of the late twentieth century. It is estimated that approximately one hundred million migrants were living outside their countries of origin in 1985.[17] The exact motivations and circumstances of all migrants are difficult to catalog. About one-fifth are designated as refugees; many others are displaced persons. Most are probably voluntary labor migrants. Although immigration has grabbed an increasing amount of press attention and policy debate in the highly industrialized countries of Western Europe and North America, the phenomenon is much broader. As many as one-third of international migrants may reside in Asia and Africa. These regions have absorbed a very large share of forced migrant resettlement, but they also are the scenes of substantial voluntary movement of persons seeking economic gain or better living conditions.

Indeed, one of the important points to recognize about international migration is that many world regions serve as both origins and destinations. Nigeria and South Africa have received labor migrants from neighboring countries during periods of economic growth. North Africans, meanwhile, constitute a visible flow of persons to France and other European destinations. Mexico sends large (often undocumented) numbers to the United States whereas it receives migrants from Central America. Hong Kong ships labor to Canada, the United States, and Australia, and receives workers from the Philippines and other Asian states.

Most migrants end up in cities. The concentration of new arrivals in major urban areas is usually far greater than that of the native population.[18] Rapid international migration can itself be the genesis of other social stress. Migrants from less-developed origins often have different social mores; these differences can be the sources of ethnic conflict and nativist reactions, as they have been in the United States, Germany, and other receiving societies.

In the realm of demographic dynamics, immigrants are likely to come from regions of higher fertility. Host population perceptions of higher fertility and alternative notions of family structure can exacerbate tensions. Some observers have latched onto international migration (and its contribution to host country growth) as a related cause of threats to the environment, although immigrants and their children tend to adjust their fertility downward fairly quickly.[19] This phenomenon parallels that discerned in our review of internal migration and urbanization. The long-term trend of immigration in high-income societies may be to offset below replacement fertility.

A great deal of the tension between recent immigrants and natives in large high-income urban settings derives from labor market competition. This is a hotly contested issue and is politically quite salient. Despite the common argument that immigrants cut into job opportunities for natives, the empirical social science evidence is equivocal. Some immigrants may take jobs that natives do not want. Studies of immigrant-native job competition have generally found only modest substitution effects, except in certain highly focused settings.[20]

Another perspective on international demography and economics is relevant. Many advanced industrial nations face the migration of jobs and industries out of the country to low-wage regions; witness the growth of manufacturing in Mexico and of textile and garment manufacturing in Asia. To cast the migration-urbanization issue as one of prohibiting immigration (and retaining high native wages) vs. permitting immigration (and presumably depressing native wages) is to miss the point. The increasing interconnectedness of the global economy pits international trade against domestic production and wages.[21] In a globally fluid economy, highly advanced nations may have a more limited choice between importing labor and exporting capital.

Given that these new urbanites arrive from foreign destinations and set up in major urban entrepôt cities, and given that the demographic shift of international migration is likely to continue, there are still issues to be addressed by the receiving societies. In many settings, debate has turned on the fiscal (public-sector) impact of immigration. Again results are equivocal, but suggest a net benefit.[22] The geographical and governmental impact of these population shifts is quite pertinent for the present discussion. Municipal governments in receiving areas (witness Los Angeles County or Paris) may spend a disproportionate share of public money on the health, education, and welfare of migrants and their children, without full reimbursement from the state and national governments that receive the payroll and sales taxes paid on behalf of or by immigrant labor.

Social cleavage, tension, and inequity are even more difficult to measure than these pecuniary impacts. Undoubtedly, the pressure to absorb thousands of new residents—many of whom speak a different language and adhere to differing cultural values—places stress on the receiving society. Each subsequent migrant wave brings with it, so it seems, an outcry about the "impossibility" of absorbing these new masses. In contemporary receiving societies, genuine problems within the polity appear to be emerging and the long-run integration of diverse groups remains a challenge.[23]

It is important to maintain a historical and comparative framework when considering the scale of immigration and its consequences. The United States provides a useful reference point. At least fifty million persons were counted as immigrants to the United States from 1820 to 1987.[24] Immigration in the early 1990s, although numerically greater than historical flows, is still rarely on the scale of that experienced at the turn of the century.

Two things *have* changed since the twentieth century began: immigrants arrive predominantly from non-European countries, and fertility has diminished, so that immigration accounts for a larger proportion of population growth. To get some sense of this compare the first decade of the twentieth century to the baby-boom era, and both to the 1980s. Between 1901 and 1910 the United States saw a number of births equal to about 30 percent of the population at the start of the decade, and another population increase of 12 percent due to immigration (see table 8.1). In the 1950s, the baby-boom era, the percentage added through births was about the same as during 1901–10, but the immigration proportion dropped to about 2 percent. The 1980s differ from

TABLE 8.1

THE IMPACT OF IMMIGRATION AND FERTILITY ON U.S. POPULATION

Decade	Starting U.S. Population	Births in Decade (prop. of initial)	Immigrants in Decade (prop. of initial)
1901–10	75,994,575	21,980,000 (0.29)	8,795,000 (0.12)
1951–60	150,697,361	41,146,000 (0.27)	2,515,000 (0.02)
1981–90	226,542,203	38,075,000 (0.17)	7,338,000 (0.03)

the 1950s not so much in immigration numbers but rather in low fertility levels. Even when undocumented U.S. immigration is added the proportion of immigration for the decade remains under 5 or 6 percent.

This simple demographic scale comparison suggests that the more recent immigrant flow to the United States is not abnormally voluminous when viewed in comparison to previous immigrant flows and to increases in the population stock due to fertility. The U.S. historical experience may be unique, but there are several parallels with other industrialized host countries. Most of the receiving countries of Europe, along with Canada and Australia, have also found that their newest immigrants are from culturally different backgrounds. The below-replacement fertility levels in host countries have also magnified the apparent impact of immigrants. As the natural increase of the native population falls and immigrants from new origins form a larger part of the population, issues of accommodation and adjustment will rise.

Conclusion

Although urbanization and urban living may have negative consequences for overall well-being in some settings, other aspects of urbanity are positive. Cities consume land and are the sites of pollution, but the careful observer must ask what would take place otherwise.

Urbanization in contemporary countries is mostly neutral, bringing with it some benefits and some costs. Urbanization is concomitant with most economic growth and is itself related to declines in childbearing and overall growth rates. There is concern, however, that the pace of urbanization and economic development in developing nations may not be keeping pace with historical transformation.

A high rate of urban growth (which is not the equivalent of urbanization) is linked to high rates of population growth. Some analysts have advanced concerns that the "bulge" in the demographic transition is especially large in contemporary developing societies and the convergence of fertility to lower mortality is lagging. The conditions that diminish fertility (education, improvements in the status of women, growth of nonagricultural employment in the formal sector, relief of concern about old-age security, and improved access to family planning and its integration with health services) might all serve to lower urban growth rates. There is reason for guarded optimism that several large developing countries will reach near-replacement fertility early in the twenty-first century.[25]

Urban settings are often the most visible sites for congestion, pollution, and income disparity. It is unclear to what extent some of these undesirable features of the urban landscape are inevitable accompaniments to the great demographic and economic transformation. Urban and population growth rates are implicated in environmental stress, but their influence seems to be outweighed by economic factors.[26] In turn, greater affluence can translate into more efforts to improve environmental quality.[27]

The public sector in some countries may overinvest in urban settings in two ways: by maintaining artificially high urban wages and by subsidizing urban public services and consumption. This can result in an inefficient allocation of resources[28] even though urbanization itself is not much to blame.

International migration adds a new dimension. Large cities are called upon to absorb many thousands of workers neither born, trained, nor acculturated in the host country. This confluence of populations creates a great deal of social and political stress, but it is not clear that continued immigration is detrimental to the immigrants or to the economic well-being of natives in a global economy.

Are cities saviors, villains, or bystanders? Cities have an important part to play in economic development, environmental conditions, and social life in any setting, yet it is unlikely that urbanization itself can overshadow other processes that impinge on everyday life.

Notes

The author is grateful to the Mellon and Ford foundations for providing support to Brown University and the Urban Institute for research on which this article is based.

[1]Alden Speare and Michael J. White, "Optimal City Size and Population Density for the Twenty-first Century," in *Elephants in the Volkswagen,* ed. Lindsey Grant (New York: Freeman, 1992), 85–97.

[2]Paul R. Ehrlich and Anne H. Ehrlich, "The Most Overpopulated Nation," in *Elephants in the Volkswagen,* 125–33.

[3]Gayl D. Ness, William D. Drake, and Steven R. Brechin, eds., *Population-Environment Analysis* (Ann Arbor: University of Michigan Press, 1993).

[4]National Research Council, *Population Growth and Economic Development: Policy Questions* (Washington, D.C: National Academy Press, 1986).

[5]United Nations, *World Urbanization Prospects* (New York: United Nations, 1993).

[6]Samuel Preston, "Urban Growth in Developing Countries: A Demographic Reappraisal," in *Population and Development Review* 5 (June 1979): 195–215.

[7]Ibid.

[8]Sidney Goldstein, Alice Goldstein, and Shenyang Guo, "Temporary Migrants in Shanghai Households," *Demography* 28 (1991): 275–91.

[9]Zai Liang and Michael White, "Market Transition, Government Policies, and Interprovincial Migration in China, 1983–88," in *Economic Development and Cultural Change* (forthcoming).

[10]The countries are Argentina, Brazil, China, Colombia, Egypt, Ethiopia, France, Germany, Indonesia, Italy, Japan, Mexico, Nigeria, Pakistan, Russia, South Africa, United Kingdom, United States, and Zaire. I use the total fertility rate (TFR) to measure fertility (adjusted for age and expressed as the equivalent number of children a woman would bear over her lifespan at currently prevailing rates).

[11]Allen C. Kelley and William Paul McGreevey, "Population and Development in Historical Perspective," in *Population and Development: Old Debates, New Conclusions*, ed. Robert Cassen (New Brunswick, N.J.: Transaction, 1994), 107–26.

[12]Michael J. White, Lorenzo Moreno, and Shenyang Guo, "The Interrelationship of Fertility and Migration in Peru: A Hazards Model Analysis," *International Migration Review* 29 (summer 1995): 492–514.

[13]Massimo Livi-Bacci, *Population and Poverty* (Liege, Belgium: International Union for the Scientific Study of Population, 1994): 11.

[14]John Caldwell, *Theory of Fertility Decline* (New York: Academic, 1982).

[15]Mead Cain, "On the Relationship between Landholding and Fertility," *Population Studies* 39 (March 1985): 5–15.

[16]El-Rayah Osman, "The Fertility Impact of Rural Development Projects: The Case of the Rahad Irrigation Project, Sudan," (Ph.D. diss., Brown University, 1995).

[17]Michael S. Teitelbaum and Sharon Stanton Russell, "International Migration, Fertility, and Development," in *Population and Development*, 229–52.

[18]Michael J. White, "Immigrants, Cities, and Equal Opportunity," in *Urban Labor Markets and Job Opportunity*, ed. George Peterson and Wayne Vroman (Washington, D.C.: Urban Institute, 1992), 283–308.

[19]Joan Kahn, "Immigrant Selectivity and Fertility in the United States," *Social Forces* 67 (1988): 108–15.

[20]Rachel M. Friedberg and Jennifer Hunt, "The Impact of Immigrants on Host Country Wages, Employment and Growth," *Journal of Economic Perspectives* 9 (spring 1995): 23–44.

[21]John Abowd and Richard Freeman, eds., *Immigration, Trade, and the Labor Market* (Chicago: University of Chicago Press, 1992).

[22]Eric Rothman and Thomas J. Espenshade, "Fiscal Impacts of Immigration to the United States," *Population Index* 58 (fall 1992): 381–415.

[23]Stephen Castles and Mark J. Miller, *The Age of Migration* (London, UK: Macmillan, 1993).

[24]Ibid., 51.

[25]W. Parker Mauldin and John Ross, "Prospects and Programs for Fertility Reduction, 1990–2015," *Studies in Family Planning* 25 (1994): 77–95.

[26]Samuel Preston, *Population and Environment from Rio to Cairo* (Liege, Belgium: International Union for the Scientific Study of Population, 1994).

[27]Gene M. Grossman and Alan B. Krueger, "Environmental Impacts of a North American Free Trade Agreement," discussion paper no. 644 (Center for Economic Policy Research, 1992).

[28]National Research Council, *Population Growth*.

Chapter 9

The Social Dimensions of Technological Change: Reshaping Cities and Urban Life

Julie A. Roqué

The Promise of Technology

Since the Renaissance, Western cultures have been captivated by the quest to develop technologies to master natural phenomena, with the ultimate goal of benefiting all humankind. Although the Renaissance was not a period of great technological advances, it was a time in which magicians and alchemists dreamed of controlling the world through spells and incantations, and changing lead into gold. Later, in the sixteenth century, natural magic was condemned by the Catholic Church and it was replaced by the mechanistic philosophies of Francis Bacon and René Descartes, which remain dominant today. Bacon viewed knowledge as power and believed that science and technology should be maintained in the public domain for the benefit of all humanity.[1] Two centuries later, Thomas Jefferson envisioned that a common understanding of science and technology would lead humankind to manage cooperatively both natural and human resources toward "satisfying of the needs of everyone, wisely and humanely."[2]

Throughout history technology has played an integral role in the development of all modern societies. Today we produce more food and other goods at less cost; we better understand how natural systems work and how they respond to human stresses; and we move information, goods, and even people around the globe faster than ever before. Because of such successes, technology has been looked to for solutions to resource and environmental constraints, as well as a range of social and economic problems.

Optimism about the power of technology to meet such challenges remained prevalent throughout the 1960s and 1970s, despite growing concerns that we were nearing physical limits with exponential population growth and the depletion of natural resources. This faith in technology was conveyed in statements quoted in the 1972 *Limits to Growth:*

> There are no substantial limits in sight either in raw materials or
> in energy that alterations in the price structure, product substitu-

tion, anticipated gains in technology and pollution control cannot be expected to solve.

Frank W. Notestein[3]

Humanity's mastery of vast, inanimate, inexhaustible energy sources and the accelerated doing more with less of sea, air, and space technology has proven Malthus to be wrong. Comprehensive physical and economic success for humanity may now be accomplished in one-fourth of a century.

R. Buckminster Fuller[4]

More recently, technology has been referred to as "the engine of economic growth,"[5] and has been credited with being "the major input to productivity, the main generator of wealth creation"[6] by Nobel Prize economist Robert Solow.

The broadest definition of technology is simply that of applied knowledge, or "anything that makes something happen."[7] Most often the term is used to refer to processes and to tools, machines, and other products that embody human knowledge in some form. Technology is what we do, or build and use to control our environments; to protect our health; to transform materials and resources into usable goods; and to dispose of wastes in ways intended to prevent harm to human health and ecological systems. Technology, as information, now is considered as fundamental to production as labor and capital. In many instances the phrase "technological development" is used synonymously with industrialization or modernization.

Technology and Urban Life: From Habitat I to Habitat II

Many of the technological advances of the twenty years that followed Habitat I were based on discoveries of previous eras: modern water supply and wastewater treatment systems, concrete and paved roads, telephones, and electricity, for example, all rely upon technologies that were developed in the nineteenth century.[8] During those two decades, however, technology proceeded to evolve rapidly. Because technology will play an increasingly important role in shaping, or reshaping, cities and urban life around the world, the impacts of technological choices and how they are made in the context of development decisions warrant explicit discussion in the light of Habitat II.

Urbanization is possible only with technological (and institutional) innovations that occur both in cities and the countryside. Hence, technological changes in rural areas, as well as urban ones, influence the growth of cities and the nature of urban life. The industrialization of agriculture in the countryside, for example, frees people to move to urban centers, or perhaps even forces them to do so as they are supplanted by machines. The influx of workers to cities provides the labor that enables the growth of urban industries—and the development of new technologies. Simultaneously, the concentration of people and economic activity that occurs in cities creates larger urban markets, which often require the transport of goods and environmental resources, such as water and raw materials, from other regions by truck, train, or plane. And as urban areas grow, the infrastructure of cities must be expanded to respond to the needs of larger and denser communities.

The twenty years from Habitat I to Habitat II lie within a continuum of technological development. In most areas, changes in technology during this period have been subtle; electricity, the internal combustion engine, air travel, and space exploration were all already in place. In certain areas, however, technological changes since 1976 have been more profound. Advances in electronics during the 1980s, for example, revolutionized both the applications and availability of computers, opening new doors through which we view communications and the use of information. But perhaps the most significant changes associated with technological development since Habitat I have been in attitudes toward technology. Although people have long been wary of some of the social impacts of technology, since the 1970s much attention has been paid, especially in industrialized nations, to the health and environmental consequences that often accompany technological development.

Benefits of Technology

The most obvious benefit of modern technology in industrialized societies has been the tremendous improvement in the standard of living by almost any measure. This is due largely to greater economic productivity resulting from new industrial technologies, but other technological developments also have provided vastly improved living conditions for most urban residents: clean water supplies, effective sanitation systems, more resilient building materials, and improved medical care. Electricity, refrigeration, and hotter stoves have improved food processing, storage, and cooking, all reducing food contamination. Infant mortality rates have dropped significantly in developed countries and people now live longer; residents of the U.S., who lived just forty years at the turn of the century, for example, now live seventy years or more on average.[9]

Since 1950, world production of consumer goods has increased sevenfold, and during the 1970s, the proportion of global industrial production in developing countries increased from 9.3 percent to 13.2 percent.[10] New industrial technologies have sped up the manufacture of goods, increased efficiency, decreased costs, and facilitated the development of new products. In fact, to remain competitive it is imperative that firms in many industrial sectors adopt new technologies such as flexible manufacturing systems, automation and robotics, and computerized tracking of entire manufacturing processes. This is especially true of telecommunications technologies, which facilitate entry into markets, improve customer services, reduce costs, and increase productivity.[11] Fortunately, it also has become apparent to many manufacturers that technologies to prevent and control pollution improve resource efficiency and avoid environmental damage that may require remediation later.[12]

Modern agricultural practices have provided more productive, large-scale food systems, and to date, the world's production of food has grown faster than its population. Between the early 1960s and the early 1980s, the worldwide supply of calories per person increased by 14 percent; developing countries overall averaged a 21 percent increase in calories per person by intensifying their use of resources and expanding their cultivated lands.[13] Some regions reaped great benefits; the Punjab in India, for example, saw real wages rise by 16 percent between 1963 and 1968,[14] and wheat production there more than tripled between 1967 and 1971.[15] Some observers have been concerned about the depletion of nutrients in soils from intensive agriculture in the countryside for food production for cities, but new technologies are being implemented in both developed and developing countries to recycle nutrients. Several cities in China, for example, have successful urban agriculture initiatives, producing 85 percent or more of their own supplies of vegetables, and recycling both garbage and sewage into fertilizer. Similarly, fish-farming using nutrients from the wastewater system in Calcutta has become a prosperous venture, producing up to twenty tons of fish daily.[16]

New systems to transport both people and goods have revolutionized our cities, allowing people to live farther from central areas and still obtain materials and finished products from across the world. Threats to air quality, uncontrolled construction of roads and highways, and the inefficient use of resources associated with urban sprawl all have been contained in some cities with proper land-use planning and transportation alternatives. The use of greenbelts and building restrictions promote dense development within urban boundaries, and model cities such as Portland, Oregon, and Curitiba, Brazil, offer alternatives to driving (such as light rail or buses) and provisions for pedestrians and bicyclists.

Since the 1970s, scientists have learned to map the genetic sequences of living organisms. The revolution in biotechnology and bioengineering has enabled us to detect and prevent certain diseases, produce new drugs, and clean up chemical contamination of the environment using microorganisms. Information and education are also more available to larger portions of the population through developments in electronics that have made computers more affordable and accessible. Although cities, with the necessary infrastructure, continue to be the nodes in the information superhighway, computer networks now connect many rural as well as urban residents to resources previously far beyond their reach.

Information and communications technologies allow private industries greater freedom in choosing locations by providing electronic access to markets across the world and integrating production within firms as well as among partners or subcontractors. Tele-working networks can provide employment opportunities in rural or peripheral regions, where labor may be undervalued, by decentralizing certain functions such as data processing, software development, telephone sales, reservations, and customer support. Workers in these networks in the United States rely primarily on telephones and answering machines, although in 1993, 36 percent (twice the national average) were reported to have personal computers as well. As many as 2 million workers in the United States telecommute at least part of the time, reducing reliance on automobiles and other modes of transportation. Despite Alvin Toffler's projections in *The Third Wave* that people would telecommute only from their homes ("the electronic cottage"),[17] telecommuting today includes working in regional, satellite, and local centers or offices.[18]

The information sector is defined broadly as the production, processing, and distribution of information and knowledge. Some commentators see information technologies as central to the evolution of advanced economies into postindustrial information societies.[19] The growth of the information sector, including banking, government operations, and the accounting and management functions of factories and farms, has been made possible by the convergence of telecommunications and computing technologies, particularly during the 1980s and 1990s. Great advances in microelectronics, software, and optics during the 1980s reduced significantly the cost of information transmission and processing, and the information sector is one of the fastest growing industries. It comprised between one-third and one-half of both the GDP and employment in OECD countries in the 1980s, and it is estimated that by the year 2000 it may account for as much as 60 percent of the economies of the European Union. The information sector also accounts for a substantial proportion of the GDP of the newly industrialized economies and the modern sectors of less-developed countries.

Information technology has become critical to economic development since attracting private firms to regions may depend on the quality of telecommunications infrastructures in cities almost as much as locational decisions depend on access to markets and customers.[20] Accordingly, construction of the National Information Infrastructure (the "information superhighway") is one of the top priorities of the Clinton administration's technology policy for the United States.[21]

Cities remain the key to these technologies. Most investments in the infrastructure for information and communications technologies are in metropolitan areas because the largest users are corporations with plants or offices in multiple locations. In the United Kingdom, for example, approximately three hundred large firms transmit 60 percent of the data sent electronically. Just twenty-five companies account for 40 to 50 percent of communications traffic on Norway's national data network, and 65 percent of all of the data communications traffic from large organizations in Canada converges in computer networks centered in metropolitan Toronto.[22]

Secondary Consequences of Technology

Although the development of new technologies generally is not undertaken with an explicit intent to reshape human societies, their introduction does influence social and cultural patterns, the health and well-being of both people and ecological systems, and the structure and needs of industrial processes. Too often these secondary, often adverse, consequences are neither anticipated nor recognized until new technologies have been integrated into industrial processes, routine public functions, or the daily lives of large numbers of people. This understanding of ill effects often takes decades, by which time it is virtually impossible to eliminate the technologies' widespread use, at least within a reasonably rapid time frame. A case in point is the international movement over the past decade to ban the production of chlorofluorocarbons (CFCs), which are associated with the destruction of the stratospheric ozone layer.

SOCIAL AND CULTURAL CONSEQUENCES

Are the physical ways in which human beings live, including their use of technology, the products of their cultures and ideas? Or are their cultures and ideas the products of their physical life? Whether technology or ideas are ultimately more powerful, the influence they have on each other is reciprocal and occurs not all at once but over a period of time.[23]

Secondary consequences of the introduction of new technologies, development projects, or technological catastrophes include social changes in traditional societies.[24] Radio and television have delivered Western ideas into previously closed Islamic cultures in the Algerian Sahara, for example, as well as other parts of the world. The complete effect of such mass communications is yet to be understood.

The mechanization of manufacturing processes, aimed at increasing productivity and the efficient use of material and energy inputs, relies upon technologies that replace human labor. Critics, including Wendell Barry and Lewis Mumford, warn that computerization and automation may lead to the breakdown of social relations and the loss of human spiritual fulfillment that depends on worthwhile work. This was the future envisioned in a 1964 episode of the television program *The Twilight Zone* titled "The Brain Center at Whipple's," which is on permanent display in the Information Age exhibit at the Smithsonian's National Museum of American History in Washington, D.C. In this program a new computer at the Whipple Corporation promises to replace sixty-one thousand workers, eliminating sick leave, vacation leave, and coffee breaks, and avoiding $4 million in hospitalization, insurance, and welfare costs. Such a scenario was also the subject of Kurt Vonnegut, Jr.'s 1952 novel, *Player Piano:*

ILIUM, NEW YORK, IS DIVIDED INTO THREE PARTS.

In the northwest are the managers and engineers and civil servants and a few professional people; in the northeast are the machines; and in the south, across the Iroquois River, is the area known locally as Homestead, where almost all of the people live.[25]

. . . Before the war, they worked in the Ilium Works, controlling machines, but now machines control themselves much better. . . . Less waste, much better products, cheaper products with automatic control.[26]

Other secondary, cultural consequences include the disruption of communities and the displacement of indigenous peoples. New transportation technologies have affected migration by enabling people to travel more easily around the globe, establishing new patterns of relocation but also weakening traditional communal ties. Nubian communities in the Nile Valley were flooded out of their homeland with the construction of the Aswan Dam, and residents of Bhopal, India, were forced to flee when a deadly chemical intermediate leaked from a nearby pesticide plant, killing more than two thousand people and blinding and injuring another two hundred thousand. Similarly, the nuclear disaster at a reactor in Chernobyl in the former Soviet Union forced the evacuation of thousands of people. Fallout from the explosion affected food production (and consumption) all across Europe.

Health & Environmental Consequences

The most obvious adverse secondary effects of new industrial technologies are emissions of exotic toxic contaminants, which are associated with occupational and public-health risks and the environmental degradation that has accompanied the industrialization of cities. The use of agricultural chemicals contaminates not only soils, but also food, water supplies, and fisheries. Significant pesticide exposures to people in both developing and developed nations result through the food chain and water supplies; during applications in farming, building, and yard maintenance; and with residential or commercial use of buildings treated with pesticides.

The industrialization of cities around the world has been accompanied by (or perhaps achieved with) great increases in the consumption of energy. Some of the richest countries, such as Norway, the United States, and Canada, consume forty to fifty times as much energy as poorer African or Asian countries for commercial use alone;[27] the average per capita use of commercial and residential energy in any one industrialized country is more than eighty times that in sub-Saharan Africa.[28]

The primary source of energy is the burning of fossil fuels, which poses local, regional, and global environmental threats. Carbon dioxide is emitted into the atmosphere, contributing to global warming, which may shift agricultural production and raise sea levels sufficiently to flood coastal cities within the next fifty years.[29] The burning of fossil fuels generates acid deposits, which can be transported great distances in some regions, and locally, fossil-fuel burning creates dangerous concentrations of particulates and toxic pollutants in the ambient air.

Other sources of energy also pose health and environmental problems. Indoor air pollution from household fuel burning is reported to present the greatest health risk from energy use, especially in developing countries where exposures, on the average, may be twenty times higher than in industrialized countries.[30] Many cities have dangerous levels of lead in the ambient air from the use of leaded gasoline in cars and trucks. It is believed that exposures to lead are causing children's IQs to drop as many as four percentage points in cities such as Bangkok. None of the twenty largest cities in the world meet the World Health Organization's standards for air quality, and as many as 60 percent of the residents of Calcutta suffer from respiratory diseases related to air pollution.[31]

Heavily polluting industries, such as those that produce textiles, leather goods, iron and steel, and chemicals, are moving to developing countries, and hazardous waste generation rates in some of the newly industrializing East Asian countries are beginning to match those of the OECD. During the 1980s, for example, the proportion of factories producing hazardous wastes in Thailand grew from 29 percent to 58 percent.[32] The greatest problem is that most less-developed countries have neither the technical capacity to manage these wastes nor the regulatory institutions to govern their handling and disposal.

Secondary health consequences of technology are not restricted to risks from industrial chemicals. Dams, for example, are constructed to control flooding and to generate electricity, and irrigation allows for agricultural expansion into areas previously uncultivated. These practices also encourage the development of floodplains, and create new areas in which insects and diseases can breed. As a result, dams and expanded irrigation may increase the spread of waterborne illnesses. One author reported, for example, that "prevalence of schistosomiasis in children living in the area around the Akosombo Dam in Ghana jumped from 5 to 10 percent before construction to 90 percent one year after the dam filled."[33]

ECONOMIC CONSEQUENCES

One outstanding trend since the end of World War II has been the increasing interdependence of economies and the globalization of capital and labor in cities around the world. New technologies have been vital to this trend. For example, 90 percent of securities trades now take place electronically, tightly linking international markets. Information management and communications technologies (as well as improved transportation systems) allow production to be decentralized across cities in different nations, although what effect these technologies ultimately will have on the geographic distribution of people and firms is not obvious. One paper reports that

> some authors suggest that the geographical delocalisation of back-office functions or production-related activities through [information and communication technologies] may not result in decentralisation of management and decision functions, therefore intensifying the specialisation of territories by providing good channels for co-ordination between related specialists and between smaller specialised places and the larger, more diversified, cities. Others, on the contrary, underline the distance-shrinking effects of [information and communication technologies] and the possibility of a more even distribution of development and wealth across territories.[34]

Changes in industrial processes and structures may influence the locational decisions of private firms as well as information and communications technologies. The relocation of industries may impose secondary consequences such as encouraging new development on the peripheries of cities, requiring new roadways and other infrastructure to be extended beyond existing boundaries. Further, industrial relocation imposes secondary, adverse effects on workers, in some instances displacing low-skilled workers and forcing them to search for jobs in other locales. Restructuring already has allowed many large corporations to subcontract work previously performed in-house, leaving people to work part-time, on temporary schedules, at lower pay, and with fewer benefits.

The mechanization and automation of production processes also displaces lower-skilled workers in industrialized societies although its not clear how, or how quickly, these workers may be reabsorbed into the economy.[35] By eliminating requirements for specialized, skilled labor, firms can move more freely. Tendencies to relocate may be reinforced by differential labor costs and health and environmental standards, and as a result, opportunities for work sometimes shift geographically, displacing workers or forcing them to follow the movements of employers if they are able. Alternatively, industries recruit migrant workers who accept lower wages with few or no benefits, and who will work for shorter periods of time without further commitments.[36] Like refugees, however, migrant workers often brave harsh living conditions with limited food and water supplies, poor sanitation, and limited or no medical assistance.

Uneven Technological Development

Infant mortality is falling; human life expectancy is increasing; the proportion of the world's adults who can read and write is climbing; the proportion of children starting school is rising; and global food production increases faster than the population grows.

But . . . in terms of absolute numbers there are more hungry people in the world than ever before, and their numbers are increasing. So are the numbers who cannot read or write, the numbers without safe water or safe and sound homes, and the numbers short of woodfuel with which to cook and warm themselves. The gap between the rich and poor nations is widening—not shrinking—and there is little prospect, given present trends and institutional arrangements, that this process will be reversed.[37]

New technologies almost always pose at least some disadvantages, but on balance we generally accept that their secondary consequences are outweighed, in some way, by the benefits they provide. (Otherwise they would not be implemented.) But perhaps the most significant secondary consequence of the introduction of new technologies is their reinforcement of existing social disparities. There is no doubt that we live in an unequal world, with large disparities in health, living conditions, and educational and economic opportunities both between groups of people and between individuals within a group. Although much of this disparity can be described spatially, by socioeconomic status, and by race or ethnicity, the causes of inequality are structural. Extreme poverty in many developing nations, for example, is due in part to uneven development strategies that have shaped power relations for centuries.

The technologies that affect us most directly are those that many of us may take for granted: water supply and wastewater treatment systems; the processes by which stable building materials are produced; cars, buses, and trains; and medical technologies that have lengthened expected lifetimes and improved quality of life for most people in developed portions of the world. But in too many areas within cities across the world these sorts of technologies are not available to most people. Whereas about one-fourth of the world's population in the developed countries consumes three-fourths of the world's primary energy,[38] two billion people remain without electricity and use dung and fuelwood for cooking.[39] And although the worldwide progress in agricultural production during the 1960s and 1970s increased the supplies of calories per person in developing countries by an average of 21 percent, the increase was less than 5 percent in parts of Africa during that same time. Further, eighteen countries in sub-Saharan Africa actually experienced a decline in the 1980s.[40]

DISPARITIES IN HEALTH

Six hundred million people in cities around the world live in overcrowded conditions that lack basic services such as adequate drinking water supplies and sanitation facilities, and basic healthcare.[41] Between 30 and 50 percent of the solid waste in urban areas of developing countries, for example, is not collected.[42] Intestinal parasites are transmitted easily through contaminated water systems and open sewers, and hundreds of millions of people suffer from debilitating intestinal parasitic infections especially in low-income, urban settlements. Between 700 million and 900 million people worldwide have hookworm, causing 1.5 million cases of disease and 50 thousand deaths annually. In a Manila slum 92 percent of surveyed children between the ages of eight months and fifteen years were discovered to have whipworm, 80 percent to have roundworm, and 10 percent to have hookworm; two or more of these species of parasites were found in 84 percent of these children. Studies in Kuala Lumpur, Malaysia, and Allahabad, India, obtained similar results.[43]

In most developing nations, housing averages between 2 and 3.5 people per room, as compared to 0.5 to 1 in developed countries; the range may be as high as 4 or more people per room among poorer people. Households have less than one square meter of interior space per person in many poor urban settlements, and beds often are shared.[44] Such overcrowding, compounded by poor ventilation, encourages the spread of acute respiratory infections, meningitis, and tuberculosis. Although tuberculosis can be treated inexpensively and effectively, it claims about 3 million lives each year, more than any other infectious disease. Only 1.4 percent of these deaths are in developed countries; more than 60 percent are in Asia and at least 20 percent in Africa, although sub-Saharan Africa has the highest proportion of its population infected. Although the cost of immunizing someone against infection is less than $6, eight million people continue to contract tuberculosis annually, half of whom are infectious. Approximately 20 million people worldwide have active tuberculosis in 1995, and when left untreated this disease has a fatality rate of about 50 percent. Another two million deaths annually are attributed to acute bacterial and viral respiratory infections.[45]

Disparities in health exist not only between rich and poor countries, but also within national boundaries between cities and even neighborhoods. Rates of tuberculosis in certain subgroups in the United States (e.g., some migrant farmworkers, the homeless) are comparable to those in developing countries. Infant mortality in the Mississippi Delta is almost two and a half times the national average, and comparable to that of a Latin American nation. Childhood mortality rates often are twice as high, or higher, for children in squatter areas of cities in developing countries than they are elsewhere in the same cities.

These great disparities in health status between nations, cities, and neighborhoods have only been exacerbated by the introduction of sophisticated technologies that primarily benefit the wealthy whereas the very basic healthcare needs of the rest of the world remain unmet. Providing basic healthcare such as immunizations, treatments for diarrhea and acute respiratory infections in children, family planning, and prenatal care has been shown to be easily cost effective.[46] Yet, some 1.6 billion people in developing countries lack access to inexpensive and effective preventative interventions; more than half of the populations of the least-developed countries do not have access to basic health services—medical technologies—at all.[47]

The percentage of children and pregnant women who are immunized has grown considerably but hundreds of millions still are not. Four million children and infants die every year from easily preventable diarrheal diseases associated with contaminated food or water, and hundreds of millions continue to suffer from undernutrition.[48] Every year five hundred thousand women die during childbirth, 99 percent of whom are in developing countries. For comparison, of every one hundred thousand births in Africa, somewhere between two hundred and fifteen hundred women may die, whereas less than ten per one hundred thousand die in most developed countries. Because women in developing countries tend to have more pregnancies, their cumulative lifetime risk of dying in pregnancy and childbirth may be as high as one in twenty. This accounts for 20 to 45 percent of all of the deaths of women between the ages of fifteen and forty-five in poorer countries.[49] Many maternal deaths could be prevented with inexpensive and simple interventions such as providing information on nutrition, family planning, routine care, and backup care for high-risk emergencies, but these measures simply are not available to most.[50]

DISPARITIES IN INDUSTRIAL HAZARDS

As with traditional or conventional health risks, disparities exist in the levels of hazards associated with industrial technologies that are borne by different individuals, and groups of individuals, especially in urban areas. Industrial hazards include both physical and chemical risks; in recent years exposures to the toxic or hazardous substances used in manufacturing and emitted routinely as wastes into the air, water, and land have become of particular popular concern. These chemicals pose significant occupational risks as well as risks to the general public when released into the ambient environment. The imposition of such risks on low-income communities or people of color who also suffer other social disadvantages has become especially significant in the United States, but the same patterns of differential exposure occur throughout the world in both industrialized and industrializing countries. Disparities in industrial hazards are even greater in less-developed societies where fewer safety precautions are imposed through regulation on manufacturing operations reliant on toxic or hazardous chemicals.

During the 1980s, the term "environmental racism" was coined by grassroots organizations to describe situations in which exposures to toxic chemicals fall disproportionately on racial and ethnic minority communities. The high prevalence of hazardous waste facilities and abandoned waste sites in lower income or racial or ethnic minority communities in the United States has been well documented, and it generally is recognized that members of these same subgroups more often live in highly industrialized, and heavily polluted, urban settings.

Charges of environmental racism and, conversely, calls for environmental justice have highlighted important concerns about disproportionate burdens of risks throughout society. Such terms, however, identify ambient environmental contamination as the root problem that needs to be contained, sometimes excluding consideration of other important industrial health hazards such as those experienced inside the workplace. The environmental justice movement in the United States also emphasizes race (and usually ethnicity) over other systemic causes of social injustice. Factors that correlate with race, such as unequal educational and economic opportunities, and lack of social and political power, exacerbate inequitable distributions of all risks. Higher rates of illiteracy and language barriers compound workplace hazards, for example, because employees may not be fully informed of necessary safety precautions.

Disparities in Economic Opportunities

Technology also may reinforce social disparities in the economic opportunities available to workers. In agriculture, disparities between richer and poorer farmers, as well as between men and women, are well recognized. Despite the fact that women grow most of the food in subsistence cultures, for example, they usually do not own or control the land. As a result, women do not benefit from development schemes that encourage the expansion of cash-cropping by offering improved agricultural technologies and seeds, using land as collateral. Similarly, mechanization tends to benefit men, who own land, making work more difficult for women, who do not.[51] Women also may be affected disproportionately in the information sector as there is some evidence that they may be exploited further with home-based teleworking systems that do not provide the same benefits as full-time employment elsewhere. Other industrial process changes such as the automation of office functions threaten jobs in the service sectors where women dominate the workforce.[52]

The "Green Revolution" involved the breeding of new varieties of staple cereals that increased average yields significantly. These new varieties mature quickly, enabling two or three crops each year, and are less sensitive to the duration of daylight so that they can be used more widely. They also produce more grain per plant. The introduction of these new varieties is accompanied by expensive inputs such as inorganic fertilizers, pesticides, and farm machinery (since multiple-cropping requires quick harvesting and replanting), so the application of this technology requires capital and credit. As a result, wealthier landowners were most likely to adopt these new techniques first since they had the capital to do so and could afford to take the associated risks. Poorer farmers were not able to reap the benefits of these technological developments until later, if at all.

The information revolution presents great potential for increasing social disparities, especially in cities and high-tech urban enterprises. In the United States, the National Information Infrastructure links individuals through computers and phones or coaxial cables to vast networks of information. Although this system promises to broaden the resources available to everyone, most investment to date has been in cities and wealthier communities that can afford both computers and the infrastructure to hook into on-line networks. According to one critic,

> The information superhighway . . . threatens to completely bypass whole communities that cannot afford the service, the hardware, the training or the time to invest in it. The result will be a kind of electronic redlining, leaving low-income communities and minorities behind. . . . Just as the Kerner Commission reported on race relations in the mid-1960s, we are standing on the threshold of two technologically separate societies. One will be driven by

increased utilization of computer networks, the other shaped by lack of access, with a further increase in unemployment and dead-end service jobs. The "best and the brightest" will be skimmed off as an information elite."[53]

The possibility of greater disparity due to differential access to information technologies has become a significant enough concern that the U.S. Congress is discussing how to guarantee equal access to the information superhighway. Representative Edward Markey, the ranking minority member of the House subcommittee on telecommunications, refers to unequal access as "information apartheid."[54] Analogous disparities also are possible between private firms. Clearly, larger and more sophisticated firms are able to take greater advantage of new information and communications technologies by linking up with national and international networks; meanwhile, others are left behind.

But perhaps of even greater concern is the possibility that future manufacturing jobs may be lost entirely. As noted, technology displaces workers in the countryside, encouraging them to move into cities, and industrial restructuring and relocation displaces lower-skilled, often urban, workers. Some fear that the application of new technologies may increase productivity so dramatically that "far fewer people will need to be employed in manufacturing industry to satisfy the demands of our home and export markets."[55] A similar effect on labor was experienced in agriculture in the United States during the first half of the twentieth century when the workforce was reduced from half of the population to approximately 3 percent as a result of the mechanization of farming.[56]

The loss of large numbers of manufacturing jobs would be disastrous, especially for cities in developing countries where under- or unemployment is widespread and the need for employment is growing. It has been estimated that by the year 2000, three hundred sixty million additional jobs will be needed to employ a potential workforce of over two billion people in the developing world.[57] Yet, the key to private firms' economic success is to rely upon sophisticated hardware and just a few highly educated workers with information-management and organizational skills.[58]

BUILDING TECHNOLOGICAL CAPACITY

The economic and social development of cities depends on building technological capacity, that is, integrating infrastructure, industrial, and other technologies into their economies. Large gaps exist between the technological capabilities of developing and developed countries, especially in the areas of particular concern for sustainable development: biotechnology, new energy sources, new materials, pollution controls, and "clean" industrial technologies.[59] These gaps can be narrowed through activities such as the international trade of equipment; the provision of expertise to less-developed countries; and collaborative research focused on problems faced by developing countries.

Because less-developed areas rely on more advanced regions for technological developments, building capacity must be achieved through the transfer of new and existing technologies. Such transfers must be appropriate; technology must be adapted to meet local needs, to fit local conditions, and to be sensitive to local cultures. Technology that may be appropriate to introduce in one place, for example, may be more complex and expensive than is needed in another. The principal barrier to technology transfer, however, is the expense of commercially developed technologies. Only 6 percent of the world's patents were held by developing countries in 1980, and most of those had been granted to nonresidents. In 1980, developing countries paid industrial countries almost $2 billion in royalties, fees, and licenses, about the amount they spent on their own research and development.[60]

In many instances, government policies regarding the adoption, use, and maintenance of transferred technologies may need to be established. Most developing countries, for example, may need to strengthen their regulations for protecting worker and public health, the environment, and natural resources. As Robert Kates, a renowned scholar in the fields of risk and hazard assessment, warned,

> New products will bring new hazards. Old products and processes in new locales will bring new hazard problems. The rapid restructuring of world industrial production will reduce the hazards in places that have learned to cope with them and move hazards to places where the knowledge and resources for control are not available.[61]

Developing countries, with only 12 percent of the world's scientists and engineers, generally do not have the technical capacity to assess and implement new technologies without the assistance of industrialized nations.[62] International institutions such as the United Nations Environment Programme, the World Health Organization, and the World Bank, however, may be sources of technical assistance for assessing and managing the risks associated with the transfer of new technologies to developing countries.

Technological Choices for a Sustainable Future

Recognition of the harmful aspects of technology can be attributed to some degree both to improved detection methods and to greater awareness of how chemical contaminants, changes in land use, degradation of natural systems, and other alterations to the natural landscape may affect human and ecological life. In 1970 we were concerned with acute and visible hazards such as smokestacks and raw sewage in surface waters. In the 1990s the hazards are markedly different, both temporally and spatially; we are concerned with chronic and complex health effects such as cancer and developmental disorders in children, and our focus has shifted from local problems to regional and even global effects. Many technologies developed since the 1940s are far more powerful than ever before and have the potential to impose disastrous effects that could affect larger regions, or even the entire planet, for great lengths of time.

New technology is essential for continued development throughout the world, and for mitigating existing environmental damage. Specific choices about its development and use, however, must be made responsibly. The complexities and uncertainties associated with the hazards of new technology challenge even the most advanced societies on Earth. In contrast to the technological optimists of the early 1970s, the World Commission on Environment and Development (better known as the Brundtland Commission) stated in 1987 with regard to the environmental consequences of technology that

> The rate of change is outstripping the ability of scientific disciplines and our current capabilities to assess and advise. It is frustrating the attempts of political and economic institutions, which evolved in a different, more fragmented world, to adapt and cope.[63]

The challenge that we face in shaping our future is not to discover still newer technologies to address all of our social problems. Rather, we must work toward developing new institutions that can capture the benefits of technology "wisely and humanely" in accordance with Thomas Jefferson's vision. Clear goals for technological development must be defined, and decisions regarding technology and its applications must be integrated with other public policies for urban and economic development, labor and immigration, health, and the environment. Further, we must better anticipate the adverse consequences of new technologies prior to their introduction, and should evaluate the distributions of the costs and benefits of new technologies within cities, across nations, and even around the world.

APPROPRIATE GOALS FOR TECHNOLOGICAL DEVELOPMENT

The Carnegie Commission on Science, Technology, and Government stated that "[t]echnological goals are usually linked to well-articulated social purposes."[64] In industrialized countries with explicit technology policies, these goals usually include national security; public health and human development; jobs and economic growth; and environmental quality. Development assistance from industrialized nations for technologies to enhance public health, environmental quality, and economic opportunities in cities would encourage their transfer to other parts of the world, but these concerns must be given higher priority relative to other goals, particularly national defense. Former President Jimmy Carter described the disparity between spending for development technologies and that for weapons in this way:

> In 1990, $880 billion was spent worldwide on weapons and preparations for war, fifteen times the total of all non-private development assistance. Military purchases by the poorest nations have quintupled in the past three decades, so that they are now almost triple humanitarian aid received. Amazingly, only 7 percent of bilateral assistance and less than 10 percent of multilateral aid is for education, health, clean water, shelter, sanitation, family planning, and nutrition.[65]

National investment in research and development also generally is not aimed toward decreasing social disparities. Instead, many of the richer countries invest in expensive, complex (high-end) technologies that will benefit few. The United States, for example, spends billions of dollars on research for constructing extremely high-end technologies: a space station; the information superhighway; advanced surface transportation projects such as "intelligent vehicle/highway systems" to better manage traffic, and magnetic levitation (MagLev) in which vehicles would glide above the ground at speeds of 250 to 300 miles per hour; and, as a means to assist American companies in capturing Pacific Rim markets, high-speed aircraft to carry three hundred passengers from California to Japan in four hours, or to Australia in seven.[66]

Yet, as we invest billions of dollars to build a space station, to put computers into every village in every nation across the world, and to develop futuristic transportation systems, we virtually ignore the sorts of technologies that touch the everyday lives of people—clean water supplies, sanitation systems, and medical care, for example. By focusing on space stations, computers, and MagLev, we buy into a sort of "trickle-down" development and redevelopment philosophy. This philosophy is grounded in the assumption that if we boost national economies and increase our surpluses of goods, the benefits of economic growth will trickle down to all, raising the standard of living of even the poorest of the poor.[67]

The problem with such a trickle-down philosophy is that is has not worked sufficiently, at least if we care about the billions of people who still do not benefit from most modern technologies. To those who may claim that social equity is not a legitimate goal and that we are not responsible for those left behind by new technologies, one can respond in two ways. First, there is the moral argument that we are indeed our brother's keepers; second, there is the self-serving argument that the problems of poverty, ill health, and environmental decline in inner cities throughout both the developed and the developing worlds do in fact affect us all. (Both of these arguments have been explored in depth elsewhere.) For neoclassical economists and technologists who believe that the trickle-down philosophy simply must be given more time to work, one can respond only by stating that we have waited long enough. There has been and continues to be sufficient human suffering to warrant a realignment of our technological priorities.

These issues must be raised in international discussions, which tend instead to address primarily the high-end technologies that dominate the news. Responsible national technology policies should not be based on the trickle-down assumption, but rather ought to have as their goal equalizing the costs and benefits of technological development. Such policies would emphasize investments not in high-end technologies such as space stations, computers, and MagLev, but would focus instead on the construction of low-end technologies that comprise the basic infrastructure of cities and directly raise the standard of living for all people. This proposal can be summed up in a question:

> I would ask you to remember something that a former prime minister of a developing country once said: "Of what use is putting the first man on the moon if we cannot reach the last man on earth?"[68]

APPROPRIATE CHOICES IN THE APPLICATION OF TECHNOLOGY

Arguing for the implementation of appropriate technologies in underdeveloped urban areas and selecting the most effective applications of technology are two very different challenges. Defining appropriate technology depends on local needs and local social, environmental, and economic circumstances. In general, therefore, there are not any technologies that can be deemed "best" for all situations. Rather, different technologies fill different niches and must be evaluated on a case-by-case basis. This is not to say, however, that general guidelines for sustainable technological choices cannot be defined.

Michael Cohen has raised questions about environmental thresholds for cities—points beyond which harm cannot be reversed. These questions include: Are there environmental thresholds for cities, and can we identify them before crossing them? How should we take thresholds into account in managing our cities? And "Do we decide, for example, that the loss of four points of IQ in school children is sufficiently serious that some of the economic costs of moving to unleaded fuels in big cities should be absorbed by the transport system?"[69] Clearly there are no simple answers here, but alternative viewpoints in the debates about health and environmental risk assessment and defining "acceptable" levels of risk provide some insight into approaching these questions. These are debates about decision-making under uncertainty, about appropriate levels of risk-aversion in public decisions, and about the values we place on intangible benefits such as clean air and protecting the IQs of children.

One general guideline for sustainable technological choices is that we ought to avoid these questions whenever possible by adopting an ethic of pollution prevention in all decisions. Instead of becoming trapped in endless debates over the magnitude of risk associated with leaded gas, we ought to first consider alternative means to the same ends that avoid weighing the trade-off of more lead in the air versus the cost of switching to methods of transportation that do not rely on leaded gasoline. These alternatives include more than simply shifting to other types of fuels or vehicles; they include options that might reduce the need to move people or goods from one location to another at all. Telecommuting, for example, reduces some need for driving, and urban agriculture bypasses the need to deliver produce from the countryside. Energy generation and use provide excellent examples of how behavioral changes and simple techniques for increasing efficiency can enable us to avoid the choice between solar, coal, or nuclear sources. Although these examples are "low-hanging fruits" and nonpolluting alternatives may not always be available, it is imperative that we evaluate potential technologies that might at least soften the trade-offs we face.

An extension of this pollution prevention philosophy is that we must strive toward zero-risk goals in the selection of new technologies, even if we do not truly believe they are attainable at present. Technological breakthroughs provide new alternatives all the time, redefining what is attainable and feasible. Technology-forcing regulations in the

United States, for example, have stimulated technological innovations in areas such as air-quality control, achieving lower levels of air-pollutant emissions than were previously feasible. (Technology-forcing regulations are those that set performance requirements beyond what standard, existing technologies can meet.)

Further, as new technologies are developed, the costs of some alternatives decrease. Greater knowledge also may affect estimates of costs and benefits, making health, safety, and environmental protection more cost-effective. Cost-benefit analyses of banning leaded gasoline in the United States that were performed during the 1970s, for example, concluded that such a regulatory action could not be justified. Looking back, however, we find that the benefits have far outweighed the costs. The benefits of removing lead from urban air are far greater than anticipated earlier, due in part to a better understanding of the severity of health effects that has evolved between 1980 and 1985. We also discovered that the cost of shifting to unleaded gasoline was lower than first estimated. Similarly, major U.S. automobile manufacturers argued that forcing them to install seat belts in all new cars would put them out of business. This, of course, never happened after seat belt requirements were imposed.

Another general guideline for assessing technological choices is that the entire lifecycles of technologies—products and processes—should be evaluated. This is especially important in choices between complex technologies, the impacts of which may not be readily apparent. Comparisons of electric vehicles (EVs) often are made to conventional, gasoline-powered cars, for example, simply on the basis of their operating costs. In particular, tailpipe emissions and the air pollution from the generation of electricity have been compared repeatedly for the two types of vehicles. But only recently has attention been paid to other components of the EV lifecycle, especially the large numbers of lead-acid batteries that will be generated as wastes if EVs are commercialized in the near future.[70]

The energy crises of the 1970s spurred manufacturing industries to increase production efficiencies, reinforcing a trend since the beginning of the twentieth century toward "dematerialization"—minimizing volumes of materials in finished products. Lighter and stronger synthetic materials are replacing metals in numerous applications, and certain products, such as electronics, have been miniaturized with the advent of new technologies. Since the 1970s, the average weight of an automobile has decreased by almost four hundred kilograms; vacuum tubes have been replaced by silicon chips; and fiberoptics are being substituted for copper wires for communications.[71]

A life cycle perspective on some of these new technologies suggests, however, that dematerialization may not necessarily constitute an environmentally beneficial technological choice in many cases. Observed decreases in the quantities of pesticides used in the United States, for example, may be attributed to the fact that many are far more toxic today. In addition, the manufacture of lighter, smaller goods also does not guarantee that they are of equal quality, and products such as toasters, televisions, and shoes may simply be discarded earlier rather than repaired. This could, on balance, require the manufacture of more of these products and actually generate more waste in both the production and consumption phases of their life cycles.[72]

EVALUATING DISTRIBUTION OF RISK

A very general model called the "risk transition"[73] provides a point of departure for exploring how we might assess the distributional consequences of technological choices more systematically. The risk transition describes the trade-off between "modern" and "traditional" health risks as societies develop: traditional risks (e.g., infectious diseases) fall, and modern risks (i.e., those associated with technology) rise. The risk transition is simply a broadening of the epidemiological transition discussed in the public-health literature, which "is the shift in the main causes of death—from infectious diseases to degenerative cardiovascular diseases and cancers . . ."[74] that are more prevalent in industrialized countries. The risk transition extends this concept to other sorts of diseases and hazards.

One troubling feature of the risk transition is that it presupposes that the traditional and modern risk curves cross; in other words, that modern risks always will replace traditional ones. This premise implies that there is only one development pathway available, or that all new technologies inevitably will present similar trade-offs. We need not always settle for new technologies that incur risks of their own, however, and there are numerous examples of traditional risks that have been mitigated or even eradicated without substitution by new risks. "Win-win" situations like this are the provision of prenatal care; improved health-care access in rural areas; the construction of basic infrastructure for wastewater treatment and clean drinking water; and the discovery of vaccines for diseases ranging from polio to river-blindness. Clearly, in these cases the modern health risks associated with these technologies never exceed the traditional risks they replace. The opposite occurs when we consider technologies that have essentially no social worth. It can be argued that the manufacture and consumption of plastic swizzle sticks, food coloring, and lawn pesticides, for example, impose modern risks but do not in any way displace traditional risks.

The risk transition raises the important issue of how we might incorporate considerations of equity into technological choices. The model assumes that total risks (traditional plus modern) will decrease, or that new technologies always provide net positive gains. This is consistent with observations of average statistics in developing countries; average life expectancies and health status generally do rise with development. But clearly, aggregate statistics mask disparities between subpopulations within societies, and the use of only aggregated statistics can be used to justify strategies that lead to uneven development. Once again, these are trickle-down strategies, intended to benefit the underclass eventually by improving the lot of the majority. It is yet to be revealed, however, whether the disparities in health and other risks will eventually narrow over time. In the United States, for example, infant mortality rates and other health risks have decreased for all groups but the disparities between groups remain.

Disaggregating statistics and illustrating social disparities in risks could provide new ways to conceptualize trade-offs between competing technologies. Accordingly, the risk transition should be redrawn with multiple curves for both traditional and modern risks that represent the different levels of risks experienced by various subgroups (rather than one aggregate curve for traditional risks and one for modern risks). The actual shapes of these curves depend on the measures of risks used, but in any case disparities remain between those who benefit most from new technologies that reduce traditional risks (and are affected least by the modern risks they impose) and those for whom traditional risks are reduced less but who bear disproportionate increases in modern risks. Squatters who lived downwind of the chemical plant in Bhopal, migrant farmworkers who are exposed to large doses of toxic pesticides, and the impoverished residents of Cancer Alley in Louisiana and the border communities around the *maquiladoras* in Mexico all are examples of people who benefit minimally from the modernization that new technologies provide, yet suffer the most from the industrial hazards they create.

Decisions about alternatives to gasoline-powered automobiles constitute one current example of how this modified risk-transition model might be used to frame technological choices and to highlight an alternative, pollution-prevention approach. California has mandated that in the near future a certain percentage of cars sold in the state by major manufacturers must be zero-emission vehicles, and at this time only EVs meet this requirement. The introduction of large numbers of EVs will incur risks, particularly from the use and disposal of large numbers of lead-acid batteries that are expected to be generated. (Other fuel cells do not yet appear to be feasible on a commercial scale.) The rationale for forging ahead with EVs, especially in Los Angeles, is that the reductions in smog regionwide are believed to far outweigh any risks from recycling or disposing of these batteries.

If one lives in any of the inland areas of Los Angeles where smog levels often are high but where there is little or no manufacturing, one will benefit most from reducing the "traditional" risks of smog and bear few or none of the "modern" risks associated with the EV substitution. But those who live in southeast Los Angeles, where both of the only two secondary lead smelters west of Texas operate, will bear the brunt of the new lead risks associated with EVs. Therefore, whether one's total risks decrease, increase, or remain constant depends upon where one lives. Calculating the net risks for all of Los Angeles depends on how we measure and weigh very different types of risks: chronic exposures to smog throughout the region against high local concentrations of lead.

In the near term, however, other alternatives can be envisioned that are perhaps far preferable to either continuing our reliance on gasoline-powered cars or shifting to EVs. Ride-sharing and mass-transit, for example, both would reduce vehicle emissions and neither would incur the risks of EVs. Electric buses use fewer batteries per person-mile, and therefore could provide even greater net risk reductions for everyone. And finally, bicycles, land-use controls that reduce the need to drive, and electronic commuting would present no air pollution risks at all.

The lessons of this sort of assessment are twofold. First, it is imperative that we avoid framing technological choices as simple dichotomies, and instead remain open to evaluating other alternatives. Second, technological development must not overlook the simplest solutions to the problems we face in managing our cities. Often the best solution to these challenges involves low-end technologies implemented locally.

The Governance of Technology

This chapter began by describing the promise and the power of technology and how it has shaped and reshaped urban life throughout history. The primary challenges we face in the 1990s, however, are not technological, but social and political. Albert Einstein stated that nuclear power had changed everything "except our way of thinking."[75] Nuclear power and other technological achievements also have not changed our approaches to, and institutions for, managing their social dimensions.

Our most urgent need is to remedy the huge disparities that exist both between cities and between sections of cities by dispersing the benefits of existing technologies to the billions of people who do not yet enjoy the many advantages of modern life. This will require constructing institutions to manage technologies safely, effectively, and equitably. At all levels of governance, policies must be established to guarantee that the secondary consequences of technology and their distributions are anticipated and weighed into development decisions. Strong national policies are needed throughout the world to promote research, development, and deployment of technologies that will improve urban life. And as mentioned previously, international organizations must be called upon to assist less-developed countries in evaluating and managing the adoption of new technologies.

To enable such policies to be effective, people in the more advanced parts of the world must acknowledge equity as a primary social goal, and be willing to reconsider both their consumption patterns and whether alternative technologies could meet their needs satisfactorily. Those optimistic about human nature might depend on more comprehensive analyses and better information about the full impacts of technological choices to modify consumptive behavior. Pessimists can turn to government to intervene with additional regulations and incentives for change. People in less-developed portions of cities also must mobilize to identify their needs and to demand the technologies they need to obtain a decent standard of living. Ultimately, it is urban residents in both developed and underdeveloped portions of cities who are the "true city-builders." These are the people whose futures are held in the balance, and it is they who provide the promise and the power to meet the social and political challenges ahead.

Notes

[1] Victor Ferkiss, *Nature, Technology, and Society* (New York: New York University Press, 1993), 32–34.

[2] Hugo A. Meier, "Thomas Jefferson and a Democratic Technology," in *Technology in America: A History of Individuals and Ideas*, ed. Carroll W. Pursell (Cambridge, Mass.: MIT Press, 1981), 33.

[3] Donella H. Meadows et al., *The Limits to Growth* (New York: Universe Books, 1972), 130.

[4] Ibid.

[5] President William J. Clinton and Vice President Albert Gore, Jr., preamble to *Science in the National Interest* (Washington, D.C.: Executive Office of the President, Office of Science and Technology Policy, August 1994).

[6]Robert Malpas, "Technology and Wealth Creation," *The Bridge* 24, no. 1 (spring 1994): 12.

[7]Ibid.

[8]·Albert A. Grant and Andrew C. Lemer, eds., *In Our Own Backyards: Principles for Effective Improvement of the Nation's Infrastructure* (Washington, D.C.: National Academy Press, 1993), 24–25.

[9]World Health Organization, *Our Planet, Our Health: Report of the World Health Commission on Health and Environment* (Geneva: World Health Organization, 1992), 147–48.

[10]Nick Robbins and Alex Trisoglio, "Restructuring Industry for Sustainable Development," in *Making Development Sustainable*, ed. Johan Holmberg (Washington, D.C.: Island Press, 1992), 161–62.

[11]Bjorn Wellenius et al., *Telecommunications: World Bank Experience and Strategy*, World Bank discussion paper 192 (Washington, D.C.: World Bank, 1993); and Bjorn Wellenius, Arnold Miller, and Carl J. Dahlman, eds., *Developing the Electronics Industry* (Washington, D.C.: World Bank, 1993).

[12]Robert Gottlieb, ed., *Reducing Toxics: A New Approach to Policy and Industrial Decisionmaking* (Washington, D.C.: Island Press, 1995).

[13]Jules Pretty et al., "Regenerating Agriculture: The Agroecology of Low-External Input and Community-Based Development," in *Making Development Sustainable*, 92.

[14]Meadows et al., *Limits to Growth*, 146.

[15]Viscount Caldecote, "Technology, Master or Servant?" in *Man and Technology: The Social and Cultural Challenge of Modern Technology*, ed. Bruce M. Adkins (Cambridge, U.K.: Cambridge Information and Research Services Limited, 1983), 12.

[16]Marcia D. Lowe, *Shaping Cities: The Environmental and Human Dimensions*, Worldwatch paper 105 (Washington, D.C.: Worldwatch Institute, October 1991), 45; and Ismail Serageldin and Michael A. Cohen, eds., *The Human Face of the Urban Environment: A Report to the Development Community*, Environmentally Sustainable Development Proceedings Series 5 (Washington, D.C.: World Bank, 1995), 21.

[17]Alvin Toffler, *The Third Wave* (New York: Morrow, 1980), 210–13.

[18]U.S. Department of Transportation, *Transportation Implications of Telecommuting* (Washington, D.C., 1993).

[19]Mark E. Hepworth, "Planning for the Information City: The Challenge and Response," *Urban Studies* 27, no. 4 (1990): 537–58.

[20]Bjorn Wellenius et al., *Telecommunications*, 1; and Robert Herman, Siamak A. Ardekani, and Jesse H. Ausubel, "Dematerialization," in *Technology and the Environment*, ed. Jesse H. Ausubel and Hedy E. Sladovich (Washington, D.C.: National Academy Press, 1989), 62.

[21]Office of Science and Technology Policy, *Technology for Economic Growth: President's Progress Report* (Washington, D.C.: Executive Office of the President, November 1993).

[22]OECD Territorial Development Service, Group on Urban Affairs, "Information and Communication Technologies and Territorial Development" (project proposal, available from the U.S. Department of Housing and Urban Development, Washington, D.C., March 1995).

[23]Ferkiss, *Nature, Technology, and Society*, 47.

[24]See, for example, Ricard E. Sclove, "The Nuts and Bolts of Democracy: Democratic

Theory and Technological Design," in *Democracy in a Technological Society*, ed. Langdon Winner (Boston, Mass.: Kluwer Academic Publishers, 1992), 139–57.

[25]Kurt Vonnegut Jr., *Player Piano* (New York: Dell, 1952), 1.

[26]Ibid., 18.

[27]World Health Organization, *Our Planet*, 146.

[28]World Commission on Environment and Development, *Our Common Future* (Oxford, U.K.: Oxford University Press, 1987), 169.

[29]Ibid.; and National Commission on the Environment, *Choosing a Sustainable Future* (Washington, D.C.: Island Press, 1993), 11–12.

[30]Gregory Kats, "Achieving Sustainability in Energy Use in Developing Countries," in *Making Development Sustainable*, 261–62.

[31]Serageldin and Cohen, eds., *The Human Face*, 1; and National Commission on the Environment, *Choosing a Sustainable Future*.

[32]Robbins and Trisoglio, "Restructuring Industry," 161–62.

[33]Kats, "Achieving Sustainability," 262.

[34]OECD Territorial Development Service, "Information and Communication Technologies," 2.

[35]Adkins, ed., *Man and Technology*, 24.

[36]Hal Kane, *The Hour of Departure: Forces that Create Refugees and Migrants*, Worldwatch paper no. 125 (Washington, D.C.: Worldwatch Institute, June 1995), 35.

[37]World Commission, *Our Common Future*, 2.

[38]Ibid., 169.

[39]World Bank (Environment Department), *Making Development Sustainable* (Washington, D.C.: World Bank, 1994), 117.

[40]World Health Organization, *Our Planet*, 61.

[41]Ibid., 198.

[42]Ibid., xxvi.

[43]Ibid., 205.

[44]Ibid., 202.

[45]Ibid., 202–3.

[46]Helen Saxenian, "Optimizing Health Care in Developing Countries," *Issues in Science and Technology* 11, no. 2 (winter 1994–95): 42–48.

[47]World Health Organization, *Our Planet*, xxvi.

[48]Ibid., 1.

[49]Jodi L. Jacobson, "Improving Women's Reproductive Health," in *State of the World: 1992*, ed. Lester R. Brown et al. (New York: Norton, 1992), 85.

[50]World Health Organization, *Our Planet*, 43.

[51]Jodi L. Jacobson, "Closing the Gender Gap in Development," in *State of the World: 1993*, ed. Lester R. Brown et al (New York: Norton, 1993).

[52]Adkins, ed., *Man and Technology*, 24.

[53]Tom Soto, "Redlining the Information Superhighway," *Los Angeles Times*, 18 April 1995, p. B7.

[54]Suneel Ratan, "A New Divide Between Haves and Have-Nots?" *Time* 145, no. 12, (spring 1995): 26.

[55]Caldecote, "Technology, Master or Servant?" 13.

[56]Willard Cochran, *The Development of American Agriculture: A Historical Analysis* (Minneapolis: University of Minnesota Press, 1979).

[57]Kane, *Hour of Departure*, 36.

[58]Robbins and Trisoglio, "Restructuring Industry," 163.

[59]World Commission, *Our Common Future*, 87.

[60]Ibid., 87–88.

[61]Robert W. Kates, "Managing Technological Hazards: Success, Strain, and Surprise," in National Academy of Engineering, *Hazards: Technology and Fairness* (Washington, D.C.: National Academy Press, 1986), 217.

[62]Adkins, ed., *Man and Technology*, 20.

[63]World Commission, *Our Common Future*, 22.

[64]Carnegie Commission on Science, Technology, and Government, *Enabling the Future: Linking Science and Technology to Societal Goals* (New York: Carnegie Commission on Science, Technology, and Government, 1992), 28.

[65]Jimmy Carter, "Global Development: Cooperation for Development Can Prevent Somalias," in Carnegie Commission on Science, Technology, and Government, *Science, Technology, and Government for a Changing World* (New York: Carnegie Commission on Science, Technology, and Government, 1993), 33–34.

[66]Office of Science and Technology Policy, *Technology for Economic Growth*.

[67]See, for example, Pursell, *Technology in America*, 1.

[68]Moeen Qureshi, "Technology in a Developing World," in *Man and Technology*, 26.

[69]Serageldin and Cohen, eds., *The Human Face*, 35.

[70]J. A. Roqué, "Electric Vehicle Manufacturing in Southern California: Local versus Regional Environmental Hazards," *Environment and Planning A* 27 (1995): 907–32.

[71]Robbins and Trisoglio, in *Making Development Sustainable*, ed. Holmberg, 161–62; and National Commission on the Environment, *Choosing a Sustainable Future*, 12.

[72]Herman, Ardekani, and Ausubel in *Technology and the Environment*.

[73]Kirk R. Smith, "The Risk Transition," *International Environmental Affairs* 2, no. 3 (summer 1990): 227–51.

[74]R. G. Wilkinson, "The Epidemiological Transition: From Material Scarcity to Social Disadvantage?" *Daedalus* (1994): 65.

[75]Adkins, ed., *Man and Technology*, vii.

Chapter 10

The Changing Agenda for Urban Health

Edmundo Werna, Ilona Blue, and
Trudy Harpham

Urbanization has long been recognized as one of the most important social changes to take place at a global level. This is particularly true in developing countries where the pace and extent of urbanization is considerable. In addition to social scientists, public-health professionals are increasingly interested in urbanization because of the specific health problems it generates and because of the specific characteristics of urban populations and the need to tailor responses accordingly.[1]

The varying patterns of economic growth in developing countries have had serious consequences on the results of urbanization: "Accompanying the explosive growth of large cities has been a plethora of problems of seemingly unmanageable proportions. These include, among others, high rates of unemployment and underemployment as urban labor markets are unable to absorb the expanding number of job seekers, soaring urban poverty, insufficient shelter, inadequate sanitation, inadequate or contaminated water supplies, serious air pollution and other forms of environmental degradation, congested streets, overloaded public transport systems, and municipal budget crisis."[2]

In their book on community health and the urban poor Trudy Harpham, Tim Lusty, and Patrick Vaughan state that "[e]stimates are that, at present, an average of 50 percent of the urban population live at the level of extreme poverty, with this figure rising as high as 79 percent in some cities."[3] As awareness of the extent and consequences of urban poverty in developing countries has grown, various case studies have analyzed particular aspects of the urban environment, sometimes explicitly involving health, in various cities.[4] It was not until the late 1980s, however, that urban health exploded as a field of study.

Although urbanization has received considerable attention during past decades, urban health has not enjoyed such focus until more recently. This is mainly because the WHO-UNICEF Alma Ata conference in 1978 emphasized the need for primary healthcare in rural areas due to a commonly held belief that urban areas were better served with health services than rural areas. Using average figures for urban areas as a whole this may well appear to be the case, but Alessandro Rossi-

Espagnet's work at WHO followed by the work of Harpham, Lusty, and Vaughan made it clear that the plight of the urban poor was as bad and frequently worse than that of their rural counterparts:[5] "The urban poor are at the interface between underdevelopment and industrialization and their disease patterns reflect the problems of both. From the first they carry a heavy burden of infectious diseases and malnutrition, while from the second they suffer the typical spectrum of chronic and social diseases."[6]

Focusing on the urban poor is important not only on humanitarian grounds, but also on economic ones because of the significant role played by the urban informal sector in the overall productivity of a city. The importance of the urban informal sector in fostering development has been widely recognized.[7] A vast literature on its advantages in production has built up since the early 1970s. It notes issues such as high flexibility of production (leading to greater responsiveness to demand and greater ability to fill niches in the market), low prices of products (leading to expansion of demand), and resilience (ensuring survival despite adverse economic and political conditions). The urban informal sector has been responsible for a large share of production in different sectors of the economy. It has also been a major source of employment and income generation. For example, the share of the labor force engaged in this sector in developing countries ranges from 20 percent to 70 percent according to the country, averaging 50 percent or more.

In addition to its general role in the economy, the urban informal sector has been particularly active in alleviating urban poverty. From the production/income side, the sector brings advantages to the poor and less-skilled producers: ease of entry, less or no need for paperwork (regarding both employees and the firm as a whole), less or no need for formal training, and less or no need for initial capital. From the consumption side, many goods supplied by informal producers would otherwise not be accessible to the poor (whether due to the lack of interest of large-scale firms in catering to this part of society, or higher prices of their products).

Recognition of the importance of the urban informal sector has generated a vast array of policy recommendations to support it. For instance, the World Bank, in its urban agenda for the 1990s, places a major emphasis on increasing the productivity of informal producers.[8] However, informal sector workers are particularly vulnerable to health problems, which may undermine, not increase, their productivity. They do not have funds to pay for comprehensive treatments in the private sector, lack the stable income needed to pay fixed monthly insurance premiums, or do not have a regulated job that gives them access to public or company assistance. Many of them may also work in hazardous activities where they generally do not use proper equipment or protection. In sum, the concomitant importance and plight of the informal sector has reinforced the emphasis on urban health.

This chapter highlights the importance of urban health inequalities within cities and their relationship to poverty. Although this relationship is frequently considered axiomatic, many international organizations, despite apparently recognizing the influence of poverty on health, do not take this finding to the level of policy formulation and action: "Policy on urban poverty and health [has been led] on a path towards narrow, ameliorative and non-structural solutions."[9] The chapter then takes the opportunity to examine two particular problems of significant importance to low-income urban populations that are neglected by current health and urban development policy: mental health and violence. Although mental ill-health and violence are strikingly different problems, neither can be adequately tackled by the health sector alone. For this reason, the final section of the chapter focuses on an integrated approach to urban health.

Although additional trends such as the privatization of the health sector and the impact of globalization on health (e.g., AIDS) are clearly of significance, it is beyond the scope of this chapter to address all of these issues. In relation to the role of the private sector and the financing of urban healthcare, a review by Margaret Thomas and Barbara McPake eloquently covers the main issues.[10] The focus of this chapter is on developing countries where the process of urbanization has led to a particular set of problems not wholly comparable to the developed world.

Urban Health Inequalities—The Growing Evidence

If poverty is the focal point in the relationship between an urban setting and health it will be important to explore this matter extensively. Peter Townsend's explanation of poverty reflects considerable insight: "People are relatively deprived if they cannot obtain, at all or sufficiently, the conditions of life—that is, the diets, amenities, standards and services—which allow them to play roles, participate in the relationships and follow the customary behavior which is expected of them by virtue of their membership of society. If they lack or are denied resources to obtain access to these conditions of life and so fulfill membership of society they may be said to be in poverty."[11]

Townsend's work on poverty, by using a phrase such as "fulfill membership of society," stresses the significance of relative inequalities. How people relate to the circumstances in which they find themselves is as important as acquiring the basic goods and facilities for quality of life to be maintained. Despite the fact that absolute poverty is bound to have some effect on health, relative poverty is a more flexible concept and allows for the fact that needs are socially determined and change over time.[12] Richard Wilkinson has taken Townsend's work on board and has attempted to make the link between inequalities in wealth and inequalities in health.[13]

Wilkinson emphasizes the research carried out in various parts of the world suggesting that it is the countries with the narrowest gap between rich and poor that enjoy the best national health, not those that spend the most money in absolute terms per capita.[14] It is the most egalitarian societies that have lower national mortality rates and Wilkinson argues that it is relative social status that is of importance in influencing health outcomes. He has put forward a thesis that the connection between low income and poor health outcomes revolves around psychosocial factors, namely cognitive comparison. The evidence to support this suggestion is that inequalities have remained even as the health events occurring unevenly across population groups of different socioeconomic status have altered (e.g., from communicable to noncommunicable diseases). Although much of Wilkinson's work refers to developed-country settings, this last point can be illustrated with data from São Paulo, Brazil, and Accra, Ghana, linking the socioeconomic and environmental aspects of cities with health differentials.[15] A study by Carolyn Stephens, Ian Timaeus, Marco Akerman, and colleagues mapped mortality differentials across these two cities, quantifying and making explicit the variance between the high- and low-income groups that had been suggested by previous work.[16] The study was carried out under the premise that knowledge of intra-urban differentials is essential for the equitable distribution of resources within a city.

Stephens, Timaeus, Akerman, and colleagues demonstrated that people living in the poorer areas of both Accra and São Paulo suffered disproportionately from both the "old" (infectious and parasitic) and the "new" (chronic and degenerative) diseases.[17] "In Accra in 1991, up to 67 percent of deaths in the adult population of the less privileged areas might have been avoided if the mortality rates of residents of the best areas had prevailed in the worst three zones."[18] In the case of São Paulo (again using data for 1991), respiratory and infectious mortality in the birth through four-year-old age group was four times greater in poor areas than in the most privileged zone. Homicides significantly burden adult (fifteen- to forty-four-year-old) men; rates are three times higher in the deprived areas. For the forty-five- to sixty-four-year-old age group, mortality from the main causes (traffic accidents, cerebrovascular diseases, and hypertension) is twice as high in the zones with the worst socioenvironmental conditions. For those over sixty-five years of age, differentials across the city appear to lessen somewhat.

The Accra/São Paulo study has been invaluable as an advocacy tool.[19] The policy implications of the findings on intra-urban differentials are being investigated and research has also been carried out into the implications intra-urban differentials have for urban management in São Paulo.[20]

The overall conclusions of the study stressed the scale of the health differentials in the two cities and the inextricable links between socioeconomic and environmental conditions and health.[21] The need for an integrated approach to urban health was evident. Psychosocial diseases in both cities were cited as worthy of further investigation, and in the case of São Paulo data on an "epidemic of violence" was provided. Both these problems will be addressed in the following sections.

This section highlighted the possible links between inequality and health with a specific emphasis on psychosocial problems. Patterns of health problems among the urban poor in developing countries are changing; an increasing burden of disease is more explicitly related to social factors. The following section concentrates on two such problems: mental ill-health and violence, for which policy formulation in developing countries is in its infancy. Although the importance of the full spectrum of health problems (including AIDS, tuberculosis, and malaria) is not denied, space constraints have led us to select these two problems, which we feel deserve particular attention.

Mental Health

URBANIZATION AND MENTAL HEALTH

Anthony Marsella sees the history of research into urbanization and mental health as having taken off within the last decade.[22] However, his writing on the history of urbanization and mental health links the topic to that of the general movement of social sciences into health dating from the eighteenth century. He cites Rousseau as the first to notably link society to disease. Blaming civilization for many of the health problems of the modern world became increasingly popular and much attention was focused on the "evils" of man-made urban environments.

Stanislav Kasl and Ernest Harburg reviewed the research on urbanization and mental health and concluded that much of it was based on aggregate data producing correlations between different urban areas and different proportions of treated cases of mental disorder.[23] The weakness of such studies is that they are prone to ecological fallacy. (Ecological fallacy is the name given to false conclusions drawn from measurements averaged over populations that have failed to take possible confounders into account.)[24] The use of such studies is limited, and their results must be viewed with skepticism. So, although an interest in the relationship between urban areas and mental disorder has a relatively long history, the validity of early findings is questionable.

However, more recent attempts to link characteristics of urban areas to mental disorder have involved the collection of individual-level data using standardized screening instruments and they therefore do not fall into the ecological fallacy trap. Although one trap is avoided, others are not, such as the problem of defining mental health across cultures, and the limitations of a purely individual focus. Various factors have been explored in the relationship between an urban environment and mental health.[25]

After reviewing the literature on mental health problems in urban areas of developing countries, and examining the comparisons between rural and urban areas, Harpham produced a conceptual model (figure 10.1) that aims to explain what factors commonly linked with rapid urbanization might be associated with high levels of mental ill-health.[26] The model concentrates on reduced social support, increased life events, and long-term difficulties because there is plentiful evidence to demonstrate that these social factors (as opposed to biological factors) are the major cause of common mental disorders. The model is not comprehensive. For example, some potential stresses related to the physi- • cal environment, such as traffic and transport problems, and high noise and pollution levels, are excluded. This is not because these factors are believed to have no association with mental health (although no literature demonstrating any independent effect was found), but because these factors are not easily conceptualized as long-term difficulties or life events, the two areas that have clear links with mental health as demonstrated by the literature. For similar reasons, the model avoids mention of the wider socioeconomic context within which mental health problems occur. This model is being used to stimulate further research on the links between urbanization and mental health.

Another publication that has addressed the links between urbanization and mental health is *World Mental Health: Problems and Priorities in Low-Income Countries*,[27] which prompted the UN Secretary General to suggest that "Priorities must change. Mental health must be recognized as a foremost challenge. . . . [An] international campaign is needed. . . . It is time for mental health problems to be seen by the international com-

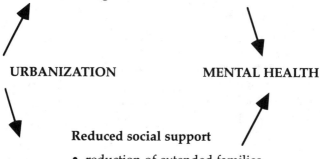

Increased stressors (life events)

A. Long-term difficulties
- poor, overcrowded physical environment
- need for acculturation if migrant
- change from subsistence to cash economy
- high levels of violence, accidents
- insecure tenure

B. Life events
- separation from partner
- loss of employment
- migration

URBANIZATION   **MENTAL HEALTH**

Reduced social support

- reduction of extended families
- increase in single-parent households
- reduced fertility
- age-specific rural–urban migration
- women's labor force participation
- under- or unemployment

FIGURE 10.1 A model of social factors of urbanization in developing countries associated with mental health. (Trudy Harpham, "Urbanization and Mental Health in Developing Countries: A Research Role for Social Scientists, Public Health Professionals and Social Psychiatrists," *Social Science and Medicine* 39, no. 2 [1994]: 233–45)

munity as what they are: a threat to individual well-being, and a threat to peace and development worldwide."[28] These statements highlight the fact that mental ill-health is certainly a problem without a policy.

EXTENT OF THE PROBLEM

Common mental disorders (sometimes referred to as "minor psychiatric morbidity") account for 90 percent of all mental disorders.[29] "The clinical features of such morbidity include a mixture of anxiety, depression, insomnia, fatigue, irritability, poor memory/concentration, somatic symptoms and somatic concern."[30] The prevalence of common mental disorders has been estimated at between 12 and 46 percent in both developed and developing countries and at both community and primary care levels.[31]

Limited information is available reflecting the individual suffering caused by common mental disorders. According to one study it is equivalent to that of major chronic conditions such as diabetes and heart disease.[32] In terms of the burden common mental disorders place on society, the World Bank's *World Development Report 1993: Investing in Health* cited depression as the fifth cause of illness among adult females in the developing world (after selected communicable diseases and maternity-related morbidity and mortality).[33] Using data for United Kingdom (UK) general practice in 1985 the costs of common mental disorders in health services at the primary care level were estimated as greater than the overall costs for hypertension in the same year.[34] All these facts justify a focus on common mental disorders.

Some of the reasons for the lack of priority accorded to mental health research in developing countries are the following:[35]

1. a stigma associated with mental problems, which is particularly acute in developing countries where mental problems are linked to superstitions;
2. a lack of research into the economics of mental health in developing countries;
3. the fact that research into common mental disorders requires the knowledge and skills of a variety of professionals (psychiatrists, psychologists, social workers, health workers, anthropologists, epidemiologists, etc.) resulting in a multidisciplinary field that is interesting and full of debate, but hard to coordinate;
4. the problem of somatization (physical manifestation of a mental problem) ensuring that many common mental disorders go undetected because repeat appointments dealing with superficial physical symptoms fail to address the psychological aspects of a patient's problem. (Not only does this result in considerable misallocation of resources, but it obscures the true level of mental disorder within a community);
5. problems associated with the definitions of mental ill-health.[36] (The idea of a universal state of normalcy on which definitions of mental ill-health could be based was counterintuitive to many. However, a study published in *JAMA*, using data from 15 coun-

tries, stressed the importance of the common forms of psychological disorder across cultures.)[37]

6. the fact that common mental disorders cause little direct mortality. (The morbidity attributable to mental problems is considerable
but until the publication of the World Bank's *World Development
Report 1993*, worldwide data on health had tended to focus on
mortality statistics, which although easier to collect do not accurately reflect the health burden of a society.)[38]

Despite the difficulties involved in getting mental health issues onto
public health agendas, within the field of urban health the frequently
detrimental impact of urban social processes is recognized and mental
health is benefiting from growing attention.

EXISTING POLICIES AND RECOMMENDATIONS

- The burden of mental ill-health (in terms of human suffering,
  resources used in health services, loss of productivity) is still not
  fully recognized.
- Policy needs to focus on reducing life events and long-term difficulties, and increasing social support. Without societal structural
  change the latter is most feasible.
- A few attempts have been made to design and evaluate such interventions: e.g., in a low-income settlement in Harare, Zimbabwe.[39]
- Low-income urban women are particularly vulnerable (typical
  prevalence of depression/anxiety is twice that of men) so attention
  (research and action) is needed.
- Urban development in general is likely to have an impact on mental
  health. The problem is truly multisectoral and must be treated as
  such.

Violence

URBANIZATION AND VIOLENCE

There is a growing emphasis by urban management specialists on the
problem of violence in cities. Evidence for this shift can be seen in the
devotion of an entire issue of the World Bank's urban newsletter, *Urban
Age*, to the topic of violence in cities and the selection of violence as the
theme for a workshop of the Latin America and Caribbean branch of
the Urban Management Program of the World Bank/UNDP/Habitat,
also in 1993.[40] The Urban Management Program is of considerable importance in the urban development arena. It is by far the largest inter-

national program of technical assistance in the field of urban development, involving three multilateral agencies and financial support from nine bilateral agencies and two private foundations.

As it has gained attention in the urban development field, violence has appeared on the public health agenda. The benefits of using a public health approach are that it moves away from a strict interpretation of violence as a judicial problem and has various advantages in terms of tackling some of the issues. Using a broad definition of health, public health professionals are well placed to collect and interpret data on violent deaths. They can also move on from descriptive statistics toward an analysis of possible causes. From this stage it is feasible that policy conclusions could be drawn and interventions developed (that need not focus on health services); any interventions implemented could then be evaluated. However, several problems may arise if public health specialists keen on studying violence do not pay particular attention to some potential pitfalls. Perhaps the main problem with using a public health approach is the tendency among many health professionals to search for single causes and solutions to complex health problems. Another potential limitation of the public health approach is the tendency to emphasize the role of the individual in disease causation rather than considering the wider socioeconomic and political context within which health problems occur. Bearing these potential limitations in mind, the following sections attempt to provide some information on the extent of the problem and future research needs and types of possible interventions.

EXTENT OF THE PROBLEM

Figures from the World Bank relating to 1990 estimate that in the developing world the proportion of the total burden of disease caused by injuries (including both unintentional, such as road accidents and drowning; and intentional, such as homicide and war) was 8 percent for women and 15 percent for men.[41] As with all health problems, the burden of violence is not evenly distributed through space and the use of such all-embracing statistics is limited. The following section gives some indication of the scale of the problem in various developing-country settings.

In South Africa in 1992, deaths due to injuries were the third highest cause of mortality, representing 14 percent of all deaths. Of these deaths, over 70 percent were due to violence (only 10 percent of deaths were considered to be of a political nature). The rate of homicide in South Africa is 57 per 100,000, approximately six times the rate in the

United States. This last point should be considered in light of the fact that the U.S. homicide rate of 8.7 per 100,000 is the highest of all industrialized nations and 2.6 times higher than the rate for the next highest industrialized nation (Finland, at 3.3 per 100,000).[42]

The issue of *Urban Age* devoted to violence provided some information on the scale of violence in various cities in the developing world: "For every 100,000 people in Cali there are now 87 murders every year."[43] In fact, the rate of homicide in Colombia increased by 50 percent between 1972 and 1982.[44] "In El Salvador, violent deaths accounted for 9 percent of total deaths in 1984, and for 21 percent of the total years of potential life lost."[45] The disparity noted between the percentage of total deaths and the percentage of total years of potential life lost highlights one aspect of violent deaths that appears to hold true across a wide variety of contexts, namely that such deaths occur disproportionately among youths, especially males. The concentration of violent deaths in young males has serious implications for the productive capacity of a city. Data for São Paulo demonstrate that 70 percent of deaths among young people (fifteen- to twenty-four-year-olds) between 1991 and 1993 were due to external causes (both intentional and unintentional injuries).[46] Among males in the same age group, over 50 percent of deaths were homicides. The consequences, both social and economic, of death at the beginning of a young man's adulthood are phenomenal.

Saul Agudelo sees the problem of violence "as the exercise of force—physical, psychological, or moral—directly or indirectly by a person or group of persons against another person, group or thing . . . although force is merely the instrument or physical expression of what is really at stake, which is power. . . . As a precondition for violence, it is essential that there be an imbalance between heterogeneous entities having unequal power."[47]

Larry Cohen and Susan Swift, although considering violence in the United States, list three root causes of violence that may be appropriate to developing countries.[48] First, the depressed economic conditions within a given community, as well as individual cases of unemployment and underemployment, lead to significantly higher levels of violence. Second, oppression, and the resulting feelings of inequality and powerlessness, are an underlying component of many types of violence. Finally, an unsupportive home life, including physical or psychological abuse, can produce low levels of self esteem in both the victim and the perpetrator. Violence begets violence; it is frequently cyclical. A sense of isolation and fear for one's personal safety can adversely affect one's ability to resolve conflict without violence.

EXISTING POLICIES AND RECOMMENDATIONS

To date there has been no systematic review to analyze the influence of urbanization on violence or to compare rates of homicide across urban and rural regions in developing countries. It is therefore difficult, at this stage, to draw conclusions about the urban aspects of violence in developing countries. Considering violence as a public health problem is still a relatively new approach so we focus on research needs and types of possible interventions.

- More detailed data must be collected on mortality and morbidity created by violence—considering mortality alone has serious limitations.
- Although the problem of violent deaths appears to be more prevalent in poorer segments of society, it is important to steer clear of blaming the victim.
- Research must clarify the distribution of violence in the home and in the street—there may be a tendency for developed countries (e.g., the United States) to be dominated by domestic violence whereas developing countries (e.g., South Africa) witness more street violence.
- Some interventions that would be appropriate for the protection of mental health (such as social support mechanisms) might also reduce violence.
- Interventions should not only focus on the individual or community (i.e., the victims), but need to reach the "national and multinational interests for whom sales of weapons, drugs and alcohol are profitable."[49]
- The complexity of violence should be acknowledged and explored in future research.

Our focus on two problems (mental health and violence) with such complex links to socioeconomic and political factors makes manifest the limitations inherent in seeking solutions wholly within the realm of health services. The need for an integrated approach to urban health problems in developing countries is apparent.

An Integrated Approach to Urban Health

Urban health problems can be addressed more appropriately through an integrated approach. In terms of health sector action this implies the primary healthcare approach that was advocated by WHO in the early 1980s, but which failed since it was not able to successfully meet the need for cooperation with other sectors. Due to the close connection between the overall process of development of a city or town and the health status of its population, an integrated approach to urban health should be, in fact, an integrated approach to urban development.

In order to better understand these issues, the links between urban development and health must be analyzed, and we must define what the integrated approach to urban development would be. The institutional aspects of integration—which are central to the approach—need to be elaborated. We will examine the WHO Healthy Cities Project as an example of how the integrated approach has been implemented, and analyze the advantages and problems of this approach.

Urban Development and Health

WHO has espoused a view of health that differs significantly from the conventional view that emerged in industrialized societies in the mid–twentieth century. In this conventional view, "health care (an activity) is often treated synonymously with health (a state of being) and the determinants of health . . . become disassociated as causal factors."[50]

WHO's view, in turn, asserts that health is a state of complete physical, social, and mental well-being—much more than the mere absence of disease or infirmity—whose attainment requires far more than the supply of health services. "That health is a state of well-being indicates that health is not an activity . . . rather it is the outcome of all activities which make up the lives of individuals, households, communities and cities."[51]

"Physical, economic, social, and cultural aspects of city life all have an important influence on health. They exert their effect through such processes as population movement, industrialization, and changes in the architectural and physical environment and in social organization. Health is also affected in particular cities by climate, terrain, population density, housing stock, the nature of the economic activity, income distribution, transport systems, and opportunities for leisure and recreation."[52]

This view has been reinforced by the Ottawa Charter, the product of an international conference on health promotion held in 1986.[53] It emphasizes that policies in sectors other than health make key contributions to health—for example, those that help create supportive environments for health in the economic and social sectors.[54] In short, in order to improve the health status of urban populations, it is necessary to act upon the multitude of issues that form a city or town. Such actions have been carried out not via specific projects, but via integrated processes.

THE INTEGRATED APPROACH TO URBAN DEVELOPMENT

Urban development policies for developing countries were heavily based on the so-called project approach until the mid-1980s.[55] In broad terms, the first phase of this approach entailed direct implementation of large-scale urban projects based on Western concepts and resources. It was followed by a second phase based on the direct implementation of small-scale projects built on the use of local resources.[56] The achievements of both types of projects have been limited by a number of problems, which included bad administration by national/local authorities, low replicability, high costs (in the first phase), and narrow impact of local resources (in the second phase).[57] This situation led to disillusionment regarding direct investment in urban projects, which in turn led to the formation of a new approach to urban development, here termed the "integrated approach."

This new approach is based on the premise that sound urban development can be better achieved through city-wide processes that integrate different sectors, than through compartmentalized sectoral projects (implemented without regard to each other).

The integrated approach is strategic to urban health. Although specific, separate urban projects intended to improve the quality of life of the urban population in different ways, and their lack of integration with the overall process of urban development or with other specific projects often resulted in failure. One classic example is the removal of slum-dwellers to housing estates. This type of action often generated disruption of job networks (especially in the informal sector), higher housing and transportation costs, and reduced access to health services and to other urban facilities. These issues have affected the health of the dwellers in different ways.[58] Another illustration is the implementation of projects heavily based on the participation of inexperienced communities and not complemented by proper training projects.[59] Other examples abound.

There is still obvious need for solid direct investment in all types of urban projects in developing countries. However, considering the failures of the past, new projects should avoid implementation via direct, strong intervention from central governments or foreign donors. The integrated approach strongly emphasizes the strengthening of local institutions, which should be the leading actors in the process of urban development and in the improvement of urban health conditions. In short, the integration of actions and projects should be achieved not through direct support, but through support to the local institutions.

The Role of Institutions

Traditional structures of local government were based on compartmental administration with few or no horizontal connections between different areas or services, and with a strong emphasis on the role of the public bureaucracy. However, since the 1980s there has been a move toward a flexible structure of urban management, with an emphasis on integration between areas or services as well as on cooperation between the public sector and the other actors involved with urban management.

These trends are central to the integrated approach. WHO, for instance, condemns the traditional systems of organization, rooted in "concepts of bureaucracy, hierarchy, paternalistic power, professional authority, disciplinary specialization, win-lose and either/or strategy and sectoral analysis."[60] Therefore, "to address the problems of the twenty-first century . . . new, holistic, flexible approaches [must be] adopted."[61]

These new approaches "cut across the old departmental lines and indeed across the different sectors—public, private, voluntary and community. None can be addressed by one department of government alone, nor indeed by city government alone. The whole community has to be mobilized and the efforts of all sectors and departments have to be combined and focused."[62] Therefore, the integrated approach works via a process of institutional integration.[63]

The Healthy Cities Project

The Healthy Cities Project is a WHO long-term development program that seeks to put health on the agenda of decisionmakers in cities and to build a strong lobby for public health at the local level. Ultimately, the program seeks to enhance the physical, mental, social, and environmental well-being of the people who live and work in urban areas. The "healthy cities" concept was developed in 1984 and the WHO Healthy Cities Project was launched in 1986. The initial network of eleven cities that initiated this project rapidly expanded. In 1993 there were 650 cities within fifteen countries, interacting through nineteen national and subnational networks. Although most of these cities were in industrialized countries, in the mid-1990s the project is expanding throughout the developing world.

The project is based on premises such as WHO's (ample) concept of health, the Ottawa Charter, and WHO's strategy of "Health for All in the Year 2000." All these premises note the connection between health and several issues that form a city or town. In short, in order to improve urban health conditions, it is important to intervene primarily in urban development. This point is illustrated by data from the Healthy City Project in Chittagong, Bangladesh.

The Chittagong Project includes seven task forces that deal with most topics related to the process of urban development, namely (1) town planning, infrastructure, and economic development; (2) slum improvement; (3) literacy and unemployment; (4) water and sanitation; (5) environmental protection; (6) drainage and wastewater treatment; and (7) primary healthcare and maternal and child health.[64]

Improvements in the aforementioned areas are to be achieved by the implementation of a plan comprising seventy-three specific actions as diverse as a transport development strategy, a mechanism to attract inward investment to Chittagong, community business investment support mechanisms, extension of technical and vocational training, legislation to prevent hill-cutting, support for ragpickers to sell and distribute low cost latrines, etc.[65]

The specific actions included in each Healthy City project are to be carried out via an integrated process based on strengthening local institutions and supporting their cooperation. In the Chittagong project, for instance, the task forces and the plan of action are under the coordination of the Chittagong City Corporation (i.e., the local government authority), and involve other actors active in urban development. These include public authorities (Bangladesh Railway, the Chittagong Development Authority, the Chittagong Port Authority, the Civil Surgeon, the Department of Environment, the Department of Forests, the Power Development Board, education departments, ward representatives, the Water and Sewerage Authority, and all the departments of the City Corporation); the voluntary sector (Association of Development Agencies of Bangladesh, Concern, Ghashful, NGO Forum, World Vision, and other NGOs to be incorporated later on); the private sector (Chamber of Commerce, leading banks, Lions Club, Rotary Club); the community (slum leaders, community associations); and international agencies (UNCHS, UNDP, UNICEF, WHO).[66]

The links between the Healthy Cities Project and urban management are further illustrated by the analysis of the onset of the Chittagong project. This analysis noted the potential of Healthy Cities to overcome the major problems found in the structure of urban management. The problems are related to cooperation, coordination, motivation, internal organization, decentralization, and community participation.[67] In sum, the Healthy Cities Project is a thorough example of the integrated approach to urban development and health.

PROMISES AND PROBLEMS

The policy of the Healthy Cities Project (and of the integrated approach in general) to concentrate investment in building sustainable processes and in enabling institutions to better manage urban development may bring more profound, longer-term improvements for the health status of the urban populations (compared to the specific projects of the past). There is still a clear need for substantial direct investment in all types of urban projects. However, considering the failures of the past, it appears sound to invest more in local people and institutions. By doing so, specific urban projects (and processes) will be sustainable even when central governments and international donors pull out of the scene; the local community and authorities will be better prepared to negotiate funds from different sources—and also to administer them.

However, the integrated approach also has problems. Analyses of the Healthy Cities Project in developing countries, for instance, reveal local institutions that have difficulty using the approach to benefit their city.[68] These problems are related to outmoded institutional structures in local authorities, lack of conceptual understanding of the (integrated) concept, absence of a public authority with enough power to coordinate the whole process of urban development, lack of cooperation between different layers of government, lack of coordination and cooperation between central government authorities that have agencies operating at the local level, and a lack of commitment. These problems illustrate that the successful implementation of programs based on the integrated approach must influence the public authorities regarding their organization, civic commitment, transparency, and accountability. Under such circumstances, the Healthy Cities Project (or any other program based on the integrated approach) may have a fundamental role as the principal vehicle for change. However, one should bear in mind that structural problems take longer to resolve. Thus, the project will need to give stronger support to the local authorities and allow a longer period for maturation (in comparison to experiences in industrialized countries).

The Healthy Cities Project has also faced difficulty integrating the activities of other sectors (i.e., private, voluntary, and communitarian) with those of the public sector. This is an expected difficulty, given that most cities and towns are not usually managed with great inter-sector integration. Thus, although the implementation of the Healthy Cities Project is carried out via the public sector, the project's team should keep a close eye on the other sectors as well. A particular problem already identified is the low level of organization in local communities. Considering that community participation is a fundamental point of the project, its team has to devise methods to deal with inexperienced communities and leaders, rather than take for granted that people will instinctively participate.

These issues are not specific to the Healthy Cities Project, but to the implementation of the integrated approach as a whole.[69] If they are not taken into consideration, the effectiveness of the approach may be jeopardized.

Conclusion

In terms of the changes in the urban health landscape from Habitat I to Habitat II, perhaps the main point is the acceptance of urban health as part of the urban development agenda since the mid-1980s. This chapter has explored the extent of polarization and inequality in living conditions and health within cities and argued that there are new public health problems, which are not yet being acknowledged and are far from having policies to address them.

These urban health problems without policies are largely linked to growing social stress within cities, which in turn is linked to the process of globalization. As Manuel Castells states, "Metropolitan regions must cope with the increasing social stress caused by the new system. Indeed, the process of globalization is selective, and highly exclusionary. Large segments of the local population could be left out, as producers and consumers, from the system."[70] Wilkinson argues that because health seems to be influenced more by the scale of income differences than by the absolute level of income, cognitive processes of social comparison are implicated in the causal chain for health. He provocatively claims that "it is less a matter of the immediate physical effects of inferior material conditions as of what the social meanings attached to those conditions make people feel about their circumstances and about themselves."[71]

In terms of action, we argue with Castells for an emphasis on local actors—an issue that is also intrinsically linked with the process of globalization. National and regional actors are losing significance. On the one hand, they are being overwhelmed by global issues, such as the expansion of the international flow of goods, services, and capital, that are beyond their control. On the other hand, they do not have the attributes to respond to the specific needs of different places within the country. In this context, local actors are assuming pivotal importance. They have the flexibility and the adaptability to respond to global changes, and to adjust them to the specific interests of each locality.[72] "Unless governments and societies of metropolitan regions design programs and build institutions to redistribute wealth and ensure community building, the developmental dynamism generated by globalization and information technology will doom the promise of human enhancement, ushering in a dark urban age."[73] Such action implies further attention to the issues of good urban governance (as distinct from government), which can be defined as the interaction between government and civil society. An "action space" has to be created that allows all dimensions of governance (institutional, political, technical, and cultural) to be openly discussed and strengthened.[74] The Healthy City concept follows this philosophy as far as health is concerned and also provides a vehicle to begin to address urban health problems without policies.

Notes

Thanks to Mark Sambrooke for his administrative support.

[1] Trudy Harpham and Marcel Tanner, eds., *Urban Health in Developing Countries: Progress and Prospects* (London, UK: Earthscan, 1995).

[2] John D. Kasarda and Allan M. Parnell, *Third World Cities* (London, UK: Sage, 1993), x.

[3] Trudy Harpham, Tim Lusty, and Patrick Vaughan, *In the Shadow of the City: Community Health and the Urban Poor* (Oxford, UK: Oxford University Press, 1988), 11.

[4] Ibid.

[5] Alessandro Rossi-Espagnet, *Primary Health Care in Urban Areas: Reaching the Urban Poor in Developing Countries*, report no. 2499M (a state of the art report by UNICEF and World Health Organization [WHO]) (Geneva, Switzerland: WHO, 1984). See also Harpham, et al., *In the Shadow of the City*.

[6] Rossi-Espagnet, *Primary Health Care*.

[7] Hernando de Soto, *The Other Path: The Invisible Revolution in the Third World* (New York: Harper and Row, 1989). See also International Labor Office (ILO), *Employment, Income and Equality: A Strategy for Increasing Productive Employment in Kenya* (Geneva, Switzerland: ILO, 1972); Carlos Maldonado and S. V. Sethuraman, eds., *Technological Capability in the Informal Sectors of Developing Countries* (Geneva, Switzerland: ILO, 1991); and Om Mathur and Caroline Moser, "The Informal Sector Reworked: Viability or Vulnerability in Urban Development," *Regional Development Dialogue* 5, no. 2 (1984): 3–12.

[8] World Bank, *Urban Policy and Economic Development: An Agenda for the 1990s*, World Bank policy paper (Washington, D.C.: World Bank, 1991).

[9] Carolyn Stephens, *Urban Environment, Poverty, and Health in Developing Countries: An Analysis of Differentials Using Existing Data* (Ph.D diss., University of London, 1995).

[10]Margaret Thomas and Barbara McPake, "Costing and Financing Urban Health and Environmental Services," in *Urban Health*.

[11]Peter Townsend, *The International Analysis of Poverty* (London, UK: Harvester Wheatsheaf, 1993), 36.

[12]Ellen Wratten, "Conceptualizing Urban Poverty," *Environment and Urbanization 7*, no. 1 (1995): 11–36.

[13]Richard G. Wilkinson, "The Impact of Income Inequalities on Life Expectancy," in *Locating Health: Sociological and Historical Implications*, ed S. Platt (Aldershot, UK: Avebury, 1993); see also Richard G. Wilkinson, "The Epidemiological Transition: From Material Scarcity to Social Disadvantage?" *Daedalus* 123, no. 4 (1994): 61–78.

[14]Ibid.

[15]Carolyn Stephens, Ian Timaeus, Marco Akerman, et al., *Environment and Health in Developing Countries: An Analysis of Intra-Urban Differentials Using Existing Data* (London, UK: London School of Hygiene and Tropical Medicine, 1994).

[16]Ibid.

[17]Ibid.

[18]Ibid, iii.

[19]Ibid.

[20]Edmundo Werna, "Urban Management and Intra-urban Differentials in São Paulo," *Habitat International* 19, no. 1 (1995): 123–38.

[21]Stephens et al., *Environment and Health*.

[22]Anthony J. Marsella, "Urbanization, Mental Health and Psychosocial Well-Being: Some Historical Perspectives and Considerations," in *Urbanization and Mental Health in Developing Countries*, ed. Trudy Harpham and Ilona Blue (Aldershot, UK: Avebury, 1995).

[23]Stanislav V. Kasl and Ernest Harburg, "Mental Health and the Urban Environment: Some Doubts and Second Thoughts," *Journal of Health and Social Behaviour* 16 (1975): 268–79; see also Robert Park, Ernest Burgess, and Roderick McKenzie, *The City* (Chicago: University of Chicago Press, 1925); Robert Faris and Henry Dunham, *Mental Disease in Urban Areas* (Chicago: University of Chicago Press, 1939); August Hollingshead and Frederick Redlich, *Social Class and Mental Illness* (New York: John Wiley, 1958); and Alexander Leighton, *My Name is Legion: Foundations for a Theory of Man in Relation to Culture* (New York: Basic Books, 1959).

[24]Kenneth J. Rothman, *Modern Epidemiology* (Boston: Little, Brown, 1986).

[25]Anthony J. Marsella, "Urbanization and Mental Disorders: An Overview of Theory and Research and Recommendations for Interventions and Research" (paper prepared for the World Health Organization's Commission on Health and the Environment, 1990); see also Trudy Harpham, "Urbanization and Mental Health in Developing Countries: A Research Role for Social Scientists, Public Health Professionals, and Social Psychiatrists," *Social Science and Medicine* 39, no. 2 (1994): 233–45; and Harpham and Blue, eds., *Urbanization and Mental Health*.

[26]Harpham, "Urbanization and Mental Health," 233–45.

[27]Robert Desjarlais, Leon Eisenberg, Byron Good, and Arthur Kleinman, *World Mental Health: Problems and Priorities in Low-Income Countries* (New York: Oxford University Press, 1995).

[28]United Nations Secretary General Boutros Boutros-Ghali, remarks at the launch of "World Mental Health: Problems and Priorities in Low-Income Countries," New York, 15 May 1995.

[29]David Goldberg and Peter Huxley, *Common Mental Disorders* (London, UK: Routledge, 1992).

[30]Andrew T. A. Cheng, "Urbanization and Minor Psychiatric Morbidity: A Community Study in Taiwan," *Social Psychiatry and Psychiatric Epidemiology* 24 (1989): 309–16.

[31]Harpham, "Urbanization and Mental Health."

[32]K. B. Wells, A. Stewart, R. D. Hays, et al., "The Functioning and Well-Being of Depressed Patients: Results from the Medical Outcomes Study," *JAMA* 262, no. 7 (1989): 914–19.

[33]World Bank, *World Development Report 1993: Investing in Health* (New York: Oxford University Press, 1993).

[34]C. Croft-Jeffreys and Greg Wilkinson, "Estimated Cost of Neurotic Disorder in UK General Practice 1985," *Psychological Medicine* 19 (1989): 549–58.

[35]Ilona Blue and Trudy Harpham, "The World Bank, *World Development Report 1993: Investing in Health* reveals the burden of common mental disorders, but ignores its implications," *British Journal of Psychiatry* 165 (1994): 9–12.

[36]Norman Sartorius, preface to *The Public Health Impact of Mental Disorder*, ed. D. Goldberg and D. Tantam (Toronto, Canada: Hogrefe and Huber, 1990).

[37]J. Ormel, M. VonKorff, B. Ustun, S. Pini, A. Korten, and T. Oldehinkel, "Common Mental Disorders and Disability Across Cultures," *JAMA* 272 (1994): 1741–48; see also H. W. Pretorius, "Mental Disorders and Disability Across Cultures: A View from South Africa," *Lancet* 345 (March 1995): 534.

[38]World Bank, *World Development Report 1993*.

[39]Melanie Abas, Jeremy A. Broadhead, Priscilla Mbape, et al., "Defeating Depression in the Developing World: A Zimbabwean Model," *British Journal of Psychiatry* 164 (1994): 293–96.

[40]World Bank, *The Urban Age*, 1, no. 4 (1993).

[41]World Bank, *World Development Report 1993*.

[42]Larry Cohen and Susan Swift, "A Public Health Approach to the Violence Epidemic in the United States," *Environment and Urbanization* 5, no. 2 (1993): 50–66.

[43]World Bank, *The Urban Age*.

[44]Ibid.

[45]Ibid., 131.

[46]Karla Soares, Ilona Blue, Eduardo Cano, and Jair J. Mari, "Violent Deaths in Young People in the City of São Paulo, 1991–1993" (unpublished manuscript, 1995).

[47]Saul F. Agudelo, "Violence and Health: Preliminary Elements for Thought and Action," *International Journal of Health Services* 22, no. 2 (1992): 365–76.

[48]Cohen and Swift, "A Public Health Approach."

[49]Alex Butchart, Mohamed Seedat, and Victor Nell, "Violence in South Africa: Its Definition and Prevention as a Public Health Problem" (unpublished manuscript, 1995).

[50]CCC-WHO (Chittagong City Corporation and World Health Organization), *Chittagong Healthy City Project—Health for All—All for Health* (November, 1993): 3.

[51]Ibid.

[52]WHO (World Health Organization), *The Urban Health Crisis—Strategies for Health for All in the Face of Rapid Urbanization* (Geneva, Switzerland: WHO, 1993), 10–11.

[53]CCC-WHO, *Chittagong Healthy City Project*.

[54]Ibid.

[55]Nigel Harris, ed., *Cities in the 1990s—The Challenge for Developing Countries* (London, UK: University College London Press, 1992).

[56]Edmundo Werna, "United Nations' Agencies' Urban Policies and Health" (paper presented at the Conference "Urban Health Research: Implications for Policy," London School of Hygiene and Tropical Medicine, 6–8 December 1994).

[57]Werna, *UN Agencies' Urban Policies and Health*; see also Harris, ed., *Cities in the 1990s*.

[58]Werna, *UN Agencies' Urban Policies and Health*.

[59]Richard Batley, *Cooperation with Private and Community Organisation*, Institutional Framework of Urban Management working paper no. 6, Development Administration Group, School of Public Policy, University of Birmingham, U.K., 1992; see also Francoise Barten, Ton van Naerssen, Jan de Koning, and G. Tom Heikens, "Urban Poverty and Health," (discussion paper on the experiences and proposed activities of WHO Healthy Cities Project and framework for discussions on possible collaboration between WHO-HCP, UNDP/LIFE, DGIS and HEC, intended for the WHO/DGIS workshop, WHO Headquarters, Geneva, Switzerland, 4–6 October 1993).

[60]WHO, "City Networks for Health," (technical discussion paper, May 1991).

[61]Ibid., 12.

[62]Ibid., 13.

[63]Trudy Harpham and Kwasi Boateng, "Urban Governance in Relation to the Operation of Basic Services" (report produced by South Bank University, London, UK, submitted to the Overseas Development Administration, UK, 1995).

[64]CCC-WHO, *Chittagong Healthy City Project*.

[65]Ibid.

[66]Ibid.

[67]Edmundo Werna and Trudy Harpham, "The Evaluation of Healthy City Projects in Developing Countries," *Habitat International* 19, no. 4 (1995): 629–41; see also Edmundo Werna, "The Chittagong Healthy City Project: Follow-Up Analysis One Year after Its Initiation"(research report, Urban Health Programme, London School of Hygiene and Tropical Medicine, January 1995).

[68]Werna, *UN Agencies' Urban Policies and Health*.

[69]Ibid.

[70]Manuel Castells, "Information Technology, Cities, and Development," *Urban Age* 3, no. 1 (February 1995): 15.

[71]Wilkinson, "The Epidemiological Transition."

[72]Manuel Castells, *The Informational City: Information Technology, Economic Restructuring, and the Urban-Regional Process* (Oxford, UK: Blackwell, 1989).

[73]Castells, "Information Technology, " 15.

[74]Harpham and Boateng, "Urban Governance."

Political Choices

THE CENTRAL ARGUMENT IN the preceding section was that there are dilemmas confronting every city that have no perfect solution and that the solution ultimately chosen is, in some sense, political. And, in many cities, there are political solutions that are so obviously less than ideal that selling them to the public relies on supreme efforts of leadership and vigilance in urban governance. For urban planners and for some politicians, this may appear a heretical idea. The former are trained to formulate ideal solutions; the latter are trained to sell their solutions as ideal.

In Part IV, the authors focus on the dilemmas of urban governance itself—how the complexities of governing cities make formulating and carrying out policies more difficult. But all is not gloom; there are also suggestions as to how cities can protect themselves, how they can maximize their resources, and how they can get help in solving their problems.

K. C. Sivaramakrishnan draws our attention to the difficulties of aggregating local units within some large cities. He emphasizes the anarchic quality of urban governance and reminds us of how difficult it is to deliver social services or to execute policies smoothly across a complex urban landscape. The other side of the coin of complex governance, according to Sivaramakrishnan, is the autonomy this provides to local groups, to civil society. This means, especially, in the poorer countries of the developing world, that the poorest of the poor in the poorest cities actually have the greatest say in their own governance. While this is certainly not an ideal situation, it is preferable to a situation in which the city governors were unable to provide for the needs of the city's population and yet were sufficiently powerful to prevent local groups from devising their own solutions to problems.

Jordi Borja offers one of the most optimistic appraisals of how cities are facing a globalizing future. Borja describes the efforts of the city of Barcelona to attract capital, to build its tourism industry, and to improve the quality of life of its citizens. Borja sees the very process of globalization as an opportunity. In the case of Barcelona, he shows how city officials used the emerging structure of the European Community to enhance its autonomy within the Catalan region and within Spain, and to enhance its ability to market itself as a city, illustrating his argument with the Olympic games and the selection of Barcelona as the European City of the Year. He makes for the city as entrepreneur and for how energetic leadership improves urban governance. Improving urban governance makes it posssible to solve urban problems not directly related to the projects on which the leadership was focused by strengthening community identity.

María Elena Ducci drives to the heart of the painful, complex issue of urban sustainability, the ultimate urban dilemma. She describes the conflicts within the city between the green agenda, the agenda for environmental conservation, and the brown agenda, that new set of environmental concerns that are associated with urban poverty and the desecration of the urban environment. Ducci explains, in a manner similar to the arguments presented by Julie Roqué and Edmundo Werna, that the political choices on environmental issues fall unequally across segments of the urban population. Ultimately, she warns, the sustainability of cities depends on the ability to reach some form of compromise in setting the priorities between the green and brown agendas in cities around the world. As with so many of the difficult choices facing cities, Ducci is convincing in her argument that the environmental issues that form the core of her chapter are as difficult for rich cities as for poor cities.

Chapter 11

Urban Governance: Changing Realities

K. C. Sivaramakrishnan

When Habitat I, the first UN Conference on Human Settlements, convened in Vancouver, the world's urban population was about 1.3 billion, a 37 percent share of the total. The less-developed countries accounted for 652 million and only a quarter of their total population was urban; their cities with a population of 1 million or more numbered fewer than one hundred. The preamble to the Habitat report stated confidently that "in developing countries, most people live in rural areas and will continue to do so, notwithstanding considerable movement to urban areas."[1] Settlement planning was articulated mainly in physical terms and public control over that process was regarded as the key function of the government. Although the conference understood the wide variety of human settlements, its understanding of institutions was mainly hierarchical, in terms of national, regional, local, and neighborhood. There was much support for "single high-level institutions as the best means of ensuring comprehensive public control over human settlement problems." Reference to "large and complex metropolitan areas" was brief and it was urged that "the search for more appropriate institutions must be a continuous one."[2]

Much has happened to change and challenge the Vancouver perceptions of urbanization. Countries long regarded as rural and as different as Bangladesh, Yemen, Mozambique, and Tanzania have doubled or trebled their urban populations. The total urban population in developing countries has nearly doubled to about 1.7 billion since the Vancouver meeting. There are 141 cities of more than 1 million people in the developing countries. While nine of the world's fourteen largest cities are in these countries, growth is not limited only to these cities. Secondary cities such as Kano (Nigeria), Surabaya (Indonesia), and Guadalajara (Mexico) have grown into metropolises of 2 to 3 million.[3] Much of this growth has overrun traditional municipal boundaries. Urban growth has taken place across the board at a frenetic pace, overtaking infrastructure and the meager instruments of planning, leaving urban governments gasping.

The Concept

"Governance," as a concept and a term, has received increasing attention in recent years. To some scholars, "[g]overnance, as distinct from

Government, refers to the relationship between civil society and the State, between rulers and the ruled, the State and Society, the government and the governed."[4] Attempting to steer clear of political dimensions and in keeping with its emphasis on economics, the World Bank's first report on the subject defines governance as the "manner in which power is exercised in the Management of the Country's Economic and Social Resources for Development."[5] The report further states that "good governance is epitomized by a transparent process; a bureaucracy imbued with professional ethos; an executive arm of the government accountable for its actions; a strong civil society participating in public affairs: and all behaving under the rule of law"—an ambitious catalogue of ideals rather than an analytical framework of a concept. Apart from recognizing that governance as a concept is much broader than government and much more inclusive of process issues, this chapter will not attempt any additional definition of the term. Rather, it will try to look at the problems faced by people in cities and their governments and how the institutions, instruments, and processes have fared in dealing with them.

What Is Urban?

Definitions of what is urban are not uniform in the census practices across the countries. Although the UN continues to be the principal source of data, its estimates and projections are based on national definitions. Let us consider the two most populous countries. In India all places that have a municipality, corporation, town committee, or cantonment board are urban. In China, on the other hand, there are at least three official sets of figures: one is of people living within the boundaries of its 517 cities (746 million), the second is the census count (324 million), and the third counts people with valid nonagricultural residence permits (164 million). Depending on the figure used, China's urban population is 64, 28, or 14 percent of the total population.

The issue is of particular significance in defining urban agglomerations and devising institutions for their governance. Whereas China has a system of cities, including within their limits agricultural areas, in India, urban agglomerations comprise mainly the contiguous urbanized areas, which are usually multimunicipal and multijurisdictional.

Apart from urban agglomerations, census definitions in most countries are based on a combination of factors such as nonagricultural occupation, density, income, level of infrastructure services, and per capita taxation. But in most developing countries the paucity of data confounds categorization and even where urban characteristics are

TABLE 11.1
POPULATION OF MAJOR CITIES IN CHINA, 1989 (in millions)

	City	County	Total
Shanghai	7.76	4.98	12.76
Beijing	6.92	3.32	10.24
Tianjin	5.70	2.87	8.57
Shenyang	4.50	1.15	5.65
Wuhan	3.71	2.82	6.53
Guangzhou	3.54	2.31	5.85

SOURCE: World Bank

patent a fear of increased taxes has prevented the incorporation of new municipalities.

In recognition of this problem in India, where villages in some states have an average population of fifty thousand, a constitutional amendment has introduced the *Nagar Panchayat*, literally the town's village council, a deliberate hybrid of town and village that can be set up in urbanizing villages, and which can access a combination of revenues and powers from urban and rural local bodies.

The situation is not very different in developed countries. Census definitions of "urban" and "rural" have been blurred by the nature of growth, communications, and admixture of occupations. The European Community, which commissioned a study on the statistical concept of the town in Europe, noted that definitions of what is urban varied from one member country to another and observed "the city walls which were once the tangible evidence of municipal status have disappeared:

TABLE 11.2
INDIA—METROPOLITAN AREAS, 1991
Constituent Units

Type of Unit	Bombay	Calcutta	Delhi	Madras
Corporations	3	3	2	1
Municipalities	3	29	—	4
Non-municipal towns	—	91	23	24
Cantonments	—	—	1	1
Village panchayats and outgrowths	—	23	—	27
Total population of the Census Agglomeration (in millions)	12.57	10.91	8.37	5.36
Population of the metropolitan area (in millions)	14.40	11.02	9.42	6.00
Area (in sq. km)	4,189.17	13.5	3,182	1,176
Area of the city	437.71	174	1,485	170

SOURCE: Census of India, 1991

statistically speaking, there is not only no break in the distribution of population aggregates; instead we have a rural urban continuum."[6]

It is therefore important to recognize that all that is urban is not necessarily municipal, and therefore municipal is not the only form of urban government. In fact, although a significant portion of urban growth takes place within existing cities, much of it spills over traditional boundaries. Whether by urbanization of villages or expansion of small towns and metropolitan areas, much of the growth takes place in pockets, within or on the peripheries of existing urban areas. Usually, such growth is spontaneous and unplanned. In many cities one-quarter to one-third of the population live in slums or squatter settlements. These settlements are variously characterized as spontaneous, informal, marginal, illegal, unplanned, or unintended. Unfortunately, many governments also regard them as ungovernable. Acts of patent hostility such as bulldozing of slums and large-scale eviction may be far less common, but they continue to occur.[7] Alternative approaches to bringing these settlements into a conscious design of urban services and management are still lacking.

Governance and the Urban Poor

The concentration and densification of poverty in the central city is increasingly considered a major problem in North American cities. This concentration "has been accompanied by soaring unemployment, increased and prolonged welfare dependency, public health problems too numerous to mention and most visible and startling, rising crime. . . . Places where the poor and politically dispossessed become concentrated, inevitably become places where environmental problems are too easily ignored."[8] Slums in American cities are not "unintended" settlements; they were very much a part of the city planned and built earlier, but have become blighted since then. In developing countries, however, the slums are primarily composed of shacks and shanties, and the sharp contrast they present to the cities that surround them is even more striking. Whether in Manila or Bangkok, Bombay or Rio, the gleaming glass and steel downtown and the well-provided, plush residential enclaves of the rich are constant evidence of this contrast.

The contrast is not just a matter of standards and services or environmental conditions. It goes deeper than the outward manifestations—to differences in legal status, fiscal base, levels of expenditure, and the continued inability overall of local and other governments to integrate these settlements into the structure of urban governance. The black townships in South Africa are a dramatic example. Of the 6.12 million people in the Johannesburg metropolitan area (Witwaters

Rand), 4.42 are in "deprived" settlements, a euphemism for black townships suffering service deficiencies. In Durban, out of a total of 3.3 million, 2.28 are in the townships. Public expenditures in the white townships are about $552 per capita, among the highest in the world and nearly ten times the national average of $62, reflecting the much lower expenditure in black communities.[9] Metropolitan institutions merging white and black local authorities have been created, but the redistribution of expenditures and the rearrangement of tax revenues remain contentious issues.

In other cities, although these settlements may be notionally within metropolitan boundaries already defined, they are beyond both the service domain and the taxation reach of such governments. One example is Cairo, where spontaneous settlements account for nearly a third of the growth in the governorate since the 1960s.[10] The proportion is not very different in Delhi, Dar es Salaam, Nairobi, or Lagos. Even in cities of more recent origin like Lusaka, Zambia, out of about 1 million people in the area, only one-third live in the city proper; the rest are in "compounds." These compounds are called "peri-urban" but in reality, it is the city proper that is peripheral. The majority of the households in the compounds are made up of the poor, who spend nearly three-fourths of their meager incomes on water, energy, transportation, rent, and education, as compared to the nonpoor who spend only a quarter of their income for the same services.[11] To the people of the compounds, the ostensible symbols of the Lusaka City Council are of little use and relevance. Much of Africa's urbanization is of a similar kind. Whether in Kinshasa, Maputo, Luanda, or Freetown, the central city of the colonial days is not where the people are. Yesterday's camp of refugees, whether driven by drought or civil strife, is tomorrow's city.

The situation is not very different in Lagos and Nairobi, which are comparatively older settlements. The bulk of the poor are not within the reach of the local governments, and in the main have to fend for themselves. Several Asian cities present the same picture: Delhi, Bombay, Karachi, and Bangkok. In cities like Calcutta and Manila, there have been conscious efforts to provide basic services and upgrade the slums but it has not been possible to avoid gentrification and consequent displacement of the residents.

Given the fact that slum settlements constitute one-fourth to one-third of most cities in developing countries and account for most of the poor, one harsh reality is that, apart from being largely outside the formal management systems of urban governments, their relationship is often one of "negative engagement."[12] Whether fighting eviction, stealing electricity or water, or resisting regulations or taxes, it is this negative engagement that stands out as a prominent issue for the municipal and other authorities. The efforts of the elite to insulate themselves from the problem is an obverse of this negative engagement. To quote Cisneros, "[i]n the U.S. middle and upper income families may flee to the suburbs but the problems of the inner cities are sure to follow them."[13] In Delhi, Manila, Rio, and Nairobi the wealthy try to ensconce themselves in well-provided but heavily fortified enclaves, called "villages" in Manila. Such negative engagement is one of the unfortunate similarities between the North and the South.

In Urban Governance, Is the Centerpiece Municipal?

Not all that is urban is municipal. Where municipalities do exist as units of urban and local governments they are not uniform in their origin, tradition, functions, or place in politics. In Europe, North America, and Latin America the mayor is a recognized political figure who can aspire to move to positions in national politics. Mayors Jacques Chirac (of Paris), Willy Brandt (of Berlin), Konrad Adenauer (of Berlin), Henry Cisneros (of San Antonio), and Comancho Solis (of Mexico City) are some examples. Belaunde Terry, an architect of repute deeply concerned with urban problems, also managed to serve as president of Peru twice. Most of the leaders of independent India, such as Jawaharlal Nehru or Subhas Bose, honed their political skills as mayors and municipal chairs. In more recent years, however, there has been a shift. Provincial and national leaders have viewed themselves as more representative of the people than municipal leaders. In many Asian and African countries, municipalities are creatures of provincial or national governments, and their powers and functions can be altered or abridged arbitrarily. In India for instance, although municipalities served as the cradle for national political leadership, at any given time since the country became independent, 40 to 50 percent of the municipalities have been under suspension. It was only in 1994 that a constitutional amendment gave the municipalities the "right to live." This far-reaching amendment made elections mandatory in the country's four thousand municipalities and added about half a million elected representatives to the body politic in the process.[14] Neighboring Bangladesh adopted direct elections to the posts of mayor and municipal chair. South Korea held mayoral elections after a gap of more than two decades, and the Philippines concluded nationwide municipal elections. After the colonial past, national sovereignty has been a zealously guarded principle in many Asian countries. The feeling that this principle might be undermined by too much emphasis on local autonomy appears to be slowly changing and there is an increasing recognition that local governments can, legitimately and usefully, coexist with national and provincial governments.

Decentralization

A World Bank study points out that of seventy-five developing countries and those whose economies are in transition with populations of over five million, all but twelve are engaged in some form of decentralization.[15] These ongoing exercises vary in type and range as well as in the political and other purposes to be accomplished. The consequences reported vary from mere disengagement of higher levels of government from certain functions to conscious devolution of responsibilities with commensurate powers and resources; from increased revenue sharing as in Brazil or the Philippines to concessions of political autonomy as have occurred in Hungary.

None of the decentralization exercises have reached a stage in history where they can be evaluated objectively. Although decentralization may be regarded overall as a positive feature, widening participation at different levels of government, it should not be presumed that it will, ipso facto, strengthen local autonomy or render local performance more effective and accountable. That will depend on several administrative, regulatory, and fiscal measures following up.

India is involved in an elaborate and complex exercise of bringing the numerous provincial laws into conformity with the 1994 constitutional amendment, in law as well as practice. This exercise includes the establishment of finance commissions in each state to determine revenue sharing and to rearrange functional and financial domains of both urban and rural local bodies. In some states compliance with the constitutional amendment has been in letter rather than substance, whereas in others, a serious attempt has been made to rationalize and strengthen the municipal structure. One may discern a common thread linking the strident demands for local autonomy in developed countries with the arduous and complex steps toward decentralization that developing countries are taking. What is happening in India, the Philippines, Brazil, and Bolivia is not just an angry reaction to "big" government, as currently witnessed in the United States, although the political rhetoric may sound similar. A major motivation for the rearrangement of functional and financial domains in developing countries is that the central governments simply do not have the resources to meet the rising aspirations and increased demands on the infrastructure in their cities. The rearrangement being sought will require a delicate balance between needs and resources, powers and accountability.

Some theorists regard privatization of public services as another form of decentralization. This may be stretching the point. In the case of basic urban services such as water supply or solid waste collection, privatization is more in the nature of contracting and the municipal authorities will continue to be responsible for the regulatory framework (such as standards of supply, parameters of tariff, coverage, etc). Indeed the establishment of such a framework may require more sophistication and sensitivity to public needs than traditional engineering departments in municipalities have demonstrated. Ensuring that citizens are not short-changed in any process of privatization is a demanding task in urban management.

Proximity

Proximity between the citizen and the government is a recurring issue in governance. In urban areas, high density and large numbers present both a challenge and an opportunity. Municipalities in most developing countries are composed of wards. In many cases, one elected councilor for each ward may be the only formal representative.

Attempts have been made to rearrange municipal wards to make them equal in size as much as possible, but on average a city of one million people is unlikely to have a municipal council of more than fifty to sixty members with ward sizes of twenty thousand to thirty thousand people. Apart from the size question, given the rather limited range of services that a city government may handle, a municipal council member may not be able to deal with all the issues. For primary healthcare or education, citizens may need to contact a state rather than a municipal agency. Municipal wards may not, therefore, be the most or the only relevant constituency for addressing citizens' needs. Furthermore, in many cities there is also a mismatch between the delineation of the electoral districts, municipal or provincial, and the physical realities of rapidly urbanizing peripheries and densification.

In many Indian cities for instance, the size of a municipal ward may vary from thirty to three hundred thousand and provincial electoral districts from five hundred thousand to two million voters. In the absence of periodic and regular readjustments of electoral districts there is considerable disparity between rural and urban constituencies. In the state of Maharashtra (of which Bombay is the capital), the assembly has 288 members, of whom 58 are elected from principally urban districts. The voting size of these urban districts exceeds the state average by 20 to 50 percent. The value of a vote in such a district is thus much lower than in the others. In the event, even in this 39 percent urbanized state, the number of urban representatives in the assembly is only 20 percent. In the country's parliament, representation from urban areas is less than 15 percent. The composition of the national and state legislatures therefore do not reflect the urbanizing character of the country. Urban issues tend to get relegated as local or municipal issues, unworthy of debate in these legislatures.

To reiterate, the question is whether municipal councilors, members of state assemblies, and the parliament should be the only representatives of the people and whether in matters of urban governance, disaggregated, community-based arrangements, however informal, would better serve the citizens.

There are numerous examples of communities mobilizing themselves to secure and in some cases maintain some basic local services, such as garbage collection and removal, maintenance of drains and footpaths, etc. Such initiatives are often a part of the people's strategies to cope with deprivation or municipal nonperformance, rather than a conscious element of governance. In the Barriadas of Lima, the Bustees of India, the Kampungs of Indonesia, and the Barangays of Manila, the scaling up of these initiatives to the city level has not been easy. However, the organizations handling these tasks at the community level have been given formal recognition. For example, the Barangay Committees and Captains in Manila are elected; the Bustee Committees in Calcutta have a formal say in capital and maintenance works in the neighborhood; and in the Kampungs of Jakarta, *Ripung Warga*, a time-honored informal group of about 150 to 200 families supervises garbage collection and drainage cleaning. The issue is not merely one of formality or informality of these community groups but rather their scaling up. In some cities, these community groups and other non-governmental organizations come together to interact on citywide issues. Although developing countries may lack several things, pervasive politics is not one of them. Depending on the identification of political parties, these associations and NGOs engage or disengage in debates and interaction with government authorities on city-level issues. Indeed their informality and the ability to engage or disengage may be a significant source of strength for these associations.

Transparency and Accountability

Transparency and the right to information are critical requirements for a positive civil society–government relationship. Unfortunately, neither is perceived as a strong attribute of city governments. City hall politics is often referred to in pejorative terms when compared to other levels of government, though there is little concrete evidence to show that graft, corruption, denial of information to the public, and inefficiency are exclusive features of municipal authorities or that provincial and national governments fare better in these respects. The potential for abuse of power may be more of an issue with regard to building and trade permits, service connections, and so on. However, it is the manner in which these functions are performed that determines the character of the "public face" of a local authority and thus provides the opportunity to voice discontent and enable corrective action. Locally elected officials cannot be far removed from their constituencies, and regular elections do provide a mechanism to correct for gross nonperformance and abuse of power. Problems of accountability may be more serious for organizations that are responsible for providing urban services but that are not elected local governments.

Given the varied character of urban growth formations, not all subnational or local authorities are municipal. There is a wide variety of agencies and organizations functioning within a city and also at metropolitan or state levels. In a few cases, they are subsidiaries of municipalities that operate specific utilities such as water companies in Latin American or Indonesian cities, but in most they are creatures of higher levels of governments, such as statewide or special purpose parastatal agencies. It is unlikely that all these organizations will be municipalized in the near future; at the same time, they will continue to have a critical role in urban governance.

Unlike elected local governments, which are prima facie accountable to the electorate, the special purpose agencies may feel more responsible to the institutions that created them or own them. A state-level water board for instance may consider itself accountable to the department in the state government that oversees it, rather than the several urban areas to which it is expected to provide water. South Asia contains several locales where such state-level boards are at loggerheads with municipalities over project scope, completion, debt liability, or maintenance. Land-development agencies or housing boards may regard their accountability more in terms of profit and financial performance than client satisfaction. Entrusting basic municipal functions such as water supply and wastewater systems to special purpose agencies or parastatals on grounds of technical competence, need for additional funds, or improved coverage has weakened the municipalities of South and East Asia. Experience shows that the reasons cited for such diminution have not been justified, have reduced accountability, and have not resulted in increased benefits to the public.

The Metropolitan Dimension

Since the conference in Vancouver, the total number of cities with populations over 1 million has increased by 141; one hundred of these are in developing countries. India and China alone have added fourteen and twenty-five such cities respectively. Africa, whose urbanization was not a strongly recognized feature at Vancouver, has increased its number of such cities from five to sixteen. Despite serious strife and severe want, cities like Luanda, Kinshasa, Douala, and Addis Ababa (in Africa) and (elsewhere) Hanoi, Ho Chi Minh City, Kabul, and Port-au-Prince have steadily grown in population. Today the metropolitan city is no longer a Western phenomenon. Indeed, natural growth and migration have carried many of the large cities in developing countries to megacity proportions. Ten of the world's fourteen cities with 10 million people or more are in developing countries; by 2015, the number will be twenty-two out of twenty-seven.[16]

All of these megacities are multimunicipal in composition; as are most other large cities. This is one point of strong similarity between the cities of the North and those of the South. More than two-thirds of the people in the United States live in over three hundred metropolitan areas, and a metropolitan area typically has about one hundred different governments.[17] Establishing a metropolitan perspective is thus an arduous process. Yet in the provision of basic urban services such as water supply, sanitation, or transport "most American urban areas have realized effective metropolitan governance without having to enact formalized metropolitan government."[18] In North American cities metropolitan or regional governments as such have never enjoyed much support. Instead, through a variety of institutional arrangements such as voluntary councils of governments (nearly six hundred in the United States); special purpose regional bodies for water, transport, or wastewater; and urban county set-ups, these cities have tried to secure the provision and coordination of urban services. The Toronto metropolitan council with its two-tier structure, metropolitan Dade County in Florida, and Minneapolis–St. Paul have been the exceptions to the rule. Despite the serious compulsions of economic competitiveness, intermunicipal fiscal disparities, poverty, crime, and environmental management, emphasis continues to be on cross-sectoral coalitions and collaborative partnerships rather than formal regional governments.[19]

Other countries have made more frontal attempts at metropolitan governance. The 1974 Constitution in Brazil created special multimunicipal organizations in the country's eight metropolitan areas for metro-wide planning and investment coordination. The 1988 Constitution abrogated this arrangement and returned the power to form such bodies to the states and the municipalities. Current efforts are limited to inter-municipal associations. Colombia, in 1979, created five metropolitan regions headed by the mayor of the central cities, but these have not emerged as metro governments. Even in national capitals like Mexico City, the 1980 effort toward metro-wide planning did not succeed.[20] In the early 1990s, this largest metropolitan area in the developing countries continues to be fragmented between three states, one federal district (population 8.23 million) and twenty-seven municipalities (population 6.81 million).[21]

Two of these municipalities, Ecatepec and Nezahualcoyotl, the latter regarded by many as a sprawling slum, have about 1.2 million people each. Of the 3.12 million households in the metropolitan area, 1.53 million have no access to sanitation. Public transport links between the federal district and the rest of the metropolitan area continue to be tenuous. Air pollution, without respect for municipal boundaries, affects the entire area.

Municipal fragmentation has occurred in metropolitan areas of all sizes. Santiago de Chile (1.21 million) is broken up into Santiago City (.998 million) and thirty-one other units ranging in population from 9,500 to 88,000.[22] São Paulo, as big as Mexico City, comprises thirty-eight municipalities; its 8,000 km² area includes municipalities as small as 14 km² and as large as 1,500 km².

By definition, tasks in a metropolitan area are multiple: a multiplicity of tasks render a multiplicity of institutions inevitable. Yet, some attempts have been made in developing countries to aggregate some of these, especially development planning and capital works, at the metropolitan level.

In the 1970s, India set up more than a dozen metropolitan development authorities. Beginning in Calcutta and after elaborate exercises at consolidation of municipal boundaries that failed, these development authorities were created by provincial governments with responsibilities for planning, capital budgeting, infrastructure works, and mobilization of funds, in conjunction with or overriding the municipalities constituting the metro area. The fact that the elected municipalities were kept under suspension in many cities such as Calcutta and Madras no doubt facilitated this process. However, given the continued demand for new services, the need for operation and maintenance of the facilities already built, and the broader thrust of decentralization, these metropolitan authorities face a moment of truth. Under the 1994 constitutional amendment metropolitan planning committees, with two-thirds of their membership comprising the elected representatives of the urban and rural local bodies within the metropolitan areas, are now mandatory for all cities with populations over 1 million. In the face of these elected bodies, the nominated development authorities are likely to yield ground and take on staff rather than policy functions.[23]

In Thailand, Bangkok and Thonburi, the city across the river, were merged in 1972 to create the Bangkok Metropolitan Administrations (BMA) with a directly elected mayor and an assembly. However, the BMA is responsible only for a limited range of services such as solid waste management, public-health services, and primary education. Water, transport, and other metro-wide services are handled by other agencies. Though the BMA survived a brief abrogation of the elective arrangement in 1978, it is under considerable control by the national government.[24]

Indeed, in most metropolitan cities of developing countries that are national or provincial capitals, metropolitan autonomy is still regarded as a threat to state and national leadership. Metropolitan Manila, which has undergone three major changes since the mid-1970s illustrates the problem. In 1975, the Metropolitan Manila Commission (MMC) was created to plan, administer, and operate many public services in an area comprising seventeen municipalities. Chaired by Imelda Marcos, then first lady, MMC was quickly transformed from a service agency to a conspicuous power. Though the MMC accomplished a significant degree of coordination, fear of an alternate power base in the nation's capital led to its dismantling in 1990 by President Corazon Aquino, and to the creation of an ineffectual Metropolitan Manila Authority (MMA) with vastly reduced powers. The decentralization process and internal revenue sharing initiated soon after helped the seventeen municipalities to reassert their position, eventually leading to "atomization" as lamented by President Ramos. In March 1995, a new law created the Manila Metropolitan Development Authority (MMDA) with the seventeen municipal chairpersons and some national agency representatives forming the governing council and a presidential appointee as the chairperson. The details of the changeover from the MMA to the MMDA are still being worked out in the mid-1990s.[25]

The abolition of the Greater London Council (GLC), long referred to as a model of metropolitan governance, is another dramatic illustration of the perceived conflict between national authority and local autonomy. Some believe that the GLC was abolished by the Thatcher government not because it failed to address metropolitan issues, but because it emerged as a significant political force, frequently at odds with the national government. The Tokyo Metropolitan Government, on the other hand, has endured with a sophisticated delineation of metropolitan and local functions, and fiscal adjustments among the fifty municipalities and special wards of the area, as well as a widely accepted pattern of autonomy from the national government.

Environment: An Issue and an Opportunity

Urban environmental problems, collectively dubbed the "brown agenda," present a new challenge to urban management. The efficient provision of basic services such as water supply and sanitation is in itself the essence of good urban environment. Yet in situations of scarcity, securing these basic services becomes even more critical. Large urban areas across the world, such as Mexico, Tokyo, Beijing, Madras, and Delhi, are literally running out of water. Industrial pollution and municipal wastes have slowly poisoned myriad streams and other bodies of water in both the North and the South. Nearly half of China's groundwater resources are polluted; so are several stretches of India's fourteen major rivers. When urban and environment ministers from over fifty countries in Asia and the Pacific gathered in Bangkok in November 1993 to discuss urbanization, the sober conclusion was "that urban growth as a key aspect of economic development in this region has entailed a sharp and significant deterioration in the environment,"[26] in terms of increased health risks and increased inability of the poor to secure any protection from pollution.

Nevertheless, as environmental degradation threatens the sustainability of cities, it also provides a platform for those affected to gather. Rivers, seas, and natural endowments have served as rallying points to bring together the different stakeholders and hammer out agreements and action. The Ganga Action Plan in India, the Med Cities network to reduce pollution in the Mediterranean, the Baltic Seas group, the Delaware and Rhine river basin commissions, and the Guarapirange watershed in São Paulo are some examples. Mexico City literally ran out of breath but has struggled to begin implementation of a multi-component plan to reduce air pollution which involves the Mexico City Federal District and all the constituent municipalities. Even in highly fragmented Los Angeles (four hundred suburbs in search of a city) some measurable improvement in air quality has been achieved by the South Coast Air Quality Management District.[27]

There also appears to be an increased convergence of problems and approaches between the cities of the North and the South as far as urban environmental issues are concerned. This has brought about some useful international and multi-agency partnerships such as the Healthy Cities Project and the Metropolitan Environment Improvement Program (MEIP). Insofar as these programs emphasize stakeholder participation in problem-solving and help to bring about closer contacts between citizen groups and government agencies, they have the potential to contribute to the substance and quality of urban governance.

Globalization

The liberalization of economies and the globalization of trade has resulted in an unprecedented flow of resources at the international level. At the same time, it is not clear that urban authorities can access this flow of resources, which may go only into the upper end of the infrastructure spectrum, reaching airports, civil aviation, and telecommunications but not healthcare, education, or water supply. Yet, along with globalization, avenues of private investment in public services are also opening up. As mentioned earlier, the capacity of traditionally organized urban governments to access the capital markets and utilize privatization for optimum public benefit is limited.

Globalization and economic reforms will also, undoubtedly, add to existing strains. Competition between cities to become the location of manufacturing and other activities that take advantage of cheap labor may bring about sharp increases in environmental deterioration and aggravate existing inequities in income and access to basic services. The rapid rise of land and housing prices is an illustration of the unintended, but real, consequences of sudden spurts of capital inflows. The 40 percent increase in commercial property prices in one year alone (1994) did not prompt any significant initiative for redevelopment in Bombay, despite an abundance of crumbling old property and derelict land. Foreign financiers, who have rushed to set up in Bombay in the mid-1990s, have discovered that a modest three-bedroom flat may cost $2 million although two-thirds of the city's 10 million residents live in one-room tenements or shacks.[28] The story amply illustrates that the marketplace alone cannot be expected to produce the right answers to these new challenges.

Although country after country embarks on economic liberalization and seeks to embrace globalization, most subnational and urban governments have not been in the mainstream of these changes. Economic reform, it has been wryly observed in India, has been by stealth rather than by a consciously developed consensus and design involving the states and the cities. At the subnational level, the gaps in knowledge about the economic changes are many: local political perceptions vary significantly (as demonstrated by the recent decision of a state government to cancel a private-sector power project agreement in India) as does the capacity to adapt to the changes.

These are some factors that constitute a significant change of scene and challenging realities of urban governance in many developing countries. Until these realities are better understood and addressed, the cities of developing countries will continue to be "rife with problems— although filled with promise."[29]

Notes

[1]Report, United Nations Conference on Human Settlements (UNCHS) 31 May–11 June 1976, Vancouver, Canada.

[2]Ibid.

[3]United Nations, *World Urbanization Prospects: 1992 Revision* (New York: United Nations, 1993).

[4]Mohamed Halfani, Patricia McCarney, and Alfredo Rodriguez, "Towards an Understanding of Governance," in *Urban Research in the Developing World,* ed. Richard Stren (Toronto, Canada: University of Toronto Press, 1994).

[5]World Bank, *Governance—The World Bank's Experience* (Washington, D.C.: World Bank, 1994).

[6]Network on Urban Research in the European Community, *The Statistical Concept of the Town in Europe* (Duisburg, Germany: 1992).

[7]"In a Scene Evoking Past, South Africa Levels Squatters' Settlement," *Washington Post,* 26 November, 1994.

[8]Henry Cisneros (secretary, HUD), in *The Human Face of the Urban Environment,* ed. Ismail Serageldin, Michael A. Cohen, and K. C. Sivaramakrishnan, proceedings of the Second Annual Conference on Environmentally Sustainable Development (Washington, D.C.: The World Bank, 1995).

[9]World Bank, *Financing the Metropolitan Areas of South Africa, Southern Africa Department,* working paper no. 8 (Washington, D.C.: World Bank, April 1994).

[10]UNCHS, Habitat, *Cairo and Madras: A Comparison of Planning and Change* (Nairobi, Kenya: UNCHS, 1994).

[11]World Bank, *Poverty and Vulnerability in Chawama, Luzaka, Zambia: Research Project on Urban Poverty and Social Policy in the Context of Adjustment* (Washington, D.C.: World Bank, 1994).

[12]Halfani, McCarney, and Rodriguez, "Towards an Understanding of Governance."

[13]Cisneros, in *The Human Face,* 9.

[14]K. C. Sivaramakrishnan, *Urban Governance in India* (New Delhi, India: Center for Policy Research, December 1992).

[15]World Bank, *Municipal Development Sector Review* (Washington, D.C.: World Bank, October 1993).

[16]United Nations, *World Urbanization Prospects.*

[17]K. C. Sivaramakrishnan, "Urban Environmental Governance: An Overview," in *The Human Face.*

[18]Ibid.

[19]Allan D. Wallis, "The Third Wave: Current Trends in Regional Governance," *National Civic Review, USA* (summer–fall 1994).

[20]Lordello de Mello, "Decentralization and Metropolitan Governance" (paper presented at the World Conference on Metropolitan Governance, Tokyo, Japan, 1993).

[21]Census of Mexico, 1990.

[22]Census of Chile, 1992.

[23]Sivaramakrishnan, *Urban Governance in India.*

[24]K. C. Sivaramakrishnan and Leslie Green, *Metropolitan Management: The Asian Experience* (Oxford, U.K.: Economic Development Institute/Oxford University Press, 1986).

[25]*Metropolitan Manila Management Study* (Manila, Philippines: Local Government Development Foundation, February 1995).

[26]"State of Urbanization in Asia and the Pacific" (report on the Ministerial Conference, ESCAP, Bangkok, October/November 1993).

[27]Sivaramakrishnan, "Urban Environmental Governance."

[28]*The Economist*, 6 May 1995.

[29]*Time*, 11 January 1993.

Chapter 12

Cities: New Roles and Forms of Governing

Jordi Borja

This chapter begins with an examination of the economic and social challenges that must be faced by cities and their governments in an era characterized by competition between regions—within the framework of a global economy—and by the concentration of social problems in the urban setting. However, my emphasis is not on the analysis of these processes, but rather on the political, legal, and organizational changes that local governments must deal with while providing leadership to the community in the search for effective answers. Creating strong leadership implies reacting to important external changes, such as contractual inter-administrative relations, public-private cooperation, strategic planning, and international outreach. Internal changes must also be addressed, such as the need for a strong elected city government, regional and functional decentralization, management of services, and civic participation aided by new communications technology.

These ideas and proposals have, above all else, a practical purpose. They do not stem from a theory of the modernization of administration, but from ongoing trends and projects. An effort was made at systematization and synthesis, based on my analytical and pragmatic experiences.

This chapter is not the product of academic research, but rather a reflection based on professional experience in three particular areas: 1) The city of Barcelona: the author was responsible for the decentralization and participation project; the "Metropolitan Area"; the draft of the Special Law; and international relations for the city; 2) At the European level, the author was the force behind and served as president of the Founding Conference on Eurocities (Barcelona, 1989). He has directed or collaborated on diverse works for the European Community (urban strategies and city networks, green book on the urban environment). Between 1989 and 1994 he actively participated in the Council of Municipalities and Regions of Europe; 3) Various Latin American cities: The author has prepared reports concerning the political-legal reforms of Mexico and São Paulo (1991–92), the decentralization of Buenos Aires (1986–87), the future of local democracy in Chile (1985–86), etc. He has edited a manual on democratic municipal management for Latin America (1987) and also a report on local governments in Latin America.

Cities as the Protagonists of Our Era

The United Nations Conference on Population (Cairo, 1994) focused on the problems generated by urban population growth. The international press, in reports prior to the conference, presented images—more or less dramatized—of the largest cities of the world. Simultaneously, the UN convoked a conference of mayors, in preparation for the Social Summit (Copenhagen, 1995). For the first time, the intergovernmental organization recognized local authorities. In reality, what was being recognized was the need to deal with social problems (unemployment, poverty, and social-cultural integration) at the local level. In the mid-1990s social, economic, cultural, and population processes are reaching a global level. Their effects, however, are mainly felt in the urban agglomerations and require integrated policy measures. Following a logical sequence, the UN called for the Conference on Habitat (Istanbul, 1996), which the secretary general dubbed "The Summit of the Cities." The twentieth century will end as the century of the cities. The twenty-first century will be the urban century, and economic progress, social well-being, and the cultural integration of cities will be determined to a large degree within the cities.

Signs of the growing importance of cities have multiplied. In Europe, the economic recession of the 1970s elicited a response by local governments and the principal urban economic and social actors. The former went beyond their legal duties to attract investment, generate employment and renovate the productive base of the city. They worked together with urban actors to promote the city. The conference on European cities (Rotterdam, 1986) was named, "Cities as the Engine Behind Economic Growth." The Eurocities movement was born and was formally established at the following conference (Barcelona, 1989). In 1995 it links the fifty most important cities of Europe. The European Community finally recognized local governments within its institutional framework with the creation of the Committee of Regions (Maastricht, 1993), which joins representatives of regional and city governments. This is something that had not been foreseen in the Founding Treaty (Rome, 1957).

The new economic protagonists often carry the names of cities. The Eurocities have been defined as "the multinational Europe" and as the European "force of the frappe" by Jacques Delors, former president of the European Commission, Pasqual Maragall, president of the Council of Municipalities and Regions of Europe, and others.

On other continents, the economic protagonism of cities is even more evident, especially in Asia: take note of Seoul, Taipei, Hong Kong,

Singapore, Bangkok, Shanghai, and Hanoi. Available economic statistics on the cities show a strong complementarity between city government and economic actors, all of which are oriented toward external markets. Asian cities have demonstrated that in the global economy the speed of information regarding international markets and the ability to act on that information, the flexibility of productive and commercial structures, and the capacity to enter networks determines success or failure much more than positions acquired in the past, accumulated capital, natural resources, or geographic location. The secret is the speed at which the network of small and medium-sized businesses is able to innovate. It is understood that this network is, in turn, connected with large businesses that maintain links with the exterior and with the domestic political power structure. This assures that the important functions of information processing and promotion are fulfilled. It also guarantees that city services are adequately provided, since the economic network and the urban network are logically interwoven. The urban political power structure, in the case of Asian cities, has developed a model with low general costs (unlike Europe), but with high social costs. It does not appear to be a sustainable model, because in the long run it diminishes the attractiveness of the city and does not sufficiently train human resources.

In the United States, cities have played an important role in changes in politics and economic policy. The exalted neoliberalism of the Reagan and Bush administrations not only brutally eliminated a large portion of welfare programs that covered the basic needs of one-third of the urban population, but also favored de-industrialization and encouraged movement away from the cities, which caused a decline in the budgets of local governments. Some cities reacted by initiating ambitious strategic programs that combined the objectives of economic growth and urban development with answers to the problems generated by environmental deterioration, increasing social inequalities, and a rising level of public insecurity. Cities such as Los Angeles, San Francisco, Detroit, and Seattle (as well as the states of Florida and Wisconsin), through strategic planning and public-private cooperation, demonstrated both the negative results of the aberrant neoliberal policy and the ability of cities to respond. A large demonstration, called by U.S. mayors, brought together half a million people in Washington, D.C., to announce the downfall of President George Bush and the implementation of new policies for cities: new infrastructure; "enterprise zones"; and the relaunching of social programs based on employment generation, education, increased access to healthcare, protection of the urban environment, etc.

The political protagonism of cities was spectacularly manifested in Eastern Europe. The fall of the state-controlled communist system was evident mainly in the cities: Berlin, Budapest, Prague, Warsaw, etc. Almost all of the social-political movements that expressed the rebellion of civil society were called "civic movements." Furthermore, it is in the cities that not only democratic organization has been reconstructed, but also the market economy has been rebuilt.

In Latin America, the processes of political democratization and decentralization of the state have reemphasized the role of cities and local governments. Nonetheless, the limitations of these same processes, the social effects of adjustment policies that have exacerbated inequalities and marginalization, the weakness of the sociocultural framework of the cities, and the serious lack of infrastructure and public services hindered the emergence of the city as protagonist. This situation changed during the 1990s. On one hand, economic reactivation has stimulated the implementation of large-scale urban programs (in some cases encouraged by privatizations) and invigorated the construction sector. On the other hand, it has sharpened long-standing contradictions and weaknesses: physical and communications infrastructure; insufficient public resources; the inability of local governments to act; low levels of social integration in the city; and weak public-private cooperation. Furthermore, the consolidation of internal democratic processes and the continued opening of the economy have increased social demands and have accentuated the feeling of a functional crisis within the large cities. The intensity and visibility of urban problems (traffic congestion, public insecurity, air and water pollution, housing shortages, and insufficient basic services) have heightened this sensation of crisis. Simultaneously, economic trends (reactivation), social trends (participation), and political trends (democratization) have created the conditions to generate possible solutions. There has been no lack of response: the passage of political and financial reforms in significant Latin American cities (Mexico City, Bogotá, Buenos Aires, and São Paulo); the protagonism of mayors of large cities who, as politicians and mediators, have also become national leaders; the initiation of strategic economic, social, and urban development plans based on wide civic participation; the decentralization of local governments; the implementation of publicly or privately initiated large urban projects; and cooperation between both sectors. Large Latin American cities are emerging, in the 1990s, as political and economic actors. Whether these roles can be consolidated will depend upon the level of support given to large city programs that rely on both the active participation of major public and private actors and widespread public support.

The Cities with Plans: From Europe to Latin America

THE EUROPEAN PRECEDENT

Large cities must respond to five different challenges: a new economic base; urban infrastructure; quality of life; social integration; and governability. Only by facing these challenges will they be able to compete in the external market and insert themselves in global economic areas, while satisfying the minimum needs of the population so that democracy can be consolidated. Responding to these challenges requires a city plan; the formulation of this plan can be encouraged by various elements. For example, in some cities the feeling of crisis has provoked a joint response by local government and principal economic actors, bringing about a transformation of urban infrastructure. This transformation facilitates the transition from the traditional industrial model to the qualified tertiary center.

Birmingham, through a strategic plan that enjoyed important support from the European Community, renovated its city center and was transformed into the most dynamic English city. Other cities, such as Amsterdam and Lyons, through strategic plans, preempted crisis by promoting infrastructure and image changes to adapt to the new demands of a global economy and international competition. In other instances, the impotence of local government has prevented strategic plans from being carried out, as was the case with the Milan Project (*Projetto Milano*).

Responding to the feeling of crisis is easier for cities that have secured and taken advantage of a large international event. Barcelona has become the paradigm. Most likely, the city's strategic plan would not have been the outline for an ambitious urban transformation project—part of which has already been achieved—without the Olympic Games of 1992. Yet Barcelona is not the only example. Lisbon, a city that carefully preserved a circle of melancholy and marginality, has started an important urban transformation and economic dynamization process through "cultural capital" (1994) and preparation for the World Exposition (1988). Glasgow also used the designation of "cultural capital" to modernize its urban infrastructure, to create an attractive location for congresses and international meetings, and to attract tourists and visitors (especially with its summer cultural festival). More recently, Manchester started along this path (as a candidate for the Olympic Games, Global Forum, etc.).

It would be difficult to provide positive responses to these challenges without personalized leadership. In many cases, the mayor plays a decisive role. This is true of the foregoing examples, especially Lisbon (Sampalo) and Barcelona (Maragall). The governmental crisis in a majority of Italian cities during the 1980s explains the failure of their strategic plans (for example, Milan and Turin after Mayors Tognoli and Novelli). The high level of international competitiveness and the positive image obtained by those cities that are not large capitals, such as Lille, Montpellier, or Strasbourg in France, cannot be fully understood without taking into consideration the strong personalities and dynamism of their mayors (Mauroy, Freche, and Trautman, respectively). In other instances, there has been a failure to take advantage of unique opportunities, due to a lack of local leadership. Two examples are Seville (host to the World Exposition of 1992) and Madrid (the "European cultural capital" during the same year). In Spain, moreover, cities that remained on the margin of the large projects in the glorious years (1986–92) have responded with a shared leadership (between public institutions and private-sector actors) and have implemented strategic plans (e.g., Valencia and Bilbao). Local leadership does not necessarily stem from political authority. In any situation, however, local leadership must be present and must contribute to the formation of shared leadership.

In all of the aforementioned cities, the urban transformation project was the sum of three factors: a sense of crisis heightened by the realization of economic globalization; a consensus among urban actors (public and private) and the generation of local leadership (political and civic); and a joint willingness and public consensus that allowed the city to grow physically as well as economically, socially, and culturally.

IS THIS ANALYSIS APPLICABLE TO LATIN AMERICA AND ITS LARGE CITIES TODAY?

These European examples are mirrored in Latin America a few years later. The challenges appear greater, yet conceptually they are the same. It is true that demographic growth, extension of the "nonlegal" city, social marginalization, lack of modern infrastructure, and weakness of local government are elements that are quantitatively different. However, other factors are more positive in Latin America than they were in Europe: less unemployment; greater economic dynamism; flexible productive structures; a good human resource quality/cost ratio; and the potential of the regional economic area.

Most likely, the key questions facing Latin American cities can be addressed and resolved by urban actors: joint efforts between public and private actors; the creation of central areas and qualified public spaces; reconstruction of the civic culture; political-administrative reform to make local government more efficient and participative; and above all else, the modernization of urban infrastructure (public services, communications, and commercial areas).

Have Latin American cities responded? Certainly. First, the democratization and decentralization of the state have reinforced and provided local government with a greater degree of legitimacy. This legitimacy has created the conditions, in many cases, for the exercise of local public leadership by mayors and governors.

Second, economic opening, both a fear-provoking and opportunity-generating factor, has mobilized economic actors. These actors have recognized the need for a competitive (i.e., attractive and functional) city endowed with modern infrastructure, that guarantees a minimum standard of living and security for its citizens. This realization has led economic actors to define objectives and actions to be carried out collectively that are also compatible with the goals of local government.

Third, dominant public and private actors have begun to understand that a city that excludes or marginalizes a significant portion of its population, or to be more precise, provides it only with substandard living conditions, is not feasible. Urban economic development based on high social costs does not necessarily bring with it lower general costs. Public insecurity, time spent in daily transit, and the degradation of public areas and of the urban environment in general also carry economic costs. A competitive city must have the capacity for the sociocultural integration of a significant majority of its population. Major socio-urban undertakings are seen as urgent and essential and, therefore, enjoy the political and economic support that they previously did not.

Fourth, and as a consequence of all of the above, the conditions are created for greater citizen action in collaboration with political sectors, professional and intellectual critics, and grassroots organizations.

Finally, the city is seen not only as a densely populated area that is the site of a great diversity of activities, but also as a symbiotic area of political and civic power, and as a symbolic area that integrates its citizens culturally and provides them with an internationally recognized collective identity. Therefore, the city is converted into a source of possible solutions to the economic, political, and cultural challenges of our era. Three examples are the need for integrated (as opposed to segmented) answers to the problems of unemployment, education, culture, housing, transportation, etc.; the need to reach compromises between the public and private sectors on the requirements for economic growth and environmental protection; and the challenge of defining new areas and configuring new mechanisms to stimulate political participation, facilitate the relationship between the administration and those under its authority, and promote the organization of social groups.

City reactions tend to take form in the drafting of a "project for the future" or "strategic plan" by the main public and private actors. In addition to Colombian cities (Bogotá, Medellín, and Cartagena), other Latin American cities have started down this path or have announced their intention to do so, such as Rio de Janeiro, Porto Alegre, Salvador de Bahia, and Recife (Brazil); Santiago and Concepción (Chile); Córdoba and Rosario (Argentina); Asunción (Paraguay); and Caracas (Venezuela). Other cities such as Mexico City and Buenos Aires have had to make pending political reform the first priority in order to create a local government with leadership capacity. In other cases, the promotion of the city, urban and economic transformation, and public-private cooperation have been expressed through simpler and more participatory master metropolitan or regional plans (like those in San José de Costa Rica and Quito), through economic promotion and international city "marketing" campaigns (witness Monterrey, Mexico), or through urban renovation and promotion of city centers (notable in Buenos Aires, São Paulo, and Bogotá).

THE CITY PLAN

The effectiveness of these plans or projects for the future depend upon a number of factors. Three of these factors are important to highlight because they are often overlooked. A project will be effective only if it encourages public and private urban actors from the very beginning and is translated into concrete actions and measures that can be implemented immediately. Only then will the viability of the plan be confirmed, generating trust among the actors promoting the plan and consensus among the population. This consensus instills a sense of loyalty and civic culture that is the principal strength of a strategic plan.

Second, a strategic plan must build or modify the image the city has of itself and the image it has in the eyes of others. A city plan may be called a communications, citizen mobilization, or internal and external promotion program as long as the plan is a response to the feeling of crisis. This response is triggered by the city's willingness to insert itself into new economic and broad cultural areas. It also attempts to integrate that sector of society that often feels excluded or ignored.

Finally, a strategic plan questions the abilities of the local government, its authority and organization, its relationship with other administrations and its citizens, its image, and its international presence.

Without a radical political reform—aimed more at pragmatic aspects than at a legal base—it will be difficult to achieve the goals set forth to respond to current challenges.

Cities and Their Governments: Leadership Assuming the Role of Promoter

The historical revindication of local autonomy that characterizes the municipal movement, further political and administrative decentralization within a modern democratic culture, and adequate public resources are not sufficient goals today. A local government capable of responding to current urban challenges, formulating a city project, and guiding that project must play the part of promoter.

Local autonomy has been understood as the city's legal right to self-organize, to have exclusive and specific authority, to be able to act in all areas of general interest to its citizens, and to have unconditional control over its own funds. The first principle that legitimizes autonomy is proximity, which allows the representative organization and administrative structure to establish a direct and immediate relationship with the region and its population. Proximity continues to be valid, as does the revindication of local autonomy. In Latin America, the constitutions of both unitarian and federal states (including the constitutions of the states, provinces, or departments) considerably limit self-organization and local authority, local public funds are shamefully insufficient (far from the European standard of a 50-25-25 division between the three levels), and legal defense of autonomy is practically impossible. Therefore, the question of autonomy has not been resolved despite the apparent need for change.

The city of the mid-1990s is a polymunicipal or metropolitan city that tends toward the functional organization of a discontinuous and asymmetrical territorial area. It is difficult to determine the size of the urban population because users of the downtown area may be more numerous than actual residents. There are numerous public and semipublic administrations active in the cities and their authority and functions are sometimes shared, at times by joint agreement. For example, in New York alone it has been estimated that more than one hundred public or semipublic organizations act with little or no coordination among them and that frequently their authority and functions overlap. This means that the three classic elements on which local government is based—population, territory, and organization—have not been clearly or sufficiently established. Above all, this is due to the fact that the big city is defined by its centrality and therefore, local government must propose actions for a population and an area that exceed its historical and legal reach. And, of course, it cannot perform these functions with a monopolistic approach.

I would like to present some suggestions for the shaping of the jurisdiction and organization of local government.

There is a new type of relationship with those public administrations considered superior (especially central governments). Although it is not necessary to grant greater recognition to the autonomy of the local authority, contractual relationships should be developed in order to share responsibilities and perform functions that require inter-administrative cooperation (for example, communications infrastructure, public transportation financing, regional economic promotion, public safety, large urban development projects, and environmental and antipoverty policies). Urban contracts are destined to become a new model for relations among public administrations. In terms of the metropolitan area, governing the region almost always requires going beyond the contractual relationship without necessarily creating a new local or departmental government that eliminates or controls the municipal governments. I will present some proposals that facilitate joint public action and shared management of services in the metropolitan region later in the chapter.

Local political organization cannot be based—as it is in 1995—upon a centralized administration, a rigid separation of the private and public sectors, and on the executive-legislative dichotomy. Forms of management and contracting must guarantee agility and transparency and respond to economic and social efficiency criteria, not to political or bureaucratic control.

Finally, local government must assume a level of responsibility derived from the use of its authority and the execution of those actions traditionally reserved for the state (for example, justice and safety) or for the private sector (for example, commercial activity in the market). This level of responsibility may result from the recognition of local government's right to act and from its possessing the means to do so, from the granting of specific legal authority, or from its capacity to perform the role of leader or coordinator in relation to other administrations and the private sector.

Prior to the development of political and administrative reforms, I believe it is more convenient to specify new roles that local governments must fulfill. Organization comes after the definition of objectives. Therefore we ask: What is understood by the local government in the role of promoter?

International promotion of the city, by developing a strong and positive image strengthened by appropriate infrastructure and the availability of services (communications, economic, cultural, safety, etc.)

attracts investors, visitors, and users, and facilitates "exports" (of its goods and services, of its professionals, etc.). Such promotion does not have to be financed, implemented, or managed entirely by local government. In its role as promoter, local government must create the conditions that facilitate the promotion of the city by public or private actors (through planning, political campaigns, and subsidies).

Cooperation with other public administrations and public-private coordination is a means of achieving international "marketing," in addition to other works and services required because of accumulated deficits, new urban demands, and changes in the size of the city. Joint planning and cooperation require political initiative, legal and financial innovation, and consensus among citizens.

The internal promotion of the city will develop among its inhabitants a "civic patriotism," a sense of belonging, a collective willingness to participate, and trust in and hope for the future of the city. This internal promotion must be supported by visible works and services, both those that have a monumental or symbolic character, as well as those designed to improve the quality of public areas and the public welfare.

Political-administrative innovation can generate numerous mechanisms of social cooperation and citizen participation. The role of local government as promoter is, to a large extent, to stimulate and direct the energies of the population toward achieving collective welfare and civil harmony. Three examples are employment; public safety; and the maintenance of public equipment, services, and areas. These are three types of problems that need to be addressed at the local level regardless of their causes and the organizations that have to deal with them. Responding to these problems also requires a significant capability for innovation and cooperation. Neither unilateral state or public actions nor the invisible hand of the market will resolve these problems.

Democratic innovation is probably the most exciting aspect of the role that is assumed by local government. I believe that this obligation must respond to three distinct challenges: citizen participation, social cooperation, and the integration of urban policies.

There is, without a doubt, a crisis in the collective identities of and participation within the representative institutions and political parties. The local environment (of a neighborhood, city, or region) is an adequate framework within which to experiment and to develop new electoral formulas for regional and functional decentralization, participation in the management and execution of public programs, etc. Democracy will be renewed through the principle of proximity, an indispensable part of the supranational political entities already in the making. In order to do so, the right to diversity and the need for creativity must be granted. For example, why not give cities the right to regulate their own electoral systems, provided that certain basic principles are respected?

Social cooperation is essential in facing problems that are new due to their nature or intensity. I have previously cited some of these problems, such as safety and the upkeep of public areas. Others can be listed, such as social services for the elderly, environmental awareness, or the promotion of cultural activities that foster the integration of a heterogeneous population vulnerable to marginalization. Public policies are inadequate because neither do they have the use of all the necessary resources nor are they able to develop appropriate methods of managing social demands. Therefore, public actions must support and stimulate social initiative. For example, only by increasing employment generation in sectors that are isolated from international competition (such as social services, urban ecology, etc.) can we resolve the imbalance that exists, even during periods of growth, between an active population and the number of jobs.

Innovation must be expressed by the exercise of authority and the performance of actions at the local level, so that integrated policies can be implemented. Problems concerning housing, poverty, the environment, education, economic promotion, culture, and so on cannot be efficiently addressed through sectoral policies and organizations. Therefore, new blocks of authority and new forms of management by local governments must be defined.

New Authority and Actions Assumed by City Government

Local government authority and actions can neither be defined by uniform national legislation nor be based on rigid divisions drawn according to a criteria of exclusion. I believe that other criteria, such as proximity, capability, cooperation, social demands, and diversity, must be included in the definition.

Cities and regional entities must be able to use all of their authority, perform all the functions assigned to them, and go beyond their natural limits in order to carry out duties that are not mandatory; the principle of proximity is an essential element for democratic legitimacy. Cities vary according to size, population, activities, quality of human resources, etc. The principle of capability means that certain types of cities can bestow upon themselves or assume additional authority because they are able to generate political, economic, social, or technical resources and as a result can accomplish such tasks as planning or coordinating police forces.

The principle of cooperation implies that we give priority to contractual relationships over hierarchical ones, in dealing with situations where administrations (or state and regional governments) are intertwined with private actors. It is a matter of developing formulas such as consortia, businesses of mixed ownership, and contract-programs.

The expression of social demands must always be taken into consideration. No local government can argue that it does not have jurisdiction over serious problems, such as unemployment or public safety. The legal system must allow and enable local governments to take action whenever social demands and political willingness coincide. This is necessary in order to face the challenges that either affect the authority of the state or are the responsibility of the private sector, whether in theory or due to legal inertia.

All of this leads to the revindication of the principle of diversity. Cities are and must be different in their features and activities. They must also be allowed to be different in their organization and level of authority. I recognize five areas for possible widening of the field of city government activity.

ECONOMIC BLOCS

Traditionally, municipal firms have only delivered and managed public services, and they have done so as monopolies. With respect to economic promotion activities, they have almost always been limited to the definition of areas—or zoning—by urban planning, and to advertising the city as a tourist destination. Economic promotion of the city requires that local government have the jurisdiction and the means—in collaboration with other public and private actors, but on its own initiative—to develop business activity zones; to create banks with capital-risk lines; to promote public and mixed-ownership businesses that are competitive with the private sector; to develop international campaigns in order to attract investors and visitors; to promote and manage fairs, convention centers, and industrial and technological parks; and to establish information offices to advise local and international businesses and investors.

URBAN BLOCS, HOUSING, AND ENVIRONMENT

Although traditionally these fall within the jurisdiction of local governments, in practice major decisions are made by the national government (such as the financing of large public works, the use of central areas or areas that are fit for urban development whether owned or managed by the state or by national corporations, the creation of housing programs, and the enforcement of environmental legislation) or private actors (who make decisions regarding investment in urban areas and about the design of construction projects and their specific purposes). Since local government uses the authority it has over city planning to force negotiation between public and private actors, priority must be given to facilitating cooperation between them.

This is one of the principal aspects of strategic planning. The role of promoter and local leader can be expressed in the design of large public works financed by the state; in renovation of obsolete areas under the control of port authorities, the military, or various ministries; in the management of housing programs; in delegating or transferring disciplinary authority in all areas pertaining to the urban environment; in the design of new planning schemes that link planning with the execution of the project; in the possibility of creating holdings, consortia, or companies of mixed ownership that could carry out large urban development operations jointly with other administrations and private actors; and in the use of underground areas that belong to the public domain, renovation of old areas of the city, usage plans, etc.

THE BLOC OF CITIZEN SAFETY AND JUSTICE

In this bloc, local government must assume authority in order to be able to perform a coordinating function based upon its capacity and the principle of proximity—for example, the coordination of the different police departments (overseeing safe areas, public buildings, traffic, petty urban crime, etc.). In some cities the national police are subject to the authority of the mayor (in spite of the existence of a local police force).

In addition local government must develop an innovative function to implement policies aimed at preventing or attacking new problems: drug trafficking and the rehabilitation of drug addicts; development and enforcement of environmental protection laws and regulations; and the elimination of racism, xenophobia, and other types of social, ethnic, and religious discrimination, for example. In certain cities the need to shape the municipal justice system has already been recognized.

SOCIAL AND CULTURAL BLOC

Local government jurisdiction and its ability to participate in social and cultural policy-making are widely recognized. In certain instances it is more than just a question of legality, it is a question of resources. The lack of means is the reason why in practice, higher level administrations take the place of local government, whether through sectoral programs or specific projects. In other cases it is the private sector that acts, without its action being part of a coherent urban program. And in other cases, a significant part of the city and its inhabitants are left without any cultural benefits or social services. The authority that must be attained is the management and coordination of public or mixed projects and programs and the development of all of the necessary types of public-private coordination.

Four fields of activity are especially relevant:

1) Housing and basic services programs with the cooperation of the area's inhabitants. Recognition of the existence of informal housing. Development of the periphery (including monumentalization, communications, urban centers, and political-administrative decentralization).

2) Employment-generating programs in sectors isolated from international competition: personal services, maintenance of infrastructure and public services, and urban ecology.

3) Availability of cultural products, directed toward both foreign audiences (attractiveness) and domestic groups (integration).

4) In some countries, education and healthcare are under municipal jurisdiction, in others they belong to the state, and in still others they are under joint jurisdiction. In general, they cannot be under the exclusive jurisdiction of local government (programs and financing must be determined at the national level so that greater inequalities are not created), yet it is beneficial to assign management of the basic network (nonuniversity education and primary healthcare) to the local government.

THE BLOC OF BASIC URBAN SERVICES, TRANSPORTATION, AND COMMUNICATIONS INFRASTRUCTURE

In this bloc there are at least three types of problems:

1) Financing of infrastructure and upkeep of basic services: public transportation, water supply, and wastewater systems, for example. Contractual agreements are required with the state and eventually with companies to be granted concessions. The model here is the contract-program.

2) The relation with public or semipublic monopolistic firms such as the telephone company or the railroad company. Local govern-

ment must attain a favorable negotiating position. A strategic plan may legitimize an intermodal transportation and communications plan that merges the regional train system with the urban network, or forces the telephone company to co-finance service centers.

3) The need to assume political authority and to manage businesses in new areas: erecting telecommunications towers; wiring and laying cable within the city; authorizing local radio and television broadcasting; and experimenting with the multimedia to reach the public, for example.

New Authority, New Resources, and New Management Methods

Many local governments say, We don't want greater authority and more obligations without increased financial resources and greater means. It is true that there is an imbalance between the increase in the actions of and demands made upon the local government and the increase in the amount of resources used to respond to those demands.

However, in many cases what is needed is greater power, greater freedom, and greater autonomy. For example, the regulation of economic activities (including simple issues such as determining business hours), the application of jurisdiction over environmental issues (over contaminating actors, for example), and the authorization of local radio and television do not require significant financial resources (including the authority over allocating resources). In other cases it is a matter of being able to find new ways of organizing in order to make contracting goods and services more flexible (always with the goal of increased transparency) or to bring about innovation in administrative procedures (to facilitate relations with citizens). That is to say, a greater degree of freedom and autonomy is achieved. What is certain is that new policies cannot be made and greater authority cannot be assumed if old organizing structures and procedures—designed to control instead of act—are maintained.

Political and Administrative Reform of Local Government

It seems evident that current local political structures, organizational plans, and management methods are inadequate to build the local leadership, assume the greater authority, and undertake those new actions that have been proposed here. Let me share some ideas for reform.

Metropolitan government and decentralization of the large city are both essential. On one hand, it is necessary to create metropolitan structures for regional and strategic planning, joint decision-making with respect to investment in urban development, and joint management of supramunicipal services. Metropolitan government must be understood as a contractual relationship or consortium with other administrations more than a hierarchical relationship, even though its decisions will be imposed on everyone. The regional metropolitan government should not pattern itself after only one level of the state government, but rather all of them (central, departmental, and municipal). Simultaneously, large cities must be decentralized according to districts or localities at both the political and administrative level.

Political organization must recognize the personalization of the leadership position, the need to overcome the legislative-executive confrontation, and the continuity of municipal management. The following reforms, among others, are proposed:

- The direct election of mayors, including local mayors or district presidents.
- Homologation among the legislative and executive majority. For example, the position of mayor would be given to the head of the list receiving the most votes, or the list to which the mayor belongs would receive a majority of seats in the council.
- Elimination of the impediments to reelection, and/or extension of terms from four to six years.
- Appointment of professionals to executive positions' through a selection process in which contracts are not tied to the duration of the political term.

Local government needs adequate financing. Doctrine and international experience (of decentralized countries that are oriented toward federal systems) suggest that 50 percent of the fiscal budget be allocated to the central state and 50 percent to the regional governments (municipalities, provinces, departments, or regions). Local governments should be able to automatically finance most of their own budgets (with their own income combined with their share of national taxes such as income tax or VAT). The state, in turn, plays a compensatory role (through a policy designed to maintain balance) or employs contract-programs or other instruments that set priorities for the allocation of funds. A significant portion of urban development projects must be able to secure financing through public appropriation of the additional value generated by the project and through public-private cooperation.

Business management of public services and activities requires finesse. I will not attempt to impose just one model, or to prescribe privatization at all costs. Quite the opposite, I believe that the diversity of management methods brings about maximum economic efficiency and social transparency. I am convinced that the local government as promoter cannot function according to traditional forms of management and contracting. Some proposals include the following:

- Autonomous management centers (which may adopt various forms: institutions, sponsorships or foundations, public corporations or consortia, etc.) could handle those activities or services that can be physically separated from general services. These centers could have their own income and control their own spending, hiring of personnel, and external services. Administrative control might be assumed at a later time.
- Businesses of mixed ownership or private firms might receive, through concessions or contracts, the right to perform certain public services. This is always perfectly acceptable provided that a public administration determines the conditions for the delivery or the quality of services and that more efficient management is achieved.

A major portion of municipal activities can be carried out through these forms of functional decentralization, from management of cultural activity to economic promotion, from the implementation of urban development projects to management of public transportation. When this type of decentralization is not possible, it is beneficial to at least expedite management and contracting procedures for goods and services.

Relations with citizens, communication, and participation are all fields in which innovation is most needed and most feasible. I offer three suggested reforms:

- Facilitate citizen access to the administration and public service corporations. For example: conducting business at a single window, conducting business by phone, validity of oral statements, housecalls, etc.
- Improve communication based on both the use of new technologies (for example, multimedia that allows feedback or citizen response) and personalized relations supported by direct elections and regional and functional decentralization.
- Increase citizen participation through concerted programs based on the cooperation of the beneficiaries, the support of grassroots

organizations and their recognition as counterparts, shared equipment management, etc.

Internationalization of local governments is pivotal. Traditionally, international relations have been under the sole jurisdiction of the national government. In the 1990s cities need to promote themselves internationally, to become integrated in transnational systems or alliances, to be part of regional or global networks and organizations of cities and local authorities, and to increase their bilateral and multilateral relations. It would be a paradox if private actors within the city (chambers of commerce, businesses, universities, professional and trade organizations, cultural entities, etc.) had global protection and an international presence but local governments did not. It falls on the national government to facilitate this international presence in a number of ways:

- Political and financial support is needed for actions that promote the city on an international level, such as those to attract public or private international events.
- The construction of alliances and networks that allow the cities of a country to reinforce their standing on the continent and in the world, taking into consideration the growing competitiveness between regions, ought to be facilitated.
- Actions before intergovernmental organizations (most of all the United Nations, but also regional and economic organizations, etc.) must be undertaken so that cities and their organizations are recognized as partners.
- The right of local governments to have access to international credit and to manage credits or subsidies provided by international organizations needs confirmation.
- In general, local governments deserve confirmation of their ability to act as political entities in the international community and before organizations that, until recently, were exclusively intergovernmental, provided that they are dealing with issues that are in their interest or under their jurisdiction.

Conclusion

A global (strategic) plan reflects the design of a city plan that integrates conclusions, determines public and private activities, and establishes a coherent framework for the mobilization and cooperation of urban social actors.

The participatory process is more important than the definition of the contents of the plan, since the viability of the proposed goals and actions will depend on participation. The final product of a strategic plan is not a law or a government program (although its approval by the state or the local government must be translated into laws, investment, administrative measures, political initiatives, etc.), but rather it is a political contract between public institutions and civil society. Therefore, the process that follows approval of the plan—i.e., the follow-up and implementation of the methods or actions—is as important, if not more important, than the definition and approval of these methods and actions by consensus.

Habitat II coincides with a historic moment characterized by economic globalization and market-opening policies; by political decentralization; by the placement of increased value on local or regional spaces and identities; and by an increase in heterogeneous social demands that remain unsatisfied in spite of state actions. Within this context, the city plan (or regional plan), based on a strategic plan that expands social cooperation, represents a great democratic opportunity. It provides an integrated response that originates where the problems of the society are expressed and where public and private actors are able to act together. On the other hand, the plan allows us to rebuild the sense of city, and of region. It does so in an era in which the diminished awareness of our limits and vanishing ideologies—those that used to support our collective projects—present us with the challenge of rebuilding the systems under which we live together.

Notes on Government Policies for Cities

In the mid-1990s, large cities are the objects of special attention from national governments for two main reasons: the issues associated with the cities go beyond the local or municipal government—in terms of territory, the affected population, and their authority and resources; and both economic globalization and the processes of political decentralization bring new and difficult challenges that can only be addressed through the concerted actions of political institutions and civil society.

A distinction must be made between those city policies that are the responsibility of the federal government, those that must be assumed by the states, and those that fall to the local governments. It is best to apply the principles of cooperative federalism to city policies, by lessening hierarchical relations and employing contractual relations. This does not mean diminishing the value of the functions of the federal government, just the opposite. The city, as an economic and cultural power, as a set of social issues and as a political challenge, requires a policy with global ambitions on the part of the government.

The federal government must guarantee a basic standard of living (equality), a large margin of local autonomy (freedom), and the implementation of balancing and redistributive actions (solidarity or brotherhood). It is more a question of political and financial cooperation than legal cooperation.

Nevertheless, this policy requires specific actions in order to optimize the use of constantly limited resources and to stimulate, not block, other initiatives (whether public or private).

The first priority is to choose to reinforce the system of large cities and cities with "centrality" (nodes of the urban network). The main action to achieve reinforcement is communications. Accessibility to and from the exterior (ports, airports, railway systems, and highways), and accessibility *within* the city (peripheral roads or beltways, massive intermodal transportation systems, and new centers) are crucial. However, integrated logistical zones (incorporating new communications technology) and telecommunications infrastructure (including teleports and other infrastructure tied to the role of the city in the global economy) are also important.

Second, national governments must face the notion of cities as "the wealth of the nation" and contribute to their ability to compete, especially with infrastructure that aids production, commerce, and trade in general. It is beneficial to stimulate the distinct elements of each city and also the infrastructure that places the cities in the best position in their regional or global surroundings through, for example, the organization of fairs and expositions and the availability of facilities and equipment for congresses, conventions, organizational headquarters, and international meetings; technological and scientific parks, teleports and other information systems (such as world trade centers) for economic activity; research and development centers that join universities with the most dynamic and competitive sectors of the economy; and a marketing campaign for cities, tourism promotions, and design and promotion of large cultural or sporting events, whether one-time or periodic.

Third, the national (or federal) policy promoting the city should be able to coordinate the different public administrations (always more difficult than public-private cooperation). Ideally, the integrated vision that cities (or in certain cases, states or regions) provide, especially if there is a strategic plan, should be coordinated with sectoral plans and federal government investment programs. The formulas are diverse; they include consortia, contract-programs, participation in the strategic plan organizations, financial holding projects, etc.

Fourth, the federal government must guarantee the availability and upkeep of infrastructure and the adequate delivery of basic services that, due to their cost and nature, surpass the means (political and financial) of local governments: water supply, wastewater systems, roads and mass transit systems, and large environmental and cultural undertakings. The federal government, in these cases, would not necessarily assume direct management or execution (in general, it is preferable that this is assumed by the local authority), but should take control and contribute financially.

Housing and social programs (education, health, employment, and poverty) are the responsibility of local and state governments. The federal government ought to be limited to establishing the legal and financial framework with the goal of promoting equality. Nevertheless, critical situations or structural deficits require concerted public policies (whether temporary or permanent) that can be driven by the federal government (for example, the contract plans between cities and the government in France, to be put into action in urban areas in crisis). In some cases it would be beneficial to have national programs that join together a variety of entities, ranging from international bodies to social organizations.

It is beneficial to have an "urban observatory" at the federal level. It should be permanently updated, so that it can serve as a *tableau de bord* to guide investment programs and promotional activities regarding the cities. For example, the "European Urban Observatory" (a network of cities in which Barcelona participates and assumes technical direction) provides a computer-accessible databank of indicators on urban policy for each city.

Chapter 13

The Politics of Urban Sustainability

María Elena Ducci

Instead of attempting to summarize the many ideas and publications dealing with the sustainability of cities, I will try to further the discussion on current and possible actions for reversing the growing environmental deterioration occurring in the cities of both the developed world and the "rest of the world." Some of the questions addressed by this chapter are

Environment as a political issue: Do we need to get serious about sustainability?

Why is the environment becoming a hot political issue?

How are decisions being made concerning the way we manage cities?

Can we reconcile poverty alleviation with environmental improvement?

What role does citizen participation play?

Can we find new alternatives for improving the urban environment?

Is Urban Sustainability a Feasible Goal for the World?

One of the distinctive features of the final third of the twentieth century is the emergence of environmental concerns and the recognition of an environmental crisis of global proportions. Little by little, what started as an awareness of the "limits to growth" imposed by the scarcity of natural resources has expanded with the acknowledgment that there is a limited capacity to absorb anthropic waste.[1] The amount of refuse has increased at an alarming pace as a consequence of the industrial revolution and the population explosion.

The introduction of the concept of "sustainable development" signaled the beginning of a new way of thinking about and debating the meaning and rationality behind economic growth and world development. An important element of this process is the original concept of sustainability proposed by the Brundtland Commission in 1987: "Sustainable development is the ability to ensure the needs of the present without compromising the ability of future generations to meet their own needs."[2]

A more functional definition of sustainable development is proposed by William Rees: "positive socioeconomic change that does not undermine the ecological and social systems upon which communities and societies are dependent. Its successful implementation requires integrated policy, planning, and social learning processes; its political viability depends on the full support of the people it affects through their governments, their social institutions, and their private activities."[3]

However, a number of these elements prove very difficult to implement in the real world, such as preventing the undermining of the social system; the integration of policies and planning; "social learning processes"; and achieving the "full support of affected people," themes that I will develop later in this chapter.

Of the current work to be done, a very important goal is the reconciliation of two apparently opposite themes: development, which uses a greater amount of natural resources to obtain economic benefits in the short term (*desarrollismo*); and "sustainability," which respects the biosphere by attempting to modify the current patterns of production and living.[4]

In spite of growing acceptance of the interdependence of political, economic, and ecological systems, these systems continue to be disarticulated in current institutional structures. This is one of the main barriers to achieving sustainable development. A number of institutional relations must be changed and "new international laws, an international court to enforce them, and perhaps a scientific council to regulate new theories on environmental changes" must be created.[5]

The Rio Earth Summit of June 1992 was a landmark in the sense that it showed for the first time that environmental concerns are present in all countries and at all levels of society (179 presidents, 18,000 NGO members from 166 countries, and 450,000 individuals attended the event). It is impossible to say, however, that the Rio summit brought about fundamental changes in national decision-making mechanisms, which, in the majority of cases, are still based on economic criteria.[6] Nevertheless, the summit increased awareness in the international community of the need to correct its course toward sustainable development.

If it is agreed that the concept of sustainability is changing the way in which development is understood and promoted, then the way in which cities are understood, planned, and managed must be changed, with a focus on the goal of urban sustainability. The urgent need for these changes is evident when the global urbanization rate and the fact that within the next twenty years most of the world population will be living in cities is taken into consideration.[7]

WHAT ARE THE MAIN ISSUES CONCERNING THE CONCEPT OF SUSTAINABILITY?

There are two types of problems, which have been grouped according to two different agendas.[8] The "green agenda" deals with global problems: global warming, ozone layer depletion, deforestation, and exhaustion of nonrenewable resources. The reinterpretation of urban problems associated mainly with poverty elicited a "brown agenda." This agenda deals with the problems of water and air pollution, the lack of basic services and green areas, the inadequate management of solid waste, and poor housing conditions.

At the Rio Earth Summit in 1992, the green agenda was highlighted because governments of and environmentalists from developed countries focus their attentions on these issues. In general, citizens of the North believe that this is where global concern should be centered.[9] However, for the nations of the South, the green agenda is not as important as the need to resolve the acute problems related to poverty. Within less-developed countries it is a commonly held belief that achieving sustainable development is not possible until the urgent problems of poverty and inequality within cities are resolved.[10]

The boundaries between the concepts of sustainable global development and urban sustainability are not clearly defined, due to their complex interrelationships.[11] For analytical and practical purposes, global and local (urban) problems can be handled separately, but in reality they are intertwined.

There has been inadequate recognition of the myriad relationships between both sets of problems, as each agenda has been addressed in an isolated fashion. The strong link between the two agendas must be understood in order to overcome the current dichotomy and to prevent governmental actions and investment in less-developed countries from having a negative effect on the green agenda in the medium term. My hypothesis is that it is possible and necessary to make advancements in both fields simultaneously.

The strong international effort that is placed on the brown agenda (national policies and programs of the multilateral agencies and donors) is aimed mostly at improving the living standards of the poorest sectors of the world, those that have neither basic services nor adequate housing. Yet, throughout this process, no one has questioned the developmental goal being pursued, or explored the effect of these programs on global environmental problems. There is an urgent need to redefine the direction of development, which will require a change in current patterns of consumption.

A number of studies have explored the feasibility of continuing to search for the kind of development that could raise the global standard of living to the levels common among developed countries.[12] An interesting analysis conducted in Canada reviewed the concept of "carrying capacity" and demonstrated that, based on the consumption rates of the Canadian population, the area of productive land needed to maintain the world population according to the criteria of sustainability is three times the current capacity of our planet.[13] "The implication is that we would require an additional Earth or two with existing technology to provide for the present world population at Canada's ecological standard of living."[14]

This chapter focuses on the concept of urban sustainability, but refers constantly to the relation between local-urban problems and global problems. First, the present situation of the urban environment, its main problems and the differences between the urban environment of the poor in the developed and less-developed countries is presented. Second, the main actors in the political arena of sustainability are analyzed, and the role that each one plays is debated. Then, I elaborate on what I consider to be one of the most important forces in the current environmental political game: citizen participation—its origin and effects. Finally, I offer some conclusions that may help in the advancement toward a socially and ecologically sustainable world.

The Urban Environment

There are at least three reasons why it is important to concentrate efforts on the improvement of the urban environment: (1) A large portion of the population of the developed countries and Latin America live in cities, and there appears to be a "natural" tendency to live in urban settlements, which stabilizes when approximately 80 percent of the population is living in cities. (Less-developed countries are experiencing urbanization at a much faster pace—people are migrating to cities with rational motives.[15]) (2) The goal of accelerating improvements in the standard of living that ensure a minimum level of universal access to basic services can only be achieved in cities (particularly cities of medium size). The concentration of people in urban areas facilitates the provision of social services and infrastructure. (3) Increases in agricultural productivity make it possible to maintain adequate levels of food and raw material production with a workforce of less than 10 percent of the world population.[16] The highest levels of productivity are reached in areas where there is less demographic pressure on the land and where technological advances—requiring less labor—are applied.[17] Therefore, in order to produce more efficiently in the countryside, it is best that the majority of the population lives in the cities.

Moreover, within the current global context, cities have become the fundamental engines behind economic growth—the source of administrative and financial brainpower, where large corporations are headquartered.[18] Thus, urban sustainability, adequate standards of living, and a sufficient level of safety are basic requirements for the economic development of a country. Yet, what is the status of today's urban environment?

Major Issues

It is difficult to distinguish between environmental problems and socioeconomic needs or deficiencies in an analysis of major urban problems. These two aspects are so intricately intertwined that it is also very difficult to separate them for the purposes of policy-making. This explains why actions aimed at the brown agenda inevitably touch on social and economic aspects and coordination among programs can increase their effectiveness.

In an interesting comparison of "pressure points" between cities of the developed and less-developed countries, Rodney White and Joseph Whitney propose the following in table 13.1.[19]

It is interesting to note that development eases the pressure on most of the elements noted in table 13.1 but, at the same time, it concentrates urban problems in three main areas: environment, crime, and housing, which remain unresolved issues even in the most advanced societies.

Housing

It is necessary to go further in the analysis of housing problems in cities, whether developed or not, because traditional housing policies must be revised in order to improve the urban environment. The poorest neighborhoods suffer from undesirable location. Whether because of an irregularity that allows the poor to occupy only land unwanted by developers, or due to market forces that select inappropriate land for urban development, the poor are concentrated in areas inadequate for living—areas exposed to such dangers as floods and landslides. Moreover, poor neighborhoods are generally disconnected from the urban

TABLE 13.1
URBAN PRESSURE POINTS

Pressure Point	LDCs (less-developed countries)	MDCs (more-developed countries)
Employment	H	L
Food	H	L
Health	H	L
Education	H	L
+Water	H	L
+Energy	H	L
+Transportation	H	L
+Recreation	H(L)[20]	M
+Environment	H	H
Crime	H(M)[21]	H
+Housing	H	H

H=High; M=Medium; L=Low.
SOURCE: Adapted from Rodney White and Joseph Whitney, "Cities and the Environment, an Overview," in *Sustainable Cities, Urbanization and the Environment in International Perspective,* ed. Richard Stren, Rodney White, and Joseph Whitney (Boulder, Colo.: Westview, 1992), table 2.1.
Strictly speaking, only the categories marked "+" can be considered part of the urban environment.

grid and isolated, making it difficult for inhabitants to take advantage of urban facilities offered in better-equipped areas.[22]

The quality of housing for the poor is substandard. The problem of low-quality housing for the poor is particularly serious in those countries where the state is the provider. Paradoxically, in countries where the poor build their own houses because the state does not have the resources to fulfill the need for low-income housing, the quality of the construction improves over time, along with the consolidation of the poor neighborhoods and their integration with the city.

Countries that have achieved a medium level of development (such as Chile) and some developed countries provide the poor with extremely low-quality housing in areas and houses that deteriorate very quickly and, in addition, deny them the mechanisms that the Third World poor use to improve their dwellings. This problem is taking priority in the political arena and has become a permanent topic of discussion among local governments.[23]

The size of homes for the poor is a topic that has been neglected, even though it has a significant effect on quality of life and on certain social problems that are among the most difficult to resolve.

Traditional housing policies have tried to provide the poor with at least a minimum acceptable amount of space in which to live. With this goal in mind, all countries set minimum standards for the size and even the design of public housing.[24] As a consequence of the limited size of these houses (and the impossibility of enlarging them), extended families have disappeared and, with them, important social capital has been lost, which only recently has been reconsidered as a crucial element for development.

Extended families include the older generation, which has been displaced due to lack of space. The isolation of senior citizens is one of the greatest problems facing the developed world. In developing countries (especially in Africa and Asia) the elderly still play an important role within the family (providing care for the children, for instance), a role that is lost elsewhere.[25]

It is also difficult to provide shelter in the small family home for poor or afflicted relatives. They are generally excluded from modern society, which is only capable of handling the needs of the "functional" nuclear family.

Another equally important consequence of the small size of housing for the poor is the lack of privacy for families and couples that is associated with low-quality design and construction. This dimension has neither been adequately measured nor been understood.[26]

Finally, the inadequate size of houses makes it extremely difficult for members of a poor family to spend recreational time indoors. As a result, children and teenagers grow up in the streets, where they come into contact with gangs, drugs, etc.

Infrastructure in poor areas is sadly deficient. It is unreasonable to expect changes in the conditions that turn poor neighborhoods into breeding grounds for crime and violence unless the urgent need for an urban environment that permits healthy social development is addressed. Providing space is not enough.

With respect to the evolution of urban areas, and particularly from the point of view of how the poorest families *feel* in relation to their environment, the most serious issue to address is not poor living conditions, but rather, the impossibility of improvement. This is fundamental because it has not been adequately treated, at least at the level of explicit policies. "What is bad is not to feel poor [a concept that is relative] but to feel that one can never improve."[27] This feeling of hopelessness is the main difference between poverty in developed countries and poverty in the informal cities of undeveloped countries.

Crime and Violence

The prevalence of violence and crime is becoming one of the most critical social problems, and one that seems least likely to be brought under control in the future. Violence and crime seem to be characteristics of the postmodern society and, although a detailed examination of this subject goes beyond the scope of this chapter, there are some elements directly related to the urban environment that must at least be mentioned.

A distinction must be made between violence in its current forms—linked to international terrorism, racism, or fundamentalism—and everyday urban violence. Cities at all levels of development are becoming increasingly unsafe. People on the streets, storekeepers, and the like are frequently exposed to violent crime; increased police activity does not seem to be the solution. This problem is related, in part, to widespread use of illegal drugs and the glorification of violence by the media. But the neighborhoods—ghettos—in which the poorest live, where the streets are a breeding ground for gangs and violence, are also partly responsible for this problem.

Social anomie, which characterizes poor neighborhoods of developed and semideveloped countries (and which seems less common in the "spontaneous" settlements of the developing world), contributes to an increased sense of insecurity. Neighborhoods where everybody knows one another generate protective networks that make people feel safer. "When I get to the barrio, the kids take care of me. . . . I have known them since they were little."[28]

The absence of a sense of belonging among residents and their inability to shape their own environment are elements that must be addressed more carefully in order to make streets safer and more livable.[29]

Environment

Environmental problems are increasingly becoming pressure points and causes for urban mobilization in both developed and developing countries.

Cities worldwide are faced with the problem of locating undesirable urban elements that are essential for the functioning of the city, yet rejected by the population because they pollute or decrease land values. Some examples are dumps, water treatment plants, cemeteries, antennas, and power lines, which, as LULUs (Locally Undesirable Land Uses), often cause NIMBY (Not in My Back Yard) reactions.

Due to misuse of the city's environmental capital, large residential neighborhoods boast completely empty beautiful parks and green areas (suburbia) whereas millions of people in poor neighborhoods live without green areas (the so-called green areas in these neighborhoods are barren, inhospitable empty lots) with no possibility of enjoying urban parks and other recreational areas.

Traffic jams and increased traffic cause higher pollution levels, which directly affect the health of urban inhabitants. The proliferation of privately owned motor vehicles is a direct result of economic development, as are the resulting traffic jams and added pollution. Some experts believe this to be a natural tendency, which cannot be restrained and which will only be resolved when the deterioration of the quality of life in large cities reaches such a level that the population is forced to move to smaller cities.[30] In my opinion, this is a serious blunder because the "modern need" to have a car has been artificially created and encouraged by specific economic interests: auto makers and oil companies.

THE ENVIRONMENT OF THE URBAN POOR IN DEVELOPED AND DEVELOPING COUNTRIES: PUBLIC SOCIAL HOUSING VERSUS THE INFORMAL CITY

Even though some of the more acute problems of the urban environment have been discussed, I believe it is necessary to explore the environment of the urban poor in more detail for two reasons. First, some of the difficulties presently observed in the cities of the developed countries could be avoided if their causes were understood. Second, it is the poor who suffer the most from adverse environmental conditions, and who are less able to enter into a process of improvement on their own.[31]

There seem to be two completely different types of urban environments and therefore of urban problems. There are the problems faced by rich countries that have enough financial resources to provide their poorer population with housing and basic services, which are able to implement urban plans to regulate the growth of their (formal) cities. At the other extreme are those problems faced by poor countries, where the majority of the population does not have enough money to access the legal market for land and housing. Those governments have no other alternative than to allow the poorest sector of the population to settle land in a "spontaneous" and irregular manner. The use of the term "spontaneous" for informal settlements is inappropriate, because this kind of habitat is the clear result of a series of specific pressures: economic and financial barriers, obstacles to landownership, etc. It is also the result of the deliberate social practices that produce the division between the formal and informal city.[32]

There is no doubt that the situation of the poor in developed countries is different, particularly in the short term, in that most of them have access to minimum levels of housing and services. This translates into immediate, positive changes in health conditions and reduces the amount of political pressure exerted on the government by the poor (still a major political issue in less-developed countries).

Although developed countries apparently face urban environmental problems that are relatively easier to manage—explaining the low priority assigned to the brown agenda—even these countries are experiencing growing environmental deterioration, which they are unable to offset. By understanding what does not work in wealthier countries, developing countries could avoid duplicating those errors in their search for development.

Public Housing Programs

Developed countries (and some that have achieved a medium level of development) have been able to respond to the demands of the poor through a number of mechanisms, such as subsidized housing markets. However, even though the cities have growth under control, market forces have defined very low standards of living for the poorest sectors of society.

The isolation of public housing projects, the poor construction of houses, the lack of a sense of belonging, and little or no interest in improving the situation result in both the deterioration of the urban environment and increasingly unmanageable social problems. These areas are hotbeds for violence, drug abuse, and gangs; they are dangerous places to live in and in them social anomie seems impossible to escape. These are neighborhoods where no one wants to live, and anyone who has the chance to escape does so immediately. This is the city of the poor in the developed countries.[33]

The Informal City

Irregular settlements on the periphery of cities—home to a large portion of the population—are quite possibly the most important characteristic of urban growth in developing countries since the 1960s. The poor residents of irregular settlements do not receive any help from the state, aside from the tolerance shown for illegal building on the city's periphery in areas ignored by developers. As a result, a large share of the urban population in the world's poorest countries has faced sanitation and health problems and housing deficiencies for ten years or more, all the while organizing to obtain legal title to their plots of land and access to basic services.

However, there is an element that has not been given sufficient attention: it is the basic social cohesiveness of the neighborhood's inhabitants that propels the process of land invasion and the long fight to gain legal status and access to services. Those who live in irregular neighborhoods need to cooperate from the outset to solve the most basic problems (carrying water, leveling the streets, etc). A social web is created that becomes the force behind the processes of consolidation and improvement.[34] The need to solve these problems and the scarcity of economic resources cause these groups to develop a system of relations that are reflected in a dynamic process of neighborhood improvement and consolidation.[35]

The best evidence of this process takes place on the periphery of any Latin American city: an empty, isolated, and dirty lot is transformed over ten years into an established neighborhood connected to the urban structure, with solid houses and buildings, colored façades, shops, and paved streets. Moreover, some residents are able to earn income by renting out part of their homes. They know one another and collaborate to solve common problems. They feel proud of what they have achieved and develop a sense of belonging.

On the contrary, in developed and semideveloped countries, ten years after the construction of a public housing neighborhood, the quality of the buildings is in rapid decline, common areas are abandoned, and residents show no interest in improving their habitat because there is no sense of ownership. Homes (townhouses and apartment blocks) are the smallest size allowed by each country's regulations. Plots of land are also very small, prohibiting expansion and improvement of the homes. Often, the residents have not taken part in any decisions about where and how they live.

The poor in richer countries may receive more from a material point of view (that is, physical capital), but they are relocated far from family and friends so social networks are broken and social capital is lost. By acquiring a material good (a house, the most important social demand in poor countries), the recipient becomes part of an alienated group. There is a lack of trust among these residents, which prevents any desire for collaboration. In the medium term, there is deterioration, neighborhoods turn into slums—ghettos of poverty and hopelessness—and eventually the inhabitants begin to abandon the area.

The urgency of ensuring that the poor have access to housing, basic services, and paved streets is evident. Nevertheless, the spontaneous generation of the informal city promises a richer and more positive social scenario, in which people work together from the beginning and take part in a "chronic" process of improvement. In spite of the pressing problems of overcrowding, poverty, and disease, it is possible to detect a feeling in these neighborhoods that contrasts with the social anomie and apathy that permeates the poorest neighborhoods in developed countries.

Furthermore, people who seize land illegally generally occupy larger plots than those provided by the state. Little by little they build, improving the quality and size of their houses according to their means. This flexibility allows residents to provide shelter to relatives (married children or newly arrived migrants) and even to generate additional income by renting out rooms, thus using the house as capital. In these neighborhoods, the process of improvement is a part of daily life (people save, plan, and work in order to improve their situation). Therefore, in the medium term, they have a greater chance of improving their environment.

Factors and Political Forces Involved

In almost every country, particularly in developed countries, environmental concerns are a significant element of political discussion. The most important social demands relate to quality of living, which is, in turn, directly linked to the environment. Therefore, this issue is taking priority among politicians and becoming a cause of controversy surrounding elections. However, in less-developed regions, such as sub-Saharan Africa and certain parts of Asia, the problems of survival take precedence over environmental concerns, which continue to maintain a low priority in the political arena and in governmental policy.

Even so, the environment is beginning to have a direct influence on domestic politics, due to its elevated international status and the effects of economic globalization. No country with hopes of integrating itself in the global economic system can afford to ignore (at least at the rhetorical level) concern for environmental issues. Globalization and greater access to mass communications are also being used as informal environmental education tools for the world population, which is increasingly aware of and concerned about the environment.

The major trends within the current political arena are globalization, democratization, and privatization. These elements mobilize national governments and international agencies (which have a strong impact on domestic policy-making), encourage citizens to organize—for protest or to work to protect the environment—and mobilize economic groups that are facing conflicting pressures.

GLOBALIZATION, DEMOCRATIZATION, AND PRIVATIZATION:
THEIR EFFECT ON URBAN SUSTAINABILITY

Globalization of both the economy and communications is changing all previous conceptions of economic development. In addition, it is creating economic entities that consider every region of the world either a source of raw materials, a production center, or an emerging market.

The fall of the Berlin Wall—a symbol of the end of the cold war and, for the most part, the end of dictatorial governments—provided a new framework for reestablishing relations between countries and regions.

The role of the state has been revised stemming from questions about its ability to manage the development process single-handedly, through direct participation in investment and production.[36] The validity of the state's role in domestic redistribution, a role assumed by the state in all democracies, has also been challenged. Here, a paradigmatic change is affecting both wealthy and poor countries: the search for new systems of government that are smaller and more efficient, and that are able to channel resources and regulate the actions of both civil society and the private sector in order to achieve social equity and sustainable development. In this context, new forms of partnership between the state and other sectors of society are being explored.

There is a new awareness of the current ecological crisis and the need to change traditional concepts of economic development—those concepts that identify progress with achieving the consumption and production patterns of the industrialized countries.

The significance of these processes is such that presently we cannot see all the implications, although we are starting to witness some of their effects. What follows is an attempt to identify and understand the relations between them and the search for sustainable development.

Globalization

A central element of the current strategy for global economic development is the expansion of international trade. Transnational corporations, headquartered in developed countries, need new markets for their products. Furthermore, technological advancements allow them to open operations in any geographical region that maximizes efficiency. Companies headquartered in developing countries are also expanding abroad. Currently, economic growth is based mainly on exports (*maquiladoras*, transportation equipment, fruit, mining, and cellulose) and in the promotion of nontraditional exports (flowers, seafood, and information services). Developing countries need to increase their investment rates and the majority of governments are taking actions aimed at encouraging the inflow of foreign capital to fuel economic growth.

As a result, the interdependence between regions and countries is increasing every day, making it essential to establish multilateral mechanisms and commercial agreements that help assure stability and set clear regulations for the expanding flow of trade.[37]

The pressures created by economic globalization are forcing all countries (regardless of their level of development) to enforce environmental regulations and policies. One form of pressure is exerted by large transnational corporations that are based in developed countries and that have had to improve technology and production methods in order to comply with stricter environmental regulations in their home countries.[38] More and more, these companies are demanding that their competitors be bound by the same standards. They exert pressure in a number of different ways, including appeals to governments and use of the media, to avoid so-called ecological dumping. That is to say, antidumping legislation is applied in order to deny market access to companies from countries where production is cheaper because environmental regulations are not enforced.

The globalization of markets also reflects, in some instances, new opportunities and pressures generated by the consumer markets. Consumers from developed countries are demanding that exporters from developing countries meet certain standards in order to access these markets with greater purchasing power.[39] In addition, a new niche for organic and natural products is being created.

Finally, exporters from developing countries, the engines behind their domestic economies, need to be able to enter international markets. This can only be accomplished if they are able to demonstrate that they have satisfied the standards of quality enforced by developed countries. As a result, these companies have converted their production methods before being required to do so by their own governments. Credibility in this area can be achieved only through international certification, a costly process if undertaken individually by each firm. Therefore, the more dynamic domestic economic groups have started to recognize the benefits of accelerating the "environmentalization" of their countries. By doing so, competition with other domestic companies that employ polluting production methods can be avoided and their countries can earn international credibility, which, in turn, allows them access to international markets.

An interesting result of global communications is the quick and effective coordination of environmental groups from different regions of the world to oppose actions that they deem dangerous to the envi-

ronment.[40] At the same time, a worldwide process of informal education has begun, through which organizations from developed countries
are transferring knowledge to their counterparts in less-developed
countries. As a consequence, environmental awareness and public demands are rising quickly in these other countries.

Democratization

The recognized failure and widespread disappearance of authoritarian
regimes has resulted, in part, from political and economic pressure
exerted by developed countries. The following editorial on the Chilean
transition to democracy and that country's interest in joining NAFTA
is a clear example:

> But NAFTA cannot afford to be any less demanding in its require-
> ments for members' democratic good behavior than the European
> Union has been. . . . The EU's policy has been a tremendous suc-
> cess, and a great example of the use of hard-headed economics
> and political idealism in support of each other. . . . The attraction
> of the EU's wealth strengthened the principles of many people in
> those countries whose previous support for elected governments
> had been minimal. The same requirement can produce similar
> benefits here.[41]

In any case, the proliferation of democratic regimes throughout the
world allows for the expression of public demands and requires greater
accountability on the part of elected officials. Simultaneously, and in
part due to the acknowledgment of the limited capacity of governments,
democratization processes are being accompanied by decentralization processes. Through this process the central government is yielding
an increasing amount of authority and resources to local governments
and civil society. As I discuss later, it is at the local level that popular
pressure for environmental improvement is beginning to appear.

In developed countries, which have long democratic traditions and
where urban environmental problems are relatively under control, the
population is demanding solutions to these problems (the green
agenda) and the implementation of higher environmental standards
within their own countries.

In developing countries, citizens demand solutions mainly to the
urban environmental problems that relate to their daily life (the brown
agenda), but even there environmental awareness is increasing. This
explains why most of the democratic political agendas that are defined
and continuously adapted according to the priorities of the electorate

(commonly through the use of polls) now list the environment among the most important issues.

Due to the fact that the general population has better access to information and has achieved higher levels of education, more environmental demands are being generated. Thus, there is no doubt that, as democratic governments become consolidated in different regions of the world, they will need to become more serious about making the search for sustainability one of their top priorities.

Privatization

Privatization, not only of the economy (which is already occurring even in countries such as China and Cuba) but also of utilities, infrastructure, and other areas that until only recently were controlled by the state, has become a priority on the international agenda. Privatization is one of the themes promoted by multilateral agencies as part of a number of structural reform measures, and also as a viable way to improve the situation in developing countries.

Just as the 1980s were a decade characterized by structural adjustments promoted by international agencies, the 1990s seem to be characterized by a trend to privatize many activities. In fact, privatization is a consequence of structural adjustment policies that consider bureaucratic centralized states incapable of leading economic and social development. Thus, these policies promote the largest reductions possible in the size and power of the state to allow private initiative to propel economic growth.

In both developed and developing countries, discussion is focused on the appropriate size of the state and what regulatory and financial responsibilities the state should assume to ensure a level of redistribution that maintains political stability.

Within this context of reduction of the size of the state, it is very difficult to create the environmental agencies and institutions needed to lead the drive to achieve sustainable development. Thus, it is crucial for the state, particularly in developing countries, to find new forms of partnership with civil society and private corporations, so that environmental problems can be approached in a coordinated and efficient manner.

THE ROLE OF THE STATE IN THE PURSUIT OF SUSTAINABILITY

In developed countries, environmental concerns have reached such prominence that, in response to growing demands, governments have had to develop and constantly revise their legal and administrative systems to ensure the enforcement of environmental standards.

These countries have the capability to respond to the urban-industrial environmental problems of the brown agenda. Day after day, however, citizens' requests are greater, and therefore environmental concerns are appearing with increasing frequency in the news as an important aspect of local politics.[42] Clearly, no political current can disregard this concern for the environment.

On the other hand, the upkeep of cities is increasingly expensive, bankrupting many large cities in developed countries. City governments do not have sufficient resources to maintain and improve infrastructure and services, so new alternatives through alliances with the private sector are sought.

In developing regions, governments are creating environmental institutions, passing laws and regulations, and training people to work in this new field of development. Yet, these government initiatives are, even in the best cases, not very effective, and decisions continue to be made based on the objective of speeding up economic development.

The main forces compelling the governments of developing countries to adopt environmental policies are increasing public pressure and growing demands from urban citizens; international economic competition, which forces large exporting companies (the main engines of economic growth) to observe international environmental legislation and to demonstrate their compliance to the international community; and pressure from international financial institutions, which exercise important influence on domestic policy-making decisions regarding development.

The main obstacles to this process are prioritizing economic growth over all other goals without attention to the cost externalities imposed on the country in the medium to long term (environmental concern is perceived as an obstacle to rapid economic development); private producers refusing to recognize the cost to society of the use or degradation of natural resources; the very difficult process of adapting existing administrative structures to "new" trans-sectoral aims (various government agencies view the inclusion of the "environmental component" as just an additional problem and perceive the need to coordinate with the new multisector as debilitating, triggering a paralyzing internal power struggle); the powerlessness of the new environmental institutions, usually ministries or other institutions that carry no real weight in the decision-making process (this weakness is revealed by their limited budgets); and a lack of citizen awareness regarding the impact of environmental problems on health and quality of life (this is particularly true in the poorest countries, where day-to-day survival is difficult and shortages of housing and basic services become the main environmental concern).

Finally, one aspect of the role of the state in pursuit of sustainability that has not yet been adequately addressed is the inability of the governments of developing countries to actually implement the policies that they enact. In spite of the efforts made by some governments, there is a very limited trained staff available to apply these policies and even fewer people capable of supervising their enforcement.[43] An immediate solution to this problem is needed because environmental laws and regulations that are incorrectly enforced may discredit environmental policies, producing negative consequences, even of an economic nature.

THE IMPACT OF INTERNATIONAL AGENCIES[44]

Although the level of direct investment by multilateral agencies is proportionally not very high, these organizations have significant influence on domestic policy-making decisions in developing countries. Guidelines set forth by multilateral agencies shape a large number of domestic policies, such as the restructuring policies currently in place in a majority of developing countries.

At the same time, international financial agencies provide partial financing for domestic programs, including housing, basic services, infrastructure, and other programs directly related to the urban environment. In many cases, the evaluation and approval processes of international agencies introduce certain standards that define national sectoral policies.

The most effective of the international agency requirements for national governments is the completion of "environmental impact assessments," mandatory for all projects financed by these entities. This measure alone has created the need for a national system of environmental impact assessment, already in place in a number of countries. In spite of its flaws, this process—which requires a country to demonstrate that a particular project will not harm the environment—is a major step toward sustainable development.

This being the case, international agencies are in the position of redefining housing standards and creating massive housing improvement programs to help overcome one of the most urgent urban problems: the poor quality and deterioration of housing in the poorest neighborhoods.[45]

Also, if it is clear that the only way to solve or lessen growing problems such as traffic congestion and air pollution in large and medium-sized cities is to change the manner in which people travel, then international agencies should favor the improvement and enlargement of mass transit systems. This would allow governments to address these issues in an efficient manner.

Economic Groups

There is a completely contradictory dynamic in the way in which economic forces and groups behave with respect to the environmental problem.

Given that economic growth is, by definition, a priority, corporations use mass media and advertising to generate new consumption "needs." They have created symbols of global status requirements, such as the need to own a car (the automobile syndrome) and the dream of a house in the "garden city." A significant part of advertising uses "green propaganda," pretending to support valid environmental concerns (with cars that pollute less, "ecological" houses, or even ecological yogurt) when actual goal is, of course, to sell the most goods or services.

As I have already asserted, transnational corporations are pressing for the adoption and implementation of international environmental standards. This is explained, in part, by the fact that there are costs associated with the protection of the environment that must be paid in order to maintain permanent growth.[46] Furthermore, implementation of these standards helps to avoid ecological dumping. Environmental regulations are now included in the negotiation of international free-trade agreements, the number of which continues to grow. This creates incentives for corporations to oversee the compliance of environmental regulations in all countries.

Citizen Reaction: The Rise of Environmental Movements

The first environmental groups appeared during the 1970s, when voices were raised concerning the situation of the global environment and the impending disaster threatening humankind. Some groups acquired remarkable strength and became relatively important political forces in countries such as Germany, Holland, and Sweden.

A transnational group, Greenpeace, has become the international paradigm of the defender of the environment. Although it has been argued that Greenpeace is a conservationist group that aspires to halt development, its contribution in raising the level of international awareness with respect to environmental problems is undeniable. Also, there has been unofficial recognition of the important role played by this group in monitoring such operations as the transportation of toxic waste, a task that no government or official agency has been capable of performing so far.

The most important impact of the environmental-ecological groups has been their contribution to the development of political pressure by raising citizen awareness and with it, interest in solving environmental problems. This is essential to drive governments to make the pursuit of sustainable development a priority.[47]

In some developed countries, environmental movements have become institutionalized and have formed political parties (the Green Party emerged in Germany in the late 1970s, and the PvdA Party is a sound political force in the Netherlands), increasing the visibility of ecological issues. In 1989, the conservative Dutch government stepped down due to an ecological controversy; it was the first time that a government had resigned due to environmental issues.[48]

In the developing countries, this process has been much slower, which is understandable considering that they are facing other serious problems such as hunger, high mortality and infant mortality rates, lack of basic services, insufficient housing, low-quality education, etc. In spite of that, and partly due to the fact that traditional urban problems have blended with environmental problems, a growing popular awareness is generating new political pressures that are starting to or will eventually affect the development and management of cities.[49]

Citizen Engagement

FROM THE STRUGGLE FOR LAND TO THE FIGHT FOR A
BETTER QUALITY OF LIFE

During the 1970s the major urban issue for Third World countries was urban social movements and their struggles for land and shelter. Habitat I officially recognized, for the first time, the potential of the poorest groups to construct their own city. All of the developing countries allowed (most without explicitly admitting it) the poorest sector of the population to settle irregularly on the periphery of the large cities. In some regions, such as Latin America, this phenomenon began in the 1960s. In other areas, such as Africa, the level of migration and "unintended" settlement in the cities is still very high.

What was seen as an unmanageable problem until Habitat I was then transformed into a tool. As a consequence, support was given to housing improvement programs and programs that provided the poor with plots of land with basic services already installed (known as *lotes con servicios* in Spanish) in order to speed up the ongoing process of urban consolidation. Nevertheless, popular mobilization for obtaining legal title to property and the use of services has been the main force behind urban growth in the developing countries since the 1960s.

The 1990s are witnessing a change in this process. In a majority of the developing countries, the natural growth of the urban population is becoming more important than social growth. At this time, a large percentage of the urban poor own their houses, yet living conditions, even in the best of cases, are still very inadequate.

In any case, the emphasis of the struggle has shifted from the rights to land and housing to the quality of life and the conditions of the urban environment in which people live.

This is where the new environmental movements emerge, and as I will argue, these movements cut across different social strata because they address problems that are affecting not only the poor. It is important to recognize that, even though environmental problems break with the traditional class divisions, these problems do not affect all groups in the same way. Moreover, the solutions to these problems are not always the same for the wealthy and poor sectors.[50]

Citizen Participation as a Key Issue

Why do I think that citizen participation is indispensable for stopping the environmental deterioration of human settlements? There are several reasons. First, structural adjustment programs and the proven inability of the state to respond to all of the needs associated with the functioning of the city make it imperative that alternatives be found to stop the growing deterioration of the urban environment. Second, urban environmental problems affect people directly at the local level. Therefore, it is the residents of the neighborhoods who are the most capable and the most interested in detecting the causes of and finding solutions to problems. Third, experience has shown that development projects that are designed with the participation of the beneficiaries, rather than imposed from above, tend to survive longer and achieve better results.[51]

Problems, Actions, and Struggles

A review of studies dealing with urban environmental problems in Latin America reveals that, from the point of view of the inhabitants, the most urgent issues are those listed in table 13.2.[52] In studies on Asia and Africa problems such as rodents, mosquitos, and animal waste are added to the list in table 13.2.[53] This signifies a greater health problem,

TABLE 13.2

URBAN ENVIRONMENTAL PROBLEMS IN LATIN AMERICA, 1995

- Public transportation, traffic congestion
- Air pollution
- Violence
- Solid waste management (litter)
- Lack of basic infrastructure (potable water and wastewater systems)
- Liquid waste management (lack of water treatment plants)
- Low-quality housing (slums)
- Noise pollution
- Lack of green areas (parks)
- Floods
- Ecological degradation (erosion, deterioration of green areas, water pollution)

but is not completely different from the situation in Latin America. Some of these problems are still present in wealthy countries in spite of so-called development. Violence, the poor quality of public housing, the degradation of downtown areas, air pollution, and in some cases noise pollution seem to be the urban environmental problems that development has not yet been able to cure.[54]

An element worth noting is the rise in the level of public opposition to the installation of certain facilities in residential areas. Dumps, wastewater treatment plants, cemeteries, and toxic waste disposal sites are facing growing opposition in the cities. Acronyms like NIMBY and LULU reflect a new kind of urban environmental problem that challenges both developing and developed countries alike, making waste management—especially of toxic waste—a particularly difficult and hot issue.[55]

Local Community Initiatives

It is possible neither to visualize general participatory strategies nor to try to arrive at conclusions that are regionally and internationally valid. Therefore, I will present a series of initiatives implemented in the early 1990s by local communities as examples.

An analysis of almost thirty studies undertaken by ICLEI (see table 13.3) shows a clear difference between environmental initiatives carried out in developed countries versus those in developing countries.

In the less-developed countries of Asia, Africa, and Latin America, the main concerns deal with waste management, transportation, quality of housing, city planning, open spaces, recovering beaches, and drainage. All of these initiatives are linked directly to the brown agenda—to local problems that affect daily life.

TABLE 13.3
LOCAL ENVIRONMENTAL INITIATIVES

LESS-DEVELOPED COUNTRIES

BOLIVIA	*La Paz*	Solid waste management
BRAZIL	*Curitiba*	Integrate land use and transportation planning
	São Paulo	Public transportation management
	Santos	Wastewater control; beach recovery program
CHINA	*Beijing*	Housing rehabilitation
ECUADOR	*Quito*	Neighborhood recycling program
INDONESIA	*Bandung*	Solid waste management: indigenous, community-based responses
SOUTH AFRICA	*Durban*	"Metropolitan Open Space System": establishment and maintenance of a comprehensive open space system

MORE-DEVELOPED COUNTRIES (OECD COUNTRIES)

AUSTRIA	*Graz*	ECOPPROFIT: produce and market successful private sector examples of economic and ecological waste minimization
	Linz	Citizen participation in the siting of waste facilities
CANADA	*Ottawa*	Environmental management strategy for the city of Ottawa
GERMANY	*Saarbrucken*	Program for Energy and Water Conservation and Efficiency: method to finance energy conservation activities
JAPAN	*Sumida City*	Rainwater management
SWEDEN	*Gotheburg*	Program to develop, test, and market less-harmful alternatives for hazardous products
	Stockholm	Wastewater management; "Measures at the Source."
UNITED KINGDOM	*Blackburn*	Partnerships for environmental and economic regeneration
	Lancashire County	Municipal environmental auditing; identifying overall environmental health
UNITED STATES	*Austin, Tex.*	Building and marketing environmentally sound residential housing
	Los Angeles, Calif.	Strategic service planning; wastewater treatment
	Muncie, Ind.	Local water pollution control, industrial pretreatment and biological indicators (biological monitoring)

Table 13.3 *(continued)*

New York City	Community-based environmental management; Bronx Community Paper Company: Recycling, waste management, income generation, and social services for the community
Newark, N.J.	Recycling business development program
Portland, Ore.	BEST (Business for an Environmentally Sustainable Tomorrow): To facilitate environmentally sustainable private sector business practices that increase efficiency and profitability
Santa Monica, Calif.	Water conservation (using water saving devices)

Source: International Council for Local Environmental Initiatives (ICLEI), case studies 1991–1995, Toronto, Canada.

On the other hand, in developed countries, three different types of actions can be observed: diminishing or containing waste (wastewater management and recycling); solving problems related to the green agenda (alternatives for hazardous products, water conservation, alternative fuels, etc); and searching for ways to increase the economic benefits derived from private sector pro-environment initiatives. Of these three categories, only waste management is related to the brown agenda.

NGO Projects

It is not possible to provide a detailed list of the causes that the environmental NGOs are presently defending. Therefore, I will just present a list (table 13.4) of the projects undertaken during the 1990s by a group of NGOs from Santiago de Chile devoted to reducing pollution levels in the city: ACpMA (Accion Ciudadana por el Medio Ambiente).

These tasks touch on all of the problems listed in this chapter, and they also include an important number of environmental education and training programs, essential for raising awareness levels and concern for the environment. The public pressure constantly exerted by these organizations on local and national authorities (through declarations, demonstrations, letters to corporations, etc.) should be noted. Their association with well-known national medical organizations is also relevant, because the levels of concern and the amount of subsequent political pressure increase rapidly when environmental issues are tied to health.[56] ACpMA, comprising, in part, local grassroots organizations,

TABLE 13.4

ACpMA (Citizen Action for the Environment)*,
Chile: Main Tasks Accomplished, 1991–95

- Created "Clean Air for Santiago" campaign (distribution of flyers, meetings)
- Conducted public opinion polls on the status of the environment (1992–95)
- Held "Santiago: How are we doing?" meetings, 1992–95: annual evaluation of environmental conditions in the metropolitan region
- Participated in talks on the "Environmental Law" bill and the attached regulatory legislation
- Organized various public demonstrations and declarations: support for the Ministry of Transportation's reorganization of mass transit in Santiago; support for the campaign to control the quality of food and other products by SERNAC (the National Consumer's Service); and support of efforts to prohibit the passage of ships hauling toxic residues
- Worked to help speed up the implementation of recycling programs; participated in the establishment of the Chilean Commission on Recycling (corporations-government-NGOs); supported meetings of people who earn their living collecting paper and cardboard (cartoneros)
- Edited and distributed 15,000 booklets on anti-pollution measures for Santiago
- Supported the "Cajón del Maipo Ecological Committee" (Maipo River Canyon area), which is working to repeal plans to build cement-mixing plants in the area, and the "Parque Environmental Protection Corporation," which opposes the installation of a toxic waste dump to be used by the country's largest paper factory in the area of Parque
- Participated in talks on the design of the new Line 5 of Santiago's subway (Metro) and, particularly, supported the "Defenders of Parque Baquedano" (a park partially destroyed by the construction of the new Metro line)
- Talked with the Ministry of Housing and Urban Development on the Intercommunal Plan for the Metropolitan Region of Santiago and its mechanisms for citizen participation
- Publicly protested (letters to the editor, to corporations, etc.) various issues, such as highly toxic products that are available for sale in Chile, improper use of "ecological make-up" ("ecological shoes"), etc.
- Participated in many seminars and other meetings on various environmental issues (as part of the training program for the group)
- Organized training and environmental awareness sessions, directed particularly toward young people and neighborhood groups (CBOs)
- Trained ACpMA members: held seminars on appropriate waste management, environmental impact systems, energy conservation, etc.
- Led "Commitment to Clean the Metropolitan Region" campaign (1993): 560,470 personal commitments signed, including the president of the republic, ministers, mayors. The majority of signatures were from young students.
- Edited several educational handbooks on community action: water conservation, reducing the use of motor vehicles, etc.

TABLE 13.4 *(continued)*

- Provided support for the preservation of Santiago's Metropolitan Park (the city's largest green area), particularly after being threatened by new CHILECTRA (Chilean Electrical Company) power lines that would have affected 130 hectares of park surface
- Advised other regional organizations outside of the city of Santiago
- Cooperated with various governmental, nongovernmental, and corporate programs in favor of the environment, including planting trees, promoting energy efficiency, engineering La Reina municipal recycling program, supporting the "Defenders of the Chilean Forest" campaign, and cooperating with the "Center for Packaging" in order to diminish garbage volume and create incentives for recycling
- Sponsored "Mano a Mano" campaign, which supports local urban environment improvement projects in collaboration with the municipality of Santiago (repairing sidewalks, painting walls and buildings, etc.)
- Maintained a constant presence in talks concerning Santiago's urgently needed new dump sites, a problem that is still pending (meetings with officials, businesses and residents)
- Participated in cooperative actions with the Chilean Medical College and Chilean Society for Pediatrics, to raise awareness of the negative effects of air pollution on health
- Worked on the Agenda 21 issues
- Engaged in talks regarding the plan to build a large campus for the University of Chile in an area that had been destined to become a metropolitan park: meetings with local and sectoral authorities, the appropriate ministries, etc.

*Citizen Action for the Environment (ACpMA) is a coordinating body for forty-eight NGOs working for the improvement of environmental conditions in the city of Santiago de Chile. It includes a number of local grassroots organizations (environmental councils of the *comunas*/municipalities) and NGOs such as Caritas, the Scouts, and CUT (*Central Unitaria de Trabajadores*, the country's main labor federation).

has made significant advances in carrying out successful collaborative efforts with corporations and government agencies.[57]

Failure and Success

What makes some initiatives succeed and others fail? The answer to this question is crucial for the analysis of environmental politics and is related to the weaknesses and limitations of citizen participation. "How real are the limits to community participation? Are communities a supplement to performance by public authorities? Is there a danger of the community being regarded as a substitute?"[58]

Unable to expand further upon this topic, I will limit myself to pointing out a few elements that seem to be important for environmental organizations to achieve their goals.

Experience has shown that when environmental organizations cooperate and coordinate among themselves their leverage with governments and corporations is increased. Growing public pressure explains, to a large degree, the trend in developed countries to set higher environmental standards, a phenomenon that is already reaching the developing world.

With respect to local initiatives on urban environmental problems, such as obtaining basic services, it is essential that the local group be well organized. However, the role of intermediate organizations (NGOs, universities) is also basic, because they facilitate the mobilization of internal resources and coordination with local governments.[59]

Capable and widely accepted leadership is another element that strengthens a local organization. This is vital in order to obtain the support of the local community and to make the residents feel part of a shared project.

The probability of success is also increased with public visibility. Therefore, support from public figures, such as popular artists and politicians, can be very effective in shaping political impact. The government can no longer ignore a problem or conflict when it has been covered by the media. From that moment on, the involved institutions (corporations or ministries) need to respond in some way to the charges, allegations, or demands—even to carry out studies to show that the issue in question will not have a negative impact on the population.

Groups with greater financial means seem to achieve success faster. This is due, in part, to their access to the media and, thus, their ability to make their demands more visible and politically relevant.[60]

Even when certain groups do not accomplish their goals (such as groups opposing the construction of a dam or the destruction of a park), the pressure they create forces the government and the corporations involved to explain their actions to the public; economic justification is no longer sufficient. Some corporations even state that projects facing strong public opposition are not profitable because they can require additional studies, meetings with leaders of the opposition movement, and project delays. As a result, corporations and governments are becoming much more aware of the need to work with the local population from the first stages of a project.

Looking Forward

Until now, to be more developed or wealthy meant to have more: higher per capita income, higher GNP, more square feet per house, more cars, more power, a greater number of consumer electronics, bigger TV sets, more . . . whatever.

Under this conception there are two alternatives. More than one-half of the world can remain poor and underdeveloped so that residents of the "North" (and also the small proportion of wealthy population of the poor countries) can continue to improve their standard of living. This trend could lead to social instability and its eventual consequences.[61]

Alternatively, development could begin to reach the poorer countries. As a result, an ecological crises of unknown dimensions might take place: global warming causing large areas of land to be flooded by sea water; unbearable pollution levels in cities; the loss of a major portion of our natural resources; or some similarly dire event.

Therefore, new meanings must be assigned to the concepts of development and progress, and certain core objectives of our society must be changed. Instead of searching for "more," we should start pursuing "better," looking for quality instead of quantity.[62]

One of the aspects of globalization, the mutual dependency among human beings (across different regions or countries), and between human beings and nature, must be understood and accepted. What takes place in one region of the world affects all of the others; what happens in the city affects its hinterland and vice versa, even though we still do not know the magnitude of this phenomenon.

In urban terms, this means that we must see urban systems as ecosystems, where humans, through their actions, produce changes that throw the global ecosystem off balance. Therefore, the challenge is to determine which actions are needed to offset the negative effects of human activities and to keep the system balanced within the parameters of sustainability. For example, if we are generating islands of heat by paving streets and building dense urban centers, we must find a way to compensate for this phenomenon.[63] Large spaces with trees and lakes, which cool down the environment, should be created, or perhaps other technical means should be developed for this purpose.

In the current political arena there are a number of actors working to achieve a sustainable world. They must join forces and refine their efforts to bring about a true change of direction. For different reasons and in the pursuit of different objectives, the more advanced corporations and environmental groups are seeking new environmentally sound alternatives to traditional forms of development. Change could be accelerated insofar as their initiatives move forward, and are coordinated and broadly adopted.

Constant controversy is to be expected, since certain activities will generate problems for specific sectors. Therefore, priority must be given to creating and improving effective conflict resolution mechanisms that allow us to move in the right direction, making decisions that negatively affect a smaller number of people.

The role of government is essential in guiding and regulating this process. Corporations need clear and stable rules (which have a tendency to become international environmental standards) in order to be able to function in the global economy. Individuals and organizations need access to effective mechanisms to solve or minimize conflicts. Yet, governments are better-qualified to plan development, to coordinate its supervision, and to ensure national observance of the rules and regulations.

Indirectly, the influence of multilateral organizations on national policy planning could accelerate this process if a greater number of environmental considerations were included in their mode of operations.

Finally, there is a great potential for the population to have a positive influence on urban change. "Participation is a process through which stakeholders influence and share control over development initiatives, and the decisions and resources which affect them."[64] To this end, there are a number of options. The first is the traditional participation of low-income populations in the improvement of their homes and neighborhoods. In many of the developing countries, this is supported by specific policies and is the only feasible way to improve the urban environment of the poor. There is the possibility of involving the population in environmental supervision, both in developed countries (where this is already occurring) and in developing countries. With an effective system in place and adequate dissemination of information, neighbors would be the most interested in ensuring that their environment is not being negatively affected. As certain large corporations have already realized, citizen participation from the very beginning in environmental impact assessments can avoid many conflicts, reduce delays, and lower costs for both the firm and the country. This requires developing effective participatory systems that go beyond the traditional acts of listening to the community and making technical decisions.

Notes

[1]Donella H. Meadows, et al., *The Limits to Growth: A Report of the Club of Rome's Project on the Predicament of Mankind* (New York: Universe Books, 1972); and Donella H. Meadows, Dennis L. Meadows, and Jorgen Randers, *Beyond the Limits* (Post Mills, Vt.: Chelsea Green, 1992).

[2]World Commission on Environment and Development, *Our Common Future* (Oxford, U.K., and New York: Oxford University Press, 1987).

[3]William E. Rees, "A Role for Environmental Assessment in Achieving Sustainable Development," *Environment Impact Assessment Review* 8 (1988): 279.

[4]Richard Stren, "A Comparative Approach to Cities and the Environment," in *Sustainable Cities, Urbanization and the Environment in International Perspective*, ed. Richard Stren, Rodney White, and Joseph Whitney (Boulder, Colo.: Westview, 1992), 4.

[5]Rodney White and Joseph Whitney, "Cities and the Environment, an Overview," in *Sustainable Cities*, 34–35.

[6]There are some exceptions among the Nordic countries (the Netherlands and Sweden) where developmental policies are being phased out in response to public demands for continuously higher environmental standards.

[7]Patricia McCarney, "Four Approaches to the Environment of Cities" (paper presented to the Center for Urban and Community Studies, University of Toronto, Canada, 1995).

[8]Michael Cohen, "Urban Policy and Economic Development: The Agenda," in *Cities in the 1990s: The Challenge for Developing Countries*, ed. Nigel Harris (London, U.K.: University College Press, 1992), 19.

[9]McCarney, "Four Approaches," 5; see also Cohen, *Cities in the 1990s*, 19.

[10]Willem van Vliet, "The United States" and Maria Di Pace et al., "Latin America," in *Sustainable Cities*.

[11]The same is true for "urban" and "rural"; the interdependence of the city and the region is such that it is impossible to understand the manner in which one of them functions without considering the other.

[12]Fritjof Capra, *Deep Ecology for the 21st Century* (Boston, Mass: Shambala, 1995); Riley E. Dunlap, George Gallup Jr., and Alec Gallup, "Of Global Concern: Results of the Health of the Planet" *Environment* 35, no. 9 (1993): 7–38.

[13]Ecologists define "carrying capacity" as the amount of the population of a specific species that can be supported indefinitely by a specific habitat without permanently damaging the ecosystem on which it depends. For human beings this must be interpreted as the maximum rate of resource consumption and waste production that can be sustained indefinitely in a given region without compromising the integrity and productivity of relevant ecosystems. See William E. Rees, "Ecological Footprints and Appropriated Carrying Capacity: What Urban Economics Leaves Out," *Environment and Urbanization* 4, no. 2 (October 1992): 129.

[14]Ibid.

[15]All of the studies of value on migration show that a clear rationality (not always solely economic) exists in making the decision to migrate.

[16]Santiago Friedmann, interview by author, World Bank, Washington, D.C., 1995.

[17]There is a sharp controversy over high agricultural productivity technologies, which increasingly use fertilizers that have deleterious environmental impacts. However, the problem lies more with the type of fertilizers used than with the use of labor-intensive technologies.

[18]See chapters 3 and 12 in this book.

[19]Rodney White and Joseph Whitney, "Cities and the Environment, an Overview," in *Sustainable Cities*, 16.

[20]White and Whitney designate recreation as a low pressure point (L) for the cities of less-developed countries. However, I consider it to be a high pressure point (H) for the poor sectors of society, because the poorer areas lack adequate green areas, sufficient

sporting areas, and the economic capacity to travel to recreational areas (such as city parks and beaches).

[21]White and Whitney designate crime as a medium pressure point (M) for cities in less-developed countries, which I also do not agree with. Studies on violence and crime show growing crime rates in all of the cities, including those in the less-developed countries. The lack of safety affects not only the upper-class residential neighborhoods, where the level of security increases day by day, but also the middle- and lower-class neighborhoods, where assaults are increasingly carried out with impunity in broad daylight.

[22]"Most cities are still characterized by a gap between an acceptable quality of shelter and the needs of the people." White and Whitney, "Cities and the Environment," 23.

[23]In Chile, the government created a National Commission of the Quality of Housing (Comisión Nacional de Calidad de la Vivienda) to respond to pressure from the debtors' groups who have refused to continue paying their mortgages because of the low quality of the houses.

[24]In order to do so, the nuclear family was used as a base, the prototype of which, for several decades in the developed countries (and in the more-developed developing countries), has been a couple and two children.

[25]"The extended family and other traditional methods of caring for the elderly are weakening, and the formal systems have turned out to be unsustainable." *Envejecimiento sin Crisis*, Informe del Banco Mundial (Washington, D.C.: World Bank, 1994).

[26]Sexual dysfunction is one of the growing reasons for medical consultations in the lower-class neighborhoods created by the state in Chile. María E. Ducci, *Health and Habitat Final Report* (Santiago, Chile: Instituto de Estudios Urbanos, 1994).

[27]Interview with a resident of a poor neighborhood on the periphery of Santiago de Chile, July 1992.

[28]Interview with a resident of a neighborhood in Chalco, on the periphery of Mexico City, about the gang of youths who gather at night in the streets, 1987.

[29]Bill Hillier and Jullienne Hanson, *The Social Logic of Space* (New York: Cambridge University Press, 1984). The authors use concepts related to the watch that neighbors maintain over public areas and how this relates to safety.

[30]Interview with Claudio Hohman, undersecretary of transportation for Chile, 1995.

[31]Jorge E. Hardoy and David Satterthwaite, *Squatter Citizen: Life in the Urban Third World* (London, U.K.: Earthscan Publications, 1989).

[32]Malick Gaye, "The Self-Help Production of Housing and the Living Environment in Dakar, Senegal," *Environment and Urbanization* 4, no. 2 (October 1992): 107. Also Peter Ward, *In Search of a Home; The Role of Self-Help Housing in Mexico City* (Liverpool, UK: University of Liverpool, 1976); María E. Ducci, *La Colonia Popular: una Manifestacion del Problema de la Vivienda* (Mexico City: UNAM, 1978).

[33]"Anyone who has a chance to get out goes to live in a better district, leaving the weakest groups behind, the poor and the old." Tjeerd Deelstra, "Cities, People and the Environment: A View Based on Experiences in Western Europe," in *Cities of Europe: The Public's Role in Shaping the Urban Environment*, ed. Tjeerd Deelstra and Oleg Yanitsky (Moscow, USSR: Mezhdunarodnye otnoshenia, 1991).

[34]It must be acknowledged, however, that this process can take too long when economic resources are tight and the situation of the country is not favorable.

[35] Larissa Lomnitz, *Como Sobreviven los Marginados* (Mexico: Siglo XXI editores, 1976).

[36]Santiago Friedmann, interview by author, World Bank, Washington, D.C., 1995.

[37]Of course, political stability is also needed to ensure that the rules of the game regarding foreign investment are observed. The lack of political stability becomes a serious obstacle to progress (witness the cases of Haiti, Sri Lanka, Burma, and Brazil).

[38]Some of these companies, during the 1970s and 1980s, preferred to move their factories to developing countries where governmental regulations practically did not exist. However, there is a growing tendency among these types of companies to raise their environmental standards in all of the countries where they work, either due to local demands or on a voluntary basis. Daryl Ditz, Janet Ranganathan, and R. Darryl Banks, eds., *Green Ledgers: Case Studies in Corporate Environmental Accounting* (Washington, D.C.: World Resources Institute, 1995).

[39]For example, there are moves to ensure that imported fruit has not been grown with the use of dangerous chemical products, that the packaging in which it arrives is completely recyclable, and so on.

[40]A clear example is the resistance of various countries to allow ships with nuclear waste, sent from one continent to another, to pass through their territorial waters. In July 1995, a network organized in Japan to protest French nuclear explosions in the South Pacific was unable to continue functioning due to the more than 3,000 responses it received on a daily basis, which saturated the computer system.

[41]"Test for Chile's Democracy," *Washington Post*, 30 July 1995.

[42]For example, California has been unable to reach a decision on where to locate a toxic waste site since the early 1990s. Tim Campbell, interview by author, World Bank, Washington, D.C., 1995.

[43]It is interesting to note that in Chile, SOFOFA (Sociedad de Fomento Fabril, the Association of Industrialists) considers this to be one of their concerns and is currently looking for ways to finance implementation and supervision by the government. They recognize this as a necessary step to achieve the kind of international credibility that importers demand.

[44]These are regional banks such as Interamerican Development Bank, Asian and African Bank, World Bank, International Monetary Fund, and bilateral aid agencies.

[45]Another subject, not yet adequately addressed, is the search for housing designs, technologies, and materials that allow the use of sustainable energy and help fight indoor pollution and global warming.

[46]Ditz, Ranganathan, and Banks, eds., *Green Ledgers*.

[47]It is interesting to note that in the United States, despite a sitting Congress (with a Republican majority) that is willing to cut government expenditures in many areas, major cuts in the budget for environmental programs have not been made. This is because such cuts would be quite unpopular among an electorate that is deeply interested in improving environmental conditions.

[48]Robert Rohrschneider, "Environmental Belief Systems in Western Europe: A Hierarchical Model of Constraint," *Comparative Political Studies* 26, no. 1 (April 1993).

[49]McCarney, "Four Approaches."

[50]For example, an annual opinion poll taken in Santiago de Chile shows that people who live in the poorer municipalities believe it is necessary to cut down on the number

of cars in the streets to reduce air pollution problems. Yet, residents of the wealthier areas are in favor of reducing the number of buses. Similar results have been found in São Paulo; see Pedro Jacobi, "Households and Environment in the City of São Paulo: Problems, Perceptions and Solutions," *Environment and Urbanization* 6, no. 2 (October 1994): 87–110.

[51]Bhuvan Bhatnagar, World Bank ENVSD, 1995. See also May Yacoob, Eugene Brantly, and Linda Whiteford, "Public Participation in Urban Environment Management: A Model for Promoting Community-Based Environmental Management in Peri-Urban Areas" (working paper for Water and Sanitation for Health Project, Washington, 1994), 9.

[52]Pedro Braile, "NGO Strategies for Urban Development in the Rio de Janeiro Metropolitan Region: The View of the NGOs," in *Towards a Sustainable Urban Development: The Rio de Janeiro Study,* ed. Alcira Kleimer et al. (Washington, D.C.: World Bank discussion paper 195, 1993). See also Jacobi, "Households and Environment in the City"; New Partnership Working Group, *New Partnerships in the Americas* (Washington, D.C.: World Resources Institute); Elsa Dawson, "District Planning with Community Participation in Peru: The Work of the Institute of Local Democracy," IPADEL, *Environment and Urbanization* 4, no. 2 (October 1992); Lair Espinosa and Oscar Lopez, "UNICEF's Urban Basic Services Programme in Illegal Settlements in Guatemala City" (1994, mimeographed); *Medio Ambiente y Gestion Urbana: Procesos Participativos en Problemas Ambientales: Taller de Experiencias,* CEDUAM, CENVI, FOSOVI, GEA, PDP, Mexico, 1994; Martha Schteingart, "The Environmental Problems Associated with Urban Development in Mexico City," *Environment and Urbanization* 1 (April 1989).

[53]UNCHS (Habitat) Community Participation in Zambia, *The DANIDA/UNCHS Training Programme* (Nairobi: UNCHS, 1992); and Yok-shiu Lee, "Intermediate Institutions, Community Organizations, and Urban Environment: The Case of Three Bangkok Slums" (Honolulu, Hawaii: East-West Center working paper, 1995). See also Yacoob, Brantly, and Whiteford, "Public Participation," 9; and David Dewar, "Cities under Stress," in *Restoring the Land: Environment and Change in Post-apartheid South Africa,* ed. Mamphela Ramphele (London, U.K.: Panos, 1991).

[54]Adversaries of the city argue that urban life is too expensive and that it wastes resources. However, all of the studies show that in the future most of the global population will be urban. "Turn up the Lights: A Survey of Cities," *Economist,* 29 July–4 August 1995.

[55]Carl Bartone and Barry G. Rabe, *Beyond NIMBY: Hazardous Waste Siting in Canada and the United States* (Washington, D.C.: Brookings Institution, 1994); see also Anne Whiston Spirn, *The Granite Garden: Urban Nature and Human Design* (New York: Basic Books, 1984), 232–35; Michael R. Edelstein and Abraham Wandersman, "Community Dynamics in Coping with Toxic Contaminants," in *Neighborhood and Community Environments,* ed. Irwin Altman and Abraham Wandersman (New York: Plenum, 1987).

[56]Cathy M. Alpaugh and Lynn Sabean, "The Politics of PCBs: A Viewpoint," in *Environmental Concepts, Policies and Strategies,* ed. J. Rose (Philadelphia: G+B Science Publishers, 1991).

[57]For instance, the "Mano a Mano con el Ambiente" (Hand to Hand with the Environment) campaign with the municipality of Santiago.

[58]K. C. Sivaramakrishnan, *Urban Environmental Governance* (Washington, D.C.: World Bank, 1994).

[59]Lee, "Intermediary Institutions."

[60]An example of a new type of NIMBY is seen in inhabitants of residential areas opposing the installation of antennas (monopoles) by cellular phone companies in their neighborhoods, because these devices are an eyesore and decrease property values. See "High-Tech Means Trouble: The Cellular Industry Wants U.S. Protection as Communities say No to a Towering Eyesore," *Washington Post*, 31 July 1995.

[61]"Crises determine social conflicts and political debates, resulting sometimes, in restructuring processes . . . other outcomes of crises are revolution, or a long period of "muddling through" social inertia." Manuel Castells, *The Information City* (Oxford: Basil Blackwell, 1989).

[62]A review of the proposals for a "new social paradigm with environmental conscience" is in P. E. Sullivan, "Environmental Science and the Coming Social Paradigm," in *Environmental Concepts, Policies and Strategies*, ed. Rose. Also, the concept of "postmaterialistic values" reflects an essential element of the change that is needed. Rohrschneider, "Environmental Belief Systems in Western Europe."

[63]The "islands of heat" generated in all large cities are the result of the heat-absorbing capabilities of buildings, the reduction of water absorption by the ground (as a result of large paved surfaces), and the artificial barriers to free circulation of air (thermic inversion). See *Sustainable Cities*, ed. Stren, White, and Whitney, 33; also Spirn, *The Granite Garden*.

[64]*Participation Learning Group Final Report*, World Bank Participation Sourcebook, (Washington, D.C.: World Bank, June 1995).

PART V

The Urban Landscape

EXPLOSIVE URBAN GROWTH AND gnawing urban decay both find expression in the physical development of the city. Changing technologies, standards of living, and demographic trends all alter how people organize their lives. Cities expand and shrink, grow upward and outward. Their physical development, in turn, determines how much arable land there may be in a given region, how sustainable a region's valued ecosystems will be, and how closely people will live together. Space may be stratified according to a variety of dimensions—economic activity, socioeconomic class, ethnicity—and, in the process, shape the human habitat.

The rapid growth of the world's cities has dramatically changed the urban landscape over the past quarter century. Cities have grown into metropolitan regions, which have expanded into massive agglomerations and conurbations. The foci of wealth in urban regions has migrated to new sites—on the periphery in North American cities, into traditional urban central cities elsewhere. Precisely how do all the trends discussed in this volume's previous chapters find spatial expression? The contributions by Galia Burgel and Guy Burgel and of Robert Bruegmann point in different directions.

The Burgels argue that spatial change has been so rapid and dramatic that few urbanites are cognizant of the new cities they inhabit. "The internationalization of the economy, trade, and information" combined with "the need to sustain economic growth and to support employment" and the futility of past "voluntarist policies of regional development and urban planning" have contributed to the failure of previous mechanisms for fashioning patterns of urban growth. Equally important, the intellectual framework used to understand the city's spatial realities is hopelessly outdated. As their empirical analysis of recent developments in their native France as well as in post-Soviet Russia suggests, the "complete victory of the city" may, in fact, prove to be "a negation of the city." For the Burgels, the true challenge of urbanism today is one of "urban experimentation." They search for small-scale pragmatic solutions to specific pressing problems that actually work.

Robert Bruegmann argues that an exciting experiment in a new urbanism is already under way, one brought about not by planners but rather by millions of individuals making up their own minds about how best to live and do business, and then acting on their conclusions. The city is shaped by "every citizen, every organization . . . every day." The result is most visible in the United States, where cities have spread out, decentralizing at an accelerating pace. "At the same time, however, there has been a countervailing tendency of certain functions to re-center, either in the traditional core, in neighborhoods around the core, or, most strikingly, at the very edge of the metropolitan area." The result is "a patchwork quilt of urban fabric that extends over immense areas of land." Driven by a middle-class search for privacy, space, and "choice of living, working, and recreation environments once reserved only for the wealthiest citizens," this new urban form is most visible in the democratized environment of the United States. Such patterns appear elsewhere, and their robustness suggests that everyone concerned with the future of the city must re-examine their basic assumptions about what constitutes "urban." Modesty in the face of such dynamic spatial changes becomes most compelling.

The Burgels and Bruegmann agree on this last point. Cities are not dying. Rather, they are so dynamic—they are transforming themselves so quickly all around us—that their vitality cannot be captured by a solitary intellectual concept, a single set of policies, or, most especially, by a unitary plan. Caution and prudence are the watchwords of the day when thinking about and operating in the turn-of-the-twenty-first-century city.

Chapter 14

Global Trends and City Policies: Friends or Foes of Urban Development?

Galia Burgel and Guy Burgel

The end of the twentieth century is replete with political and economic upheavals. But urban history appears to be even more tumultuous, especially fraught with contradiction. For a long time now, some people have been predicting that the death of the rural environment would be followed by the death of the cities, which would become diluted into the outer rings, crisscrossed with highways and exchanges, the pace of life dictated by telecommuting and dissemination of information on computer screens. But in fact, the age of the great metropolis has enjoyed a resurgence with the new national and international ambitions of cities: world capitals (New York, Tokyo, London, Paris), the number of which is all the more limited as their playing field is universal; city-states (Hong Kong, Singapore), which with the expanse of their hinterlands recall the great metropolises of ancient Greece; and teeming Third World cities overflowing with misery, but also with hopes for development. Thus, there are two forms of urban growth: on one hand, the further expansion of steadily growing outer rings, and on the other hand, the reinforcement of the center, both in terms of cultural life and in the control of economic interests. Likewise, administration of large urban organizations, extending their large-scale development and their transport and communications networks over vast areas, will call for institutions uniquely designed and planned. But at the same time, the inhabitants and industrial and commercial enterprises are not cognizant of this reality. Detached from it all, they carry on, torn between their roots in a particular sector of town and their attachment via travel, pleasure, or markets to a much larger dimension than that of the urban region: the nation, the world.

There is a crisis of opposing realities and even more so perhaps, a crisis in the logical systems underlying intellectual reconstructions. But to conceive a more integrated and balanced model of life in the cities of tomorrow, we must first understand the social and economic mechanisms that drive them. Technological innovations, economic decisions, and political resolutions must be supported by a social analysis of the material reality of the city and its structured spaces.

Even more to the point, there are three challenges for world urbanization in the modern era. Internationalization of the economy, trade, and information will not lead to more uniform spaces, cultures, and urban landscapes; local particulars and histories are what will determine how the universalization of processes will be interpreted. We need to sustain economic growth and to support employment in the countries of the North, while developing activity in the South confronts the ever more pressing demand for sustainable development that protects the natural environment and ecological framework of cities. Voluntarist policies of regional development and urban planning, which provided solutions during periods of growth, turn out to be useless in resolving the contradictions that arose.

From this angle, the analyses and reflections here are intended to contribute to an understanding of the mechanisms that maintain and even reinforce urban identity, and evaluate their prospects for survival and potential for transformation in a world that has been brought closer together due to failure of the Soviet system in the East, and accelerated growth of capitalism in Southeast Asia. We also intend to test on some key sectors the comparative pertinence or effectiveness of urban policies applied in a more or less similar manner all over the world: for example, new cities as alternatives to both peripheral dilution and internal recycling of city space, different methods of combating social and ethnic segregation, and job creation are selective but demonstrative approaches to critical evaluation and would also constitute a necessary return to creative imagination.

Urban Heritage Put to the Test

Following World War II, city models were established that owed as much to a long history as to the consequences of a political division of the world. Under the influence of the internationalization of economic processes (multinational corporations and trade) and dissemination of information and cultures, these models evolved abruptly, losing their equilibrium but retaining their specificity of response to universal appeals.

In the 1970s, a program of comparative urban studies could still be legitimately based on several large macroscopic divisions of the world: the uneven distribution of wealth (between North and South), the diversity of sociopolitical systems (among East and West), the influence of cultures (in Latin countries and Anglo-Saxon cultures), and the effect of local or national regulations (whether traditions of state interventionism or decentralized initiatives).[1] At the intersections of these fault lines were large territorial groupings within which cities tended to look the same: the cities of old Europe, American megalopolises, Soviet conurbations, and Third World cities represented characteristic landscapes as much as they did ideal urban models.

In the mid-1990s, although these typological systems have not disappeared, they have been weakened under the two-pronged action of major historical change and the appearance of more diffuse but significant processes. Thus, the deceleration and fluctuation of economic growth in Western Europe and the United States, rapid acceleration of the pace of development in Southeast Asia, and the opening of Eastern Europe and the former Soviet Union to the market economy bring the world together in its modes of accumulating wealth, although heritage and political uncertainties still ensure ultimately uneven results in urban spaces and societies. In the same spirit, decentralization arguments have gained ground everywhere, whether incorporated into the legislative process as they are in France, or in a more vague aspiration to local democracy as found in the Russian conurbations.

On the other hand, and in a more subtle way, a more or less universal restructuring of the relations of societies to their territories appears to be underway, juxtaposing upheavals of spatial continuity in cities within a region or nation and also in social groups and economic enterprises within a given conurbation. The place of a city is no longer determined by its rank and role in the hierarchical and interlocking organization of territories, but by its capacity to weave a network of distant influences with equivalent cities. In the same way, neighborhood community spirit and the objective advantages of local economics are being replaced by a dissociated system somewhere between near and far, between a fragmentary knowledge of the city and global changes, between impact study and international organization of markets.

For the future, the central question remains how to retain the unique features of each urban society both in its formal manifestations (space, landscapes, and social practices) and in its capacity to adapt and react to universal appeals. Is it a matter of temporary constancies, determined by the disparate rates at which processes take place—for example, the adoption of American suburbanization in Europe? Is it a matter of the durability of the physical framework of a city? Are there deeper cultural roots that could justify more permanent constancies, living manifestations of urban dynamism?

Here, we will discuss the concomitant protection of geographic heritage and homogenization of urban societies by analyzing five broad themes. They are a selective but revealing illustration of the two trends that divide cities in the modern world.

SPATIAL OVERFLOW OF REGIONAL SYSTEMS

In Western countries, the second half of the twentieth century marks the end of the classical opposition between city and country. This is significant first of all for demography and society. Originally a more or less considerable part of the total population, the contemporary city now encompasses almost all of the national society. In France, roughly one-fifth of the population still lives in communities statistically considered rural, but the lifestyles of all the inhabitants are urban, including modes of consumption and thinking, means of communication and transportation, and types of activities. Although there are statistical variations due to national definitions, this fact has become commonplace in all the developed countries; the veritable revolution since the 1960s is that it now touches the Third World. Linking a dramatic rural exodus and high fertility for the first time in human history, urban areas are growing twice as fast in the Third World as the demographic explosion, and also twice as fast as in the cities of rich countries.[2] Everywhere, the city, which has long (if not always) determined the organization of the country with its markets and dominant classes, has absorbed and urbanized the territory.

To a certain extent, this complete victory of the city is a negation of the city. What was the traditional city? A place with a high density of population and of structures, surrounded in its isolation by a more sparsely settled rural environment, which was dependent on it. For a long time—up to the mid–nineteenth century in the European city—great walls materially defined this enclosed and unique space. For another century, with the triumph of the Industrial Revolution, modes of construction and transport, particularly railroads, continued to promote compact agglomeration; the suburbs proliferated, even extending along the main highways, but they formed a continuous whole with the historic city. The real spatial upheaval came after World War II in Europe, but began earlier (in the 1920s) in the United States because of the popularity of the automobile. It was actually the car that stretched the city into areas increasingly farther away and more isolated from the central areas. From that time on, there were two opposing forces in contemporary urbanization: the center, the historic seat of power, innovation, and territorial and social exception; and the periphery, ever more sprawling and diluted, formed by the universalization and democratization of the modern city.

Since the 1960s, France has been a good illustration of these historic and spatial oppositions. They span all dimensions of the territory, from the organization of the nation to the internal structure of cities. They are all the more dramatic in France as two distinctive elements of French identity caricature their features without actually deforming them. On one hand, rapid urban growth after World War II allowed France to catch up on urbanization, an area where it was lagging behind the leading Western countries (England, United States, and Germany). On the other hand, Paris remained the demographic and economic capital, far and away the queen of the French urban hierarchy, with one-fifth of the population, one-third of the economic potential, and almost all of the country's administration in 2 percent of the national territory.

Two groups of facts will be presented here to support the proof.[3] Map 1—representing the population of urban units in 1990—shows a compelling image of the framework of French cities: the amorphous groupings of the North and East, heirs to the industrial age, Parisian sprawl, linear growth along the Rhône and the Mediterranean, and equal dispersion elsewhere, dating from the prefecture system in France at the time of the French Revolution (1789). In spite of the size of large conurbations, the linear development along valleys and coasts is still formed by populated points, which do not run into one another, where each center is individual.

Map 2 shows evolutionary trends in the population of French départements between 1962 and 1990. Map 1 reveals the stagnation of location of cities taken individually. Map 2 shows how contemporary urban diffusion has dissociated the nation and reformed the territory into homogenous compact masses at the same time. Only two large areas with markedly high demographic growth make up one-third of the French départements and are supported by the largest cities in the country: the large Parisian region, which extends to Normandy, Val-de-Loire, and small border areas of Brittany (Rennes, Nantes); the southeast of France, which—ranging from Lyon to Marseilles, Montpellier and Nice—has expanding high-growth areas.

Outside of these continuous spaces, only some isolated large cities (Strasbourg, Bordeaux, and Toulouse) are making their départements exceptions to the rule affecting nearly two-thirds of the national territory: the relative stagnation or decrease of the population. Because of these urban dynamics, usable space has receded on a national scale and, at the same time, has become diffused in a certain small percentage of regions.

In an entirely different ideological, economic, and political context, the same tensions exist in the evolution of urbanization in Russia.[4] (This subject will be discussed later in more detail inasmuch as it is less well known and the representativity of the trend is more valuable as an example due to the unique national traits characterizing the former

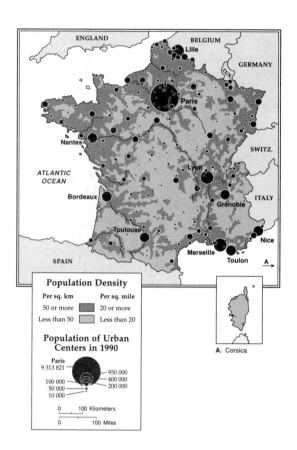

MAP 1. Distribution pattern of French cities

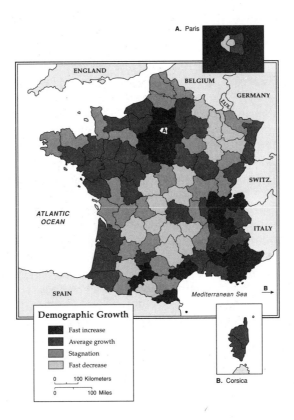

MAP 2. Demographic evolution of French départments under the impact of urban regions

Soviet Union.) The Soviet national and regional plan has traditionally been that the city had two functions: to build a network in the territory, which was its primary but not exclusive mission within the "general system of population"; and simultaneously, in its role as an "economic base," to ensure technical profitability of investment in order to multiply the productive resources of the USSR and optimally satisfy the material and cultural needs of the population.[5] Obviously, in the vast laboratory that was the Soviet Union—not only the experimental grounds of the intellectual and functionalist revolution, but also of the counterreform of an authoritarian and arbitrary voluntarism—something was lost between the intention and the act. The cities, especially in the eastern part of the country, remained isolated population centers, and most of them never served as anything but the pathetic tools and workshops of an industrial growth that ran out of steam, eventually coming to a complete stop.

The same conflicts seem to beset modern Russian cities. For all the leaders, from Mikhail Gorbachev to Boris Yeltsin, to maintain a certain territorial unity—whether it was the Union, as the former hoped, or the Russian Federation, as the latter more modestly states—the central question remained: What will substitute for the omnipresence of the Communist Party, which was, much more than the constitutional administrative architecture, the glue which held the Empire together; not in the center, not around the periphery, but as a single influence, pervading every place at every time? The dream is obviously to replace these ubiquitous tentacles with networks of cities organized into hierarchies, controlling interlocking territories, in an all-in-all Chrystallerian logic. This is obviously an illusion, because not only is the urban maturity of the Russian system a matter of doubt, but—considering dispersion and low population densities—the continuities necessary to this political scheme may not exist, especially the capability of cities to adhere to these unified requirements. Russian leaders are much more likely to look for outside economic alliances or services to satisfy their citizens than to worry about the needs of federal or even territorial cohesion.

How has urban, demographic, and spatial growth evolved since 1985 in Russia? The question is all the more acute as the Soviet period was marked by a considerable acceleration in the pace of urbanization and acquisition of new territories by the conurbations (new cities or extensions of suburbs). The continuation of this trend may indicate a new political course for Russia, by very reason of the fact that contradictory mechanisms will be brought into play: Will industrialization— which was the almost exclusive engine of urbanization in the USSR—

be helped, in the current production crisis, by the further expansion of notoriously deficient services? How will the never-specific effects of economic and political problems (difficulties with supplies, unrest, even riots, urban guerrillas, and civil wars) combine with the potential mobilization of millions of rural residents still mired there due to the weakness of agricultural productivity and restrictive rules on internal migrations? Finally, looking at this expansion in terms of political risk, urban dynamics could reveal either confidence in the virtues of the democratic melting pot or a retreat to national values more oriented to landownership.

If the most recent statistics are to be believed, the current state of affairs has relieved these opposing tensions with a clear reversal of the trend: urbanization has apparently stopped in Russia, even reversed, over recent years.[6] After fairly rapid pursuit of urbanization in the 1980s (over 11 million new city-dwellers between 1979 and 1989), the cities of Russia hit their peak population in 1992 (96 million), then lost close to 1 million inhabitants in two years (table 14.1). The reversal is especially striking in the largest conurbations, those with over 1 million inhabitants, which apparently lost 1.5 million of their residents; their number went from eight in 1979, to thirteen in 1992, then decreased to twelve in 1994. Volgograd can no longer call itself a city of 1 million people.

Three mechanisms have usually been responsible for the reversal of absolute volumes and rates: a negative natural movement, which is the most indisputable determining factor in the change of urban demographic pace; a limited migratory threshold, which can be explained by the persistent difficulties in finding food, the poor housing, the continuous rise in the cost of living, and the increasing insecurity; and finally, the administrative declassification of many "urban-type localities," which in both the tsarist and Soviet tradition had been given the status of city.

Attempts to find the logic of regional organization behind these urban dynamics are thwarted by the ambiguity of the information and the immensity of the territory. But a few significant geographic trends are enough, and three characteristics are immediately obvious. The first, once again, concerns the historic heritage of post-Soviet Russia. East of the Urals and in the northern parts of the country, the urban reality is still of limited scope, even though people in the cities compose the great majority of the regional population. Out of 167 cities of over one hundred thousand inhabitants in 1994, only 38 were eastern areas (economic regions of western Siberia with Novosibirsk, eastern Siberia with Krasnoyarsk, Far East with Vladivostok, and 7 in the northern

TABLE 14.1
URBAN POPULATION OF RUSSIA, 1979–94
(by city size)

Size of cities	Number of cities				Urban population (in millions of inhabitants)				Rate of annual variation in urban population (in %)		
Number of inhabitants (non-exhaustive categories)	1979	1989	1992	1994	1979	1989	1992	1994	1979–89	1989–92	1992–94
50,000–100,000	135	163	169	171	9.1	11.2	11.5	11.6	2.3	0.9	0.2
100,000–250,000	87	87	90	92	12.9	13.1	13.4	13.7	0.2	0.8	1.1
250,000–500,000	41	44	45	44	14.1	15.1	15.7	15.5	0.7	1.3	-0.7
500,000–1 million	18	22	21	21	12.7	14.0	13.3	13.7	1.0	-1.7	1.7
Over 1 million	8	12	13	12	19.0	25.1	26.2	24.7	3.2	1.5	-2.8
Total (all sizes)	999	1,037	1,057	1,059	83.3	94.4	96.2	95.3	1.3	0.6	-0.5

SOURCE: Olga Medvedkov and Yuri Medvedkov, *Turning Points in Russia's Urbanization* (Columbus: Ohio State University Press, 1994).

Murmansk region. This fact, which can be easily explained, reveals how Soviet planning and well-intentioned zeal failed to subdue and domesticate an immense and hostile natural environment and pass from urban colonization of space to an actual urban population.

This fundamental asymmetry is all the more remarkable as it may have become more dramatic over the last years. The main reason for this is the combination of natural and migratory urban movements, which in Russia is a definitively unusual occurrence. Whereas they often go hand-in-hand in Western countries (continuous immigration causing a renovation of aged structures, which in turn produces a statistical increase in the birthrate), the two types of dynamics oppose one another in Russia: the cities of eastern regions retain a naturally low growth rate, but experience a high net emigration. Conurbations in the Russian Far East even experience all the negative factors already mentioned: negative natural threshold, negative migratory balance, and maximum urban declassification. What these symptoms must certainly indicate is not only the economic failure of isolated mono-industrial centers, but the doubtless continuing inability of these cities to keep the people they attract: immigration, in a demographically cyclic pattern as a function of natural booms and busts, which replaced the forced movements of populations, convict labor, and the gulag, is slowing or stopping completely; repatriation to European Russia is continuing, even accelerating; and soon the natural threshold will fluctuate.

Finally, urban particulars have indisputably come to disturb regional orders. In the current state of disorganization of the country's administration, transportation infrastructures, and commercial trade, every city is fiercely protecting its autonomy and thus its ability to keep its inhabitants, attract others, or turn away undesirables as long as the city holds onto a scarce resource (mineral, energy, or industrial production) serving as its medium of exchange, and especially keeps local leaders both sufficiently well advised about and capable of using this situation to the city's advantage. Without returning to feudalism, Russian cities are becoming the strongholds of influential and autonomous politicians who were formerly only party puppets.

Once more, in spite of everything that separates France and Russia, it is impossible not to notice the convergence of mechanisms and results, whether the acquisition of these mechanisms is more or less recent or structural. Cities are no longer holding territory in a continuous network; their dynamism is associated less with their place in the national and regional hierarchy than with their internal ability to form far-reaching alliances.

URBAN SPRAWL AND CONTRADICTIONS OF CENTRALISM

On another scale of spatial analysis, urban sprawl is for European cities, and especially French ones, a significant qualitative mutation, which leads to the same result of double concentration and diffusion of the urban system.[7] Thus, once again using Paris as an example, the administrative region of Paris swelled by over 2 million inhabitants in 30 years (1962–1990). At the same time, the total population of the country increased by a little over 10 million inhabitants, growing from 46.4 million to 56.6 million. But behind this remarkable demographic growth of a very old, industrialized country, and the no-less-remarkable stable demographic status of its capital region (18.24 percent of the national population in 1962, 18.83 percent in 1990), two major reversals took place in this period. They are of disparate dimension, disparate duration, and above all, they appear to be contradictory (table 14.2).

There has been rapid growth of the peripheral area of the city, external to the spatial development of the city during the industrial era (the nineteenth century to the first half of the twentieth century). The five new cities established by the Regional Master Plan of 1965, the small isolated cities (Fontainebleau and Rambouillet), and in particular the diffuse urbanization of rural population centers increased by roughly 1.7 million people, out of 2.2 million in total growth. In this relaxation of the periphery, voluntarist policies have only a small effect: the new cities, established by the central government, account for only 500,000 inhabitants. At the same time, the city of Paris, heart of the capital region, lost over 600,000 inhabitants.

TABLE 14.2
EVOLUTION OF THE POPULATION OF ILE-DE-FRANCE, 1962–90
(by large sectors of the conurbation)

Geographic sectors	Total population (in thousands)		Annual variation (in thousands)			
	1962	1990	1962–1968	1968–1975	1975–1982	1982–1990
Central Zone conurbation	7,261	7,725	80	13	–28	11
Paris	2,790	2,152	–33	–42	–18	–3
Peripheral Zone	1,209	2,935	50	77	55	62
new cities	112	617	6	13	24	26
Total Ile-de-France	8,470	10,660	130	90	27	73

SOURCE: *Atlas of Ile-de-France*, vol. I (IAURIF-INSEE, Paris, 1991)

On the other hand, since 1982, this movement has leveled off and a recovery of demographic vitality is evident in the most central areas of the capital. The municipality of Paris continues to lose inhabitants, but at a rate ten times slower than in the 1970s. Five arrondissements out of twenty located in the east, formerly a working-class and industrial area of the capital, even gained inhabitants. The first ring of suburbs is no longer losing inhabitants, and the peripheral zone, although still more dynamic, has seen its rate of advance decrease by a factor of two. So the great city has there again split into two urbanization fronts: the peripheral diffusion and the return to the center.

There is no need to focus in great detail on the universal reasons—outside of the examples of Paris and France—for this oscillation of contemporary space. They are well known. The "forces of innovation" are driving the system toward reinforcement of centralities in all dimensions (a giant city center, large urban regions, and the richest and most industrialized countries); these forces encompass both more and less traditional reasons of economic efficiency, which seek to capitalize on the cumulative heritage and wealth of a network of dense relations, and cultural reasons linked to big-city consumption (such as museums, theaters, and people-watching). At the same time, there is a diffusion and relaxation in democratic and free-enterprise societies. More and more citizens want more living space, want to be closer to nature—even man-made nature—and are willing to pay for these with long commutes. Businesses, for reasons relating to the increase in property values at the center and more efficient facilities, are taking the same route. And governments, for reasons of territorial equity and social equilibrium, are putting decentralization policies into practice. The French government is not slacking in this area. Thus political authorities and the inhabitants together will guide the opposing forces of centralism and diffusion.

But these universal mechanisms come up against the heritage of acquired spaces, their chronological disparity in development, and certainly, in a more dynamic and enduring way, different urban cultures. To continue with a comparison of the urban regions of New York and Paris,[8] the structural irregularity of suburban expansion is evident in terms of both population and employment (maps 3 and 4). In the center of the megalopolis of the American northeast, the metropolis of New York (with 20 million inhabitants) is expanding by great leaps and bounds, over 300 kilometers from north to south and from east to west. Although the French capital (with its 11 million inhabitants) is also experiencing a wave of outward migration to the periphery, it remains a city in spite of the advance of the urbanization front. Areas of imbal-

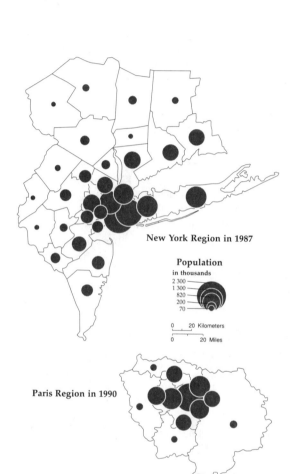

New York Region in 1987

Population
in thousands

2 300
1 300
820
200
70

0   20 Kilometers

0   20 Miles

Paris Region in 1990

MAP 3. Distribution of population in urban regions of Paris and New York

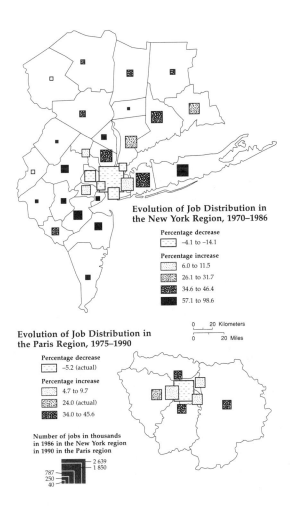

Evolution of Job Distribution in
the New York Region, 1970–1986

Percentage decrease
-4.1 to -14.1

Percentage increase
6.0 to 11.5
26.1 to 31.7
34.6 to 46.4
57.1 to 98.6

Evolution of Job Distribution in
the Paris Region, 1975–1990

Percentage decrease
-5.2 (actual)

Percentage increase
4.7 to 9.7
24.0 (actual)
34.0 to 45.6

Number of jobs in thousands
in 1986 in the New York region
in 1990 in the Paris region

2 639
1 850
787
250
40

0   20 Kilometers
0   20 Miles

MAP 4. Distribution of jobs in urban regions of Paris and New York

ance are much more dramatic for the distribution of employment. In 1990, over 90 percent of Parisian jobs were still located within the actual conurbation, whereas in 1986, close to 53 percent of New York jobs were dispersed into the suburban zone.

These differences are not just urban curiosities. For French cities, and more generally for European cities, they create difficulties in managing mobility and the environment that Americans would never suspect. The juxtaposition of a dense historical conurbation that still holds the majority of jobs, and a vast, diffused periphery that is essentially residential and low density, which developed over the last forty years under the influence of the automobile, gives rise to serious contradictions. The collective transportation networks, designed for the dense city, must be adapted to the diluted periphery. Autos will enter and jam the city. It is a double threat (due to pollution and nuisances) to the physical framework and daily life in the historic city, and to the natural environment in the urban region.

AN UNEQUALLED BUT INEQUITABLE ECONOMIC EFFICIENCY

Although the spatial organization of cities is changing and new problems are arising, their economic role in growth and material well-being is always being strengthened and expanded. However, this assessment was not advanced when the best observers were announcing not only the end of cities,[9] but the historic decline of their technical supremacy, condemned by deindustrialization and tertiary explosion; telecommuting and the information and communications revolution would disperse employment. But the reverse happened. In the richest countries, like the United States and Japan, the internationalization of trade, the influence of international groups, and the ubiquitous diffusion of the same products created, on the contrary, a need for and reinforcement of urban centers for decision-making and management of the world economy in global cities.[10] Even more recently, and in the kingdoms of suburbia that are the American cities, specialists praise the merits of the city centers for effective business economics.[11]

This revolution of spirit and reality is still more dramatic where the city previously had the reputation of either taking from the bountiful riches of the nation's agricultural development, as in the South, or exacerbating the unequal exploitation of resources and economic and social distribution of benefits, as in the Soviet Union and Eastern Europe. Thus does it apply to most Third World countries when we speak of "extravagant cities rife with nepotism"[12] and await the veritable take-off of green revolutions—"miracle wheat" or "miracle rice"—that are supposed to boost yields and agricultural production. They have not come to fruition or kept their promises, whereas the growth rate, first reached by the "dragons" of Southeast Asia (Singapore and Hong Kong), followed by South Korea, certain urban areas of Latin America (Mexico and Brazil), and today by the cities in South China, is forcing a revision of the insulting idea that urbanization is only parasitic. Here, as in nineteenth-century Europe, the city, under other conditions of technical, demographic and economic history, and with an incomparable acceleration of processes, is about to demonstrate, amid its sufferings, exploitation of human labor, and political battles, that it is the incomparable melting pot of wealth accumulation and democracy.

This is the bet in any case, the results of which we will see in the former Soviet Union after seventy years of distrust of large cities, which were traditionally suspected of increasing spatial and social inequalities. In fact, based on the collapse of industrial production and the explosion of small business and services, in the midst of the mafia excesses and rivalries between federal and municipal authorities (a good example of which is the wrangle between the mayor of Moscow, Yuri Luzhikov, and President Yeltsin), the Russian urban economy is confronted with the process of privatization and the increase of regional disparities. The theory was that in this period of mutation they would increase and that the cities already considered the most competitive, under the Soviet system, would grow further, since they would not be hampered by egalitarian planning. In fact, since Gorbachev, everyone has been waiting for Moscow, with one-quarter of the country's scientific potential, seven hundred thousand students, and 45 percent of invested capital, to take full advantage of a policy that is placing the emphasis on efficiency instead of regional equity for a change. More recent but also more limited observations tend to confirm these disparities. Shopping and service providers in the currency-exchange business are mostly concentrated in the two "capitals" of the country (Moscow and St. Petersburg) and in the "free economic zones" of Kaliningrad and Vladivostok. They reveal a certain entrepreneurial capacity as much as they do a large potential clientele. Thus the first car rental agency recently opened at the Moscow international airport, Sheremetovo-2. But at the same time, a "peasant" clientele has also sprung up—in fact, there have always been Georgians from Moscow—which is fond of luxury products, boosted by the free sales of agricultural products. Moreover, this clientele almost certainly also favors big city commerce.

However, the geography of these new inequalities between cities may not be so simple because of the aforementioned dynamism of the municipal authorities, who now tend, in the confusion and disengagement of economic and political power, to promote their cities in a manner that is more autonomous and more independent of both the law and simple urban hierarchies. Of course, these are still Moscow and St. Petersburg, whose initiatives were cited first. But is this because they are the most visible and most visited? It is in the capital of Russia that the Total French Petroleum Company signed a much-needed contract for redeveloping service stations with Moskomneft' Produkt (Moscow Petroleum Products Commission). The mayor of Moscow, Yuri Luzhkov, uneasy over the almost-total disappearance of taxis in the city after their privatization, reconstituted a fleet of municipal taxis. (They are recollectivizing!) And this is the same person who, more ambitiously, wanted to establish an alliance between the three largest cities in the country—Moscow, St. Petersburg, and Yekaterinburg (formerly Sverdlovsk)—to make them free-trade zones, exempted from the customs barriers President Yeltsin wanted. However, in Nizhniy-Novgorod, a city closed to foreigners until 1991, the enterprise reforms seem the boldest: under the impetus of local administration and the Union of Industrialists, the city is starting up an international fair, accelerated privatization, a new social policy, regional conversion funds, access to property for peasants, and a land bank. In Russia the surprise is always in the detour from the map.

This universal and perennial ability of the city to rebound is not universal and could even be structurally threatened by the repetitive shocks of the economic crisis in the last quarter of the twentieth century.[13] Thus, in Europe, particularly in France, the economic structures of enterprise are often rigid and have difficulty responding quickly to the ever more abrupt and changing demands of the world economy. The social welfare laws, to which European societies are greatly attached, reinforce this timidity. The results are delayed industrial conversion, less wide-ranging tertiarization, particularly in the less-skilled fields, and underdeveloped division and flexibility of work time. Few jobs are being created. From 1975 to 1990, only 400,000 jobs were created in the region of Paris, the most dynamic in France, with an increase in population of close to 1.2 million inhabitants. At the same time, between 1970 and 1986, 1.8 million jobs were created in the urban region of New York, although the demographic growth there is zero (table 14.3). These unequal flexibilities reflect not only differences in social and political agenda, but uncertainties vital to meeting one of the largest urban challenges of our time: providing jobs for all the men and women who demand them—even if a great many jobs require few skills, are unstable and low-paying—and ensuring that gains in productivity continue to increase.

TABLE 14.3

COMPARATIVE EVOLUTION OF EMPLOYMENT STRUCTURE IN
URBAN REGIONS OF PARIS AND NEW YORK DURING THE 1970S AND 1980S

Jobs (in thousands)	Paris (Ile de France)		New York (tri-state region)	
	1975	1990	1970	1986
Total employment	4,673	5,076	9,067	10,844
Industry	1,376	990	2,093	1,568
Tertiary sector (private and public)	2,883	3,730		
Private tertiary sector (Private nonfarm)			5,243	7,240
Public sector (Government and government enterprises)			1,338	1,453

SOURCES: for Paris: General Censuses of the Population, INSEE; for New York: *Rutgers Regional Report, vol. I: Job, Income, Population, and Housing Baselines* (Camden, N.J.: Rutgers, 1989).

THE FRACTURE OF THE URBAN MIDDLE CLASS: THREAT OR CERTAINTY?

The growth of the middle class is the true dimension of the contemporary city.[14] The fairly systematic recourse here to French analyses and statistics must not mask the essential proof. Socioeconomic transformations of urban populations look to be the same everywhere, at least over the short term. Only levels of economic development, the particulars of national histories, and political systems entail, in a general process, speedier developments, faster dynamics, and more mature stages of evolution. But neither the Third World countries—the sites of an explosion of urban growth and uncertainty of economic development, the effect of whose social extremes have been much too often exaggerated—nor the former communist countries, recently mired in a drop in the level of salaries and skills, appear to be strangers to the historical logic of how societies operate. Paradoxically, the beginning of economic growth in contemporary urban systems causes a simultaneous increase in regional inequities, an accentuation of social disparities, and the formation or expansion of a middle class. The presence or absence of these factors is an indicator of development, because they are both engines and results of change. This is how the veritable social revolution of the twentieth century took hold: the large-scale rise of white-collar employees and the more relative but still more significant increase of mid- and senior-level executives caused an upheaval in industrial societies and in the view of cities as robotic. The old ideas of the "worker" and the "boss" are evolving into "the employee" and the "executive."

TABLE 14.4

FALL OF TRADITIONAL SOCIAL CATEGORIES AND
RISE OF URBAN "NEW STRATA" IN FRANCE, 1962–90

(as a percentage of the category in the working population of France)

	1962	1968	1975	1982	1990
workers [laborers]	36.8	37.7	37.7	35.1	29.4
craftsmen, tradesmen, manufacturers	10.6	9.6	7.9	7.4	7.9
white-collar employees	12.4	14.7	17.6	19.9	26.5
middle management	7.8	9.8	12.7	13.8	20.0
upper-level management and professionals	4.0	4.9	6.7	7.7	11.7

SOURCE: Daniel Noin and Yvan Chauviré, *The Population of France*, 3rd ed. (Paris, France: Masson, 1992).

For a long time now, the steady growth of the middle class, first in the United States, then in Western Europe, has been an effective political response to the widening of gaps. Income distribution was very unequal, and places of residence rapidly segregated. But the majority of the population was united in its respect of skills, diplomas, and merit, all having the same aspiration, if not access, to all the material goods industrial society offered. Social permeability was the best barrier to growing inequalities. Its solidity is less certain today, and although the methodological errors in the Marxist urban sociology of the 1970s are still there, as demonstrated by its continued theoretical reductionism in societal analysis, it may have been more correct in its specific prediction for the future of societies.[15] The global revolution has strayed from its course. Are "urban battles" impending?

There are still not enough detailed studies to confirm with certainty the change, the slowing down, and the turnaround of the urban integration model. The dimensions of the process, the historical newness of the logic, the omnipresence of the movement, will ensure beyond doubt that it is influential and long-lived, which further validates the general picture that has been laid out. But since at least 1985, Western cities have been seeing obvious signs of fractures in society. The novelty lies less in the marginality than in the exclusion, less in the neglect of the poor than in the frustration of growing parts of the urban population. The fissure is no longer on the margin of society, but rather at the very heart of the system. In a simplistic manner, and thanks to an economic crisis with sudden revivals and the fits and starts of the recovery (the surge of 1986–90, followed by a new recession), the middle class seems to have split up.

For 10, 20, or 30 percent of the urban population—the level certainly varies, depending on the country and the city, and the unequally dramatic volumes for individuals and policies—the vicious cycle of exclusion is in motion.[16] Its characteristics determine not so much absolute thresholds of poverty or distress as they do accumulations of rejections, accompanied by the feeling, and often the reality, that the future holds no return to normalcy, for oneself or one's children. School dropouts, delinquency, drugs, unemployment, and disease are symptoms of an urban evil, all the more perceptible since it tends to hit certain groups and certain areas of the city: unemployed youth, the elderly, single women, and foreign workers concentrated largely in crumbling central neighborhoods, old industrial suburbs, or, in France, in the large cohesive blocks (*grands ensembles*) of the 1960s, soon abandoned by upwardly mobile, skilled workers and employees who, twenty years earlier, saw in it the symbol of their promotion and access to a comfortable lifestyle. Observed in its broad outlines, this spiral of collective eviction and geographic segregation is breaking up social continuities that used to be the basis of the unity of the Western city. It is this profound and new marginalization that threatens its vitality. Is the crisis reaching the center of contemporary urban societies?

The difficulty of the answer lies at least as much in the assessment of emergent mechanisms as in the diversity of their national expression. It is certain, to keep to the simple comparison between France and the United States, that differences about settlement, citizenship, and community radically affect the manner in which marginality and social exclusion are to be interpreted and handled. "France, a country of immigrants, continues to think of itself as a homogeneous country and is experiencing a fictitious ethnification based on the image of a community of men sharing the same origin, the same history, the same culture, the same values."[17] This is far from the respect or even the exaltation of differing ethnic and cultural features, which are sublimated in the hope of the American Dream. In spite of the reversal of spaces in the city, the connections between the crises in the French suburbs and peripheries, and those of the American inner cities, these distinctions in representations and ideologies are significant in the overall profile of urban poverty and decline in value of city neighborhoods. We are speaking in one instance of youth, underemployment, and social development, in another of African-Americans, Latinos, or ethnic integration. Is it the same reality?

URBAN SOCIETIES TORN BETWEEN LOCAL AND INTERNATIONAL

All these ambiguous tendencies in the evolution of societies and urban spaces are worsened by the contradiction between the representations and practices of the players in the city.[18] The results of a poll taken across various social strata in the new town of Saint-Quentin-en-Yvelines, one of five new towns in the Paris region, are a good illustration of the division of populations, torn between their attachment to the very near (their homes and neighborhoods) and the very far (the nation). This dissociation of spatial ideologies seems rather indifferent to social membership. At the outside, as is normal, the rank-and-file workers, with stronger roots and less geographic and social mobility, are more attached to local values than are executives. Likewise, living in the urban periphery may reinforce this feeling of fragmentation and division of territorial dimensions, but the observation can be generalized. It tallies in fact with all the results of studies carried out on very large cities: the dimensions and the complexity of urban regions are such that no one can think in terms of the entire territory of the city. More than ever, the mental map and the actual map of the city cannot be superimposed (figure 14.1).

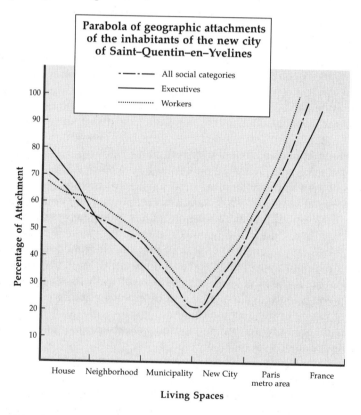

FIGURE 14.1. Parabola of geographic attachments in a new city near Paris

The observation goes beyond symbolic representations of urban populations; it also applies to their practices with regard to space. In a big city, commuting and pleasure travel generate particular and repetitive itineraries that divide the actual territory into sectors. The choice or obligation to live or work in a certain place, to use certain transportation networks, and to have certain social affinities and cultural tastes determine for everyone which parts of the city they know. The collective sum of these practices is the true fragmentation of urban social space, even beyond the classical ethnic segregation and the residential division of professional categories (of opposition between center and periphery, and between socially mixed cities and those with separated populations). At the same time, both for commuting and leisure, city-dwellers are traveling more and more, farther and farther out into the world. It is easier to take transcontinental trips, to exchange ideas or plans with professional colleagues, than it is to travel across—to know—all the geographic sectors of one's own urban region.

This dissociation of space is not reserved for social players. It is happening to economic investors, the business world. A curious evolution should be pointed out here. Technological revolutions in energy sources (electricity and hydrocarbons), in materials (the development of synthetic products), and in the means of conveying information and decisions (upheavals caused by fax and Internet networks) have classically delocalized investment. Technically, anything is possible anywhere. Of course, economic costs (property values, wages, and expected markets) are determining factors in development decisions. But they only affect the major geographic elements: for a Japanese investor, for example, choosing between England and France. For the final choice, the factors to be considered will be values of a local nature: natural or cultural and ethnic environment, available housing (especially for executives), the proximity of schools and universities guaranteeing quality and security for children, and accessibility to highways and an international airport. Thus there are international companies with attachments to the strictly local. Between the two, there is nothing, unless you count airline routes and telexes.

This lifestyle of individuals and societies obviously does not correspond to the physical reality of large cities. They have a scope, a territorial continuity, however diluted at the periphery, and modes of administration that require the city to be taken into account as a whole. Collective transportation networks (subway and suburban commuter lines) and those that support individualized traffic patterns (roads and highways) are more or less plotted out, more or less interconnected, but in any case do not coincide perfectly with the realities of traffic and commuting.

On the other hand, and in a similar fashion, the political and administrative map of cities is necessarily a map of continuous and contiguous space.[19] Even though it is fragmented into relatively autonomous units, there is no such thing as empty space in it. The urban region of Paris—Ile-de-France—comprises 1,300 municipalities, all of which have had urban powers since the decentralization laws in 1982. The tri-state region of New York has 780 municipalities. Even Eastern Europe and the former Soviet Union, which had demonstrated at least pro forma its noble pretensions to unity in the territorial management of urbanization, are experiencing the double decline of authoritarian power over the city, from the top and from the bottom. The state is fading away, as much in its grandiose visions of urban regulation as in its more modest role—but a necessary one to our Western eyes—as technical and legal guardian of local collectivities. The large municipalities, heirs to vast administrative territories, which are the essence of the extension of conurbations, and extended means of management, which territorial officials greatly envied them, are often inexperienced, and must deal with vague desires to create autonomous communities, based on local egoism or actual neighborhood solidarity. In Russia, beginning with Gorbachev, the formation of cooperatives of youths to build their own housing—first at Sverdlovsk, under the guidance of the local first secretary at the time, Boris Yeltsin, and then in Moscow—had greatly promoted the growth of territorial powers. It is not certain whether this assists in the resolution of urban problems, except as an apprenticeship for democracy.

And there it is—the cornerstone of the contemporary city. In addition to the conceptual difficulty—that the city-dweller lives in a fragmented and discontinuous urban space,[20] whereas the engineer and the politician are administrators of a global and continuous space—there is also a more ethical dimension: the universal trend, although less driven in the South and in Asia, toward individualism in societies that are increasingly numerous, concentrated, and multiple, necessarily leading to the egoism of small territorial units, public or private, at a time when problems seem to demand a global vision. The recent emergence of the concept of "governance" may be a response to this two-pronged testing of urban realities and policies.

Urban Policies: Acid-Tested by Doubts and Realities

The contradictions of the modern era must lead neither to the pessimistic abandonment of any political will, nor to recourse to a spatial voluntarism of doubtful effectiveness. This first observation comes from similarities exhibited by all large cities in the world, no matter what urban policies were applied. Of course, the reality is never as bad as the caricature: Paris is a little more than public planning policies, New York cannot be boiled down to a savage war of builders and speculators—which is what comes to mind when Robert Moses's actions are remembered—and Tokyo is not only divided into several large financial companies, which is what comes to mind when metropolitan government actions are examined. But these three giant cities are fairly good symbols of the different terms of engagement of the public sector and of the private sector. In all three, however, the same diagnosis has been made: traffic congestion, increasing insecurity (even in Tokyo since the metro gas attacks), and social segregation. In sum, an ambiguous feeling is rising in the city: a recognition of its economic efficiency and its cultural attractions, but a rejection of its pace of life as well as its physical and moral pollution.

The hopes that were pinned on radical solutions in the 1960s and 1970s, either with a qualitative change in lifestyles and spatial configurations, or with application of specific city-planning policies, now seem more remote.

The reality of economic and even demographic movements has challenged theories of "counterurbanization."[21] This new victory of the city, technological as much as cultural, dashes the hope or fear of seeing urban problems lessen or disappear in the generalized dilution of profligate suburbias. But even when they are physically partially realized, as in the United States (far from the only model), they do not resolve problems of urban concentration, social mix, protection of the natural environment, and lasting development. More than ever, the necessary improvement of the material conditions of urbanization depend less on the utopian and certainly dangerous hope that cities will decline, than on a collective recognition of the desired objectives and the policies needed to attain them. Reevaluating the role of urban planning, redefining the targets of efficiency and equity in the city, and devising different methodologies of action could well be the master text of this new program.

REEVALUATING PUBLIC POLICIES

As often happens in periods of great change accelerated by the proliferation of studies, reports of all types, and international exchanges between specialists, dominant philosophies in the area of urban planning have been vacillating since the 1960s between a naive confidence

in the effectiveness of voluntarism and in the power of urban specialists, and a pure and simple surrender to full-scale economic and societal trends, more or less disguised as a condemnation of these same
urban specialists and architects, who are accused of being responsible
for all the evil in the city. The city, however, deserves better than these
two extremes. The differences between declared objectives and actual
accomplishments, the often serious dysfunctions that have been revealed, are what most often force a reconsideration of the logic behind
society, rather than the verified consequences of specific policies of city
planning.

Observation of urban policies that have been applied for thirty years
in Paris only supports this obvious truth. The worst failure of the
Regional Master Plan of 1965 had less to do with the fact that it did not
complete the spatial segment intended for transportation (the Regional
Express Network) or for new towns, and more to do with its turnaround of three major characteristics of French society: the decline in
fertility, the considerable slowing of migratory movements to the capital, and the economic crisis, which completely warped the objectives
established for growth of the city. However, relenting to a deep-seated
trend may be a measure of success; the current focus in planning for the
region of Paris is on recovery of central areas (the first ring of suburbs)
and is certain to succeed, due to the attractions of the central region.

Unfortunately, this formal reclamation of center cities, even when
successful in an aesthetic sense, fails to eliminate the most serious problems in the city. This has been true in France for policies of renovation
(1960s and 1970s) and rehabilitation (1980s), which correspond to a
strong collective will in French society (unlike any in American culture)
to recover and reinvest in already urbanized territory. The verdict on
these activities is uncertain.

Recovery and reinvestment are effective tools for eliminating urban
decay and making urban structured space better conform to contemporary society. But studies show that they have also been accelerators
of gentrification and social and spatial exclusion of the most disadvantaged who live in these old neighborhoods. Likewise, the government
policy of building public housing, which is one hundred years old in
France, and which expanded in scope after the Second World War, has
ceased to be a means of social integration. The large groups of collective buildings (*grands ensembles*), which in the 1960s signified an aspiration to modernity for the upwardly mobile middle class (skilled
workers, white-collar employees, technicians), have become ghettos of
rejection and social exclusion. Since the 1980s, in spite of unprecedented amounts of spending in that area, spatial policies for disadvan-

taged neighborhoods have universally failed under the aforementioned weight of societal fractures.

Even more generally, lurking behind these intellectual failures of urban policy is certainly a methodological defect: the idea that spaces can be treated in the hopes of engendering an effect on society. Masked by the pace of change in the countries of the North, in a period of high economic growth and demographic dynamics, this error of understanding appears in all its glory when the economy loses impetus, and when demographics settle down. One of the challenges of the city today is exactly that: it is confronted with modifications of its fundamental mechanisms of development and, at the same time, with a realization of the insufficiency of traditional tools for intervention in these spaces. Moreover, the failure of the ideological revolutions in the East should necessarily make us hesitate to embrace a voluntarism that is trying, with the best intentions, to tackle global society. As the authors of this chapter, we are familiar with voluntarism's authoritarian and even criminal attempts to outflank political democracy, and the dramatic slowdown of economic development. And we repeat emphatically: it will not be possible to eliminate serious urban disorder in rich or poor countries if economic development does not continue. Thus we are being forced to innovate.

REDEFINITION OF OBJECTIVES: SPATIAL EGALITARIANISM OR
TERRITORIAL EQUITY

Finally, in the East and South, as in the West, most urban policies are based on the utopia of spatial egalitarianism. In the Soviet Union, the country had to be raised to the level of the city, the small town to the level of the urban center, and the metropolis to the level of the capital, to obtain territorial harmony. Within the city, the leveling of lifestyles into uniformity as a large collective group was supposed to result in a classless society. The result exceeded all hopes, from the monotony of the countryside to social atony, economic impotence, and political deviance. In the West, it did not proceed that far. But the same illusions still haunt us in other forms, the spirits of politicians and technical specialists, fortunately in a general context of liberty, and so economic growth continues, on the scale of history. Thus, the equality between the regions, the reclamation of rural space, the parity between cities, the social mix in neighborhoods, and equilibrium in distribution of jobs and housing provide a common basis for egalitarian discourse and populist proposals. This is to forget that all of urban reality is inequitable in its spatial distributions, in its social divisions, in its economic capabilities. These disparities do not appear to be negative attributes of growth, but are a part of its very substance. To try to equalize districts of the city is to take the risk of altering its wealth of creation, culture, even liberty. Suppose that the means became available to do so, what politician would agree to do the job? Do we have to give up equality to achieve efficiency?

This is an old moral question. Its urban response can be found partially in the concept of territorial equity. Spatial egalitarianism is a fatal illusion; territorial equity, a necessary utopia. Not all districts in the city can aspire to equal distribution in location of activities, of technical or cultural infrastructure, or of the socioprofessional composition itself. But all inhabitants of the city, all its citizens, have inalienable equal rights to a job, access to educational and leisure resources, and the means of meeting their need or desire for geographic and social mobility—in sum, equal rights to develop themselves to their fullest ability. This reversal of approach, which is nothing more than a return to the values of the French Revolution of 1789, would mean a true revolution in the philosophy of urban policy: What the territory *cannot* provide everyone is the requirement of a civic morality and a law that would restore it to everyone.

This conviction explains why there is a certain mistrust of the batteries of statistical indicators instituted here and there to measure the success or failure of urban policies and establish classifications for cities, as if they were football or baseball teams, with standardized rules of play: the number of permanent jobs created, the percentage of atmospheric pollution, cumulative totals of hours of traffic congestion, enumeration of the forms of criminal behavior, etc. This skepticism is caused not only by a methodological uncertainty as to the scientific precision of this desired urban quantification, but also by a moral reluctance to further accentuate feelings of injustice by designating "good" and "bad" cities. Moreover, most of the time those municipalities classified as "bad," or even their inhabitants, become indignant over these results, accusing the figures of stigmatizing them and exacerbating their situation, frightening away even more potential investors or potential inhabitants who would raise the value of the area. In fact, the main opposition to the method pertains to the radical impossibility of applying the same standard of quality to all the districts. The right to be different is claimed not only by individuals, but also by urban spaces and societies. Still, these differences cannot be allowed to become privilege, and inequality cannot be allowed to become injustice.

In this regard, and much more so than the indicators previously cited and critiqued, the most revealing and unacceptable urban disparity in moral terms lies in the inequity of the tax burden between cities.[22] Thus, in the urban region of Paris, Ile-de-France, it is of course normal for taxable wealth to be calculated based on the general distribution of jobs and of the population: poor rural towns in the outer ring, and districts brimming with activities and inhabitants in the center. But in the densely populated area, other even more revealing characteristics are turning out to be unacceptable. The tax burden is greater for the poor than for the rich: "working districts overtax their businesses (professional tax) and their property owners (developed real estate), and to a lesser degree, their inhabitants, whereas in the middle-class districts, hardly anyone is overtaxed."[23] The overall results are inconsistent and show the accumulation of territorial inequities. In working districts, the inhabitants pay more taxes in proportion to their resources—which may discourage businesses and overwhelm the residents—but receive an inferior social net in return (table 14.5).

The unequal tax burden is not the worst of urban injustices, but it cries out to the collective conscience because it reflects on the equality of citizens. It is easier to understand that of all the measures taken in France for cities, it was the small redistribution of the tax burden among the districts that caused the most hostility, especially in the region of Paris. For the first time perhaps, an urban policy did not address the inequality of districts, but rather the equity of society. For the first time, an appeal was made to the solidarity of the city to maintain its efficiency; it was no longer space, but democracy that was the topic.

INVENTION OF NEW METHODOLOGIES

These small advances in urban policies show the direction that it will be necessary to follow in order to innovate and conceive those urban constructs and especially those modes of social functioning likely to produce more harmonious cities. Without abandoning traditional

TABLE 14.5

INCONSISTENCIES OF LOCAL TAX BURDENS IN THE PARIS REGION, 1987

	Tax base (community per inhabitant)	Taxable resources per inhabitant	Percentage of household revenue expended for local taxes
Working districts	12,380 F	–2,790 F	3.7
Middle-class district	28,560 F	1,860 F	2.0

SOURCE: Olivier Jean, "Taxable Wealth and Poverty of Ile-de-France Districts," *Regards Sur Ile-de-France*, 1990

routes (reclaiming abandoned spaces on all scales, or advancing economic and cultural support of disadvantaged populations), which should be pursued persistently and continuously, it is because elimination of these symptomatic measures—though insufficient by themselves—would aggravate urban crises that we must break new trails in thinking and doing. They will be aimed at three serious problem areas that have appeared over the last few decades: employment, mobility, and environmental protection.

Employment

Though spatial policies are dubious, employment policies, because they are difficult to implement, may become the real issue in contemporary urban societies. If we want to effectively combat the disparity of rates of development in the city, it will no longer be enough to rehabilitate the formal envelope of the city, or even to embellish it in a more equitable fashion; we will also, and as a matter of priority, have to ensure that as many people as possible have genuine access to training, and beyond that, to materially and morally gratifying work.

This compelling moral necessity presupposes that we can rise above the sterile antagonism between spatial and sectoral policies.[24] To date, employment policies had been divided between measures for planning spaces (planning and setting up business parks while awaiting investors) and economic incentives (a given sector of activity will be supported regardless of its location). The choice is now a false one. Zoning of territories—industrial or service zones—would be dangerous due to the spatial division that it entails on a number of levels. It is no longer justified by the nature of the work, all too often more harmful for the urban environment than in the past. Moreover, a space for employment will never generate jobs until it has first been galvanized by commercial dynamism. To focus on one type of business activity over others is to ignore the aforementioned sensitivity of economic decisionmakers to local particulars (policies of housing, culture, leisure, and respect for nature).

But in this overall policy, which marries the economic to the social, local, and international, it should be understood that we are no longer reconstituting the old framework of regional economic alliances. In France, the city-planning elite and technical specialists are very attached to their jobs by political function or professional commitment. Thus, in certain new towns of the region of Paris, the hope is to build technopolicies around electronics, computer science, and desktop publishing, where businesses, research labs, and locations will interrelate structurally. The reality, at least in France, does not completely answer these hopes: Silicon Valley is not a transferable model, and it is now being found that locations can be welcoming and attractive to economic players without their wanting to weave strong supportive bonds of mutual services and reciprocity there.

From that point on, progress will have to be more flexible, and ambitions, even utopias, defined gradually. It may first be a matter of discovering those deep inclinations that, outside of economic changes, form the true urban continuities. Thus, in Paris, there are two good examples of these turn-of-the-century challenges. In upscale neighborhoods of the capital, the departure of Renault automobile factories may become just another urban drama if office buildings and apartment complexes are simply allowed to spring up there. But this may be a victory of the intellect if we can manage to retain there the spirit of technological innovation and social progress symbolized by business—that is, to plan research laboratories for that area, in particular high-technology ones, which could not otherwise locate there because of property values and real estate speculation. Likewise, the doubling in size of the neighborhood of *La Défense* business center, its access to the banks of the Seine, in the middle of former industrial and blue-collar housing zones, will mean something different depending on whether it can or cannot incorporate the existing university campus—the University of Paris X–Nanterre—which is both the tangible and intangible symbol of the accumulation of knowledge, and also, to a certain extent, of social mobility.[25]

Even if we were to fail in these prospects for spatial integration, the least that could be done would be to fiscally redistribute economic growth and income engendered by the creation of the most dynamic jobs. Bold policies of redistributive adjustment of local taxes are being implemented here and there. Unpopular in the rich districts, these measures are nevertheless necessary to fight municipal narcissism and eventually diminish, with material resources, the hopelessness and clashes that are the natural result of economic marginalization, even more unacceptable than the discomfort of substandard housing or social segregation. But these are historically stopgap methods. In theory, if we look at the long-term evolution of employment and productivity in developed countries, only worksharing would make it possible to ensure that everyone had a job, and that the available jobs were more evenly distributed. We already see that this necessary utopian society goes beyond business, local cooperation, and national alliances, to address international understandings. Taking into account commercial competition, actual policies of urban employment are no longer made on a national scale, or on the scale of large territorial groupings (like the European Union or the United States of America), but rather on a worldwide scale.

Like biology, the urban economy has entered the era of ethics. It is less the functioning of employment, trade, or money that is the problem, than the moral and civic conduct of urban societies. We can perform in vitro insemination, make money without producing anything, and produce without working. We must learn to share, among ourselves and with others, to save the working life of the city and certainly also the city itself.

Mobility

Mistrust of the abuses of voluntarist spatial policies—policies that are considered the be-all and end-all of social equilibrium—does not mean that they cannot be used to improve the functioning of the city and the quality of life of its inhabitants as long as the problems and objectives are considered carefully. Mobility and transportation policies are a singular illustration of this. In all the giant cities of the world, travel has increased in terms of the number of trips and distances. It is futile to think that these difficulties can be solved by better parity of zones of employment or residence, or to indulge in ineffectual magical thinking to the effect that exclusive priority can be given to mass transportation means. On the other hand—and this is a source of happiness and enrichment in a complex society—the structural mobility of populations is increasing and will continue to do so, for their work, their personal relationships, and their leisure. The expectation that these movements can be reduced via infrastructural planning is a dangerous illusion. Moreover, expansion of urban regions, their dilution into ever more diffuse megalopolitan zones, make the organization of collective transportation networks technically complicated. At any hour of the day or night, there is some urban resident in some sector of the city traveling to another sector. In Paris, there is an obvious lack of harmony between the still-impressive improvement of railroad networks, essentially radial, and the increase in mobility, which is essentially tangential. To think in terms of megalopolis instead of metropolis when drawing up future plans is not a panacea. How will it be built and how can it be made profitable in the more extensive but less dense peripheral areas of urban regions? In this primary area of urban mobility, boldness and imagination are the watchwords: to exploit and develop technologies, to be wary of anything a priori exclusive (i.e., making the mistake of viewing public transportation as one aggregate and automobile transportation another), to protect against overly strict accounting (to make the users pay for it all would be prohibitive), and in particular, take great care that these services be regular and safe, even or especially in the geographic layout of the networks.

A revolution is underway, of the same type as was begun by the automobile earlier in this century. It goes beyond simple technical aspects (electric cars) to a global vision of the city, in mobility as much as in economic activities and protection of the urban environment, both in the city center and on the periphery (see the work of Allen J. Scott of UCLA on the post-Ford dynamics of Los Angeles).[26] Moreover, this globalization of transportation and mobility problems features prominently in the outbursts that result from the predicaments in which distressed neighborhoods find themselves. Frustration with a lack of access to the vital city center and material isolation appear to be triggers and exacerbating factors in social and economic marginality. This is another indication that the city is more social stage than planned space.

Protection of the urban environment

Likewise, protecting and safeguarding the environment cannot be viewed simply in negative terms of prohibitions. Environmental protection must simultaneously take into account the idea of urban risks and that of democratization of the material and cultural consumption of city-dwellers themselves. The urban risks, whether natural (earthquakes, floods, and storms) or man-made (pollution, social unrest, and terrorism) are necessarily heightened by the demographic buildup, which we do not know how to limit. They are also accentuated by the scope of the aforementioned social disequilibrium. Although a society with no risk would seem to be an illusion, it is no less an illusion to think that technology is all that is needed to limit the human and material consequences of natural disasters. Thus, in the most seismic and most urbanized regions of the globe (California, Japan, Mexico, and the Mediterranean), tragic episodes show that prediction of earthquakes, although it may indeed improve in the future, is insufficient and would doubtless cause mass panics with consequences even more dramatic than the earthquake itself. Prevention of damage, with increasingly more rigorous earthquake-resistant construction regulations, is incapable of eliminating disasters by itself. It is therefore critical, since from Mexico to Los Angeles to Tokyo cities have always managed to rise again from their ashes, to add to the technical measures continuous education of society, especially economic and political acceptance of the mandated regulations. Insufficiently supervised construction and public contracts signed hastily or adulterated by fraud are at least as fatal as the tremor itself. Of natural origin, a major earthquake in an urban region is always a social pointer and catalyst.

The rise of middle class, and of the associated material and cultural consumption, maintenance of which is one of the conditions we have identified for success of the city, generates in itself conflicts in management of the peri-urban environment. It is easier to protect a forest or coastal region, especially in sensitive natural areas (the Mediterranean regions or Californian coast), when they are reserved for the exclusive use or pleasure of a limited few instead of a more democratic practice. A balance is needed between the action of safeguarding an area—such as a prohibition against construction or even trespassing—and opening up the area to anyone and everyone. There again, solutions lie only in political will and in the acceptance by and education of citizens, even before spatial definition of the perimeters of the area to be protected. The action undertaken in France by the Coastal Conservancy is a good and still all-too-rare example of these new methodologies: scientific inventory of the endangered resources, patiently conducted property acquisition, but also public education. In contemporary urban societies, policies more and more frequently demand both rigor and creativity.

Thus, possible new paths of action are forming. Cities, in the material expression of their structured forms, are turning out to be actual experiments of the stage of societies with their continuities, options, distractions, and turnarounds. Could we artificially, voluntarily, accelerate this course to avoid the extremes of history, also known as the misfortune of man, the crises of the city, the death of civilizations? In a world that is becoming completely urbanized, this is the true challenge that urbanism faces. The issue is "urban experimentation." The difficulties seem to be considerable. Contrary to pure substances manipulated by a chemist in a laboratory who can repeat as many physical reactions as he likes to discover and predict laws, human collectives are neither regular nor transparent, but are in fact constructed in a barely legible manner; we need patience to decode them and courage to act. In the contemporary city, this experimentation will require three things: imagination, for overly rigid societies that talk about long-term perspective while eyeing acquired rights and inherited usage, and confusing architectural heritage to be preserved with mental structures to be demolished; an aptitude for taking risks in urban choices; and acceptance of error, at the possible price of destruction, which after all is not a failure for the city, but its rule for survival. Utopia? If we do not aspire to a utopia and content ourselves simply with the expression of beauty or rationality, the city will surely be lost to us.

Notes

[1]Guy Burgel, "En Guise de Présentation: La Géographie Urbaine Comparative," *Villes en Paralléle* 1 (1978): 1–3.

[2]Guy Burgel, *La Ville Aujourd'hui* (Paris, France: Hachette, 1993), 220.

[3]Guy Burgel, "The Big City: Audacity and Necessity," in Guy Burgel, ed., *The Age of the City: The City of Vitality Tomorrow* (Osaka, Japan: Senri Foundation, 1992): 35–45.

[4]Guy Burgel, "Interrogations sur L'Urbanisation Russe," *L'Information Géographique* (1995): 1–9.

[5]Guy Burgel, "Formation et Structure des Régions Urbaines en France et en Union Soviétique," *Villes en Parallèle* 3 (1980): 178.

[6]Olga Medvedkov and Yuri Medvedkov, *Turning Points in Russia's Urbanization* (Columbus: Ohio State University Press, 1994), 30.

[7]Guy Burgel, "La Périphérie Urbaine Revisitée," *Espaces, Populations et Sociétés* (1991–92): 359–66.

[8]Guy Burgel, "A Propos de Paris—New York, les Mots et les Choses," *Villes en Paralléle* 20–21 (1994): 11–33.

[9]Paul-Henri Chombart de Lauwe, *La Fin des Villes, Mythe ou Réalité* (Paris, France: Calmann-Levy, 1981), 246.

[10]Saskia Sassen, *The Global City: New York, London, Tokyo* (Princeton, N.J.: Princeton University Press, 1991).

[11]Michael E. Porter, "The Rise of the Urban," *The State of Small Business* (1995): 104–17.

[12]René Dumont, *L'Afrique Noire est Mal Pertie* (Paris, France: Seuil, 1962), 287.

[13]Burgel, "A Propos de Paris."

[14]Burgel, *La Ville Aujourd'hui*.

[15]Manuel Castells, *La Question Urbaine* (Paris, France: Maspéro, 1970), 461.

[16]Burgel, *La Ville Aujourd'hui*.

[17]Sophie Body-Gendrot, "New York, la Ville Mosaique," *Villes en Parallèle* 20–21 (1994): 125–43.

[18]Burgel, *La Ville Aujourd'hui*.

[19]Guy Burgel, "Lettre de Perse: Comment Peut-on être Intercommunal?" *Pouvoirs Locaux—Les Cahiers de la Décentralisation* 16 (1993): 55–57.

[20]Guy Burgel, "La Ville Fragmentée," *Villes en Paralléle* 14 (1989): 264.

[21]Brian J. L. Berry, "Urban Population Densities," *Geographic Review* 55 (1963): 389–405.

[22]Burgel, *La Ville Aujourd'hui*.

[23]Olivier Jean, "Taxable Wealth and Poverty of Ile-de-France Districts," *Regards sur Ile-de-France* (1990): xx.

[24]Guy Burgel, "Politiques Urbaines et Emploi," *Informations Sociales* (April–May 1991): 47–51.

[25]*Université et Ville: Paris X—La Défense, le Défi* (Nanterre, France: Laboratoire de Géographie Urbaine, 1993), 149.

[26]Allen J. Scott, ed., *Policy Options for Southern California* (Los Angeles: University of Southern California, 1993), 198.

Chapter 15

The American City: Urban Aberration or Glimpse of the Future?

Robert Bruegmann

One of the most obvious things that has happened to American cities since the Habitat I meeting in 1976 has been their continued spread. Already built at considerably lower densities than cities in most other parts of the world, American cities' tendency to decentralize has, if anything, accelerated since the 1970s. At the same time, however, there has been a countervailing tendency of certain functions to re-center, either in the traditional core, in neighborhoods around the core, or, most strikingly, at the very edge of the metropolitan area. Together, these transformations have resulted in a patchwork quilt of urban fabric that extends over immense areas of land, dense in some places and exceedingly dispersed in others, defying traditional notions of urban form and blurring distinctions between urban and rural.

Although there has been a great deal of literature on certain changes in the built environment of American cities,[1] this literature has tended to concentrate on a few conspicuous pieces of the landscape, notably the old downtowns and the large outlying business centers like Tyson's Corner outside Washington, D.C., or the Post-Oak Galleria area of Houston. It is symptomatic that, even after several decades of writing about the latter, no commonly accepted term for them has emerged.[2] This deficiency suggests that individuals with various political viewpoints from differing disciplinary backgrounds have looked at forms on the ground and have tried to assimilate them to existing urban models but with limited success. I would like to suggest that a lack of adequate models for describing the new city, a difficulty in collecting data about it, and a concentration on the question "Are these new urban forms good or bad?" have all worked together to frustrate attempts to comprehend contemporary urban America. In this chapter I will discuss the problems in describing the physical fabric of the American city and offer some tentative answers to a different kind of question: Are these patterns new, distinctly American, and potentially an aberration in urban history, or are they a continuation of processes long at work in cities everywhere and a portent of what many cities around the world may eventually be like?

FIGURE 15.1. Typical U.S. suburban view. Air view of Schaumburg, Illinois, 1994. Clustered around a high school, a single-family residential neighborhood of cul-de-sac streets spreads itself out on ample acreage. The most striking thing about the recent American city has been its continued outward expansion. (*Photo by Robert Bruegmann*)

I will argue the latter position, suggesting that the decentralization that is so strikingly evident in the United States has been due in great part to a process of democratization. Here, more than anywhere else in the world, the broad middle class has been able to obtain for itself some of the privacy, space, and choice of living, working, and recreation environments once reserved only for the wealthiest citizens. That this process has created negative by-products, no one would deny. But it appears that efforts to stop the process of decentralization and to reform the city by forcing it into more familiar settlement patterns ignore desires deeply felt by much of the population. They also fail to solve the problems and often even aggravate them.

The Contemporary City: An Overview

From some perspectives, many cities have characteristics that distinguish them from other places. Some, like Hong Kong, are extremely tightly packed into a very small area. Others, like Los Angeles, sprawl across the landscape in a highly episodic way. In a city like Bangkok, a cluster of high buildings of steel and concrete near the center gives way almost immediately to an almost continuous fabric of densely built low wooden structures. São Paulo, on the other hand, is marked by clusters of tall buildings that dot the urban landscape up to twenty or thirty miles from the historic core. In many major European cities the urban center has a clear structure. Even from the air, a visitor can discern the trace of the concentric boulevards that resemble rings of growth in central Paris, for example, or the canals of central Amsterdam. By contrast, there are few such clues in a place like Phoenix, a city that appears to have been extruded across the landscape with little trace of hierarchical order.

If, from one perspective, cities appear to be quite different from one another and American cities emphatically different from European ones, from a different perspective the reverse is true. From an airplane, miles and miles of urban fabric, of residential neighborhoods, parks, and industrial areas, crisscrossed by railroad and highways, seem almost interchangeable in every large city. It is often all but impossible for many travelers to get any sense of where they are unless they can spot large-scale natural features like lakes and rivers. In fact, what is most surprising, given all of the variations in local history, topography, demography, climate, and planning policy, are the startling similarities between cities that grew at the same time for similar uses.

Certainly it is true that central Paris does not resemble suburban Los Angeles, but Paris was already a large city in the nineteenth century, when much of the fabric of its central core was constructed, whereas

Los Angeles was a small frontier outpost. If one of the fundamental characteristics of cities is that they are about process and change, it would seem necessary to compare changes that occur at given moments in the past rather than merely comparing the overall physical form at a given moment in time. In the case of Paris, anyone who has gotten into an automobile and driven the autoroutes and streets at the urban edge can testify that enormous portions of it that were built in a given era, for example the 1980s, despite all of the efforts of government to channel growth into self-contained, relatively high density new towns, look similar to what was built in the Los Angeles metropolitan area during the same years. There are the same single-family houses, gasoline stations, office parks, and shopping centers. Any real comparison of cities would have to address the problem of correlating geography with chronology. This effort has rarely been attempted, however, in large part because of problems of collecting, interpreting, and presenting "data."

Modeling the City

One of the great obstacles to effective description of cities in the United States and comparison of them to those across the world is bound up with problems of measuring and describing. The attempt to understand and to describe whole cities and systems of cities, rather than just specific areas or themes, has been a peculiarly modern enterprise and one of the great goals of the social sciences. This quest has been pursued with special vigor since the early postwar years, driven by the expectation that American prosperity might offer the means to alleviate urban problems. There followed a golden age of social science–writing and a torrent of literature in geography, sociology, urban economics, planning, and history. This literature fed directly into policy-making in the fast-expanding planning bureaucracy at all levels of government.[3] It appears, from the perspective of the mid-1990s, that optimism about our ability to understand the city, let alone to fix it, was misplaced.

One of the things that appears obvious from the perspective of the 1990s is how much the reigning assumptions at the time when data are collected skew the way they can be used thereafter. A good example might be the use of the terms "urban" and "rural." At one time this distinction was grounded in observable reality. The city looked quite different from the country, and city-dwellers lived in very different ways. By the late twentieth century, on the other hand, these distinctions began to lose significance. A major debate in the 1970s on the question

FIGURE 15.2. French suburbia, St.-Quentin-en-Yvelines, 1990. Despite all of the efforts of the French government to control outward sprawl by concentrating growth in certain well-defined, relatively high density new towns, the desire by many French citizens to acquire single-family houses and automobiles has led to landscapes that look increasingly like those in the periphery of American cities. (*Photo by Robert Bruegmann*)

of "counterurbanization," or a perceived trend of Americans to move away from metropolitan areas, proved to be mostly a problem of statistical classification. What appeared at first glance to be a move of city-dwellers to rural areas was in great part only the further move of city-dwellers into the loosely populated areas at the far fringe of large cities, areas sometimes labeled "exurban."[4] In fact, with better communications, transportation and delivery systems, and vastly more second homes and tourism, the very categories "urban" and "rural" are by now largely useless in a country like the United States, where even the most remote areas can participate, if the inhabitants wish, in many aspects of a culture that was once reserved only for city-dwellers.[5]

In other cases the biases and anachronisms in data collection categories were deliberately exploited. One of the most rancorous debates in the United States has been based on the assumption that race is a dominant factor in the move of city-dwellers to the suburbs. The very terms of this debate, however, force the evidence into categories that were defined according to specific ideological positions. In this case, the categories "white" and "black" and the term "minority" are based at least as much on social construction as they are on biological fact. Their use in census data makes out of individuals of diverse backgrounds a single class of people. The distinction between city and suburb is even less defensible. These boundary lines do not correspond to any real geographic or sociological division but to the vagaries of annexations at given moments of the past. It was because of the bias built into them that all of these categories were eagerly embraced by many practitioners of the New Urban History of the 1960s, who already believed that large numbers of suburbanites were racists and were intent on fleeing civic responsibilities. Comparisons between the percentages of minorities in central city and suburban communities may possibly have been enlightening in describing older cities in the Northeast, such as Boston or Newark, in the 1960s but even then such comparisons made no sense at all in places like Houston, where the core city covered a major part of the metropolitan area. By the 1990s, they make even less sense; American suburbs as well as central cities are a mosaic of racial and ethnic groups and a large percentage of the black middle class finds itself in the suburbs. No statistical measure, moreover, even begins to assess a phenomenon as complicated and as profoundly ambiguous as the interplay of class and race. Rather than the increasing segregation that some observers find in the urban landscape, there seems to be good evidence that spatial and physical barriers (gated communities, for example) have been created precisely because earlier means, both legal and customary, for segregating people of different races and classes are disappearing. Even the most sophisticated indexes of integration used today only suggest the relative positions of residence and place of work. They fail to describe the complex spatial and social interactions that flow from land-use patterns, and they are of interest only if one believes that integration is inherently better than segregation, a proposition many Americans of every demographic group consider dubious at best.

The same problems apply to the graphic representations used to model the city. The most famous city diagram of the twentieth century, the concentric circular diagram of Chicago sociologists Robert E. Park and Ernest W. Burgess, for example, was based at least as much on subjective preferences as it was on observed reality.[6] By the 1920s, even a brief examination of a city like Chicago, which Park and Burgess used for their model, would have revealed a complicated, asymmetrical, multinucleated city, not at all the simple progression of less-dense bands radiating out from a single center. To try to capture some of this irregularity and something of the dynamism of the city, the economist Homer Hoyt proposed a sector theory of residential development in the 1930s, which split the Park-Burgess circle into sectors, each of which had its own characteristics. Immediately after World War II, the geographers Chauncey Harris and Edward Ullman took this process a step further when they introduced a highly asymmetric, multinucleated city model.[7] There have been a number of attempts to push its logic further, for example in the diagrams of the planner Kevin Lynch[8] or models of the urban periphery by the geographer Peirce Lewis.[9] None of these models has been widely adapted, nor have the suggestive diagrams developed for other uses—for example, maps made by transportation planners since the 1960s showing "transportation desire lines" or commuter sheds. These diagrams, like those used to record fluid flows or DNA, start to capture, in a useful way, the complexity of city systems and some sense of the order that underlies apparent disorder.

It is conspicuous that recent texts on the city either abandon any mention of these kinds of graphic representation or return to the relative simplicity of the Park-Burgess conception.[10] At first glance it might appear that this is simply a matter of necessary simplification, a degree of abstraction useful in distinguishing underlying structure from surface incident. But the use of the concentric circle model fundamentally falsifies the actual structure of today's city. The reasons for the continued attachment to it, moreover, go well beyond convenience. They are deeply rooted in Western culture. The similarities between the Park-Burgess model and commonly used "ideal" diagrams of the atom and the solar system betray a common desire to see the world as a logical and organic whole, part of a purposeful and ultimately rational system. Likewise the similarity of the Park-Burgess diagram to the diagrams made to show growth of medieval walled European cities suggests a longing for political power and moral order emanating from the center. Of course, any twentieth-century scientist knew that the atom and solar diagrams were a fiction. The earth did not go around the sun in perfect circles nor did electrons around a nucleus. This realization did not have a negative effect on the complex calculations that scientists needed to make in order to calculate the actual path of a satellite around the earth. Social scientists also recognized that cities were not as orderly and symmetrical as the diagrams appeared. They recognized, moreover, that the European city that the diagrams most accurately represented was the European city of the age of Absolutism. To the extent that diagrams of cities started to capture the episodic, apparently disordered actual fabric of the city, however, they lost the power to reassert the order that social scientists of previous decades wished to find. More important, they lost the power to suggest simple, powerful solutions to urban problems that could be taken over by planners and politicians. The result has been a series of planning proposals, still based on the concentric circle diagram of the city, all of which attempt to force the urban areas of the present and future into the forms of the pre-industrial city.[11]

As an architectural historian, I would also suggest that one of the most neglected but fruitful areas of research is the direct observation of the built environment. Consider the case of inner-city gentrification, the process by which older neighborhoods have moved upward in socioeconomic status. From a small, relatively contained phenomenon in the late 1960s and early 1970s, gentrification has greatly expanded. Today it is immediately apparent to any observer on the ground. From small, tell-tale signs like miniblinds and the typefaces used on doorbells to much less subtle indications like the Volvos and Jeeps parked in the driveways and the professional landscaping of front yards, the visual evidence is often unmistakable. For the social scientist, these direct observations of the built environment do not constitute adequate documentation. Statistical measurement of gentrification is extremely difficult, however. The edges of a gentrifying neighborhood are notoriously porous and in flux. It is hard to distinguish the declining population in neighborhoods where single families are buying multifamily houses and converting them to single-family use from the declining population seen in neighborhoods where buildings are abandoned or in areas that all of the working-age adults are leaving. It is just as difficult to find gentrification through income statistics because many of the

FIGURE 15.3. Boston gentrification, South End, 1979. One of the most conspicuous developments in almost every American city is the simultaneous abandonment of the central city by a large segment of the middle class and a gentrification of certain neighborhoods near the core by another. The gentrifiers are often quite similar in their socioeconomic status to inhabitants of affluent outlying suburbs and there is considerable movement of individuals between the two. (*Photo by Robert Bruegmann*)

first gentrifiers of any neighborhood are young with, in many cases, no more or sometimes even less income than the people they are displacing. Most available statistical evidence is much too crude to measure the extraordinary subtleties of class distinction visible on the ground. This has led many social scientists to dismiss or minimize the extent of gentrification. The tools of the student of visual culture are perhaps more useful in this case.[12] Another interesting thing that can be learned from a close look at gentrified neighborhoods is that, despite an initial appearance that was quite different from communities of similar socioeconomic status at the urban periphery, they have started to look increasingly similar to them as nonconforming uses are driven out and new construction is dominated by the same building types, notably the row house and the strip mall. This is actually not surprising since urban gentrifiers, far from being opposed to suburban living, as they may have seemed in the late 1960s, have proven themselves capable of moving back and forth from center to edge with considerable ease as life cycles and family demands have changed. In fact, one of the reasons Americans have been willing to move more often than city-dwellers anywhere else in the world is that they can move from city to city and find a wide choice of settlement types quite similar in social, economic, and physical characteristics to those they left. One result is a striking convergence in appearance between certain communities at the center and those at the very edge of the metropolitan area.

Explaining the New American City

Having discussed the difficulties in describing cities we must return to the initial questions: Are the transformations of American cities since the 1970s a new phenomenon, unique to the United States and potentially a short-lived aberration? Or are they merely the continuation of long- standing trends and a portent of what cities elsewhere might look like in the future? I argue for the latter case.

Perhaps the best place to start is with the most conspicuous new element in the American metropolis, the outlying business centers, sometimes called "edge cities." In the abundant literature on this subject, perhaps the most influential line of thought has been that this is a new and distinctly American phenomenon, the result of a particular American or at least Anglo-American distrust of dense cities and attraction to mobility.[13] According to this argument, the traditional American city, containing a dense core with most of the jobs and surrounded by fairly dense city and suburban neighborhoods, persisted until World War II when a large segment of the middle class moved to far suburbs.

Regional shopping centers brought a large amount of retail out to them. After the 1970s, according to this line of thought, jobs likewise moved out to the outlying areas, effectively spelling the end of the traditional suburb and creating a newly reconfigured "city" at the edge.[14]

This plot does not satisfy. American suburbs have never been solely bedroom communities, and the business functions of American cities have been decentralizing since they began. At no point has the traditional downtown contained even a majority of jobs in any American city. By the first decades of the early twentieth century, a great number of manufacturing, warehousing, and distribution jobs were already located far from the traditional downtown either in locations within the city, in the numerous industrial suburbs, or in satellite industrial cities. This was due both to push and to pull factors. Many activities moved out because central area land was expensive. They also moved, however, because many workers and their supervisors found it convenient to work nearer to their places of residence.[15] This was true already before World War II, for example, for the research and development arm of many industrial firms and for many insurance companies. In both cases, the workforce consisted primarily of well-paid professionals who did not need to be in the center city. The move from central locations was facilitated by new means of transportation and communications after the war. The only thing that has changed since the 1970s is the scale of the move of upper-middle-class managerial workers to outlying locations, but this move represented only the increment of a relatively small segment of business activity. It was because these workers were upper-middle-class professionals, individuals the urban historians were likely to know personally, and the "edge cities" to which they moved so physically conspicuous, that many observers have fixed on them as the most important recent urban trend. In fact the creation of new outlying business centers is only a continuation, on a different scale and using different transportation means, of the tendency already visible in the early twentieth century of cities to spawn new centers, such as Midtown Manhattan, Hollywood, or the New Center in Detroit.

Another problem with many formulations of recent American urban history is that by concentrating on decentralization the countervailing tendency to centralize has been largely ignored. Although it is certainly true that most American urban areas are larger and settled at a lower overall density than they once were, it is also quite conspicuous that many areas of cities, particularly of Western cities, are becoming denser. Nowhere is this more apparent than in Los Angeles. Supposedly the archetypal, low-density sprawling automobile city, many newly developed areas of Los Angeles are often considerably denser than those in other parts of the country, due to high land costs. Furthermore, some areas of Los Angeles, such as the broad band extending west from downtown toward Santa Monica, have redeveloped as some of the densest districts in the country. High densities also characterize the expanding Latino neighborhoods east of Los Angeles. In both cases there is a heavy use of public transportation, a reminder that Los Angeles, despite commonly accepted wisdom, has one of the most extensive systems of public transit in the country.[16]

The question of whether these complex urban transformations are peculiar to the United States is more difficult to answer. As I have already remarked, much of the fabric of any city that has grown quickly since the 1970s looks like what we usually see at the edge of American cities. In fact, it is notable that many cities outside North America that have grown very fast since the 1960s have jumped ahead of American cities in some respects. The move of white-collar prestige business out of the core has occurred even faster in São Paulo, for example (where even major banks have abandoned the old center for the Avenida Paulista, the Avenida Faria Lima, and the Marginal), than it has in the United States. The development of Orchard Road in Singapore with enormous mixed-use shopping complexes has been a more spectacular decentralization of retail than can be seen in any American city. All of these things suggest that business has been moving out and recentralizing in cities around the world in the same way that it has in the United States.

In the case of residential development, it has often been asserted that Americans have a particular love affair with the single-family house and the automobile and a unique problem with racial relations. If so, the low-density settlement pattern of the United States could be safely written off as an anomaly. The evidence suggests otherwise. Car ownership, for example, seems inevitably to follow levels of affluence. When European or Japanese city-dwellers have been able to afford automobiles, they have bought them, despite staggering economic disincentives. As to the desire for a single-family house, the issue is more complex. I would argue that the history of cities in both Europe and the United States, since at least the beginning of the Industrial Revolution, has been marked by a process in which the amenities once possessed only by the rich have gradually been acquired by a broad middle class. Of these amenities, few have been as important as privacy, the ability to control one's surroundings. Although the search for privacy and choice has led to many different residential patterns, the overall direction has clearly been toward more dispersed housing options.[17]

FIGURE 15.4. São Paulo, Avenida Paulista, 1995. While North American cities like Chicago and Los Angeles were among the fastest growing in the world in the late nineteenth and early twentieth centuries, this distinction is now claimed by cities in Latin America and Asia. Businesses in many of them have decentralized faster than businesses in American cities. The Avenida Paulista, which became the effective business center of São Paulo in the postwar decades, is now losing much of its prestige to areas even further from the historical core. (*Photo by Robert Bruegmann*)

Of all of the residential building types, none has been more important or seen a faster rise than the single-family detached house. Whereas only royalty and very wealthy urban-dwellers could afford this option before the nineteenth century, it has become the housing of choice for a large percentage of the population in all Western cities. Although, for various economic, political, or social reasons, the single-family house has not been an option for much of the population, polls in European countries show that it and not the apartment block is where a large percentage of the population would like to live. It is also interesting to note how tenaciously many inhabitants of the Latin American *favelas* or the Asian shantytowns resist being moved to public housing, often with much better sanitary conditions, preferring to cling to their own makeshift dwellings on their own plot of land, no matter how small and unsanitary. In the matter of race, it has been asserted that the clash between white and black Americans has been a unique factor in the decentralization of American cities. Although no one denies that race has had a major effect on all aspects of American life, the evidence seems to suggest that it has not been a dominant factor in the reshaping of American cities on a large scale. If it had been, we would expect to see major differences between cities based on the size of their African American populations. In fact, this does not seem to be the case.[18]

Why are American and other cities reorganizing themselves? According to one line of reasoning, very often used by Marxist theorists, these new landscapes are the result of a new postindustrial economic system and a globalization of the world's economy.[19] One problem with this interpretation is that it assumes a fixed set of cause-and-effect relationships, that the underlying reality is economic and the changes in the landscape are symptoms. It seems just as reasonable to describe changes in the economic structure as the result of a desire for certain living patterns. The rise of the automobile industry was just as much the result of a desire for less-dense living as less-dense living was a result of the rise of the automobile industry, for example. Likewise, a company may move out of a downtown to the periphery because land prices or taxes are lower, but all evidence seems to suggest that it is just as likely the desire of many employees to be near their places of residence that drives the decision, and that land prices remain lower than at the center because there is no desire to build at higher densities.

Another problem with determinist formulations is that the landscapes used as examples do not support the hypothesis. Silicon Valley in California, for example, supposedly a prime example of a high-tech or postindustrial landscape, hardly looks different from any other recently developed industrial area in the country.[20] In fact, the entire notion that American cities are postindustrial seems to be questionable. A great number of things are still produced every day in every American city. The major change is only that the extreme centralization and labor-intensive practices of previous periods are no longer necessary. Likewise the notion that globalization has brought any significant changes to a given American city is hard to support. Economic competition and change have always led to new land-use patterns. For any given city, the origin of economic competition or of investment funding for new construction hardly matters, however. It appears, rather, that it has been not the global economy but the globalization of notions of individual freedom and mobility and the global acceptance of the market economy that has freed city-dwellers everywhere to seek the same things, among them privacy, space, and choice.

In fact, the reason large-scale patterns seem to be converging worldwide but appear to be increasingly disparate at the single-city level has been the increasing ability of families the world over to alter and experiment with their living, working, and recreational environments. In a single American family, for example, the desire for privacy and space, which might lead to the desire for a single-family house on large acreage, is often counterbalanced by the desire to be closer to the center in order to be nearer existing friends, neighbors, and community institutions as well as to potential job sites for multiple household members. The desire to live in an extremely low-density site beyond the edge of the metropolitan built-up area, likewise, is often balanced by the desire for the good schools, cultural amenities, and alternate transportation means found closer to the center. Add to this already complex mix of needs and desires a preference for a new house, or an old house in a historic district, the desire to be near a lake or the mountains, a wish to be near an airport or well away from the airport, a goal of spending very little time in the city at all and as much time as possible at a weekend house, and it becomes clear how endless are the permutations. These permutations are compounded as the continued outward movement of the affluent causes a chain reaction throughout the metropolitan area and provides new choices for the less affluent.

Policy Options

Needless to say, not everyone is happy with the recent transformations of cities, least of all everyone in the United States. According to critics, the decentralized American city is inefficient, environmentally unsustainable, inequitable, and ugly. By the 1970s, these criticisms had led to strong movements that attempted to channel urban growth into specific directions, to conserve natural areas and farmland, to preserve the built environment, to discourage automobile use and encourage public transportation. All of this was to be done by careful government planning, preferably by larger regional governments that could create efficient systems for entire metropolitan regions. In most of these directions, U.S. planners echoed the kind of directives contained in the report of the Habitat I conference and endorsed by academic planners in both Europe and the United States. The 1960s and 1970s saw an outpouring of regional plans in which growth was to be pointed in certain directions (usually based on some variant of the concentric circle diagram), sprawl was to be contained, and excess population channeled into self-sufficient New Towns. Two different means of achieving results were tried. On one hand were economic incentives and disincentives. Tax incentives were especially popular because they appeared to involve no out-of-pocket expenditures. On the other hand there were restrictive measures, outright prohibitions against building in certain ways and in certain places. For many the latter seemed a more equitable way to regulate scarce resources since it did not favor the affluent.

Although some of these movements enjoyed a certain degree of success, none was able fundamentally to change the course of the American city. American governments at all levels were able to hire many more planners, in part because of federal dollars to support planning activities, but Americans were unwilling to give much autonomous power either to the planners or to large, regional governments. If anything, grassroots movements and special interest groups demanded even more attention from local officials, and many land-use decisions made at upper levels of government were overturned at the most local level. Despite considerable exertion by planners, the regional plans were rarely successful in stopping the continued spread of the city. Even in the face of a major fuel shortage in the 1970s and major governmental subsidies for mass transportation, the modal switch from public transportation to the private automobile continued. The New Towns, notably such highly publicized efforts as Reston, Virginia, and Columbia, Maryland, although they did achieve some of their goals on a small scale, failed in other important ways and certainly did not alter the course of American urban development.

Although all of the same criticisms and the same suggestions can still be heard in the 1990s,[21] there is ample evidence of an intellectual crisis in the "progressive" branch of the social sciences and planning profession.[22] Certainly there are more land-use laws on the books in the late 1990s than there were in the 1970s, covering everything from wetlands preservation to protection of endangered species, from height and bulk regulations to historic preservation. Still, for many critics, none of these regulations even begins to tackle what they regard as the fundamental problem, the continued low-density patterns of American urban settlement or "sprawl," the word reformers use for middle-class, low-density development.[23] If anything, the rhetoric in the 1990s is even more shrill as critics warn of numerous economic, social, and environmental crises, including the crisis of the urban underclass, the crisis of declining cities and regions, and, ultimately, the crisis of global warming.[24]

There continue to be attempts to address these crises. Perhaps the most conspicuous example of urban land-use reform in the 1990s has been the growth management movement, which although not new has achieved a greatly increased respectability since the mid-1980s. Growth management programs in Florida, New Jersey, and Oregon, for example, aim to constrain sprawl by drawing up coordinated statewide and local plans to limit outward growth around cities; force new development into infill areas, making the center more compact, thereby cutting down the costs of new infrastructure at the edge; preserving valuable farmland; and creating densities more conducive to mass transportation.

Although it is too early to judge the success of efforts of this sort in most areas of the United States, where such planning has been mandated but where cities have not yet seriously run up against the growth constraints, the fate of these efforts elsewhere does not give much reason for optimism.[25] Perhaps the most important of these has been the British attempt to control the growth of London. Since the 1930s there has been a greenbelt, a growth boundary, extending in a circle around London, and a policy of channeling any further growth into tightly controlled New Towns on the periphery beyond the greenbelt. Both ideas were legacies of Ebenezer Howard and the British Garden City movement and betray the same attachment to ideas about ideal city shape later seen in the Park-Burgess concentric ring diagram. Although the greenbelt was successful in stopping most development at the expanding edge of the built-up area of London, it was completely unsuccessful in more important ways. It drove up the price of land within the belt and forced much growth out beyond it, creating for many people even longer commutes than they would have had without the growth boundary, and extending the reach of the London conurbation even further out into the countryside.

In North America, the idea of the New Town at the edge of the metropolitan area has also been revived in another guise as the New Urbanism or Traditional Neighborhood Development.[26] This neotraditional planning movement, which aims at reforming the American suburban landscape, co-opts virtually all of the ideas embodied in the New Towns. It is again too early to judge the success of these efforts. The few neotraditional towns that have been started have seen residential construction, but they have, so far, been conspicuously unable to become self-contained communities. It is quite likely that these towns will achieve popularity among a certain upper-middle-class population, but there appears to be no reason to believe that they will be any more successful in the long run than were the New Towns for many of the same reasons, the most important of which is that the supposed crisis of American suburban development patterns appears to be largely nonexistent. All available evidence shows that Americans living in suburbs, despite unhappiness with certain problems, notably traffic congestion, are on the whole quite happy, at least as happy as their counterparts in small towns or in large city centers.[27]

It remains an open question whether any of the large-scale experiments in prescriptive planning have had any major influence at all. It is difficult, driving around the edge of metropolitan Toronto, which has had a considerable history of regional planning aimed at creating a compact, transit-friendly city, to see how it is different from a city like Houston, which has been famous for its antagonism to planning, even to zoning.[28] Nor is it easy to see how one can judge the work of the private entrepreneurs of Houston, each of whom did his own planning as he went along, any more harshly than the built landscape that resulted from the elaborate public planning mechanisms in Toronto. By allowing growth to occur in any direction, the price of land in Houston has remained low. By allowing families and companies to locate according to the dictates of the market rather than through planning, the average length of commute has decreased and there has been a better balance of jobs and residences across the metropolitan area. In fact, it can be argued that the history of urban planning reforms, including greenbelts, New Towns, urban renewal, public housing, residential rent-control measures, zoning bonuses, and pedestrian shopping streets, has been marked at least as much by unintended consequences and backfires as it has by successes.[29] The lesson to be learned from these stories appears to be that cities, like all human systems, are infinitely complex. Any attempt to alter one part of the system creates changes throughout, often changes that are more dramatic in their negative implications than the conditions that the changes were supposed to fix.

It is perhaps for this reason that many cities in the world are experimenting with quite different ways of thinking about planning. In the United States it was long thought by many, even conservatives, that the changes in economic, social, and land-use policies that were put into place by liberals during the period from the New Deal to the 1960s were permanent fixtures in the American political landscape. These measures, many believed, were inevitable because they represented the necessary intrusion of government into the private market to correct the inequities caused by the capitalist system. By the mid-1990s, this picture has started to look quite different. There has been a massive assault on liberal planning ideals of the 1960s and 1970s. One overt challenge has come from "wise use" or "property rights" advocates who have challenged the legal and scientific bases of conservation, preservation, and environmental regulations. Another has been the assault on public housing. Government welfare and public housing policies, critics suggest, not only had very little effect in alleviating problems, but they, in fact, aggravated them by creating a large group of people dependent on various kinds of subsidies including public housing, which was quickly transformed from a temporary refuge to permanent housing for the underclass. All of the policies, according to conservatives, created a vicious cycle of dependence.

For many conservatives, the argument that government must protect citizens from unrestrained private enterprise has fostered the development of a government that is more repressive and monopolistic than business ever was. Far from restraining the operation of the market, they would like to see market principles used to remake government. For a government body to reduce rush-hour congestion, according to this line of thought, the worst method is to simply restrict driving. This would be counterproductive because it discourages mobility and is probably not enforceable in any case. The best method might be to charge a fee for all highways and a premium for driving during peak times. In this way the price paid by each individual would more nearly reflect the costs of his actions to the whole community and might push him to alter behavior.[30] Better yet, one could privatize the highways. Pushing this logic even further, in the "public choice" school of thought, transportation, schools, social housing, and land planning might be better accomplished by private organizations than by government. In the matter of housing, for example, a conservative would argue that far from aiding in the creation of housing, government intervention in the private housing market has had the opposite effect. Instead of improving the lot of the poorest citizens, decades of reform regulations had the effect of driving up housing prices and limiting the supply of affordable housing.[31]

Many conservatives also argue that larger, more regional governments are actually less efficient in governing than the multiple layers of smaller government because they are more remote and bureaucratic and less subject to competition. One of the great virtues of the intricate mosaic of overlapping municipal jurisdictions, school boards, and special purpose governmental bodies like water districts, it could be argued, is the element of competition. Many different patterns of land use can be tried and no government body can escape competition from other jurisdictions and from private organizations. Direct privatization has been tested so far primarily in areas like trash removal and toll superhighways, but in a more indirect fashion, police functions have in many places been taken over by private security companies and a substantial portion of mail service has been effectively supplanted by private express companies. It appears that this kind of privatization could bring the country full circle back to the early nineteenth century when many of these functions were handled by private organizations. With the dismantling of the system of compulsory taxation for public schools, the privatization of American cities could be pushed beyond anything yet seen in the country.

It can be argued that this process is already well advanced, but it has been done in such small increments that it has gone virtually unnoticed. Already in place in many American cities are vast numbers of homeowner associations, condominiums, and other common interest housing developments. Like so much else in American urban history, these are devices once used by the wealthy to protect themselves but are now widely used in middle-class developments. They provide regulations often infinitely more far-reaching and intrusive than those instituted by any government body, but they are private. Affecting large amounts of the landscape of fast-growing American cities, they have greatly reduced the role of traditional local government.[32]

The more radical ideas of the conservatives are even less tested than those of the liberals, of course. No one has any idea how the unregulated, invisible hand of the market would work in today's world since our society has become so complex and governments at all levels in the United States have moved so far away from laissez faire. Certainly many of the conditions created by the relatively unfettered operation of private industry in the late nineteenth century give little reason to be optimistic. What appears most likely at this juncture is a period of intense experimentation in which some places will opt for more centralized governmental planning and others for less, some for rapid privatization, some for more government intervention. It is likely that there will be endless hybrids and combinations of overlapping public and private initiatives.

Urban Futures

Despite the objections of critics, it appears likely that the drive for increased mobility, space, and amenity will lead to a yet more dispersed American urban settlement pattern. A major factor will be the ways in which new technologies can be harnessed to permit further changes in the environment. One of the most potent forces that has constrained low-density development to date has been the high cost of providing urban infrastructure. Not only is it possible that much of this infrastructure might be provided privately, as it was in the nineteenth century, but it is possible that basic infrastructure, which was necessarily highly centralized during the industrial era, can itself be greatly decentralized. With low-enough densities, more efficient technologies, and sufficient funds, many homeowners or small groups of homeowners could revert to septic fields or self-contained waste treatment facilities for liquid waste disposal and to improved wells or even desalination for fresh water delivery, and they could generate much of the power they would need through wind and solar energy. It is possible to imagine an urban landscape that would resemble the farm landscape of New England but with widely dispersed dwellings interspersed with high-density business and residential settlements, all connected to the rest of the world by a sophisticated communications systems and electric vehicles on highly efficient ground and aerial guideways. Some of the features of this kind of development were already visible in Frank Lloyd Wright's Broadacre City project in the 1930s. Other features are visible in places like Long Grove in the Chicago area or Paradise Valley in the Phoenix area, both of which have large lot requirements and a high level of privatized services. In fact, quite large areas, for example the North Carolina Piedmont or much of western Connecticut, now function in this way with areas of extremely low-density residential development interspersed with scattered business centers, some of shopping centers, others gentrified older town centers.[33]

At the other end of the spectrum is the traditional center, the downtown. It might seem possible, since the forces of the early industrial period that made centralization necessary are no longer in place, that dense city centers are no longer necessary as the cases of Detroit, Michigan, or Camden, New Jersey, seem to suggest. But centralization is hardly dead as the increasingly dense centers of Troy (outside Detroit) or Cherry Hill (outside Camden) attest. In many other cities, especially some of the most dispersed like Los Angeles and Houston, exactly the opposite occurred in the 1980s, as high-end global financial services centralized even further and these cities acquired gleaming new skylines. But even in these cases, future directions are hard to predict. In Los Angeles and Houston, the growth at the core was eclipsed by the growth of outlying centers. Post-Oak Galleria in Houston, which represents the furthest development of this kind, has already become, by many traditional measurements, the de facto downtown of the Houston area. Indeed the Post-Oak Galleria area now shares with the traditional downtown most of the problems associated with city

FIGURE 15.5. Inner Detroit, Michigan, Central Station, 1993. Among large American inner cities none has experienced such a sharp contraction of population and such visible signs of distress as Detroit. The metropolitan area as a whole, however, has remained surprisingly stable, considering the dramatic problems of the automobile industry, which has been the mainstay of the city's economy in the twentieth century. *(Photo by Robert Bruegmann)*

FIGURE 15.6. Houston's new "downtown." View of the Post-Oak Galleria district from central Houston, 1988. The largest of the new outlying business centers in relation to its historic downtown, the Post-Oak Galleria, with its huge shopping center and surrounding office buildings and apartments, has more first class office space and hotel rooms than downtown and faces many of the same urban challenges. In fact, most Houstonians now consider it as part of the central business district. (*Photo by Robert Bruegmann.*)

centers, and many Houstonians now view it as part of downtown Houston.

With the rapid development of telecommunications, it is possible that the demand for office space may decline sharply as employers and employees explore alternative work environments. There are some indications that even as important a business center as Downtown Manhattan could become obsolete as a business center as new communications technologies and competition from other business centers, notably Midtown Manhattan, make the cramped location and high costs uncompetitive.[34] Still, it is unlikely that the Wall Street area will be abandoned. The fixed investment in buildings and infrastructure is simply too great, and the location provides easy access to many urban amenities. It may well serve a very different function in the future, however. In fact, this has already occurred to a considerable extent in the most vibrant of America's central cities, places like San Francisco and Portland, Oregon, where the city centers have changed from working industrial and port cities to highly specialized centers of high finance, culture, tourism, and high-end residential living. Downtown Portland has often been compared to a theme park. The comparison is apt and need not be thought of as derogatory. It may well be that Lower Manhattan will survive in the same way, as a residential area for wealthy cosmopolites wishing to enjoy traditional urban amenities in the elegantly recycled shell of a former business center.

Although transformations at the very edge and at the center of the American city have been accompanied by changes in all of the fabric in between, these transformations, because they have been less dramatic, have not been the subject of much analysis. Some outlying communities have remained stable and affluent, but even in these places considerable change has often occurred through the subdivision of estates, "tear-downs" (the demolition of smaller houses and their replacement by larger dwellings), the replacement of everyday retail stores by specialized boutiques, and the expansion of upscale office and retail uses on less-desirable residential land. Other communities, particularly the inner suburbs of older cities, have experienced dramatic changes in ethnic and racial composition. This has produced urban transformations that no one could have predicted even a few decades ago, for example the mansions of the Syrian Jews along Ocean Parkway in Brooklyn, the astonishing multilevel Vietnamese strip malls along Bolsa Avenue in Westminster in Orange County, or the Hindu temples in west suburban Chicago. In some cases this ethnically and racially based development has resulted in neighborhood rejuvenation, higher incomes, and improved socioeconomic status. In others it has created what many

FIGURE 15.7. Little Saigon, Bolsa Avenue, Westminster, Orange County, California, 1993. The notion that American suburbs are overwhelmingly middle-class, white, bedroom enclaves has never been accurate. Today, the diversity of outlying areas is instantly visible. Vietnamese Americans have made this street one of the most vibrant shopping strips in the country. (Photo by Robert Bruegmann)

observers describe as a downward spiral in socioeconomic status. Critics paint a picture of a continuous and wasteful process of abandonment and deterioration as more affluent populations continue to move outward. The same process could be described in quite a different fashion. From the perspective of the African American or Latino moving from an inner-city neighborhood to a once middle-class white neighborhood, this is not deterioration but a marked improvement. The most recalcitrant problem, of course, has been the existence of an urban underclass in the city center. Most efforts aimed at rebuilding the inner city have not worked. There is little evidence that the money would not have been better spent helping the poorest residents to leave. That there are vast, illegal sweatshops in the inner cities of New York or Los Angeles is likewise no secret, but it is much less clear that traditional ideas of how to transform what are clearly substandard conditions, for example by enforcing minimum wage standards, would not destroy the very jobs on which some of the poorest Americans depend and damage the economic viability of the city centers that depend on cheap labor.

Conclusion

The result of all of the changes I have described is an infinitely complex cityscape forever mutating as market forces, constrained and channeled by government regulations, act on the center, the periphery, and all parts in between, creating convergences in some places and sharp divergences in others and a dizzying new array of land-use options. Individuals in every generation, at least since the birth of the Industrial Revolution, have thought that they were watching the most rapid changes ever seen in history. They have all been correct. Many have been dismayed by the changes and have felt that they were witnessing a cataclysmic decline of the city. This is not surprising since individuals in each generation take the city that they see around them as they grow up as their baseline and then react to the realization that this city is fast disappearing. It is conspicuous, for example, that many mid-nineteenth-century Londoners used the same arguments about their city then that we hear about cities today. London, in their impassioned rhetoric, was too big, too congested, too polluted, too devoted to private gain, and too little concerned with the public welfare, especially of the poorest citizens. In fact, most of these kinds of assertions, then as now, cannot be easily supported by the available statistics. For all the concern about crime in American cities today, there have been many times and places in American history that have been at least as violent. It is also apparent from polls that fear of crime has little direct rela-

FIGURE 15.8. South Central Los Angeles, street view, 1993. Although this area of Los Angeles has often been used as a synonym for urban pathology, particularly since the 1992 riots, the houses are larger and better equipped than the dwellings of most urban dwellers in most countries of the world today. *(Photo by Robert Bruegmann)*

tionship to actual crime levels and that, in fact, many categories of violent crime seem to have been on the wane in the largest American cities for several years now, although no one seems to understand why. Despite the cries of environmental doom, urban American air and water are, on the whole, getting cleaner. Despite all of the jeremiads about limited resources, it is not clear that there are any real limits on, for example, energy sources—only obstacles to be overcome on costs and by-products.

Even in areas of cities that are usually described in the bleakest terms, the evidence does not seem to support the notion that things are getting worse, only that things are changing. In fact, the most dramatic evidence used to support the notion that conditions are bad, such as the Los Angeles riots of 1992, can well be seen as evidence of the opposite. South Central Los Angeles, as any observer can see by driving down the streets, is far from the worst physical environment in the world today. Using almost any indicator, from the quality of the housing stock to the average income levels, the residents of South Central Los Angeles are better off than most citizens of most cities in the world today or at any point in the past.[35] In fact, it seems likely that it was the very dramatic rise in expectations that accompanied decades of booming economy, expectations shared by the poorest residents of Los Angeles, that created such a sharp feeling of deflation at the moment when the problems in the Southern Californian economic system became so obvious in the early 1990s. To the extent that the rioting was not opportunistic, it can be argued, it was about the frustration of heightened expectations.

At base, the notion that we could identify any existing large-scale urban settlement pattern as inherently good or bad is highly problematic. Every urban system that has ever existed has benefited some and harmed others.[36] It would be reassuring to believe, along with social scientists of previous decades, that we can identify the evils in our cities and propose remedies for them. It seems more realistic to admit that cities are such complex and dynamic systems that we are hard put to describe them, let alone suggest sweeping remedies. To those who would argue that this is a pessimistic proposition, leading to inaction, let me suggest that it is nothing of the kind. Every citizen, every organization makes planning decisions and acts on them every day. It is only a question of the scale of effective planning and who does it. A proper modesty about the effectiveness of sweeping remedies, however, may go a long way toward relieving individuals of the burden of believing that they need to remake the entire city around them and reform the lives of their fellow citizens.

Notes

In preparing this paper I had the benefit of the wisdom of a number of individuals, chief among them the members of the working group assembled by the Woodrow Wilson Center to produce this book. I am particularly grateful to H. V. Savitch, Richard Stren, Blair A. Ruble, and Joseph S. Tulchin. The latter proved to be an extraordinary editor, able to hone in on problems of logic but invariably encouraging. I would also like to thank Dennis McClendon, Evan McKenzie, Mitchell Schwarzer, and Scott Jorgenson for their advice and counsel.

[1]Among the more interesting recent books describing various parts or aspects of the contemporary American city are Michael Sorkin, ed., *Variations on a Theme Park: The New American City and the End of Public Space* (New York: Noonday Press, 1992); Carl Abbott, *The New Urban America: Growth and Politics in the Sunbelt Cities*, rev. ed. (Chapel Hill: University of North Carolina Press, 1987); John Findlay, *Magic Lands, Western Cityscapes, and American Culture after 1940* (Berkeley: University of California Press, 1992); and Mike Davis, *City of Quartz* (London, England: Verso, 1990). Many older works, particularly those by Jean Gottmann, Kevin Lynch, Hans Blumenfeld, Peter Hall, James Vance, and Melvin Webber, can still be consulted with profit. An essay by Webber entitled "Order in Diversity: Community without Propinquity," in *Cities and Spaces: The Future Use of Urban Land*, ed. Lowdon Wingo (Baltimore: Johns Hopkins University Press, 1963), perhaps explains, better than any other single statement, today's urban forms. For an updated view of Webber's thinking see his "The Joys of Automobility" in *The Car and the City: The Automobile, the Built Environment, and Daily Urban Life*, ed. Martin Wachs and Margaret Crawford (Ann Arbor: University of Michigan Press, 1992), 274–84.

[2]An effort to chronicle the various names given to these places from the "urban realm" of James Vance in the 1960s through the "Suburban Business Center" described by Hartshorn and Muller in the late 1980s can be found in Michael Romanos, Carla Chifos, and Tony Fenner, "Emergence of Metrotowns in the American Metropolitan Scene: Definition and Evolution of the Concept," in *The City of the 21st Century*, ed. Madis Pihlak (Tempe: University of Arizona, Department of Planning, 1988), 143–47. The most widely read of the books on this topic is Joel Garreau's provocative *Edge City: Life on the New Frontier* (New York: Doubleday, 1991).

[3]A model endeavor of this kind was the great Chicago Area Transportation Study undertaken between 1956 and 1962 with results published 1959–62.

[4]For a good recent survey that explores the complexity of the counterurbanization theories see *Counterurbanization: The Changing Pace and Nature of Population Deconcentration*, ed. A. G. Champion (London, UK: Edward Arnold, 1989). On exurban development see Arthur C. Nelson, "Characterizing Exurbia," *Journal of Planning Literature* 6, no. 4 (May 1992): 350–68.

[5]Perhaps the best statement about the way most of what was traditionally thought of as urban in the United States has become effectively urban can be found in a brilliant essay by geographer Peirce Lewis, "The Galactic Metropolis," in *Beyond the Urban Fringe*, ed. Rutherford H. Platt and George Macinko (Minneapolis: University of Minnesota Press, 1983), 23–49.

[6]The famous Park-Burgess diagram can be found in Ernest W. Burgess, "The Growth of the City: An Introduction to a Research Project," in Robert E. Park, Ernest W. Burgess, and Roderick D. McKenzie, *The City* (Chicago: University of Chicago Press, 1925), 47–62.

[7]Chauncey Harris and Edward Ullman, "The Nature of Cities," *Annals of the American Academy of Political and Social Science* (1945): 7–17.

[8]Kevin Lynch, "The Pattern of the Metropolis," in *The Future Metropolis*, ed. Lloyd Rodwin (New York: George Braziller, 1964), 103–27.

[9]Peirce Lewis, "The Urban Invasion of the Rural Northeast," in National Rural Studies Committee, *A Proceedings* (1991), 11–21. Another attempt at an urban diagram was made in James Vance, *The Continuing City, Urban Morphology in Western Civilization* (Baltimore: Johns Hopkins University Press, 1991), 504.

[10]A good example of this can be found in Edward Soja, *Postmodern Geographies* (London, U.K.: Verso, 1989). If ever one would expect a new kind of diagram it might come from a book with a title like this that focuses on a city as notably multinucleated as Los Angeles has been. However, when one actually looks at the diagram of a typical city (p. 174), one discovers how strong is the pull of the old Park-Burgess model. The city still has the same basic structure as in the Park-Burgess model, only with outlying centers scattered throughout the outer rings.

[11]From the garden cities of Ebenezer Howard to the greenbelts of London to the satellite cities and new towns of postwar America and Europe, the concentric circle view of the city has found its way into the site plans of new communities.

[12]Authors who have attempted to achieve this kind of synthesis include Larry Ford, *Cities and Buildings: Skyscrapers, Skid Rows and Suburbs* (Baltimore: Johns Hopkins University Press, 1944), and Deyan Sudjic, *The 100 Mile City* (London, UK: Andre Deutsch, 1992).

[13]Joel Garreau, *Edge City: Life on the New Frontier* (New York: Doubleday, 1991). Also describing the new outlying centers was Robert Fishman, *Bourgeois Utopias: The Rise and Fall of Suburbia* (New York: Basic Books, 1987).

[14]This is the plot line of the Garreau and Fishman books cited in note 13. It is also used in Kenneth T. Jackson, *The Crabgrass Frontier: The Suburbanization of the United States* (New York: Oxford University Press, 1985).

[15]One of the major reasons this outward movement has been so little studied is that the New Urban Historians of the 1960s, with their fixation on the central city, were not really interested in the vast areas around these centers. When they went to the census data to chart job movements, they found this data most readily accessible in the categories of city vs. suburb; these were the fundamental distinctions for the social scientists who worked at the census bureau. These statistics masked the continuous outward movement of jobs since job movement only registered when jobs actually crossed a municipal boundary. For older cities in the Northeast, the cities these historians were most familiar with, the final move out of the city was visible primarily after World War II, but it was actually only a final step in a continuous process that any examination of the vast industrial tracts of the outlying parts within any central city would have confirmed.

[16]Bus headways along Wilshire Boulevard are as little as 90 seconds in rush periods. In fact, although Los Angeles does not have the density of usage of public transportation of some eastern cities, it actually has a larger fleet of buses than Chicago. *Jayne's Urban Transport*, 13th ed. (Coulston, Surrey, U.K.: Jayne's Information Group, 1995), 76, 185.

[17]This point is succinctly made in Peter Hall, *The World Cities* (New York: World University Library, 1966), 234–35.

[18]Phoenix, for example, or San Diego, with some of the lowest percentages of African Americans, are among the most dispersed American cities.

[19]Among the more important works of this genre are Mark Gottdiener, *The Social Production of Urban Space* (Austin: University of Texas Press, 1985); Manuel Castells, *The Infor-*

national City (Cambridge, Mass.: Basil Blackwell, 1989); David Harvey, *The Urbanization of Capital: Studies in the History of Theory of Capitalist Urbanization* (Baltimore: Johns Hopkins University Press, 1985); and Manuel Castells and Peter Hall, *Technopoles of the World: The Making of the 21st Century Industrial Complexes* (London and New York: Routledge, 1994).

[20]For an example of the attempt to link high-tech industry with distinctive urban forms see Allen J. Scott, *Metropolis, from the Division of Labor to Urban Form* (Berkeley: University of California Press, 1988).

[21]An extremely well-reasoned summary of different kinds of planning remedy can be found in Anthony Downs, *New Visions for Metropolitan America* (Washington, D.C.: Brookings Institution; Cambridge: Lincoln Institute of Land Policy, 1994).

[22]On the crisis in planning see the very interesting analysis in Peter Hall, *Cities of Tomorrow* (Cambridge, Mass.: Basil Blackwell, 1988), 343–61.

[23]It is conspicuous, for example, that older, affluent, low-density suburbs are hardly ever described as sprawl. For an early and still useful investigation of the concept of "sprawl" see Jean Gottmann and Robert A. Harper, *Metropolis on the Move: Geographers Look at Urban Sprawl* (New York: Wiley, 1967).

[24]Just one example from this vast literature is John Jakle and David Wilson, *Derelict Landscapes, The Wasting of America's Built Environment* (Savage, Md.: Rowman and Littlefield, 1992).

[25]On American growth-management programs see Scott A. Bollens, "State Growth Management, Intergovernmental Frameworks and Policy Objectives," *APA Journal* 58 (autumn 1992): 454–66. For Oregon, see Carl Abbott, Deborah Howe, and Sy Adler, *Planning the Oregon Way: A Twenty Year Evaluation* (Eugene: Oregon State University Press, 1994).

[26]The best introduction to these ideas is found in Andres Duany and Elizabeth Plater-Zyberk, *Towns and Town Making Principles* (New York: Rizzoli, 1991).

[27]For some interesting observations on the preferences of Americans for living environments see Alden Speare Jr. and Michael J. White, "Optimal City Size and Population Density for the Twenty-First Century," in *Elephants in the Volkswagen: Facing the Tough Questions about Our Overcrowded Country*, ed. Lindsey Grant (New York: Freeman, 1992), 85–97.

[28]A major statement about the differences between the United States and Canada was made by Michael A. Goldberg and John Mercer in *The Myth of the North American City: Continentalism Challenged* (Vancouver, Canada: University of British Columbia Press, 1986). More recently, planning in Canada and the United States is described in Donald M. Rothblatt, "North American Metropolitan Planning, Canadian and U.S. Perspectives," in *APA Journal* 56 (autumn 1994): 501–20. His conclusion is that the differences are increasingly overshadowed by similarities. One of the major set-pieces in any analysis of differences between U.S. and Canadian cities was the comparison of the metropolitan government of Toronto with city and suburban governments of most large U.S. cities. The recent dissolution of the Toronto metropolitan government may mark a major shift for future analyses.

[29]A good study of how planning efforts have led to exactly the opposite of their intended effects can be found in Peter Salins and Gerard Mildner, *Scarcity by Design: The Legacy of New York City's Housing Policies* (Cambridge, Mass.: Harvard University Press, 1992).

[30]This was one of the major recommendations in Anthony Downs, *Stuck in Traffic* (Washington, D.C.: Brookings Institution, 1992). On issues relating to the automobile and urban form, see the interesting collection of essays in Martin Wachs and Margaret Crawford, eds., *The Car and the City: The Automobile, the Built Environment, and Daily Urban Life* (Ann Arbor: University of Michigan Press, 1992).

[31]This was the message of the "Kemp Report": U.S. Department of Housing and Urban Development, *Not in My Backyard: Removing Barriers to Affordable Housing* (Washington, D.C., 1991).

[32]On the Common Interest Housing Development (CID) see Evan McKenzie, *Privatopia* (New Haven, Conn.: Yale University Press, 1994). McKenzie finds the rise of the CID ominous whereas others argue that it is a highly effective form of voluntary, democratic governance.

[33]The existence of large areas of continuous, overlapping urban fabric, often at low densities, was suggested by Hans Blumenfeld in "Metropolis Extended," *Journal of the American Planning Association* 52, no. 3: 346–48.

[34]It is quite possible to view Downtown Manhattan as doomed to lose its battle with Midtown as the center of finance in the 1950s and to see an ambitious program of private urban renewal initiated by Chase Manhattan Bank and other key players as only a brief delay in this process.

[35]The median family income in South Central Los Angeles, according to the 1990 census, was $18,991, higher than that in the majority of countries in the world.

[36]One of the most interesting aspects of the spate of recent books purporting to rank American cities is the extreme variation in overall totals resulting from slight shifts in the weighting of various categories. Thus, in some ratings New York City appears near the top of the ratings of American cities by "livability." In others it comes out near the bottom. These studies are also very interesting for the comparative data they provide. The most extensive collection of data is found in the various editions of David Savageau and Richard Boyer, *Places Rated Almanac* (New York: Prentice-Hall Travel, 1881, 1885, 1889, and 1993).

PART VI

Ways of Learning for the Urban Future

THERE IS A HEALTHY tension between the academic world and the world of public policy. Often practitioners, laboring in the trenches of managing cities, heap scorn on academics for being hopelessly esoteric in their studies or for being unrealistic in their proposals for solutions to urban problems. For their part, not a few academics criticize those who govern our cities for being shortsighted, for failing to see clearly logical solutions, or for failing to take into account the wishes and interests of the cities' residents. But the fact of the matter is that academics and practitioners cannot get on without one another. Both are vital to the effort of helping cities survive and to understanding how they cope with global pressures and local forces.

While it is far beyond the scope of this volume to summarize the scholarly literature on cities, which is vast, it is indispensable to our enterprise to explain how we study cities, because the way we study cities is the prism through which we understand the urban experience. Although practitioners certainly contribute to shaping the academic agenda by helping us focus on what they would call urban reality, it is equally true that scholars affect urban practice by crafting the framework within which we understand that reality, by formulating the language we use to discuss urban issues, and, most importantly, by debating and selecting the paradigms we use to guide us in suggesting policy and in formulating a new research agenda.

In this section, Richard Stren offers a valuable summary of the evolution of urban studies over the past several decades and focuses our attention on the essentially interdisciplinary nature of urban studies. His chapter is both an explanation and a justification of an interdisciplinary or holistic approach to the study of cities. Part of his argument that we must study cities in an interdisciplinary manner is based upon his observation, supported by many of the chapters in this volume, that effective policy requires a holistic approach, an approach that crosses sectoral or disciplinary lines. Stren comments on the powerful forces of disciplines or departments within universities and how they inhibit research on cities. His chapter is both an appeal for interdisciplinary research and a subtle demonstration of the linkages between scholarly research and public policy.

Lisa Peattie appeals for a return to careful case studies. But her concern with case studies is not a provincial argument for the specific or the peculiar. It is a sophisticated approach that insists on appreciating the specific within the broader framework of general issues. Peattie begins her chapter with a review of urban studies paradigms over the years since Habitat I. She demonstrates how each of those paradigms, relating to questions of development, of size, and of income distribution, constrained the elaboration of research agendas and insisted too much on urban similarity or convergence. She argues that in formulating a new paradigm, the case study method is the best way to get the balance right between the unique and the general.

Chapter 16

Urban Research in the 1990s

Lisa R. Peattie

The writing and reinterpretation of history is as much an affair of shifting perspectives among historians as it is the discovery and assemblage of facts about people and settings. In this tradition, this chapter makes little or no attempt to elucidate changes in cities over the last decades; rather, it proposes an evolving transformation in the practice of urban research. I shall argue that the sorts of broad generalizations implied by "studies of urbanization" or inquiries into "urban poverty" are neither terribly helpful nor terribly interesting at this point, and that we should be striving instead for something else: a repertoire of analytic concepts that help us to understand similarities in process within diverse settings. This proposed style of urban research does not see as its preferred output broad generalizations, either as to process or as to practice, but rather focuses on the development of analytic concepts of wide applicability and their use in the analysis of a variety of particular cases. There are various arguments for this approach; I shall come to them later. First, in the spirit of historiography; I shall make some guesses as to why this seems appropriate.

To begin with, the old categories that organized research and its funding have themselves dissolved. For the field of development studies as it evolved during the 1950s and 1960s, the basic categories were "First World versus Third World" and "socialist economies versus capitalist ones." These served not only to characterize diverse terrains into specializations of subject matter, but also also to play up the diversity of the terrains in a way that rendered "out of order" comparisons based on the idea of certain recurrent patterns cutting across these divisions.

The practice of development work was anchored in the distinction between "developed" and "underdeveloped" countries and on the potential and difficulties of building institutional capacity by transferring expertise and resources from the developed to the underdeveloped. Thus, although it was proposed that such institutions as savings-and-loan societies and agricultural extension services might flow from one category to the other, the contexts into which these were to fit were thought of as radically diverse—in effect, incomparable. Meanwhile, the problems of urbanization and cities attending the development process in the Third World were thought of as quite different from those that characterized cities in the First World. Indeed, there was a substantial literature on urbanization in Latin America that argued—erroneously I believe—that the relationship between city growth and economic change there was strikingly different from that relationship as it evolved when Great Britain and Europe were developing.[1] As for "socialist" and "capitalist," the differences in theoretical approach to explanation combined with policy differences, in particular the restriction of migration to cities, to make the Iron Curtain an intellectual as well as a political boundary.

These categories seem less and less appealing as ways of slicing up the intellectual terrain. As for the socialist and capitalist categories, it is rather obvious what happened: the Soviet system collapsed. The categories were probably at no time useful ways of analyzing the working parts of any one national system. It was a shock to me when I spent a month in Cuba in 1968 and a similar period of time the following year in Yugoslavia to realize that these two "socialisms" were more different from each other in basic organizing principle than either was from my own "capitalist" society. But since the end of the cold war, it has become clear that the terms were never much more than team designations, and the collapse of political structures in the socialist world has uncovered issues and processes that seem quite familiar to those on the other side of the curtain.

Meanwhile, the developed versus underdeveloped schema has been breached by the identification of newly developed countries, some of them the object of envious admiration by the former leaders of the development path, and by the realization that there are a number of sorts of underdeveloped countries and a variety of paths to development. It has been found that it is possible for the developed world to borrow programs, such as sites and services projects, from the Third World, and that phenomena first identified in the Third World have their analogs in the First World—e.g., the informal sector.

As Alejandro Portes pointed out in an article on the evolution of the sociology of development, the development of world systems theory (itself a response to the globalization of economic institutions) calls into question both basic assumptions of the earlier sociology of development: the "existence of a qualitative gap between societies and economics of the advanced and less developed countries,"[2] and the assumption that "individual societies were the appropriate units of analysis."[3] "Instead," he says, "the field as a whole seems to have shifted toward a new interest in the forms of articulation of different actors—nation-states, cities and social classes—into the global system and the strategies and resources available to them. If 'development' means anything in this new context, it is the analysis of alternative modes of adaptation by nations and other collective actors to broader structures which condition and constrain their options."[4] Since such analysis has made it "increasingly clear that strategies of multinational . . . corporations, processes of cultural diffusion and global transfers of capital and technology tend to reproduce fairly similar structures in countries at quite different levels of industrialization,"[5] we are invited by this perspective to focus on comparative case studies of these structures.

An additional and probably even more important factor leading in the same direction is the growing demand for research help in the design of particular programmatic interventions. For program design, broad generalizations are not very helpful. Broad theories of urbanization such as those around "push" and "pull" factors or of practice along the lines of "get the prices right," while no doubt useful in focusing attention on certain sorts of issues, have done little to illuminate actual policy at the programmatic level. Their role has lain more in the realm of supporting ideology, a principle that can be invoked often, I fear, as a substitute for close analysis of the situation in which it is to be applied. For sensible program design we need a sharper manner of looking at particular situations.

A recent paper has suggested that we might well follow Aristotle in distinguishing different sorts of knowledge and singling out that variety particularly useful for action.[6] Aristotle, writer Bent Flyvbjerg tells us, distinguished three different kinds of knowledge, each with its own singular importance.

The first is *episteme*, knowledge that is universal, eternal, and can be demonstrated to be true. This term, which is represented in English by the derivative "epistemology," is the ideal of pure science. The second, *techne*, also has its English cognate in "technique"; it is the knowledge of the art or craft of bringing something into being. It is the third kind of knowledge, *phronesis*, which has no English derivative, that concerns us here. This term, often translated as "prudence," is the knowledge of what to do in particular circumstances. Aristotle says that "prudence is not concerned with universals only; it must also take cognizance of particulars, because it is concerned with conduct, and conduct has its sphere in particular circumstances."

Because conduct has its sphere in particular circumstances, research to guide conduct must be particularistic and contextual. It must be a study focused on cases in their specific and contextual richness, rather than a research of broad descriptive generalization. Such research also sharply brings out the values and interests at stake in lines of action and the structure of power within which intervention must maneuver.

In this kind of work, the prescriptive issues of what "we" ought to do are clearly embedded in the context of what others want to do, and in the institutionalized constraints on action by any of us. As in our system of case-based law, we are not permitted to pronounce "in general." We do enunciate general principles, but we are required to apply them to complex particular circumstances, recognizing that circumstances alter cases and that more than one principle is likely to apply.

Analytically, too, the focus on cases leads us, I believe, to a richer understanding than does the attempt to interpret broadly via descriptive generalizations. In this way of working, we are permitted to use more than one analytic concept at a time. For example, we may analyze peasant behavior via the concept of culture, and in so doing, focus attention on the way in which particular practices relate to each other and constitute a system of meaningfulness. But we can also work from the concept of peasant rationality, and through this focus on the constraints and practical possibilities that shape action. We do not choose between these concepts; we do not say that peasant behavior is rational rather than cultural, or cultural rather than rational. Rather, we say it is something of both, and we will show you here how that works. To take an example from urban studies, we can think of rural–urban migration as a kind of lottery for the migrants,[7] thus giving us a framework for delineating the overall advantages and disadvantages of such migration. At the same time the concept of migration chains[8] focuses attention on the social structuring of such migration that makes it anything but a lottery. Both concepts yield real understanding, although of different aspects of the situation.

Finally, in thinking about the role of case studies, I find it important to insist that cases are, practically speaking, the source of believability when it comes to causality. There are two general strategies for grounding ideas of causality. One is logic; relationships that appear to us inherently true. This strategy was employed with great success by Malthus when he proposed a relationship of causality from higher wages to increased food consumption, to higher fertility, to an increased labor force, to lower wages. Even at the time that he put forth this idea, there was evidence that his model was an oversimplification. But its inherent logic was so compelling (and its use so convenient to the employing classes) that it dominated social-policy thinking for a hundred years. This strategy has been developed a great deal in the mathematical models of economists in our time. The other strategy for creating persuasive proposals of causality is to present a situation with enough closeness of detail that one is bound to agree: Oh, that's how it works.

The two strategies overlap to a degree. Models have real-world referents and are accompanied by stories about lotteries and prisoners, and the case accounts appeal to the inherent logic of the analytic argument. But they are somewhat different in their structure and are practiced by rather different sets of professionals.

I believe that the closer we come to the world of practice and recommendations the more we find ourselves appealing to cases to support our views of causality. As an example (a case!) in point, I note the most recent World Bank housing policy paper.[9] Even as the bank advocates in generalization "the reform of government policies, institutions and regulations to enable housing markets to work more efficiently, and a move away from the limited, project-based support of public agencies engaged in the production and financing of housing," and urges governments to "adopt an enabling role of managing the housing sector as a whole," the argument in its various particulars continually appeals to the evidence of cases. Indeed, the more general text is interspersed with boxed cases from various parts of the world.

Let us pause here to acknowledge the validity of an objection that may well be made at this point as well as later in the argument: Couldn't someone proposing a different analysis equally well present a number of case examples to support *that* one? Yes, they could. This should not make us uncomfortable. The world is complex; multiple forces are at work; policy analysis will tend to focus on the forces relevant to what seem like real possibilities for action; causal analysis grounded in cases does not produce, or propose to produce, a description that covers everything to be seen in the field. We are simply asked to believe that those forces we see at work in the cases presented are at work in similar situations, not that they are the only forces at work there, or that it would be impossible to find a sort of case for which a different sort of analysis is demanded. The particulars of the cases, as these are brought out in analysis, help to keep us aware of all this.

This may be an appropriate place to respond to a question that has been raised with respect to the foregoing discussion of methodology: What is the *particular* relevance of this to the study of Third World cities? The answer, I believe, is none. It is equally applicable to the study of First World cities, and of issues other than specifically urban ones. Indeed, I believe that the segregation of First World/Third World, urban/nonurban into bounded and separate intellectual domains has not been, generally, a productive intellectual strategy.

Another aspect of the appropriate methodological approach is not sufficiently brought forward in the Aristotelian discussion of knowledge for *action;* the need for analytic concepts of very broad applicability. To say, as the theorist Bent Flyvbjerg does, that we should work with "small questions" is not to say that our analysis should be picky and particularistic. The "thick data" and the "small questions" will appear as boring detail and parochial concerns unless we have the conceptual tools to bring them together with other cases and questions in such a way that we see broader patterns of meaning.

In sociology, I believe that the most stimulating concepts have been those that brought together as instances of "the same thing" phenomena that otherwise would have been thought of as falling into quite diverse categories. A classic example is Freud's "unconscious," which made it possible to trace common implications from jokes, slips of the tongue, and dreams.[10] Erving Goffman's *Asylum*[11] opened up a new view of supposedly therapeutic services by joining the asylum to the prison via the concept of a "total institution." Although there are those who object strenuously to Gary Becker's extension of economic analysis to marriage and the family,[12] I find his use of such economic ideas as "opportunity cost" to relate family structure to labor markets exceedingly helpful.

Some areas in our general topic of urban research either have been or seem to be ripe for the development of such analytic concepts of broad applicability. I will not, however, engage a question that certainly deserves serious attention: How do we know when we have a general concept that really works? It is not enough to find a category that makes it possible for us to join together phenomena in different times and places. "Poverty" and "Third World" are examples of such categories that have organized data without, I believe, really advancing thinking about it. We need analytic concepts that help us to use case analysis and case comparisons to advance our understanding of process. What the properties of such concepts are is something we could well think about.

Another general subject that I will not much engage here is the relationship of this kind of work to the idea of science, of *phronesis* to *episteme*. I would, however, like to point out that in linking thickly described cases via general analytic concept, we preserve at the level of generalization a sense of the particular instance that keeps the general idea grounded in a way often lost when we strive for broad general assessments on urbanization or poverty. Our summary statements in this work tend to take the form of pattern identification, and some discussion of the conditions under which a certain pattern is likely to arise: for example, the conditions structuring real estate markets within which home-ownership is likely to remain a possibility for persons with limited incomes, or the conditions under which a lively small-business sector is likely to arise. Such pattern-identifications and contextualizations do not sound like science on the pattern of *episteme*, but they are in their groundedness rather more responsible to data than much of the material we get on the pattern of scientific generalization. They are even getting a certain professional respectability as the pattern of generalization offered by chaos theory.[13]

Again: We will understand any particular pattern identified, and any one of the broad analytic concepts used to develop such pattern identifications, to be one among a number of possible conceptual tools and patterns. If one set succeeds a preceding one in historic time, we are not to assume that the later sets are truer, only that they appear to be more fruitful in the circumstances of a given period, especially including new information. We are not entitled to select a concept or a pattern just because it suits our purposes and the circumstances of the moment; the grounding of research in dense data at the case level is to keep us intellectually responsible in the search for useful truths. At this point, Portes's argument around the evolution of the social context via internationalization meets Flyvbjerg's argument in proposing a kind of research focused not on broad generalizations but rather on identifying recurrent patterns within case-specific settings. In summary, I am arguing that to develop urban research that is both intellectually lively and productive of better social action, we should focus less on topics, and look instead for recurrent issues and for analytic concepts of wide applicability. We should think of the output of our work not as scientific generalizations or as programs of general applicability, but rather as the kind of issue-animated case studies focused on identification of contextualized patterns that can guide action in those cases and serve as models for analysis and analysis-guided policies in other cases.

An example substantiating this view is the evolution of ideas around housing the poor. Some years ago, the conventions were to look at this topic as it was presented under socialism and in the capitalist states, and in the First World and the Third World. Even analysts from the nonsocialist West implicitly adopted the position of the socialist states that since socialism treated housing as part of welfare policy, rather than as a market commodity, analysis should center on the progress or lack of progress of the state in meeting housing needs. There was little attention to the way in which people were housed who were not in the official housing system; (even though such persons were more often than not in the majority)[14] they were thought of as waiting for the deficit to be made up.

It was, therefore, a substantial contribution when Ivan Szelenyi[15] brought together material on the socialist systems of Eastern Europe around the concept of a housing system, and argued that by defining housing as an issue of welfare rather than as part of the economy, the state had created a system privileging the better-off part of society. Subsidies went to the official urban housing, to which only a privileged part of the population had access. The rest of the workers, living perforce in substandard housing outside the city, commuted in to work where they created a surplus that constituted, in part, the funding for the regressive housing subsidies. The thrust of Szelenyi's argument was a comparison between state and market; he saw welfare policy treatment of housing as producing a more unequal outcome than the market might. This approach leads to a way of placing socialist systems and capitalist systems in the same frame of reference, as recent political changes are causing planners to do. Although Szelenyi himself does not make this argument, when I read his work I at once made the analogy to the housing systems in Latin American countries, with the workers in informal settlements playing the role played by Szelenyi's commuters. For me, his vision also made it possible to bring the cities of the Third World into the framework.

Returning to the divided intellectual framework within which we have looked at housing, it may be proposed that the conceptual separation between First World and Third World had a somewhat different logic than that separating the analysis of capitalist and socialist systems. The settings were deemed to be so different at the level of basic economics and demography that there could be little carryover of ideas. First there were the demographics: in Third World cities the defining problem was rates of urbanization, which, whatever their absolute levels, were in all cases perceived as high enough to constitute the leading problem of city life. As for issues of housing, the barrier to crossover here was income levels. While housing policy for the well-to-do might draw on First World analogs of construction and funding, a large proportion of the population had income levels so low as to apparently defy any borrowing of ideas.

There was another deep division of the conceptual territory that operated across both First World and Third World research and separated thinking about the reputable housing for the well-to-do from thinking about the housing for the poor, otherwise known as slums. In both the First World and the Third World the housing for the poor, by being disreputable as to standard, also lost its standing as a serious topic either of urban economics or of social policy. Instead, slum housing, shantytowns, or *favelas* appeared as subtopics in the literature of social problems from which it was an easy jump to appearing in the agenda of urban policy as a topic for clearance.[16] It was a "problem" that should be "eradicated."

Research in the Third World made a dramatic breakthrough in this conceptual apparatus. The British architect John Turner, working with anthropological colleague William Mangin in Peru, concluded that squatter settlements were not only housing but a kind of housing superior to any that the official system of provision was capable of generating. Squatting, Turner and Mangin announced, was not the problem but the solution.[17] The settlements were perceived to represent "a process of social reconstruction through popular initiative." As a means of housing production the self-help efforts of the settlers were said to contrast most favorably with the "material diseconomies, social dysfunctions and general counter-productivity of centrally administered housing systems."[18] This approach was rapidly taken up by architects and planners, and came to constitute in large part the intellectual base for the sites-and-services approach pushed by the World Bank.

As an intellectual revolution, however, it was an incomplete one. Although Turner and Mangin proposed a kind of ordinary progression of urban migrants from central city slum to home- (if not land-) ownership in the periphery, the interest in irregular settlements did not at the outset find itself grounded in a larger understanding of housing submarkets. In particular, the rental market within squatter settlements only gradually came to the attention of researchers. Turner's respect for owner-directed incremental building as a form of self-definition and self-assertion helped the idealistic architects who were the spearhead of the pro-squatter movement among the technocrats to underestimate the role of commercial builders and commercial motives in this housing stock. For somewhat similar reasons, I believe, a focus on land invasion delayed recognition of the role of commercial, if strictly speaking illegal, land-developers in the formation of irregular settlements.

The enumeration of these deficient themes in the first wave of interest in squatter settlements shows in itself how research has deepened our understanding since the 1960s. There is now a large and interesting literature on Third World rental markets both in the central cities and in the periphery,[19] on the role of rental in financing incremental building,[20] and on the operations of commercial land-developers in the formation of irregular settlements.[21]

This housing submarkets perspective, largely developed by First World scholars, should next, I believe, come to be integrated with other perspectives more characteristic of scholars in the Third World, especially in Latin America: that of the community study[22] and of the human settlement pattern as an outgrowth and expression of the structures of society as a whole[23] or as the source of social movements affecting that society.[24] For real estate submarkets are very much social units as well as economic ones, and real estate is one of the most heavily politicized of markets.

A phase of the intellectual revolution that is only now beginning to be completed is the application to cities of the industrialized world of the understanding that what has been looked at as slums are also, however inadequate for the role, the housing resource for the poor. There are, I believe, two sources for this understanding. One is the fairly recent attention in the Third World to the housing stock and its inhabitants in the aging buildings of the central city;[25] here the parallels to New York and Philadelphia are much more obvious than when we were dealing with squatter settlements and Levittowns. The other source is the rapid and upsetting rise of homelessness in the cities of the industrialized world, which stimulates a sudden solicitousness for SRO hotels and the social and financial arrangements that might maintain abandoned buildings or those in the process of disinvestment as habitable structures.[26]

Once we begin to look at cities in terms of the concept of housing submarkets, a number of other intellectual developments become possible. (1) We can look more closely at how people actually get housed, rather than defining our problem around official housing programs and the housing that governments recognize. Shlomo Angel's point, made in 1976,[27] that despite the huge housing deficit in Bangkok almost everyone is living *somewhere*, has been followed by studies (like that of Tomasz Sudra in Mexico City) that identify the various forms of habitation in particular cities,[28] and at least one handbook of methods for making such identifications.[29] (2) We can look at housing programs as part of larger complex systems including transportation planning, fiscal policy, municipal finance, and political structures. (3) We can look at how such systems evolve over time, and the ways in which the evolution of housing markets shapes the evolving social opportunities for people. Studies such as Gilbert and Varley's *Landlord and Tenant*,[30] and those currently sponsored by the Ford Foundation[31] ask questions such as Are land costs rising in specific cities? What factors govern land-cost changes and how do such changes impact on access to home-ownership for the poor, recognizing that generalizations must always account for the specifics of answers from city to city?

In a discussion held at MIT in October 1992 we recognized that placing the same conceptual lens over the housing of the poor as that of the well-to-do and looking at U.S. cities as we do at those of Latin America raised new questions of the sort that call for *phronesis*. We are looking now at a system of real-estate submarkets. Who profits from these markets? Home-ownership is not simply the acquisition of a roof over one's head; it is the acquisition of a capital asset. How general is access to what assets? On what terms? What benefits do they derive? Will the asset appreciate in value? Edel, Sclar, and Luria's study of home-own-ership in Boston[32] and a World Bank study of land values in Bogota[33] both show the rapid prices rises taking place in the periphery, and leave clouded (in the Boston case doubtful indeed) the possibility that lower-income people can benefit. These studies should make us look critically at the assumption, which has been quite general, that home-ownership is necessarily the bottom step of an economic escalator. Can the dwelling space be used as productive infrastructure? My study of the shoe industry in Bogota[34] and Solomon Benjamin's monograph on the development of the coated–copper wire industry in a residential neigh-borhood in Delhi[35] are both case studies of industries almost entirely housed in residential stock. Simon Fass, in a study in Port-au-Prince,[36] found productive activities so general that he treats housing simply as infrastructure. Can the dwelling unit be used as a source of rental income? Will the legally tenured acquisition of land and dwellings by a set of city-dwellers at one point in time tend to preempt such acqui-sition by latecomers? When government agencies manage the devel-opment of housing projects for the poor, how does the production process itself differ from that in the irregular settlements, particularly with respect to the question of who profits?

These questions rose directly out of applying the same lens to *all* housing (First World/Third World, middle-class home/slum); we looked at housing not simply as shelter, but also as a capital asset that shapes people's life chances, and differentiates those chances accord-ingly. We found ourselves asking, If the poor can get shelter only as publicly subsidized tenants is this not still exclusion from the income opportunities of ownership? Are we providing only *shelter* for the poor while the better-off get *real estate*?

These questions came out of the study of cases, animated by a sense of issue and by the use of the broadly applicable concept of real estate submarkets. These are good questions, not only because they are of real social importance, but because the attempt to answer them is bound to open up our understanding of how cities, institutions, and social sys-tems work. But the answers will not be broad generalizations; they will be the description of patterns of process, with identification of the rel-evant factors of context that shape these patterns. This is a way of look-ing at the world that can be truly helpful for program design.

A second example of the uses of case study analysis involves the favorable appraisal of a concept that I have long argued is fatally flawed and in need of replacement: that of the "informal sector." On the basis of my own attempts to study the operations of street vendors, petty shopkeepers, very small shoemaking enterprises, and other such "informal" activities, I have argued that the term is exceedingly fuzzy, serving as a semantic blanket over a variety of enterprises sharing the attribute of being "off the map" for statisticians and economists, the equivalent of the "There Be Dragons" of ancient cartographers. A fuzzy concept produces fuzziness in policy thinking. Why should a single programmatic approach be appropriate for sandalmakers and component producers for large factories? Or for the peasant woman selling a little pile of vegetables on the street and the dealer in contraband radios? Or for paid artisans in informal settlement building and un-official taxi or bus lines?[37] It has served as the entry into issues that need to be picked apart analytically: the role of government regulation vis-à-vis industrial development, the role of services within the economy, and the sources of poverty.

I have argued in print that we would be better off substituting for the term "informal sector" phrases such as (according to purpose and context) "family firm," "self-employment," "small enterprise," and "working poor."[38] Nevertheless, I believe that the concept has been enormously fertile for our growing understanding. This declaration does not constitute a refutation of my prior argument because of the following circumstances: The concept of "informal sector" has opened up our understanding to the degree that it has been applied to the widest variety of contexts, First World and Third World, socialist as well as capitalist, and to the degree that it has led to case studies rather than to broad general appraisals and recommendations.

The term came into existence in the early 1970s as the invention of a British anthropologist trying to make sense of his fieldwork with poor city-dwellers in Ghana. It was popularized by the ILO as an intellectual strategy by which the ILO tried to deal with its traditional focus on employment income in a setting (Kenya) where most people were occupied in and supported by a variety of economic expedients among which a regular job was the exception rather than the rule. The sector was loosely defined as a "way of doing things" characterized by (a) ease of entry; (b) reliance on indigenous resources; (c) family ownership of enterprises; (d) small scale of operation; (e) labor-intensive and adapted technology; (f) skills acquired outside the formal school system; and (g) unregulated and competitive markets.[39] It was sharply contrasted with a "formal sector" with the opposite characteristics.

This initial debut was followed by a number of studies, many supported by the ILO, to ascertain the magnitude and distribution of the informal sector in various Third World cities.[40] I believe it would be fair to say that most of these are quite unmemorable. It is not that they were badly done, although it is of course hard to manage data when the category is "a way of doing things" with a number of overlapping and nonmeasurable characteristics; it is more that the data in question, assembled in a spirit of general assessment, did not seem to answer important questions of either interpretation or policy.

During this early period of measurement, Richard Webb made a more interesting use of the statistics by tracing the amount of formal and informal activity in Peru over a single time line, and finding that they varied together.[41] The exercise was directed at the belief of many Latin Americans that those practicing informal activities had been driven into them by weakness or decline of the formal part of the economy. Although Webb's data were more tantalizing than definitive, the papers did at least make it appear relatively certain that this could be, at best, only a very partial explanation.

It was not until researchers began to do case studies of particular informal-sector industries that we began to get a more grounded and more interesting comprehension of what had been the terra incognita of one-person and family businesses and what the Victorians had called "casual labor." Interestingly, the first such study to really bring into question the notion of a "sector" was the study by Chris Birkbeck of one of the most irregular and most denigrated of occupations; the trash picker.[42] Birkbeck was able to show that those who picked through the trash in the dump in Cali were at the bottom of a long chain of transactions; the base of a materials-reprocessing industry topped out by the corporate Cartón de Colombia. Since this pathbreaking study, there have been a number of others focusing on the links, both backward and forward, making informal activities an essential part of economic systems and the operations of formal firms.[43]

Once we moved from the general concept of an informal sector particular to the Third World to thick descriptions of various occupations, it became easier to recognize their analogs, particularly in sales and services, in cities like New York. A recent collection of papers joins an account of the cocaine economy of Bolivia with one on the vibrant small-firm economy of the Italian "Red Belt"; it finds the informal sector in locales scattered from Moscow to Miami, from New York to Malaysia.[44] It has been possible to link studies of small enterprises in the Third World to the literature on "flexible specialization" in Europe and use this comparative approach to open up some general issues in the understanding of development.[45]

But as the informal sector came to be seen everywhere, its specifications have become ever more salient. We are becoming more critical of the general term[46] and more rigorous in the methodology of investigation. A recent paper on subsector analysis[47] views small enterprises as interacting with other firms, both large and small, in vertical production and distribution systems, and outlines how to study enterprises and develop policy within this framework; the authors of this paper do not even use the term "informal sector," but I believe that their work is a direct outgrowth of the informal sector case studies cited here.

In summary, I believe that the concept of the "informal sector" is fatally flawed as a tool of analysis or policy-making. But the attempt to make use of it has done a great deal for urban research. It has, in the first place, opened up our understanding of the essence of economic activity. It will never again be so easy for someone to say, as an African bureaucrat once did, "There are no industries there—only a lot of furniture works, bakeries, maize mills and soda water factories."[48] In putting all this activity "on the map," the concept has opened up issues that, inextricably joining fact and value, are the proper material for *phronesic* research. What is the role of government regulation in the distribution of economic opportunities? What should it be? What are the roles of gender and of ethnicity in structuring what we like to call "labor markets" and other economic institutions? What are the differential effects of macropolitics on economic activity and on income distribution in various parts of the economic system? How should we be adjusting macropolicies with respect to these effects? How can economic institutions at the bottom adjust to them?

But although the term "informal sector" served us well by making it possible to look at economic activities previously thought of as unworthy of serious attention, and by bringing together in a single frame activities in both First and Third worlds, and both socialist and capitalist economies, it cannot take us much further. We now need a focused attention on analytic concepts driven by the various different issues that impel our research, whether into economic growth, social welfare, or equality. Then we will use these concepts for the comparative study of cases that can generate contextualized pattern identifications and guidance for policy.

Here as candidate for an analytic concept of wide general applicability I propose that of "in-kind bargaining" presented by Wang Yukun in his paper[49] at the Beijing meeting of the Ford Foundation urban research project. The argument was that such interactions—usually referred to in the United States under the heading of "public-private partnerships"[50]—raise issues not only as to the balance of who loses and who benefits but also as to the process by which benefits are apportioned. Wang argued that when the trade-offs are made in kind the process becomes opaque to outsiders and, he implied in a way quite resonant with the U.S. political tradition, lends itself to abuse. A New

Yorker like myself, listening to this, thinks at once of the tortuous and fairly opaque negotiations between Donald Trump and the City of New York over the proposed West Side development, and the conflicts over what public amenities and subsidized housing should be included in the package. I was especially interested after hearing a contemporaneous presentation of Susan Fainstein's look at the way in which government in London and in New York, relying on private developers to expand the tax base and produce certain amenities in the process, had to pick up the consequences of office-space overbuilding and insufficient infrastructure when the market slumped.[51] As the World Bank and other lenders pressure municipal governments to increase their capacity, the tax base will become more of an issue and the dilemmas of public-private interaction more salient. Meanwhile, the radical changes in socialist states are producing situations that are, at least in some respects, similar in a variety of new situations. Perhaps we will find when we look at these that the dilemmas are not wholly new, but were concealed by past inter-institutional negotiations under the blanket of socialist planning at the local level.

General references to "urban management" or the desirability of public-private partnerships provide very little guidance in these situations. On the other hand, the specific negotiations and institutional forms in particular settings would benefit from a broader framework. Comparative case studies built around one or two key concepts could provide that framework.

Now I turn to the question of why there is not more of the kind of research I am advocating. If it's so useful, why is it not proliferating? Actually, the answer must begin with the admission that in many places case studies abound. I have had occasion to cite many here. Graduate student theses, in particular, often consist of community or institutional case studies. In Latin America, sociology students less commonly do fieldwork but social workers almost always do as part of their training. The problem is that the case study is thought of as work to be carried out by those who have a low opportunity-cost for their time, a kind of informal sector of research, and being little-esteemed and done by the inexpert it is not often driven by important ideas.

An illuminating case study based on field research is a work of craftsmanship. It takes time, skill, and focused attention. It is only the unusually skilled craftsperson—in my Bogota shoe-industry study the experienced made-to-measure shoemaker, in our professional world an Elliot Liebow or a Herbert Gans—who can derive attractive rewards from the time-consuming, personally taxing work of preparing, one by one, single works of craftsmanship. For most researchers, it is far more appealing to be the administrator of a grant under which a number of lowly research workers will gather the data to be assembled by the senior researcher, much as auto workers combine their efforts to produce a car designed and marketed by others. Conception is separated from execution for reasons having more to do with the management of financing than the quality of the final product. In fact, as in the production of other goods, the management of production in this way actually shifts the grounds of excellence. The rewards center around grant acquisition and conference papers rather than around the interpretation of field studies. Since intellectual initiative is critical in the making of the kind of cases I am proposing, the separation of conception and control from execution renders it almost impossible to do the illuminating case study in much the same way that modern systems of food production and distribution have made it impossible to obtain a tomato that tastes like a tomato.

Here, again, we may find some clarification by borrowing a concept. A recent work on small enterprises in the development process[52] emphasizes that the small enterprise needs some sort of support system that can provide for it some of the protection that the big enterprise gets by internalizing its forward and backward linkages. One of the solutions noted therein, becoming the subcontractor of parts for a large firm, is, as I have stated, not really suitable for the product I am advocating, since the clarifying case studies that make up a working *phronesis* cannot be closely specified and designed in advance.

Another form of protection sometimes used for small manufacturing can be and sometimes is applied to our product: this is the special subsidy program. Such programs as the Inter-American fellowship program have been important in underwriting work in Latin America. Where else, and by whose initiative and what bodies' continuing support can this pattern be extended elsewhere? The obvious administering bodies here are universities, since they are already in existence and structured to provide both guidance and (within limits) help in dissemination of findings, our form of marketing. A third way in which small enterprises get shelter is by collectivizing either to reduce the cost of inputs or to build markets. The second of these seems to be particularly important, as in the import-export firms that have been the secret of Hong Kong's small-firm development miracle, and it is this function that I think we should think about seriously with respect to our case studies.

The crafts analogy helps us see that this sort of research can be well nourished in an atelier format. My colleague Judith Tendler recently carried out an interesting version of this solution by building a sort of atelier with seven first-year master's students in city planning. After carrying out a workshop with the students at MIT, she went with them for a summer's research in the state of Ceara, Brazil, supported financially by the state's government, and then returned to MIT to carry out joint discussions of the writing-up. It was not a single project; it was a set of projects, related by certain general themes and interests and by the mutual support of the common discussions in the field and at the university. But those who did the case studies benefited not only from financial support and critical comment, but also by having a real audience in the officials who listened to their presentations and the professionals in the university and lending-agency world who were introduced to the work by Tendler. This particular project no doubt depended on an unusual academic initiator and unusually generous support by a Brazilian governor. But work on human settlements and housing carried on in a similar atelier pattern at the Asian Institute of Technology in Bangkok shows that if we do not see the pattern more commonly it is not because it is inherently impossible.

There is a particular rationale for the case-study approach that I cite here merely to make clear that the prior discussion does not rest on this particular rationale: this is the use of the case-study approach as a way of engaging the people who must do problem-solving in the area being analyzed. Donald Schon and Chris Argyris, two theoretically minded organizational consultants, developed this idea in the context of issues of organizational remediation and organizational learning.[53] In this approach, people in organizations function as co-researchers, with the hope that not only will the information gathered have more validity, but that the persons involved will themselves come to use the research process in a more active way within the organizational setting. An interesting paper on community-based approaches to environmental management in Asian cities outlines a similar research approach through involving the communities concerned in the basic investigation at the local level, and linking these local case-building efforts via wider research teams, publications, and national and international forums.[54] I very much agree with these statements. But in taking part in participatory research, we must be clear that the community or organizational case study is likely to be rather different from the case study that is part of a cluster used to ground a pattern generalization, and there is every reason why it should be. Indeed, any inquiry that draws on case studies will structure the cases differently to bring out the features of particular interest. We must not imagine a permanent file of cases that can be used for this or that. Our questions will change and become more sophisticated as we work with the cases we have; we will bring in new concepts that will, in turn, surface new aspects of the situations in our case analyses and raise new questions.

In thinking about the organization of research we should therefore avoid thinking in terms of the single research project, and strive instead to build research institutions that will have the sort of flexibility and capacity to adapt on the basis of experience that can support this sort of cumulative *phronetic* learning.

Notes

[1] Richard Morse, "Urbanization in Latin America," *Latin American Research Review* 1, no. 1 (1965); Andre Gunder Frank, "Lumpenbourgeoisie: Lumpendevelopment Dependence: Class and Politics in Latin America," *New York Monthly Review Press* (1972); and Fernando H. Cardoso and Jose Luis Reyna, "Industrialization, Occupational Structure, and Social Stratification in Latin America," in *Constructive Change in Latin America,* ed. Cole Blasier (Pittsburgh: University of Pittsburgh Press, 1968).

[2] Alejandro Portes, "The Sociology of Development in the Mid-Eighties: Implications for Taiwan," in *Taiwan: A Newly Industrialized State,* ed. Hsin-huang Michael Hsiao, Wei-Yuan Cheng, and Hou-Sheng Chan (Taipei, Taiwan: Taipei Department of Sociology, National Taiwan University, 1989), 501.

[3] Ibid., 497.

[4] Ibid., 500.

[5] Ibid., 501.

[6] Bent Flyvbjerg, "Aristotle, Foucault, and Progressive Phronesis: Outline of an Applied Ethics for Sustainable Development," in *Applied Ethics: A Reader,* ed. Earl R. Winkler and Jerrold R. Coombs (Oxford, U.K.: Blackwell, 1993).

[7] John R. Harris and Michael Todaro, "Migration Unemployment and Development: A Two-Sector Analysis," *American Economic Review* (1970); and John R. Harris and Richard Sabot, "Urban Unemployment in Developing Countries: Towards a More General Sectoral Model," in *Essays on Migration and the Labor Market in Developing Countries,* ed. Richard Sabot (Boulder, Colo.: Westview, 1982), 566–739.

[8] For a review see Monica Boyd, "Family and Personal Networks in International Migration: Recent Developments and New Agenda," *International Migration Review* 23 (fall 1989): 638–70.

[9] World Bank, *Housing: Enabling Markets to Work,* a World Bank policy paper (Washington, D.C.: World Bank, 1992).

[10] Sigmund Freud, "The Unconscious: A Conceptual Analysis," in *Works: 1953–1974* (London, U.K.: Hogarth Press Institute of Psychoanalysis, 1957).

[11] Erving Goffman, *Asylums: Essays on the Social Situation of Mental Patients and Other Inmates* (Garden City, NY: Anchor Books, 1961).

[12] Gary Becker, *The Economic Approach to Human Behavior* (Chicago, Ill.: University of Chicago Press, 1976).

[13] James Gleik, *Chaos: Making a New Science* (New York: Viking, 1987).

[14]Phillippe Annez and William Wheaton, "Economic Development and the Housing Sector: A Cross-National Model," *Economic Development and Cultural Change* 32, no. 4 (July 1984): 749–66.

[15]Ivan Szelenyi, *Urban Inequalities Under State Socialism* (Oxford, U.K., and New York: Oxford University Press, 1982).

[16]Lisa Peattie, "More and Better Slums," *SPURS Newsletter*, no. 32 (summer 1992): 1–2.

[17]John C. Turner, "Squatters and Urban Policy: A Review Essay," *Urban Affairs Quarterly* 2, no. 3 (1967): 111–15; John C. Turner, "Barriers and Channels for Housing Development in Modernizing Countries," *American Institute of Planners Journal* 33, no. 3 (1967): 167–81; W. Mangin, ed., *Peasants in Cities* (Boston, Mass.: Houghton Mifflin, 1970); Mangin, ed., "Uncontrolled Urban Settlement: Problems and Policies," *International Social Development Review* (United Nations document ST/SOA/Ser. 4/1), no. 1 (1969): 107–30; also in *The City in Newly Developing Countries*, ed. G.W. Breese (Englewood Cliffs, N.J.: Prentice-Hall, 1969), 507–54; and in Breese, "Housing Priorities, Settlement Patterns and Urban Development in Modernizing Countries," *American Institute of Planners Journal* 34, no. 6 (1968): 354–63.

[18]John C. Turner, *Housing by People: Towards Autonomy in Building Environments* (London, U.K.: Martin Boyars; New York: Pantheon Books, 1976), 169.

[19]See, for example, Michael Edwards, "Cities of Tenants: Renting Among the Urban Poor in Latin America," in *Urbanization in Contemporary Latin America*, ed. A. Gilbert, J. Hardoy, and R. Ramirez (Chichester, N.Y.: Wiley, 1982); also in Alan Gilbert and Ann Varley, *Landlord and Tenant: Housing the Poor in Urban Mexico* (London, U.K., and New York: Routledge, 1982).

[20]Praful Soni, "Self-help Planning Construction and Management in Sites-and-Services Project in Nairobi, Kenya," *Ekistics* 48, no. 286 (1991).

[21]W. A. Doebele, "The Private Market and Low-Income Urbanization: The Private Subdividers of Bogota," *American Journal of Comparative Law* 25, no. 3 (summer 1977): 531–64.

[22]Larissa Lomnitz, *Como Sobreviven los Marginados* (Mexico City: Siglo XXI, 1975); and Lomnitz, "Mechanisms of Articulation between Shantytown Settlers and the Urban System," *Urban Anthropology* 7, no. 2 (1978).

[23]DESAL, *La Marginalidad en America Latina: un Ensayo de Diagnostico* (Barcelona, Spain: Herder, 1969).

[24]O. Kowarick, ed., *As Lutas Sociais e a Cidade: São Paulo: Pasado e Presente* (São Paulo, Brazil: Paz e Terra, 1988); Manuel Perlo and Martha Schteingart, "Movimientos Sociales Urbanos en Mexico," *Revista Mexicana de Sociologia* 46 (1984): 105–27.

[25]Gilbert and Varley, *Landlord and Tenant*.

[26]Charles Hoch and Robert A. Slayton, *New Homeless and Old: Community and the Skid Row Hotel* (Philadelphia: Temple University Press, 1989).

[27]Shlomo Angel, Stan Benjamin, and Koos H. DeGoede, "The Low Income Housing System in Bangkok," *Ekistics* 44, no. 261 (1977): 79–84.

[28]Thomasz Sudra, "Housing as a Support System: A Case Study of Mexico City," *Architectural Design* 46, no. 4 (1976): 222–26.

[29]John M. Baldwin, *Guide for Survey-Evaluation of Urban Dwelling Environments*, Education/Research Program, Urban Settlement Design in Developing Countries, School of

Architecture and Planning (Cambridge, Mass.: Massachusetts Institute of Technology, January 1974).

[30]Gilbert and Varley, *Landlord and Tenant.*

[31]Richard Stren, ed., *Urban Research in the Developing World*, 4 vols. (Toronto, Canada: Centre for Urban and Community Studies, University of Toronto, 1994–95).

[32]Matthew Edel, Elliott D. Sclar, and Daniel Luria, *Shaky Palaces: Homeownership and Social Mobility in Boston's Suburbanization* (New York: Columbia University Press, 1984).

[33]Rakesh Mohan and Rodrigo Villamizar, "The Evolution of Land Values in the Context of Rapid Urban Growth: A Case Study of Bogota and Cali, Colombia," in *World Congress on Land Policy 1980,* ed. Matthew Cullena and Sharon Wollery (Lexington, Mass.: D. C. Heath, Lexington Books, 1982).

[34]Lisa R. Peattie, "What Is to Be Done with the Informal Sector? A Case Study of Shoe Manufacturing in Colombia," in *Towards a Political Economy of Urbanization,* ed. Helen I. Safa (New Delhi, India: Oxford University Press, 1981).

[35]Solomon Benjamin, *Jobs, Land, and Urban Development: The Economic Success of Small Manufacturers in East Delhi* (Cambridge, Mass.: Lincoln Institute of Land Policy, 1990).

[36] Simon Fass, *Political Economy in Haiti: The Drama of Survival* (New Brunswick, N.J.: Transaction Books, 1988).

[37]See discussion in Helmut K. Anheier, "Economic Environments and Differentiation: A Comparative Study of Informal Sector Economies in Nigeria," *World Development* 20, no. 11 (1992): 1573–85.

[38]Lisa R. Peattie, "The Informal Sector: An Idea in Good Currency and How It Grew," *World Development* 15, no. 7 (1987).

[39]International Labor Office (ILO), *Employment, Incomes and Equality: A Strategy for Increasing Productive Employment in Kenya* (Geneva, Switzerland: ILO, 1972).

[40]Kalmann Schaefer, *São Paulo Urban Development and Employment* (Geneva, Switzerland: ILO, 1976); S. V. Sethhuraman, ed., *The Urban Informal Sector in Developing Countries: Employment, Poverty and Environment* (Geneva, Switzerland: ILO, 1981); ILO, *Calcutta, Its Urban Development and Employment Prospects* (Geneva, Switzerland: ILO, 1974); ILO, *Urbanization and Employment in Jakarta* (Geneva, Switzerland: ILO, 1975); and ILO, *Urban Development and Employment in Abidjan* (Geneva, Switzerland: ILO, 1975).

[41]Richard Webb, *Income and Employment in the Urban and Traditional Sectors of Peru* (Washington, D.C.: World Bank, 1974).

[42]Chris Birkbeck, "Garbage, Industry, and the 'Vultures' of Cali, Colombia," in *Casual Work and Poverty in Third World Cities,* ed. Ray Bromley and Chris Gerry (Chichester, N.Y.: Wiley, 1979), 161–83.

[43]Victor E. Tokman, "An Exploration into the Nature of Informal-Formal Sector Relationships," in *The Urban Informal Sector: Critical Perspective on Employment and Housing Policies,* ed. Ray Bromley (Oxford, U.K., and New York: Pergamon, 1979).

[44]Alejandro Portes, Manuel Castells, and Lauren A. Benton, eds., *The Informal Economy: Studies in Advanced and Less Developed Countries* (Baltimore: Johns Hopkins University Press, 1989).

[45]Hubert Schmitz, "Flexible Specialisation: A New Paradigm of Small-Scale Industrialization?" discussion paper no. 261, Institute of Development Studies (May 1989).

[46]Peattie, "The Informal Sector," 851–60.

[47]James J. Boomgard, Stephen P. Davies, Steven J. Haggblade, and Donald C. Mead, "A Subsector Approach to Small Enterprise Promotion and Research," *World Development* 20, no. 2 (1992): 199–212.

[48]Quoted in I. Livingston, "Creating Employment in Kenya: The ILO Mission Report," *Journal of Administration Overseas* 12/13 (1974): 374–82.

[49]Wang Yukun, "China: Urban Development and Research Towards the Year 2000," China's Urban Development Research Group, Development Research Center of the State Council, People's Republic of China (August 4, 1992).

[50]See Bernard J. Frieden and Lynne Sagalyn, *Downtown Inc.: How America Rebuilds Cities* (Cambridge, Mass.: MIT Press, 1989).

[51]Susan S. Fainstein, *The City Builders* (Oxford, U.K., and Cambridge, Mass.: Blackwell, forthcoming).

[52]Gary Loveman and Werner Sengenberger, "Introduction: Economic and Social Reorganization in the Small and Medium-sized Enterprise Sector," in *The Re-emergence of Small Enterprises: Industrial Restructuring in Industrialized Countries,* ed. Werner Sengenberger, Gary Loveman, and Michael J. Piore (Geneva, Switzerland: ILO Publications, 1990).

[53]Chris Argyris and Donald A. Schon, *Organizational Learning* (Reading, Mass.: Addison Wesley, 1978).

[54]Mike Douglass, "The Political Economy of Urban Poverty and Environmental Management in Asia: Access, Empowerment and Community Based Alternatives," *Environment and Urbanization* 4, no. 2 (1992): 9–32.

Chapter 17

The Studies of Cities:
Popular Perceptions, Academic
Disciplines, and Emerging Agendas

Richard Stren

Cities, like beauty, are very much in the eye of the beholder. Just as there are many ways of seeing and even imagining cities, there are many ways of thinking about them, studying them, diagnosing them, and even suggesting "cures" or solutions for their predicaments. In many respects, the city is a mental artifact. Because cities include such a large proportion of the world's people, and incorporate within their spatial boundaries a range of complex activities that are at once political, cultural, social, and economic, our understanding of them is bound to be both incomplete and highly fragmentary.

In the postmodern 1990s, to state that knowledge of cities is partial and fragmented because it is based on subjective understanding may seem banal in the extreme. But there are principles underlying this partiality and fragmentation that both impose limits on an otherwise almost infinite production of different visions of the city and its problems, and suggest some common paths to desirable outcomes. The first principle may be called "common understandings," while the second principle may be called "disciplinary perspectives." The burden of the argument in this chapter will rest on a discussion of the second principle.

Given the fact that so many of us who observe and are affected by cities also live within their borders—whether these are legal and jurisdictional, or cultural and social—a common vocabulary of phenomena and problems has grown up around our everyday experiences. This vocabulary, or "popular urban discourse," focuses on a number of key elements common (though in different ways) to cities in the North and the South. For example, the growth of cities in both population and land area is constantly referred to in the press and popular media as a problem that needs to be addressed. In North America, cities are growing from the inside out, as many central cities stagnate and high-level jobs and residential investment move to the suburbs, whereas in many parts of the South (especially in Africa) cities are growing from the outside in, as migrants from impoverished rural areas continue to flow into them. In this process of growth, cities all over the world are faced with the challenge of limiting the damage to the natural environment (such as rivers, the watershed, and the air) caused by effluents from industrial and household activity. Horror stories of dead rivers, foul and polluted air, water-borne and heavy-metal-based diseases are common all over the world and, since the 1980s, have entered the common currency of urban management practice. Not to be left out of this increasingly universal discourse are the growing congestion, inefficiency, and cost of urban public transport systems; the persistent inability of the public sector to make serviced land available to poor urban migrants, leading to a further expansion of marginal and largely unserviced neighborhoods often called "squatter villages" or "shantytowns" in the poorest countries; the recurrent financial and political problems of municipal authorities, particularly in the face of central or regional governments that resist granting more financial and political autonomy; the plight of the unemployed and low-paid workers and vendors; ethnic and racial conflicts; and crime and violence in all their forms.

I can illustrate at least some of these impressions—formed over many years of visiting cities around the world, reading their newspapers, and organizing comparative research—by drawing on press accounts of the contemporary urban scene. As this chapter was being written, I decided to summarize the articles in the "Metro" section of the *New York Times* for a single week.[1] I choose the week, from Monday to Saturday, of July 31 through August 5, 1995. In all, some sixty-one substantive articles about New York City were published in this section over the six-day period. The subjects were of great variety, but three major themes tended to prevail. The main subject of the week was crime and violence; the continuing investigation of the World Trade Center bombing, the rape and murder of a lesbian couple, and the killing of two homeless men by a youth gang were presented as major articles. The next most visible subject was traffic and transport, with a variety of stories appearing about bad traffic accidents, proposed fare increases in the public bus and subway system, and particularly noticeable traffic and commuter tie-ups. Third was the local political scene, featured in stories about the political pronouncements of the city's mayor and the governor of the state of New York. Other significant subjects, in declining order of prevalence, were: business and commerce (and the location or decline of local businesses and industrial plants), the police, the weather (this was during the summer during a very hot spell), lifestyle and health, and housing and redevelopment. Had another week been chosen, or another American city, of course, many of the details would have been different, but at the same time the overall themes would have borne at least a family resemblance.

Contrasting this with a typical week in a southern city proved to be difficult, because of the immediate unavailability of comparable newspaper materials. But six days of the major Tanzanian newspaper, *The Daily News,* were available in the Tanzanian Embassy in Washington for the month of May 1995. These copies contained thirty-five articles on events that either took place within Tanzanian cities and towns, or were announced by urban institutions. As in New York, the most prominent theme in terms of the number of articles was crime, almost all of it urban. Since most crime reporting in Tanzania relates to court cases, articles dealt with cases such as a resident of Dar es Salaam appearing before the magistrate, charged with the theft of four chicken gizzards; a Dar es Salaam businessman charged with stealing tires worth approximately $1,100; and an attack by "unknown thugs" on a business in Moshi, seriously injuring the watchman. In this sample, the violence of the crimes does not reach the level and intensity of the crimes in New York. Second, there were various stories on politics, such as the defection of the son of the former president to an opposition party, and the prospective employment of ten thousand polling agents for the upcoming general election. The third most prominent theme was the decline of public infrastructure, including stories urging Tanzanian residents to be more careful with the use of water; the announcement of a contract with a Japanese company to install new telecommunication services across the country; and the seizure in Dar es Salaam of vehicles owned by the Tanzania Electric Supply Company, for nonpayment of taxes. These themes reflect important concerns of Tanzanian urban dwellers. The newspaper stories are different in tone and even in content than those in New York—as one would expect—but the overall interest in the quality of urban life and the political process underlying urban development is common to both urban America and Tanzania.

Because these issues are so varied, and because the city itself is so complex and multifaceted, the scientific study (or should I say the "social scientific study") of cities has moved along two rather distinct paths: an interdisciplinary path and a disciplinary path. The interdisciplinary path, which is represented by interdisciplinary programs of study, by centers and institutes focused on urban studies or urban research as a generic category of activity, and by generic urban journals and publications, has been a persistent feature of the urban field since the postwar expansion of Western universities took its full measure in the 1960s and 1970s. Running parallel to this interdisciplinary structure is the much more powerful and deeply ingrained disciplinary system.

This system consists of university teaching departments based on the central social science disciplines—sociology, economics, political science, geography—and supplemented by research-granting systems largely based on the same disciplines, journals, regular meetings, and other collegial activities. In spite of the potential advantages of undertaking interdisciplinary research on cities, disciplinary research has been the norm over the twenty years discussed in this book. This is not necessarily a detriment to good work, as a brief survey of some of the leading works over the two decades will show. But it presents real difficulties for nonspecialists who wish to understand the problems and functions of cities in their totality. Let us begin to discuss these issues with an overview of a perennial question in urban studies: the disciplinary dilemma.

Disciplinarity and Interdisciplinarity in the Studies of Cities

Over the last century, the scholarly (or scientific) study of man and his environment has become largely the province of individual disciplines. Although this process, and the development of a powerful university structure that incorporates the disciplines, got under way in the second part of the nineteenth century in both Europe and North America, it was in the twentieth century that it accelerated "with a vengeance so that today the basic disciplines have not only clearly identified themselves, but have subdivided internally into many subfields; and often even within these, specialization continues apace." As one Chinese scholar put it, researchers are "looking at the sky from the bottom of the well"—and the wells are decreasing in diameter and increasing in number![2]

In the urban field, the major academic disciplines in the social sciences are economics, political science, geography, sociology, and urban planning. Each is associated with a number of specialized, prestigious journals (which accept for publication only a small fraction of articles submitted to them and screen these articles very closely through an anonymous peer-review process), train their best doctoral students rigorously in a handful of graduate schools to which access is highly rationed, and promote their young professors to quasi-permanent tenure according to the collective judgment of other highly placed professionals in their field. Two interesting aspects of this disciplinarity have been noted. In an article on scholarly reputation in the social sciences, Mattei Dogan and Robert Pahre have developed the idea of the "patrimony" of a discipline, consisting of the capital contribution of many scholars' labor over time. This patrimony is common property to all disciplines and even subdisciplines. "All scholars know the classics of their patrimony, and these exemplars are the standard against which innovation is measured."[3] This patrimony, which changes over time as innovative articles and books are added and others removed (through lack of citation in current work), provides an intellectual map to the most important ideas guiding research and teaching. It is questionable whether such a patrimony exists in an interdisciplinary field such as urban studies, although the subdisciplines of urban economics, urban sociology, urban geography, and even urban politics surely have classics and research protocols to which many scholars refer on a regular basis.

The disciplinary patrimony is part of a wider cluster of beliefs and behavior that constitute a scholarly cultural system. The idea of the faculty culture of the university seems to have originated with the British scientist and novelist C. P. Snow. In his 1959 Rede Lecture at Cambridge University, Snow caused a storm with his thesis that two mutually incomprehensible cultures had grown up in British (and by extension, in American) universities. On one side were the "literary intellectuals," or scholars in the humanities and the arts; on the other side were the "scientists," consisting of teachers and researchers specializing in physics, chemistry, and the "hard" as well as the "life" sciences. According to Snow not only were scholars in one culture ignorant of the most basic texts and principles of the other, but they tended to be recruited from different sociological backgrounds (the scientists from relatively poor families, the literary intellectuals from more affluent families), and held different political beliefs (in Britain at the time, the scientists were apparently more progressive, whereas the literary intellectuals were more conservative) as well. Between these two cultures, said Snow, there was "a gulf of mutual incomprehension—sometimes (particularly among the young) hostility and dislike, but most of all lack of understanding."[4] There was considerable discussion of this thesis following its enunciation in England,[5] and there is evidence that similar patterns exist in North American universities. Based on a questionnaire sent to over one thousand full-time faculty members in six American colleges and universities in the fall of 1968, Jerry Gaff and Robert Wilson concluded that faculty cultures indeed existed in the United States (based on four clusters of disciplines: humanities, social sciences, natural sciences, and professional fields). From responses to a wide range of questions about elements such as teaching practices, orientation toward student participation, political party preference, and religious affiliation and religiosity, the authors demonstrate statistically significant differences between the different clusters of disciplines.

Their conclusion is unequivocal: "Faculty members are ensconced within their respective cultures."[6]

Little that we have learned since the 1970s would lead us to alter this overall judgment about the pervading influence of faculty cultures. Indeed, looking at the phenomenon from the other side—the socialization of doctoral students *before* they enter academia—reinforces the argument. In 1991 a colleague and I carried out a study of doctoral students and those holding recently completed doctorates at my own university, the University of Toronto.[7] From fourteen hundred usable replies to a mailed questionnaire, we found major differences across disciplines with respect to a range of factors describing both the dissertation experience and the nature of the dissertation itself. Dividing the disciplines into the humanities, the social sciences, the physical and engineering sciences, and the life sciences, the data showed clear alternative patterns in both the social characteristics of doctoral students in these different clusters, and in the level and nature of financial support offered, the nature of doctoral supervision, and the time taken to complete the degree. Although the exact details are not important for our purposes here, the most extreme differences between doctoral student subgroups were between the humanities students (or C. P. Snow's "literary intellectuals") and students in the physical and engineering sciences (similar to Snow's "scientists"). Typically, students in the humanities develop their own ideas for a dissertation, choose their own supervisor, work on the dissertation with relatively loose supervisory control, and complete their dissertation after six or seven years of work (on average) in the form of a lengthy manuscript which might, in principle, eventually be published in book form. In the physical sciences, students are often assigned a supervisor, develop the thesis idea in close collaboration with the supervisor and others working on a single project, and (after about four years) complete a number of defined, published papers (often carried out with others) that together certify their scientific ability. Although the greatest differences in academic culture can be observed between the two extremes of the physical sciences and the humanities, the continuum includes the social sciences (more similar to the humanities), and the life sciences (more similar to the physical sciences). Not only is the subject matter very different among the disciplines and discipline clusters, but the experience of being a graduate student—for many one of the most formative periods in their lives—is also a distinct function of the academic culture in which the student is placed.

On the surface, these observations about the strong persistence of discipline-based academic cultures among university scholars may seem remote from the subject of this chapter: the studies of cities. But they are not. The difficulty of writing both engaging and analytically sound prose about those complex and changing phenomena we call cities has preoccupied scholars for some time. Writing in 1973, the geographer David Harvey pointed out that, although the city was "manifestly a complicated thing," our problems in dealing with cities could also be ascribed to conceptual limitations due to

> academic and professional specialization on certain aspects of city processes. Clearly, the city cannot be conceptualized in terms of our present disciplinary structures. Yet there is very little sign of an emerging interdisciplinary framework for thinking, let alone theorizing, about the city. Sociologists, economists, geographers, architects, city planners, and so on, all appear to plough lonely furrows and to live in their own confined conceptual worlds.[8]

Ten years later, Manuel Castells, a sociologist, lamented what he called "an increasing gap between urban research and urban problems." He argued that over the previous thirty years there had been substantial progress in many specialized fields such as land-use planning, urban design, and regional development. "Yet, we are still helpless when we wish to act on cities and regions, because we ignore the courses of their social change and fail to identify with sufficient accuracy the political processes underlying urban management." He concluded that in spite of "serious efforts at gathering data and elaborating theory in the aftermath of urban crises and protests," scholars had not yet satisfactorily understood "the fundamental processes at work in the production of the material basis of most of our experience: the city."[9]

Both of these scholars, outstanding in their own disciplines, were making a serious charge. The academic study of cities, they said, had not come to grips with the actuality of city life. Perhaps their own studies were intended to remedy this failure, but in spite of their best efforts, the tension between academic research and writing on cities, and the evolving reality of cities all over the world, has remained an acknowledged feature of this field. Can the tunnel vision of academic specialization be overcome by its logical opposite, interdisciplinarity? In principle, there are very good arguments for interdisciplinary studies at the university level. If we define "interdisciplinary studies" as an approach to thinking and research that integrates the contributions of several disciplines to a problem or issue, the approach can be justified on intellectual, practical, and pedagogical grounds.[10] Intellectually, interdisciplinarity can overcome overspecialization and fragmentation of subject matter; practically, most real-world problems have many aspects (sociological, economic, political, and geographical, to name just a few) that overlap and interrelate; proper comprehension requires complex understanding of these differential aspects. Finally, the argument is frequently and cogently made that an elusive "unity of knowledge" represents the best traditions of the university; this unity can at least be approached by undergraduate students in the programs of liberal education.[11]

While collaboration among disciplines has been taking place throughout the academic world in the North as well as the South, the path has not been an easy one. Many influential scholars who are themselves in favor of advances in interdisciplinarity admit that little progress has been made over the past twenty years. Nathan Keyfitz, for example, a sociologist and demographer who has done important work in the urban field, argues that "[t]he best one can say for each discipline is that in abstracting one aspect of what it deals with it projects the real-world round phenomenon onto a flat screen; the representation can be recognizable, but it is never self-contained."[12] He further argues that interdisciplinary study is more difficult than had been anticipated, partly because of the recondite organization of academic life into disciplines; and partly because mastering one discipline is difficult, let alone mastering two or more, which, in principle, is necessary to be truly interdisciplinary. (Being truly interdisciplinary appears to be as difficult as being truly bilingual, or even trilingual!) And even in so-called area studies programs (where the focus is on the study of the interrelated aspects of a single region of the developing world), the experience in the United States, at least, is that the best graduate students take courses almost entirely in their own major discipline; and that the tendency for the teaching staff "is for more and more disciplinary specialization."[13]

Falling short in reaching the goal of functional interdisciplinarity is not for lack of trying. In the urban field, for example, there are numerous undergraduate programs in urban studies throughout the United States and Canada, in which students are taught general urban subject matter by professors from a variety of different home disciplines. At the undergraduate level, the Urban Affairs Association listed twenty-eight urban studies bachelor's degrees in the United States and Canada in its 1994 guide. The same guide listed sixty-five masters programs (the bulk of which were in urban planning), and twenty-seven doctoral programs.[14] There are, in fact, many more programs than this, since membership in the association was a prerequisite for listing. But at the master's, and even more at the doctoral level, training, research, and dissertation work tends to fall into disciplinary areas, even when professors from a number of different disciplines work and teach together in the same program. Indeed, a careful evaluation of thirty-three urban studies and urban affairs (US/UA) programs at both the master's and doctoral levels in the United States, carried out in the early 1990s, showed that "[a]s a multidisciplinary enterprise, US/UA tends to be defined more by its subfields than by a central paradigm. Faculty in these subfields are still primarily drawn from allied social science disciplines to which their allegiance can be expected to remain strong."[15]

The cumulative importance of disciplines in writing about urban America was a central element in Russell Jacoby's thesis, published in the late 1980s as *The Last Intellectuals*. In this widely discussed book, Jacoby laments what he considers the almost total absence of a generation of visible, young, critical intellectuals in American life. In his view, the main reason for this is the co-optation of intellectuals by the universities, and in the process a bureaucratization of their critical message. The socialization of these young intellectuals into the academic culture was highly focused on the experience of the doctoral dissertation, the planning and execution of which—"often ridiculed by the outsider—loomed large. . . . For many young intellectuals it was the cultural event and context of their lives. When completed it could not be ignored; the dissertation became part of them. The research style, the idiom, the sense of the 'discipline', and one's place in it: these branded their intellectual souls."[16] The gradual loss of arresting intellectual expression is particularly conspicuous, says Jacoby, in the urban field. He argues that, at the same time as there was an expansion of urban studies in the universities, the "universe of independent journalists and scholars" was dwindling. And as urbanist intellectuals moved from the large cities to the suburban and small-town university campuses, their contact with the realities of the urban crisis was further attenuated. "For this reason urbanism shares with other fields a peculiar cultural trajectory: a rising curve of compelling writings that crests at the end of the 1950s, and afterward a steep decline with few additions by younger thinkers fired by the same caliber of imagination, boldness—or writing."[17]

Disciplinary specialization in urban studies in the North is paralleled by a somewhat similar pattern in developing countries. A large-scale survey of urban research and writing in forty-one countries, supported by the Ford Foundation and carried out by developing-country researchers themselves, established two prominent tendencies. In the first place, urban research in each of the three main regions studied—Latin America, Africa, and Asia—tended to be dominated by one or two major disciplines.[18] These disciplines set the tone and asked the major questions that animated urban research over long periods in these regions. In Latin America, the dominant disciplines were sociology and architecture/urban planning; in Africa the single dominant discipline in the urban field has been geography; in Asia, economics and regional planning have been dominant. Other disciplines have played an important role in some countries, but overall one is struck by the clustering of disciplines—and, by the same token, by the major questions being discussed—from region to region. A second tendency, which is a more direct reflection of the northern academic system in which so many of the leading southern intellectuals have been trained at the postgraduate level (this influence is particularly strong in the Francophone countries of Africa), is that interdisciplinary work has played, at best, a marginal role. Notwithstanding the fact that the last decade-and-a-half has seen an enormous increase in the sheer bulk and variety of urban research in most parts of the developing world—an increase for which local, rather than expatriate, researchers are largely responsible—compartmentalization of work has remained a major problem. One important reason for this boundary mentality is the increasing attractiveness of research consultancies to individual researchers, an influence that has the effect of privatizing a great deal of scientific work. Another persistent factor is what a Tanzanian writer calls "professional parochialism." As Mohamed Halfani observes, urban research studies in East Africa

> are conducted within the confines of single departments and institutes, thus reinforcing the disciplinary orientation of the particular department and even that of individuals. At this time, when we need to understand the broader dynamics of urban development as they are impacted by a number of forces, the need for networking is more than just a functional requirement. Compartmentalization tends to undermine that process.[19]

Multiple Visions and Common Problems: The Urban Research Agenda from the 1960s to the 1990s

As they struggle with the tension between an emerging (and always changing) urban reality and the development of their disciplines, researchers tend to be influenced in their choice of subject matter by a succession of overarching themes, established both within and often outside their own specialties. These themes are part of a research agenda—a complex of currently fashionable ideas, methodological approaches, and policy goals—that provides a focus for research and links (at least to some extent) the researchers to the real world of cities.

To illustrate the existence of such a (changing) research agenda, we will take a brief excursion into the proximate history of urban studies. This short journey will be far from complete as an intellectual history of the last three decades, and inevitably subjective, but it will serve to illustrate the influence of an external framework of exemplary works and urban ideas on a great deal of the research of the scholarly community. Our excursion will also illustrate the partial nature of leading studies in the field, and the continuing tension between academic work (often but not always highly disciplinary in style and content) and the real world of cities.

The starting point for much of the work on cities—at least in North America—was the ecological model of the Chicago school of sociology, a model that explained urban processes as a result of the interaction between the economics of space and land use on the one hand, and population movement on the other. Writing of a period during the 1920s and 1930s, when large numbers of immigrants were moving into American cities and experiencing difficulties in achieving social and economic integration into American society, this influential group, working in the Department of Sociology at the University of Chicago, focused on such themes as marginalization and integration, and the prerequisites for the achievement of urban community life.[20] Since many of the new migrants came from rural areas (in either the United States or Europe), the city represented a major cultural transformation from close, supportive social structures to competitive, impersonal life. This new culture of the city was central to the classic article by Louis Wirth, "Urbanism as a Way of Life," published in the *American Journal of Sociology* in 1938.

While many sociologists in North America were writing about the processes of urban integration (or marginalization), urban planners all over the world were designing new city forms that were heavily influenced by old ideas. Particularly important in the English-speaking world (including the colonial cities of Africa and Asia) were the ideas of Ebenezer Howard (a visionary court reporter) for the planning of a new kind of town (the "Garden City") where the urban poor might live closer to nature. Howard's planning ideas, together with the influence of Patrick Geddes (a Scottish regional planner) and the reinforcement of American planners led to principles of urban planning that focused on the provision of wholesome housing; separated residential, commercial, and industrial uses of urban land; stressed the value of suburbs and small towns rather than large, diverse metropolises; and conceived of an overall planning function in terms of central direction from a government planning or development agency. The New Towns in postwar

Britain, and the extensive urban renewal movement in the United States (involving 912 municipalities between 1945 and 1968)[21] were physical embodiments of many of these ideas. Arguing that these ideas were profoundly mistaken, Jane Jacobs presented an alternative in her powerful book, *The Death and Life of Great American Cities*, published in 1961. Jacobs, a writer and journalist, was concerned to show that large cities can be productive and socially useful if planners recognize that cities are the site of "a most intricate and close-grained diversity of uses that give each other constant mutual support, both economically and socially."[22] Using a wealth of examples based on her close observation of functioning downtown American neighborhoods, Jacobs looked at the micromechanisms and design principles leading to active street life, thriving petty commerce, and supportive patterns of social interaction that produce tightly knit, diverse communities even when most of the people are poor. Her solution to the government of large cities was to decentralize their administration; local administrators would have a close understanding of the originality and complexity of their individual districts. These ideas had a profound effect on generations of planning teachers and students, but they also reinforced resistance in Canada and the United States to large-scale, often very expensive schemes to build more freeways through decaying neighborhoods, to the continued building of large-scale "housing estates" for the poor and not-so-poor, and to principles of suburban planning that separated residential from small-scale commercial land use.

Jacobs's book raised many issues of local political responsibility for the solution of urban problems. As it was being published, a major examination of the local political process was released. This was the landmark study by Robert Dahl on New Haven (a city of approximately 165,000 in Connecticut, north of New York City) entitled *Who Governs?* The more revealing subtitle of the book was "Democracy and Power in an American City."[23] Written less as a study of a city to understand urban politics than as a study of a city to investigate wider patterns in the American political system, the book's argument that local (and by extension, national) politics were a system of dispersed rather than cumulative inequalities in which political resources were widely distributed and problems could be solved by leaders working within pragmatic coalitions, was a powerful influence on debates over American democracy in the 1960s and 1970s. A number of Dahl's students became important political scientists in later years;[24] and his ideas of local pluralist democracy were widely discussed, particularly in the heated atmosphere of the Vietnam war and its aftermath. Partly because of Dahl's probing and spirited work, a generation of political scientists were drawn to urban studies, which until then had been largely the province of sociology and geography. But in this stage of its development, political science proper (as distinguished from public administration) turned its attention to relatively small cities and towns, rather than the large, much more complex and confusing metropolitan centers. Major reasons for this were that manageable doctoral dissertations could more easily be undertaken in relatively small towns; and that many of the country's major university campuses were located in small towns where professors could carry out fieldwork with a minimum of dislocation and expense.

The political problems of the large cities—as the turbulent 1960s and 1970s demonstrated in both Europe and North America—were much more intractable. By the 1970s, the political geography of large northern cities was beginning to shift. This shift was clearly demonstrated in an important collection of essays edited by the geographer Brian Berry, entitled *Urbanization and Counter-Urbanization.*[25] What the most recent census figures were showing—at least in Western Europe and the United States—was that the hitherto rapid growth of the largest metropolitan areas had begun to decline, whereas medium-sized cities and the metropolitan fringe (outside what are often called the "suburbs") gained significantly in population and employment. This economic and population shift led Berry to state unequivocally, "Counterurbanization has replaced urbanization as the dominant force shaping the nation's settlement patterns. A similar tendency has been noted in other Western nations."[26] Whereas the process in Britain and France seems to have been a response to affluence (better road and commuter transport and positive government policies helped to develop new towns and regional growth poles outside the largest cities), in the United States transport and affluence were combined with a reaction by middle-class whites to the troubled conditions of the central city. "[T]he accompaniment of the process of counterurbanization is urban decay and the abandonment of the nonachieving social underclass; ghetto growth is a product of the white exodus."[27] Since the 1970s, urban geographers and planners have paid considerable attention to the changes in urban systems that these population movements represent; but the consensus, even in the 1990s, is that the operation of economic forces on urban-settlement configuration is much more powerful than the sporadic attempts of planners and elected city officials to achieve a "more desirable" urban form or regional distribution pattern.

At the same time as the largest cities in the North were losing relative power and demographic weight, cities in the South were adding enormous quantities of new migrants on a yearly basis, without the economic growth to absorb their numbers in an equitable fashion. Indeed, the apparent contradiction between massive urban population growth and the limited expansion of secondary manufacturing employment was the central theme in a superb study, *The Southeast Asian City*, by the Australian geographer T. G. McGee. Juxtaposing the European experience with urban development, which he called the "true urban revolution," with the current situation in the majority of Third World countries that were "undergoing a phase of pseudo urbanization" in which urban growth was not apparently connected with economic development, McGee expertly and subtly explored the history and current socioeconomic conditions of the major Southeast Asian cities. He argued that the enormous explosion of low-paying tertiary sector jobs (such as street hawkers, pedi-cab drivers, domestic servants, office peons) was symptomatic of the failure of the political elites (who lived comfortably in the cities) to come to terms with the needs of the countryside in formulating development policies. But it was the poor slum-dwellers and street hawkers, not the elites, who were "the 'real' people of the Southeast Asian city. Their struggle for a livelihood dominates all and their poverty is all-pervading."[28] Much of the analysis of the book was a spirited and informed dialogue with other urban researchers studying Asian cities, for whom a major concern was the question of whether cities had a "parasitic" or "generative" relation with the rest of the country.[29] McGee's inclination was to lean to the "parasitic" side in most cases (the most extreme being South Vietnam), while showing great sympathy for rural-urban migrants who "come to the city to alleviate their rural poverty, only to find it is replaced by urban poverty."[30]

As the magnitude and implications of Third World urbanization began to dawn on researchers and international agencies based in northern countries, two major themes occupied a central position in the research and policy agenda during the next decade: employment and housing. Underlying both, and in some ways the most profound preoccupation of many in the North, who were concerned lest Third World cities explode, or at least become increasingly unstable, thus affecting their countries' chances for sustained development, was the issue of poverty.[31]

During the 1950s and 1960s, as urban growth in the developing world became a visible problem, the first response of social scientists was to look at the source of this growth. Thus, studies proliferated on the demography of cities, and on the causes and consequences of the most important component of this growth—rural–urban migration. Anthropologists and sociologists were prominent in the study of the migration process, looking at both the small rural communities that prospective urban migrants left, and the microprocesses of adaptation to the drastically changed circumstances of life in the city. But the paradox of so many migrants leaving agricultural areas for a life of almost certain underemployment and poverty in the city was a puzzle until an econometric model was developed by two American economists, John Harris and Michael Todaro, attempting to explain the process in Africa. In their article, published in the *American Economic Review* in 1970, Harris and Todaro explain the logic behind rural–urban migration in Africa by rural dwellers' perception of their eventual chances for high-paid, secure urban employment, even though high levels of urban employment persist in the short run. The Harris/Todaro model, which assumed rational choice and eventual equilibrium between urban and rural wages (at least in the long run), provided an important intellectual bridge for the entry of a new cohort of development economists into the urban field in the Third World. Many of these economists worked on labor markets: specifically on the parameters and policy implications of dual labor markets—the relatively high-wage sector characteristic of large firms, the government, educational institutions and the like; and the relatively low-wage, unprotected sector in which small-scale enterprises and marginal workers competed for subsistence. This unprotected sector came to be called the "informal" sector, following a major report on Kenya by a mission of the International Labor Office (ILO) in Geneva, published in 1972. The leader of this mission was the British economist Hans Singer, of the University of Sussex. The informal sector had been explicitly identified by the anthropologist Keith Hart in his study of urban migrants to Accra, Ghana,[32] but it was measured and more precisely defined by the ILO study. At the time of the ILO study, for example, economists estimated that from 25 to 30 percent of total urban employment in Kenya was in the informal sector, with the caveat that this figure "seem[ed] rather low by comparison with other African countries for which similar data [were] available."[33]

Following the pathbreaking ILO report, a great deal of research was published on the informal sector throughout the developing world. The ILO itself took a leading role in sponsoring many of these studies, publishing them in the five United Nations languages and distributing them throughout the world. Much of this work was carried out by economists, some of whom worked in the neoclassical tradition, and some of whom were Marxists. In many ways the geographical counterpart to the publications of the neo-Marxist economists was a work by a Brazilian geographer trained in France, Milton Santos. Santos's book, *The Shared Space: The Two Circuits of the Urban Economy in Under-*

developed Countries attempted to come to grips with the interaction between economic and spatial dualism in cities of the developing world.[34] In the tradition of the "underdevelopment" approach (according to which Third World economies were not proceeding along the same paths that northern countries had followed), Santos developed a "two circuit" model to deal with the extreme disparities and lack of articulation between major sectors of southern urban economies. Simply, the upper circuit consisted of "banking, export trade and industry, modern urban industry, trade and services, and wholesaling and trucking." By contrast, the lower circuit was made up of "non-capital-intensive forms of manufacturing, non-modern services generally provided at the 'retail' level and non-modern and small-scale trade."[35] In practice, the lower circuit, with its typical income generation and uses of space, was dependent on the upper circuit; subordination of the poor to the rich, and the perpetuation of poverty was one of the key features of the lower circuit. Each circuit had its logic. Moreover, more-developed cities, which ranked higher in terms of infrastructure and amenities, tended to attract more upper-circuit activities, whereas less-developed cities tended to attract a higher proportion of lower-circuit activities. Although this model was essentially descriptive, it had the ability to integrate spatial and economic variables, and to generate thinking about how governments might integrate the lower with the upper circuit. Santos suggested that governments promote the concept of social, rather than economic, productivity but he readily admitted that, in the absence of major transformations in the organization of technology and capital, there would be a "difficulty in making this model operational."[36] Whatever its practical value, the book served for many years as a major bridge between the geography of underdevelopment and the newly apprehended reality of the informal sector.

But arguably the most influential (or at least thought-provoking) study was a book by Hernando de Soto, a Peruvian lawyer working through a nongovernmental organization in Lima. A translation of the book, which had been originally published in Spanish in 1986, was released in English in 1989 as *The Other Path: The Invisible Revolution in the Third World*. This book has become important for three reasons. First, it is written in simple language, following an outline designed to convince a nonspecialist audience. The foreword to the book, written by the novelist Mario Vargas Llosa, compliments the writer for telling his story well: "based [as it is] entirely on Peruvian reality . . . unlike run-of-the-mill economic and sociological essays on Latin America, which seek to be abstract and end up distanced from any specific society, *The*

Other Path never strays from the real world."[37] Second, it presents a great deal of fascinating and original information on both the scope and functioning of various informal sector activities in Lima (informal housing, trade, and transport in particular). For example, we learn that 47 percent of Lima's population lives in informal housing, worth some $8.3 billion; that there are 91,455 street vendors, who support over 314,000 relatives and dependents; and that 93 percent of the urban transport fleet is in the hands of informal operators.[38] Third, the book offers a complex yet highly credible explanation (followed by proposals for reform) for the persistence of a two-sector economy that is so costly in terms of lost productivity. This is a model of Peru as a mercantilist country, in which powerful economic interest groups control the executive branch, which in turn passes laws that redistribute wealth from the poor to the rich. The reaction against mercantilism in Peru, says de Soto, is the revolution of informality. To support the positive aspects of this revolution, and to build human capital in the process in the form of entrepreneurial and managerial skill, the author proposes a number of legal reforms including more accessible property rights for the poor, simplification of legal institutions, decentralization, and deregulation. Because these proposals accord with the general principles of neoliberal economics, the book and its author have won a large following in the North.

From a planning point of view, one of the most important areas of concern was the increasing incidence of slums and squatter settlements in the cities of the developing world. In these areas, typical residents were poor recent migrants living on unserviced and often marginal land (near swamps, on steep hillsides, in river valleys subject to flooding) to which they had no legal title. Because of the lack of tenure, building permission for the structures was absent, and the quality of the dwellings was often extremely flimsy. As the proportion of the urban population living in these areas began to rise to over 20 percent, and even over 30 percent during the 1960s, planning agencies felt threatened, and health authorities (fearful of outbreaks of disease) were alarmed. Meanwhile, church groups and volunteer agencies took the side of the squatters on humanitarian grounds. Authorities battled the onslaught of squatters whose numbers rose steadily. A new approach to this dilemma, based on support for the legitimate aspirations of the squatters rather than resistance to them, began to unfold in Peru. It was reflected in the writings of the English architect John F. C. Turner, who worked in Peru during the 1950s and 1960s. Turner's first important paper was delivered at a technical seminar of the United Nations in 1966, but was not formally published until 1969. In this paper Turner

argued that slums and shantytowns were, rather than retograde phenomena, actually "forward-moving vehicles of social and economic
change." By contrast, the typical substitute for these settlements (once
they were bulldozed out of existence), the large-scale, publicly
financed housing projects, were overly costly to the state and ineffective in meeting the needs of their lower-income tenants. Turning conventional wisdom on its ear, Turner said, "The basic problem of the
slums is not how to eradicate them, but how to make them livable."[39]
In a major book entitled *Housing by People: Towards Autonomy in Building Environments*, which appeared in 1976, just in time for the first Habitat conference in Vancouver, Turner continued to develop his ideas on
the benefits of self-help housing, bringing in further experience he had
with the American self-help and owner-built housing movement. A
crucial principle expressed in this book is that large-scale organizations
(such as central-government planning and construction agencies) cannot possibly respond to the great variety of individual economic and
social needs expressed in any typical community. As examples of individual sweat equity responses to changing family needs during different periods of the life cycle (from the need for a single room of the first
male migrant to the need for a much larger house and even commercial facility of a more mature family with older children or even older
dependents), squatter communities function in a more flexible and economically efficient manner. Turner's overall message was that people
can plan their own housing better than governments can, although they
do need some support in the form of infrastructural services and policy guidelines. An avowed "conservative anarchist," Turner's spirited
and energetic promotion of his ideas had a great effect on the policies
of international agencies from the late 1960s through the 1970s. And
although he would have rejected the attribution of parentage, it seems
clear that his ideas contributed strongly to the development of the
World Bank's sites and services program that cut a large swath through
the urban development world during the 1970s.[40]

Although Turner's writings on popular settlements were applicable
to other parts of the developing world, the fact that the discussion
more often than not centered on Latin America was a result of two
factors: the more advanced level of urbanization in Latin America as
compared with other Third World regions; and the high quality of
intellectual and technical debates in Latin America on the subjects of
development and marginality. Two important studies, both of which
appeared in the mid-1970s, address different aspects of these debates.
The first to appear in English was *The Myth of Marginality: Urban
Poverty and Politics in Rio de Janeiro*, written by Janice Perlman, a plan-

ner trained in sociology and anthropology, who looked at the plight of *favela* (slum) dwellers in Brazil's second largest city, and examined the impact and implications of the government's attempts to eradicate their settlements.[41] Based largely on her own surveys and close observation of *favela* dwellers in three communities, Perlman was able to argue that, far from being marginal and threatening to the society (as was often claimed), the urban poor performed a number of valuable functions within Brazilian society; in fact, they were an integral and necessary part of the system. Eradication of *favelas* (which took place in some cases during the period of her research) and eventual relocation of the families to new housing estates was not only costly and inefficient as Turner showed, but morally wrong considering the burden that the urban poor already carried, and unwise given their importance to the continued economic life of the city. But repression and arbitrary action against the *favelados* during the period of the military government in Brazil gradually became much more widespread and uncompromising than it had been during the period before the military coup in 1964, when the *favelados* could vote at least for the governor and local officials. Aside from its revisionist arguments about marginality, which struck an important chord within the Latin American development community, Perlman's book presented its ideas clearly and attractively (with maps and photographs), looking at the urban field from the vantage point of planning, politics, economics, and sociology. A foreword to the book, written by the well-known economist Fernando Henrique Cardoso (currently president of Brazil) commends the author for her "empathetic understanding" of the people she studied.

Another outstanding study of a low-income urban community—in this case, a shantytown in Mexico City—similarly dealt with the question of marginality. A classic case study of an urban settlement, the Mexican anthropologist Larissa Lomnitz's book *Networks and Marginality: Life in a Mexican Shantytown* explored the survival strategies of the urban poor. Her study of a small, peripheral shantytown that sprawled over the slopes of a ravine looked at the reciprocal social and kinship ties and networks that the settlers used for support in spite of their marginal economic position in the larger system.[42] In a compelling examination of the functioning of such traditional institutions as *compadrazgo* (fictive kinship or godparenthood) and *cuatismo* (a form of male friendship), which are used in reciprocal relationships, and the concept of *confianza* (loosely translated as trust, or confidence in someone), the author shows how this community manages to organize mutual support under difficult circumstances. Aside from a dense network of extended family ties, the community (of 176 households) had four football teams, a medical center (originally financed and organized by a middle-class woman from the adjacent neighborhood), and a number of temporary associations for specific purposes, often formed by small groups of neighbors. While the marginals of this community had to struggle for survival in a city that afforded them only leftovers ("leftover jobs, leftover trades, leftover living space, and homes built of leftovers"[43]), they were able to convert social resources into some level of economic security. Later studies of social organization in popular settlements in Latin America and elsewhere were to look more closely at the role of women in organizing and maintaining social networks.

Underlying and reinforcing the interest of social scientists in the phenomenon of urban marginality was an emerging, essentially Marxist approach to urban sociology and social geography. The intellectual history of this period is complex and multifaceted, but suffice it to say that the analysis of the subordinate role of Latin American societies in the world economy (and the logic and mechanisms of class subordination at the local level) was explained by such concepts as "underdevelopment" and "dependency." This southern perspective was supported by a robust Marxist approach to social questions in the North, an approach that focused on the role of the state in capitalist societies as it represented, to a greater or lesser degree, class interests or fractions of capital in serving its long-term interests. Two of the leading writers taking this approach in the urban field were David Harvey and Manuel Castells. In *Social Justice and the City*, the geographer David Harvey explored a wide range of theoretical questions concerning space, "urbanism," and social justice.[44] The book was an extended commentary on various important urban issues of the time, interpreted through a dense thicket of neo-Marxist categories and distinctions, and drawing heavily on contemporary European writers. The longest chapter in the book, entitled "Urbanism and the City," attempted to develop a "socialist formulation" of urban phenomena, based on the premise that process and conflict in the city reflected capitalist dynamics in the wider society. Its appealing title notwithstanding, the obdurate language and elaborate scholarly discourse of this book made it virtually impenetrable to non-academic readers; but within intellectual circles of geography and urban sociology, Harvey's book raised important issues of both methodology and substantive interpretation of the contemporary urban crisis.

Somewhat more accommodating in its language and theoretical formulations—at least to the world outside the confines of the university—was the important book by Manuel Castells, *The Urban Question:*

A Marxist Approach. The book, which originally appeared in French in 1972, was finally published in English in 1977.[45] Much more grounded in the issues of everyday urban reality than Harvey's work, Castells's book also sought to develop an all-embracing Marxist approach to the urban, in his case drawing heavily on the formulations of the French philosopher Louis Althusser. (In his preface to the English edition of the book, Castells makes an interesting reference to "the excesses of the Althusserian language," and the fact that "certain discussions around the concepts employed were superfluous and . . . the degree of formalism in my construction was useless at the actual research level."[46]) Although the book seeks to confront a number of important issues (such as the formation of metropolitan regions, the U.S. urban crisis, urban political-economic structures, and urban social movements) through the lenses of Marxist analysis, its most enduring influence in the urban field is a critique of the Chicago school of sociology. With telling force, Castells challenges the "universalistic" qualities of urban life proposed by Wirth in his famous definition of the city. These qualities, which included social relations that were impersonal, superficial, transitory, and segmental, are attacked by Castells as a function of a particular moment in capitalist evolution, which the Chicago sociologists presumably could not see since they looked at the city in narrow, ideological terms.[47] Looking at received sociological precepts in this fashion had a major impact on urban sociology elsewhere in the world, particularly in Latin America, where Castells' work was well known because of his earlier studies in Chile and his publications in Spanish, and because he worked within the French school of sociology which has always had a major influence over urban sociology in Latin America.[48]

Further evidence of the French influence on Latin American urban sociology came by way of the proliferation, from the 1970s through the mid-1980s, of urban social movements in many countries. These movements, reflecting broad-based, often multiclass, coordinated activity at the local level to achieve specific improvements in living conditions or collective consumption goods (such as public transport, water, or other urban amenities) were a feature of many Latin American countries during the later period of military rule. Based on the French experience of the events of May 1968, and the emergence in France of many single-issue movements contesting various aspects of everyday life, Alain Touraine developed an approach to these developments that he called "class struggle without classes," or "social movements."[49] Supported by Touraine's work, but drawing from a vast range of historical and contemporary sources in both the North and the South, Castells produced a mammoth work on urban protest movements, *The City and the*

Grassroots, published in 1983.[50] Combining such disparate cases as the Castille commune in the sixteenth century; the Paris commune in 1871; trade-union movements and housing protests in Paris; the gay community in San Francisco; and squatters, marginality, and the state in Latin America, Castells attempted to put together a comprehensive interpretation of local activism. In his formulation, contemporary urban social movements are attempting to reassert the intrinsic value of their neighborhoods, as against the tendency to commoditize urban living and urban services; to create, or to maintain, a sense of autonomous local culture; and to gain increasing power at the local level. Since the movements express the objectives of a wide variety of citizens who are not normally involved in formal institutions (such as political parties), they have a spontaneous, democratic quality. One way of interpreting their actions, argues Castells, is to suggest that these movements are groping toward an "alternative city" that has more meaning to them than the current structures in which they live. Castells argues that the emphasis of these movements on what is local is due to the fact that national structures no longer seem accessible. As Latin American countries decentralize in the 1990s, and newly democratic local government structures form alliances with community groups in a context of shrinking government resources for services and amenities, the ideas of the social movement theorists continue to have relevance.

To complete my selective overview of the exemplars of urban studies as we approach the Habitat II conference, I must mention two final works on northern cities. The first, by the sociologists John Logan and Harvey Molotch, is entitled *Urban Fortunes: The Political Economy of Place*.[51] This book, which grew out of a much earlier article published in the *American Journal of Sociology* in 1976, develops and elaborates on the idea that the most significant shared objective of urban leaders in the United States is to enhance economic development in all its forms. Thus, to the authors, the American city is primarily a "growth machine," whose leading coalition (comprising elected politicians, civic officials, and business and community leaders) pursues various strategies to attract investment and to distribute the income from this investment among its members. To the extent that cities in other countries have strong local political autonomy, combined with a laissez-faire capitalist culture that permits the widespread commoditization of land, say the authors, they should also be described by this model. In any case, the most active players in this growth-oriented coalition are such groups as real estate developers, utilities, and newspapers, although auxiliary players such as universities, cultural institutions (such as

museums, theaters, and expositions), professional sports owners, organized labor, and small retailers are also supportive. The pursuit of
growth (based on the importance of exchange values) undermines such
goals as social integration, the protection of the natural environment,
and the maintenance of a relatively low level of population density (all
of which are "use values"), thus leading to conflict in the community.
Molotch and Logan explore the dynamics of such a model of urban
political economy with respect to the role of government and the multiple issues presented by housing and community development. A significant implication of this model is that American cities—like cities in
so many other parts of the world—are becoming much more dependent on international business trends and capital movement than ever.
Among the most important aspects of this study are that it looks at the
dynamics of local leadership in relationship to the community's economic needs, and that it presents the competition between cities—a feature that has become important since the 1980s—in a coherent and
credible framework that helps to explain the interaction between local
and international.

The last influential work to be highlighted in this account is *The
Global City: New York, London, Tokyo,* by Saskia Sassen, a professor of
planning at Columbia University in New York.[52] In the increasingly frenetic climate of globalization and transnational economic competition
that has characterized the current decade, this book has become a classic for its analysis of the effects of this globalizing process on the
world's major cities. Other chapters in this volume (notably those by
Savitch and Wu) discuss aspects of the globalization theme. The contribution of Sassen's book resides in three key areas: its demonstration
of the emergence and magnitude of new patterns of direct foreign
investment as a result of mobility of capital and advanced telecommunications; the association of the financial industry physically in the
dominant world capitals (particularly New York, Tokyo, and London)
and the development of affiliated services (such as management consultants, accountancy firms, stock markets, financial instrument
houses, and cultural institutions) connected to the financial industry;
and the social and spatial effects on world cities of these phenomena.
In terms of the book's identification of new forms of urban development, what is most striking is the social polarization which seems to
result from extreme concentration of financial institutions in individual
cities. In the three major cities studied, for example, Sassen finds evidence of the accumulation of high-paying (though often insecure) professional positions related to the financial industry on the one hand,
combined with high-income gentrification and the high-end consump-

tion patterns that this entails; and on the other hand, an increase in low-wage, repetitive jobs in the service sector, along with an increase in casual and informal labor with no fringe benefits and no returns to seniority. In spite of the wealth generated by the financial industry and its associated subsectors, overall unemployment figures are up, certain racial groups tend to cluster in the lowest-paid and least-secure jobs, and the local and even national governments have little control over the disposition of economic activity. Among the many important questions posed by this book is the question of trade-offs: At what point does the increasing poverty of large numbers of workers lead to a political and social situation that directly affects the performance of core industries? "How many times do high-income executives have to step over the bodies of homeless people till this becomes an unacceptable fact or discomfort?"[53] These questions are being asked in many large cities throughout the world, but even more, apparently, in the global cities that sit at the very top of the urban hierarchy.

The research story does not end here. As scholars and urban activists put their minds and their efforts toward the organization of the Habitat II conference in June 1996, many other themes are rising to the surface. For example, as I mentioned in the first section of this chapter, urban violence is a preoccupying issue in many cities, both in the North and in the South. Although there has not yet been a strong effort to write about this in the research community (perhaps there are too many occupational hazards), it is certain to attract more interest, particularly because of the gendered nature of violence and risk. Another issue that is currently collecting converts is the question of local governance—as understood broadly by the relationship between civil society and government. Within this broad relationship are important questions about what some analysts call "social capital," defined by Robert Putnam as "features of social organization, such as trust, norms, and networks, that can improve the efficiency of society by facilitating coordinated actions."[54] Since these features are most often visible at the local level, it is important to learn how different societies can organize themselves to promote more effective local governance. Finally, there is the question of the environment, and the role cities, their governments, and their citizens can play in controlling pollution and noxious environmental effects and in the process improving (or at least maintaining) the quality of their lives. The challenge to researchers, as they respond to emerging issues presented by the changing urban reality, is to disseminate their message more effectively to the wider policy and activist community, while maintaining credible levels of logical argument and scientific integrity. The two goals are not incompatible.

Conclusion

There is always a tension between the rapidly changing reality of the modern city, as understood by ordinary people and the popular media, and the reality that is conveyed by scholarly researchers. As I have argued, one of the reasons for this tension is the fragmentation of understanding created by the division of the academic world into disciplines and subdisciplines. These divisions derive their logic from the historical development of the university research enterprise, as well as from the difficulty of treating the very complex problems of society in a holistic manner. Although this fragmentation shows no immediate signs of being successfully overcome, there are many initiatives at the level of both the academy and of donor agencies to look at urban problems from an interdisciplinary, rather than a purely disciplinary, perspective.

In spite of the powerful institutional forces that continue to drive the disciplinary perspective in the urban field, there have been exemplary studies of the city that, in most cases, are easily accessible to nonspecialists. Some of the key works are discussed in this chapter, but there are many more that could not be included. These studies set the tone for the field of urban studies in both the North and the South, and at the same time become the focus for the major issues on the urban research agenda. Although these issues are often studied segmentally, they also have a broader resonance within both the research and the policy communities. To take three examples from the works presented here, Jane Jacobs's pioneering study of urban street life had a significant effect on community battles with developers for many years after her book appeared in 1961; Manuel Castells's work on urban social movements helped to reinforce the powerful urban forces in Latin America that were actively demanding democratic local governance; and the work by Saskia Sassen on global cities has been an important part of a new debate on the real effects of the globalization of capital, labor, and technology. To better understand and cope with the fascinating and complex world of the emerging city, we need more excellent research. But we also need researchers to remember that there is a potentially large and very important audience of readers and political activists outside the boundaries of their academic disciplines.

Notes

[1] I wish to thank my intern for the summer, Caeli Quinn, for her excellent work in summarizing the contents of the *New York Times* and the Tanzanian *Daily News*. Her imagination and initiative in helping me with other research tasks connected to this chapter are much appreciated.

²David Easton, "The Division, Integration, and Transfer of Knowledge," in *Divided Knowledge: Across Disciplines, Across Cultures*, ed. David Easton and Corinne S. Schelling (London, U.K.: Sage, 1991), 11.

³Mattei Dogan and Robert Pahre, "Scholarly Reputation and Obsolescence in the Social Sciences: Innovation as a Team Sport," *International Social Science Journal*, no. 125 (August 1990): 419.

⁴C. P. Snow, *The Two Cultures* (Cambridge, U.K.: Cambridge University Press, 1993), 4.

⁵See, for example, the introduction to the new edition of C. P. Snow's book, by Stefan Collini (in ibid., vii–lxxi).

⁶Jerry G. Gaff and Robert C. Wilson, "Faculty Cultures and Interdisciplinary Studies," *Journal of Higher Education*, no. 42 (1971): 198.

⁷The University of Toronto study has not yet been published, but was presented formally to the university in the form of a report. See Joseph Fletcher and Richard Stren, "Report on a Survey of Recent and Current Doctoral Students at the University of Toronto" (University of Toronto: School of Graduate Studies, 1992).

⁸David Harvey, *Social Justice and the City* (Baltimore: Johns Hopkins University Press, 1973), 22.

⁹Manuel Castells, *The City and the Grassroots* (Berkeley: University of California Press, 1983), xv–xvi.

¹⁰Marilyn Stember, "Advancing the Social Sciences Through the Interdisciplinary Enterprise," *Social Science Journal*, 28, no. 1 (1991): 1–14.

¹¹Interdisciplinary programs are an element in liberal curricula, although they cannot respond to all the challenges of a liberal education. For a strong, partisan statement of the liberal education position, see Alan Bloom, *The Closing of the American Mind* (New York: Touchstone Books, 1988), especially the final chapter, "The Student and the University."

¹²Nathan Keyfitz, "Interdisciplinary Analysis in Four Fields," *American Academy of Arts and Sciences Bulletin*, 45 (December 1991–May 1992): 5–15. On the influence of the disciplines, Keyfitz states, "Calls to interdisciplinary study go unheeded because of the organization of academic life. Disciplines are practiced in separate departments, with separate budgets, separate national societies, separate journals. Each has its own criteria for selection of students, its isolation of practitioners starting with the beginning of graduate study, its distinct vocabulary. Students are selected and ultimately given degrees; they are hired as assistant professors and elevated to tenure or not, their researches are funded or not, all according to the judgment of practitioners in one single field. That does not make a discipline a mutual admiration society. Work with any discipline is subject to the harshest of criticism, but always by other practitioners of the same discipline, with both the critic and the criticized animated by the same loyalty to a certain body of thought" (6).

¹³Richard D. Lambert, "Blurring the Disciplinary Boundaries: Area Studies in the United States," in *Divided Knowledge*, ed. Easton and Schelling, 186.

¹⁴Urban Affairs Association, *University Urban Programs* (New Orleans, La.: University of New Orleans, College of Urban and Public Affairs, 1994).

¹⁵James G. Strathman, "A Ranking of U.S. Graduate Programs in Urban Studies and Urban Affairs," *Journal of Urban Affairs* 14, no. 1 (1992): 84. The author concludes by stating "that US/UA has not yet developed to a level where its participants identify more closely with each other than with their parent disciplines in the social sciences" (91).

¹⁶Russell Jacoby, *The Last Intellectuals: American Culture in the Age of Academe* (New York: Basic Books, 1987), 18.

¹⁷Ibid., 56.

[18]The published findings of this project can be found in Richard Stren, ed., *Urban Research in the Developing World*, 3 vols. (Toronto, Canada: Centre for Urban and Community Studies, University of Toronto, 1994–95), on Asia (vol. 1), Africa (vol. 2), and Latin America (vol. 3).

[19]Mohamed Halfani, "Urban Research in Eastern Africa: Tanzania, Kenya, and Zambia—Towards an Agenda for the 1990s," in *Urban Research*, vol. 2, *Africa*, 153.

[20]On the work of the Chicago school and its influence, see Martin Bulmer, *The Chicago School of Sociology: Institutionalization, Diversity and the Rise of Sociological Research* (Chicago: University of Chicago Press, 1984). Two of the basic works of this school are *The City*, ed. Robert E. Park, Ernest W. Burgess, and R. D. McKenzie (Chicago: University of Chicago Press, 1925), and Louis Wirth, *The Ghetto* (Chicago: University of Chicago Press, 1928).

[21]Figures from Manuel Castells, *The Urban Question: A Marxist Approach* (London, U.K.: Edward Arnold, 1977), 286.

[22]Jane Jacobs, *The Death and Life of Great American Cities* (New York: Vintage Books, 1961).

[23]Robert A. Dahl, *Who Governs? Democracy and Power in an American City* (New Haven, Conn.: Yale University Press, 1961).

[24]Two of the most prominent were Nelson Polsby and Aaron Wildavsky. The early work of both scholars, who were prolific writers, was in the field of local politics and community power.

[25]Brian J. L. Berry, ed., *Urbanization and Counter-Urbanization*, vol. 11, Urban Affairs Annual Reviews (Beverly Hills, Calif.: Sage, 1976).

[26]Ibid., 17.

[27]Ibid., 25.

[28]T. G. McGee, *The Southeast Asian City: A Social Geography of the Primate Cities of Southeast Asia* (London, U.K.: G. Bell, 1967), 92.

[29]This distinction was the subject of an important article by the economist Bert F. Hoselitz, "Generative and Parasitic Cities," in Hoselitz, *Sociological Aspects of Economic Growth* (Glencoe, Ill.: Free Press, 1960).

[30]Ibid., 85.

[31]For example, Robert McNamara, the president of the World Bank, said in 1975, "[I]f cities do not begin to deal more constructively with poverty, poverty may well begin to deal more destructively with cities." World Bank, *Address to the Board of Governors by Robert S. McNamara* (Washington, D.C.: World Bank, 1975), 20.

[32]Keith Hart, "Informal Income Opportunities and Urban Employment in Ghana," *Journal of Modern African Studies*, 11, 1 (1973): 61–89. Hart's paper was originally presented to a conference in 1971, before the ILO mission to Kenya completed its work.

[33]International Labor Office (ILO), *Employment, Incomes and Equality: A Strategy for Increasing Productive Employment in Kenya* (Geneva, Switzerland: ILO, 1972), 225.

[34]Milton Santos, *The Shared Space: The Two Circuits of the Urban Economy in Underdeveloped Countries* (London, U.K.: Methuen, 1979). The book was translated into English by Chris Gerry, a prominent British geographer.

[35]Ibid., 18.

[36]Ibid., 209.

[37]Mario Vargas Llosa, foreword to Hernando de Soto, *The Other Path: The Invisible Revolution in the Third World* (London, U.K.: I. B. Taurus, 1989), xiii.

[38]De Soto, *The Other Path*, 13.

[39]John F. C. Turner, "Uncontrolled Urban Settlement: Problems and Policies," in *The City in Newly Developing Countries: Readings on Urbanism and Urbanization*, ed. Gerald Breese (Englewood Cliffs, N.J.: Prentice-Hall, 1969), 326.

[40]As they were designed and implemented by the World Bank, USAID, and a number of other international agencies during the 1970s and early 1980s, sites-and-services schemes involved the allocation of serviced plots in large subdivisions to low-income applicants, who would (with some assistance in the form of training and materials loans) be expected to build their own houses within a specified period of time. These schemes were discontinued because the services and administration were too costly, and because large-scale "filtering" of middle- or upper-income households into the schemes took place in some countries.

[41]Janice E. Perlman, *The Myth of Marginality: Urban Poverty and Politics in Rio de Janeiro* (Berkeley: University of California Press, 1976).

[42]The original book, in Spanish, was published as *Como Sobreviven los Marginados* (How the marginals survive) (Mexico City: Siglo XXI, 1975). The translated English version is Larissa A. Lomnitz, *Networks and Marginality: Life in a Mexican Shantytown* (New York: Academic Press, 1977).

[43]Ibid., 208.

[44]David Harvey, *Social Justice in the City* (Baltimore: Johns Hopkins University Press, 1973).

[45]Manuel Castells, *The Urban Question: A Marxist Approach* (London, U.K.: Edward Arnold, 1977).

[46]Ibid., ix.

[47]Ibid., especially chapter 5. Castells's attack on Wirth was strategic, since according to Peter Saunders (with whom I have no reason to disagree), Wirth's paper, "Urbanism as a Way of Life," "is arguably the most famous article ever to have been published in a sociology journal." Peter Saunders, *Social Theory and the Urban Question* (London, U.K.: Hutchinson and Company, 1981), 92.

[48]Manuel Castells, of Spanish origin, received his doctorate in France, and later taught at the University of California at Berkeley.

[49]Alain Touraine's most important work translated into English on this subject is *The Voice and the Eye: An Analysis of Social Movements* (London, U.K.: Cambridge University Press, 1981).

[50]Manuel Castells, *The City and the Grassroots: A Cross-Cultural Theory of Urban Social Movements* (Berkeley: University of California Press, 1983).

[51]John R. Logan and Harvey L. Molotch, *Urban Fortunes: The Political Economy of Place* (Berkeley: University of California Press, 1987).

[52]Saskia Sassen, *The Global City: New York, London, Tokyo* (Princeton, N.J.: Princeton University Press, 1991).

[53]Ibid., 329.

[54]Robert Putnam, *Making Democracy Work: Civic Traditions in Modern Italy* (Princeton, N.J.: Princeton University Press, 1993).

Contributors

NEZAR ALSAYYAD is an architect, planner, and urban historian. He is currently the executive director of the International Association for the Study of Traditional Environments (IASTE) and associate professor of architecture and planning at the University of California, Berkeley, where he teaches courses on housing and urbanism in the developing world. He is the author of *The Streets of Islamic Cairo* and *Cities and Caliphs: On the Genesis of Arab Muslim Urbanism* and the editor of *The Design and Planning of Housing; Dwellings, Settlements, and Tradition;* and *Forms of Dominance: On the Architecture and Urbanism of the Colonial Enterprise.* Since 1989, he has been editor-in-chief of the journal *Traditional Dwellings and Settlements Review.*

ILONA BLUE is a research assistant in urban development and policy at South Bank University, London, UK. Her research interests include urban health, intra-urban health differentials, and mental health, all with a focus on developing countries. She co-edited the book *Urbanization and Mental Health in Developing Countries* with Trudy Harpham.

JORDI BORJA I SEBASTIA has undergraduate degrees in political science and sociology and an MA in urbanism and geography. He has been a professor of urban sociology and urban geography at the School of Architecture of Barcelona, the Universidad de Barcelona, the Universidad Autónoma de Barcelona, and a visiting professor at the Universidad Politécnica in Barcelona.

He has held several positions in public administration, serving as deputy in the Parliament of Cataluña, and successively, deputy mayor for decentralization and citizen participation, alderman for foreign affairs, and vice president of Barcelona. As an expert in planning, he was the co-director for the Strategic Master Plans for Rio de Janeiro and Bogotá, and also participated in the planning process for Barcelona 2000, Lisbon, and Asunción, Paraguay, among many other Latin American cities. He is currently serving as adviser to the organizing committee of the U.N. Habitat conference.

Among his most recent publications are *Estado y Ciudad; Las grandes ciudades en la década de los 90; Barcelona, Planificación, Estratégica y Territorio; La carta municipal: El régimen especial de las grandes ciudades; Barcelona en el mundo;* and *Barcelona un modelo de transformación urbana.*

ROBERT BRUEGMANN is an architectural historian and professor in the History of Art Department at the University of Illinois at Chicago. He has written on modern architecture, urbanism, and landscape and city planning. Among his recent publications are *Modernism at Mid-Century: The Architecture of the United States Air Force Academy* and *Holabird & Roche/Holabird & Root, Chicago Architects 1880–1940,* 3 vols.

GALIA BURGEL is a researcher in the Department of Urban Geography at the University of Paris X—Nanterre. She is managing editor of the journal *Villes en Parallèle.* Her area of specialty is Russian and Soviet cities, on which she has published several articles.

GUY BURGEL is professor and director of the Department of Urban Geography at the University of Paris X—Nanterre. He is editor and publisher of the journal *Villes en Parallèle,* which has published many thematic issues on comparative urban studies since 1978. The most recent issue explored Paris–New York (1994). He has authored many articles and papers on the topic of the city and urban planning, including his most recent publication, *La ville aujourd'hui* (The city today).

MICHAEL A. COHEN is senior adviser to the vice president, environmentally sustainable development, the World Bank. Since joining the bank in 1972, he has worked as an economist, senior project economist, advisor, and as division chief. From 1989 to September 1994, he was chief of the Urban Development Division, Transportation, Water, and Urban Development Department, where his responsibilities included policy, research, technical assistance, aid coordination, and project and sector work. As coordinator of the Urban Poverty Task Force, he was co-author of *Task Ahead for Cities in Developing Countries,* principal author of *Urban Policy and Economic Development: An Agenda for the 1990s,* and author of *Learning by Doing: World Bank Lending for Urban Development, 1972–1982.* Cohen has participated extensively in formulating the bank's urban policy.

Cohen received a Ph.D. in political economy from the University of Chicago in 1971, where he wrote *Urban Policy and Political Conflict in Africa: A Study of the Ivory Coast,* the first study of urban policy in Africa. In 1971, he worked at the Urban Institute conducting economic and financial analyses for the U.S. President's Commission on School Finance.

MARÍA ELENA DUCCI is research professor at the Institute of Urban Studies of the Catholic University of Chile and is currently the executive secretary of the Environmental Studies Program of the university. Trained as an architect in Chile, she received her M.A. and Ph.D. degrees in urban studies from the Universidad Nacional Autónoma de México (UNAM), where she worked until the late 1980s. In Santiago, she works closely with environmental NGOs and as a consultant for various government agencies. She is founder and member of the organization Acción Ciudadana por el Medio Ambiente. Her recent publications include *Análisis critico de la vivienda en Chile; Políticas de Vivienda y Mujer; Evaluación del Programa de Vivienda Progresiva* (with M. Greene); and *The Mental Health of Low-Income Urban Women: Case Study from Chile.*

ALLISON M. GARLAND is a program associate at the Latin American Program of the Woodrow Wilson International Center for Scholars in Washington, D.C. She received her M.A. in international affairs from Johns Hopkins University, School for Advanced International Studies. She is currently co-editing a book with Joseph S. Tulchin entitled *Argentina: The Challenges of Modernization.* Her research interests focus on economic development and social policy.

MOHAMED HALFANI is a Tanzanian academic who teaches at the University of Dar es Salaam. He has published widely on political as well as urban development in Africa. From September to December 1995, he was a visiting research fellow at the Urban Division of the World Bank. He is now a visiting professor in the Department of Political Science at the University of Toronto. He continues to serve as Africa's regional coordinator in a global network of urban researchers.

TRUDY HARPHAM is professor of urban development and policy at South Bank University, London. Previously, she headed the Urban Health Programme of the London School of Hygiene and Tropical Medicine (1990–95). Her research interests include the impact of urbanization on health (both mental and physical); the links between health services and environmental health; and the revaluation of city-wide health master planning. She has written extensively on urban health in developing countries and has co-edited three books including the widely cited *In the Shadow of the City: Community Health and the Urban Poor.*

LISA R. PEATTIE is professor emeritus and senior lecturer at the Department of Urban Studies and Planning, Massachusetts Institute of Technology, where she has taught for many years. She has also been a visiting professor at the University of California, Berkeley, and the

University of Hong Kong, and a consultant to the World Bank and the United Nations. Trained as an anthropologist, she has published articles on housing issues in developing countries and the United States, on "informal" enterprises, and on the politics of planning. She is the author of *The View From the Barrio; Thinking About Development; Making Work* (with William Ronco); *Women's Claims* (with Martin Rein); and *Planning: Rethinking Ciudad Guayana.*

JULIE A. ROQUÉ is an assistant professor in the Department of Urban Planning at the University of California, Los Angeles. During 1994–95, Roqué took leave from UCLA and served as a senior policy analyst in the Office of Science and Technology Policy in the Executive Office of the President. Her research revolves around questions about the interpretation and use of scientific information in public policy, particularly in the area of environmental health and safety.

BLAIR A. RUBLE is director of the Kennan Institute for Advanced Russian Studies of the Woodrow Wilson International Center for Scholars in Washington, D.C. Ruble has edited five volumes, including two reference works and three collections of articles, and has published three monographic studies. His most recent publications include *Russian Housing in the Modern Age* (co-edited with William Craft Brumfield) and *Money Sings: The Politics of Urban Space in Post-Soviet Yaroslavl.*

H. V. SAVITCH, professor of urban and public affairs, School of Economics and Public Affairs, College of Business and Public Administration, University of Louisville, Kentucky, is the author of *Post-Industrial Cities*, which was nominated as the best volume on urban politics by the American Political Science Association. He has co-edited *Big Cities in Transition* and serves as co-editor of the *Journal of Urban Affairs.* His articles have appeared in *Polity, The Journal of the American Planning Association, Economic Development Quarterly, Urban Affairs Quarterly, National Civic Review,* and *International Journal of Urban and Regional Research.* Savitch has researched, taught, and lectured abroad, including as a Fulbright scholar (France) and as a visiting scholar at the London School of Economics and Political Science, the Institute for Urban Planning in Warsaw, and the Institute for Cultural Research in Moscow. He has worked for the former mayor of New York City, David Dinkins, and served as a consultant to the U.S. Mayors' Urban Summit. Savitch is a member of the Governing Board of the Urban Affairs Association and is currently working on a book, tentatively titled *Cities in an International Age.*

MARTHA SCHTEINGART is an architect and urban sociologist. She is a professor and researcher at the Center for Demographic and Urban

Studies at El Colegio de México, and a national researcher of the National System of Researchers in Mexico. Her research on land and housing problems in cities, urban structure, cities and the environment, and poverty and living conditions in popular settlements appears in numerous edited books and scholarly journals published in Mexico, other Latin American countries, the United States, Canada, and Europe. She is also the author of seven books published in Argentina, Mexico, and France, including her most recent work, *Poverty, Living Conditions and Health in Mexico City*, to be published by El Colegio de México. She is currently coordinating several research projects on governance, poverty, and social policies in Mexico and other Latin American countries.

K. C. SIVARAMAKRISHNAN is a senior adviser in the Urban Management Division of the World Bank. He was the secretary of the Ministry of Urban Development for the government of India. He has held several public positions at the national and metropolitan level, including secretary of the Ministry of Environment of the Government of India, secretary of the Department of Environment and the Department of Public Health Engineering for the government of West Bengal, and chief executive of the Calcutta Metropolitan Development Authority. He served as vice president of the National Institute of Urban Affairs in New Delhi from 1987 to 1993. Among his most recent publications are *Metropolitan Management: The Asian Experience; Regional Review of Urban Policy Issues in Asia: UNDP; Basic Infrastructure Services for the Urban Poor;* and *India's Urban Environment—A Status Report.*

RICHARD STREN is professor of political science at the University of Toronto and director of its Centre for Urban and Community Studies. He received his B.A. in economics from the University of Toronto and his M.A. and Ph.D. in political science from the University of California, Berkeley. Since 1967 he has carried out extensive research on African cities, doing fieldwork in Nairobi, Mombasa, Dar es Salaam, Abidjan, and Makurdi. His main research areas include urban politics in the developing world and comparative public administration. His major publications include *Housing the Urban Poor in Africa; African Cities in Crisis* (co-edited with Rodney White); *Sustainable Cities* (co-edited with Rodney White and Joseph Whitney); and *An Urban Problematique.* He is currently coordinator of the global project Urban Research in the Developing World, which is supported by the Ford Foundation and the World Bank.

JOSEPH S. TULCHIN is the director of the Latin American Program of the Woodrow Wilson International Center for Scholars in Washington,

D.C., where he conducts research, supervises study groups, and coordinates international meetings on issues of concern to the academic and policy communities. Before moving to Washington, he was professor of history at the University of North Carolina, Chapel Hill, for twenty years and at Yale University for seven years before that. Tulchin served as associate editor and then editor of the *Latin American Research Review*. The author or editor of over one hundred publications, his most recent monograph is *Argentina and the United States: A Conflicted Relationship*.

EDMUNDO WERNA is a researcher and consultant in urban development in Third World countries, with special interest in urban management, the environment, and health. He has published several articles in academic and technical journals, the book *Arquitetura e Energia* (Architecture and Energy), and is co-editor of the forthcoming book *Urban Health Research: Implications for Policy*. At present, Werna is a visiting research fellow at the South Bank University, London, and an associate researcher at the University of São Paulo.

MICHAEL J. WHITE is professor of sociology and faculty associate of the Population Studies and Training Center, Brown University. He received his Ph.D. in 1980 from the University of Chicago. He has taught at Princeton University and served on the staff of the Urban Institute in Washington, D.C. His most recent book is *American Neighborhoods and Residential Differentiation*. His published articles include work on internal migration in the United States, Peru, and Malaysia; studies of residential segregation; and analysis of immigration to the United States. His current work examines demographic change in northern Ghana and the adaptation of immigrants in the United States.

WEIPING WU recently joined the Department of Urban Studies and Planning at Virginia Commonwealth University as an assistant professor. Prior to this, she was a research fellow at the Brookings Institution and a consultant for the World Bank in Washington, D.C. Her research interests include comparative urban policy, economic development, international investment, and economic geography. She has published several articles on foreign direct investment and export processing zones in developing countries. As a native of the People's Republic of China, she is also interested in urban development and economic policy in China and East Asia. She is currently co-authoring a book on urban industrial restructuring in China.

Index